The Shell Guide
to the
Gardens of
England and Wales

Title page illustration:-   Neat box-edged beds beneath
the topiary at Levens Hall.

The Shell Guide
to the
Gardens of
England and Wales

Sarah Hollis and Derry Moore

ANDRE DEUTSCH

First published 1989 by
André Deutsch Limited
105−106 Great Russell Street, London WC1B 3LJ

The name Shell and the Shell emblem are registered trademarks

Shell UK Ltd would point out that the contributors' views are not
necessarily those of this company

The information contained in this book is believed correct at the time of
printing. While every care has been taken to ensure that the information
is accurate, the publishers and Shell can accept no responsibility for any
errors or omissions or for changes in the details given.

A list of Shell publications can be obtained by writing to:

Department UOMC/D
Shell UK Oil
PO Box No. 148
Shell-Mex House
Strand
London WC2R 0DX

ISBN 0 233 98391 0

Printed in Italy

Contents

View of the river and the Britannia on the bridge from the gardens at Iford.

Foreword

Between two and six o'clock on the morning of 16th October, 1987, a couple of months after the last garden had been photographed and visited, a storm of unprecedented ferocity swept across the southern and eastern counties of England. This hurricane or whirlwind, the worst in living memory, caused unparalleled devastation to the treescape and, consequently, gardens in this part of the country. A decision has been taken to describe them as they were so that this book stands as a comprehensive record, as well as a guide. It will take some years to appreciate the full extent of the storm damage and for the owners to decide what is their wisest course. Some might wish to replant trees as they were, others might take a different attitude and completely redesign and alter the character of what had been a woodland garden. Having overcome the heartbreak of seeing what has taken many years to mature swept away in a few hours, owners will once again be looking to the future. It is, after all, a gardener's nature to focus on what is to come; hope springs eternal.

Chiswick House; a replica of Palladio's Villa Capra.

Introduction

The very real passion for gardening and garden-visiting amongst the British could be called a national obsession and the last decade has seen an unrivalled growth of interest. Gardens open to the public can now be numbered in thousands, visitors in millions, and horticulture in general has become a thriving and important industry.

The recent increase in interest might be phenomenal but a love of gardens has been a national characteristic for centuries. The medieval monk would cultivate his herb garden, the Crusader knight return home with a rose for his lady's 'flowery mead', and the Elizabethan courtier bankrupt himself to embellish his house and lay out gardens for his sovereign's pleasure. The size and beauty of a gentleman's property advertized to all his wealth, power and good taste. Seventeenth-century milords would invite writers to admire their formal gardens and landscapes, knowing full well that they, like newspaper diarists today, would make flattering or trenchant comments on their host's 'good taste' and modernity. Descriptions of gardens by John Evelyn in the seventeenth century and Horace Walpole in the eighteenth, still make entertaining reading and are invaluable to historians and those involved in period garden restoration.

Gardens have been open to the general public for very much longer than might be imagined, the garden visitor being far from a twentieth-century innovation. The head gardener would give conducted tours of his master's 'landskip', or a century later point out the newly planted pinetum or mouthwateringly rare exotics in lavishly planted stove houses. Even that most private of monarchs, Queen Victoria, opened the gardens of Hampton Court to the people.

For the visitor of the past there was an exciting voyeuristic element about an expedition to a splendid private property, and this still holds true with regard to stately homes. Few of us can resist a glimpse of how the other half lived or lives, and part of the pleasure of exploring grand gardens is being impressed by their extent, richness, high standards of upkeep, period design and historic associations — their splendour rather than any similarity to our own gardens. They are an important part of our heritage and reveal how tastes have changed over the centuries and our culture evolved. Like everything else in life, gardens are affected by political and economic climate, advances in communications, scientific progress and man's ever-changing attitude to his environment.

One of the most interesting developments over recent years is the enthusiastic and painstaking restoration of period gardens that would otherwise be lost for good. The desire to preserve our historic, as well as our natural heritage (period gardens and buildings being as vulnerable to desecration or neglect as wild life and places of natural beauty) is possibly a result of our shaky confidence in the future. Progress often demands a high price; our good health and the stability of our environment are frequently threatened by financially rewarding technical advances. There is nothing new in this, but we have now all been made more aware of how easily the good things in life can be eroded or lost, and perhaps we have become more discriminating.

Another dramatic change and much welcomed development in garden-visiting is the opening, usually for charity, of thousands of private gardens to the public. Infinitely diverse in size, situation and character, smaller than their grander forebears but equally influenced by garden-making styles of the past, their great popularity lies in their being easy to relate to. Common ground is shared between owner and visitor, a mutual pleasure taken, useful tips exchanged and inspiration to alter or improve one's garden gained. No gardener is averse to having his handiwork admired or his advice sought and enthusiasts are on the constant look-out for new ideas that can be translated to their own patch. The opening to the public of such gardens and the fact that the average age of the amateur gardener is now very much lower than it was — for gardening is no longer considered a hobby of the middle-aged — have encouraged a new breed of garden visitor. A huge percentage of owners commented on the increasing numbers of young that now turn up on open days to take photographs and notes, and ask questions and advice on how to make what is, more often than not, their first garden. Many people now wish to learn from rather than simply admire an imaginatively designed and planted garden.

The spectrum of gardens now open is extraordinarily wide, as this guide will show. Its compilation takes into account every sort of variation in climate, terrain, design and size: the sub-tropical woodland gardens of the balmy south west; that most noteworthy of English innovations, the sublime or noble landscape; the town garden measured in feet rather than acres; seaside, suburban and stately home gardens. There are some that have been carved out of rocky mountainside, nurtured on rugged moorland, created on an old council tip, or made on a city rooftop. Some have been tended by scores of gardeners, some by several generations of the same family, some solely by the present owners. Battles fought against salt-laden winds, fleeting summers and harsh winters, dramatically high or low rainfalls, difficult soil conditions and awkward situations, have resulted, if not in victory, then in successful truces.

Some of the gardens included are endangered by their popularity with the visiting public and are slowly being eroded by the garden-lover's enthusiasm, but these are balanced by those hidden gems that leave the visitor with that happy feeling of having made a 'find'.

All tastes have been catered for, though 'taste'

Foxgloves along the apple walk at Heale House.

is a tricky word, begging to be qualified as good or bad. Gardens are as subject to vagaries of fashion as the hemline, and what was considered good taste in one century, or even decade, has been abhorred in another. Garden-making styles and plants used are constantly falling out of favour or being newly appreciated. All garden lovers have their favourite sort of garden, but none has the right to say that so-and-so is in good taste, or this or that in bad. The criterion taken by this guide is that whatever the owner has set out to achieve has 'worked' and that the garden has a particular harmony and well-defined character. As all gardeners would agree, the struggle to achieve one's ideal is unceasing; no garden is perfect throughout, and experiments are constantly being assayed.

Some users of the guide may feel that certain entries should not be classified as gardens at all, that they are simply a collection of unusual plants, a flowery meadow or a deceptively natural landscape. But each entry has an historical or horticultural significance and contains something of interest either to the plantsman, garden designer or historian, amateur or professional, or even to those who open their own gardens. Unfortunately, the latter have little time during the season to visit gardens, all their energies being taken up with caring for their own. Perhaps a guide book should be written for garden-owners, so that they could share and benefit from each other's experiences and ideas. Some have an especial talent for making the visitor feel at home, or for making a visit more entertaining; some have imaginatively organized their gardens to keep in step with the rising standards demanded by the public.

Gardens and gardening seem to bring out the best in people, and gardeners are widely acknowledged as most generous people. They are always happy to pass on knowledge, plants, or cuttings. A good number of the gardens are open specifically to raise funds for charity or to finance the upkeep of what would otherwise be left to decay. Plants for sale propagated from those on show help to boost these funds but unfortunately there is always the odd vandal who helps himself to this source of income, snipping off the odd shoot or even taking the whole plant. The overall effect of a garden can be ruined by this, and the pleasure of countless other 'guests' spoilt. The success of Neighbourhood Watch in deterring burglars should now, perhaps, give birth to Garden Watch. If any of us sees a plant being attacked, we should tap the culprit on the shoulder and remind them of the

Rhododendrons and azaleas reflected in the lake at Ramster.

facts; one of the most important being that nine times out of ten the owner would be happy to give a fellow-plantsman a cutting if asked — but perhaps from a less conspicuous plant.

Latin names have been used sparingly in this book as they can make for dry reading. Indeed, identification in general has been used sparingly, as there is always a danger that by the time the garden is visited the plant mentioned may no longer exist. No garden stands still and certain elements are frighteningly ephemeral. Honey fungus might rear its destructive head, an important focal point might be lost from old age or in a severe winter or drought. Our weather is becoming ever more eccentric and vital shelter belts can be lost, as happened in the terrible storm of October 1987, discussed in the Foreword. A disaster like Dutch/Elm disease may strike. Other factors such as owners moving or being unable to tend their gardens properly can also cause changes or even bring about the closure of a garden. The sight of the odd weed usually cements a sympathetic bond between an owner and visitor rather than prompting critical comment, but there is a limit both to the visitor's tolerance of neglect and the owner's of criticism.

Except for a handful that have an especial importance, all the gardens chosen here are open regularly or by appointment. To invest in such a guide only to find that a large proportion of the gardens described are open only once or twice a year would prove cruelly frustrating. Exact times of opening have not been given as these can change from year to year and users must check these in the annually printed publications or with the organisations listed below. The owners of gardens open by appointment must be contacted well in advance to avoid disappointment. To turn up unannounced could prove a sad waste of time as well as provoke understandable irritation.

Gateway to the terrace of Heale House.

We are uniquely fortunate in this country in having organizations such as the National Trust, Historic Houses and Gardens Assocation, and English Heritage. They have saved so much of our inheritance from extinction, and their energy and expertise set high standards. A swift contemplation of the country devoid of the many properties they own or have restored is not pleasant. It quickly alerts us to a new appreciation of their work and prevents us from taking them for granted. The same could be said for all the volunteers who give their time and energy to raise funds for charity. If it were not for the National Gardens Scheme, the Red Cross, the Soldiers', Sailors' and Airmen's Families Assocation and many other good causes, the garden-visiting scene would be sadly impoverished.

The very great pleasure taken in visiting what came to a total of approximately four hundred gardens all over England and Wales, can be imagined. To see so many gardens in just under two years was a privilege and to hear of and observe for myself the hard work, determination and talent that has gone into their creation and upkeep, humbling. The highly enjoyable task opened my eyes not only to the diverse beauty of this tiny island, but to the kindness and friendliness of its inhabitants. I would like to thank the many owners who gave me so much of their time, the county and other organizers of charities such as the National Gardens Scheme, and those well aquainted with the gardens open in their particular area who advised me about what to visit. I shall not forget those who helped me when I lost my way, tolerated my appalling mispronunciation of certain place names — especially in Wales, gave first aid to my car when it misbehaved, or helped me, late at night, to find a bed for the night. Especial thanks go to Jo Brogden, Sarah Cotton, Valerie and John Cross, Heather Sutherland, Anne Pinkney, Patricia Richards, Caroline Weeks and most of all to my family who had to put up with my being away from home for long periods and much else.

Handbooks are published annually by the following and are available in bookshops:
The National Trust, 36 Queen Anne's Gate, London SW1.
Historic Houses, Castles and Gardens in Great Britain and Ireland (published by British Leisure Publications, Windsor Court, East Grinstead House, East Grinstead, West Sussex.)
The National Gardens Scheme, 57 Belgrave Street, London SW1.

Other organizations that can supply details of gardens open:
local branches of the Red Cross and Soldiers', Sailors' and Airmen's Families Association.
local Tourist Board offices (addresses can be obtained from the English Tourist Board, Thames Tower, Black's Road, London W6)
local libraries.

The Information Centre for South Wales,
8-14 Bridge Street,
Cardiff.
Cardiff (0222) 27281

The Information Centre of Mid Wales,
Machynlleth,
Canolfan Owain Glyndwr,
Powys.
Machynlleth (0654) 2401

The Information Centre for North Wales.
Colwyn Bay,
77 Conway road,
Clwyd.
Colwyn Bay (0492) 531731

The Japanese garden at Tatton Park.

Our Gardening History

ROMAN, MEDIEVAL, TUDOR AND ELIZABETHAN GARDENS

They say the late convert is always the most fanatical and this is certainly true of the people of this island when it comes to gardening. While we were struggling merely to exist, elsewhere in the world others were growing plants not simply as a source of food or for religious rites but to enhance their surroundings. The Chinese, Persians, Egyptians and Greeks were tending their roses, creating water gardens, and causing (albeit through wars) the movement of plants from one part of the world to another. Soldiers who valued medicinal or aromatic species inadvertently became the first amateur plant-collectors.

When the Romans invaded Britain in 43AD they must have been appalled at the conditions prevailing and wondered whether it had been worth the effort. Although no longer nomadic, the early Briton's life lacked sophistication; he raised a few crops and grew woad but these were used to feed the family and to produce warpaint rather than enhance his homestead. Consequently, our first gardens were created not by the natives but by a sophisticated invader impatient to make himself feel at home and to enjoy a few comforts in what must have seemed a barbaric land. It is thought that, as at home, the Romans decorated their secluded courtyards with mosaics, box topiary, ornamental pools and the few plants then available. They added variety to the daily diet by importing herbs and fruit trees, and vegetables such as cabbages, leeks, onions, garlic, cucumbers, radishes, as-paragus and globe artichokes. They introduced the lime and the mulberry tree and also thought it worthwhile — the climate being warmer than it is today — to import and plant grape vines. They made themselves more comfortable during their occupation, but totally failed to inspire a love of gardens or gardening in their crude hosts. When they left, their cultivated life went with them; some of their edible plant introductions were adopted, but not their aesthetic tastes. The Dark Ages descended, and survival rather than progress absorbed the energies of the population.

In 1066 it was thanks to another invading force, the Normans, that a gradual and better-rooted conversion to garden-making and the study of plants came about. Being channelled through the monasteries, this interest developed in a protectd environment. The monasteries were not only a refuge for those in trouble but sanctuaries of learning. Set apart from the rest of society, entirely self-supporting and not vulnerable to the vagaries of war, they were able to push forward the boundaries of civilisation and create communities which could feed, house and educate themselves in a way much in advance of the lay population. The remains of the twelfth-century Fountains and Rievaulx Abbeys in Yorkshire give an idea of how well-organised these establishments must have been been, and reveal how efficiently they fed, clothed and accommodated up to eight hundred souls, a daunting prospect even today.

Nursing the sick has always been an important role of the church and in the monasteries' small infirmary gardens herbs and healing plants were first nurtured in ordered beds. There were rules on what time of the day or the year these should be gathered to ensure their maximum potency, and ancient Christian doctrine dictated that certain flowers were allied to Satan and others to

Christ, symbolising purity, sanctity or fertility. The cemeteries of the monks were also planted with fruit trees, cherries, apples and pears, and lilies were grown for religious rituals and to adorn altars and statues. In the kitchen garden, beds protected by hedges or fences contained onions, garlic, leeks, peas and parsnips, and culinary herbs such as saffron, parsley, savory, fennel and mint, to aid digestion, flavour drinks and make the often far-from-fresh meat palatable. Others were used as dyes for the inks the monks needed to produce their illuminated manuscripts. New plants were introduced by monks who, thanks to their calling, could travel great distances without being molested. Gradually records of these, and of the plants already being cultivated, began to be kept, and knowledge could be exchanged.

Life in the castles remained under threat from warring factions, for a long time, but knowledge spread slowly from the monasteries and the standard of living rose. Small ornamental gardens were created within the confines of secure walls, forming secluded open-air rooms, which offered escape from the hurly-burly and overcrowding of the great halls. Old illustrations show a geometric pattern of paths, 'flowery mead' and raised beds planted with irises, lilies, columbines and gillyflowers (carnations), together with scented plants such as rosemary and lavender. Roses were grown over arbours, the forerunners of pergolas, and the surrounds of turf seats were planted with aromatic herbs and wild flowers. Mounds were built to view the countryside beyond the castle walls, and though still in its infancy the garden began to be an aesthetically pleasing, rather than a purely functional, adjunct to a dwelling. Queen Eleanor's Garden next to the Great Hall in Winchester, though not authentic, is a carefully-researched and laid-out example of such a medieval garden.

In time it was felt safe to venture beyond the confines of the castle, which was itself changing its nature, becoming more of a dwelling than a fortress. The inmates no longer left its secure confines only to make war, embark on a crusade or a long journey, or to go hunting, but began to enjoy the pleasures of orchards strewn with wild flowers and of small fenced or hedged plots.

The long period of relative peace under the Tudors during the late fifteenth and sixteenth centuries enabled the arts to flourish, and the Dissolution of the monasteries brought about a greater distribution of wealth. Fine houses, built from the stone which had once sheltered religious communities, were still designed to look inward on to a central courtyard, as at Holme Pierrepont, Nottingham, but the handsome appearance of a house was beginning to take precedence over its ability to withstand attack. A similar attitude prevailed in the garden, which became increasingly formal and decorated — a complete contrast to the wildness of the parks and forests outside.

Set within walls rather than hedges and fences, these gardens were often also protected by moats. Though still similar to medieval gardens, by the sixteenth century they had evolved into highly-ornamented 'rooms', which reflected the intricacies of the architecture and the interior decoration of the house. The raised beds, hedged with santolina, lavender or rosemary, which were in turn surrounded with painted rails, were later transformed into knot gardens, laid out to resemble the carved wooden or plaster ceilings of the house. They were placed near the house and could be admired from its windows or from the raised walks constructed around the perimeter of the garden. Mounts (small man-made hills) served a similar purpose and became increasingly intricate, decorated with spiralling paths which led to a gazebo or a banqueting house where sweetmeats and drinks were served while the view was enjoyed. Fountains, waterworks and mazes of low-growing plants or turf appeared, and colourful heraldic beasts of painted wood and statues enriched the scene. Shakespeare's plays and sonnets bear witness that flowers were loved for their beauty as well as for their particular properties. The herbs, violets, lilies and columbines of medieval gardens were joined by sweet williams, lilies-of-the-valley, crown imperials, peonies, pansies, Christmas roses, auriculas and pot marigolds. The garden at Charlecote Park, near Stratford-upon-Avon, has a walk decorated with plants mentioned by Shakespeare in his plays and poems.

The wealthy preferred to live in the country rather than in the unhealthy towns; travel had become much safer, and the host felt duty bound to entertain and impress guests with his wealth and modernity. The popular outdoor pursuits of the time, bowling and archery, had their prescribed place in the garden, which now played an aesthetic, entertaining and functional role in the lives of the nobility. Chroniclers like John Aubrey were assiduous in noting down all that had impressed them on a visit, and were as quick to judge a man by the state of his property and his standard of living as by his character. The cost of upkeep of such estates, and provision for large households, was considerable, and visits, particularly by royalty, could impoverish a noble. When the wily Elizabeth I (1558–1603) feared that a nobleman was becoming too power-ful she would 'grace' his home with a visit involving the housing and feeding of a huge retinue for several weeks, beggaring his resources.

Stew ponds ensured a supply of fresh fish, dovecotes (such as that at Cotehele) a source of fresh meat when others had been exhausted; honey from the beehives sweetened the palate and newly-introduced varieties of fruit and vegetables would give savour to the daily diet. Apples, pears, mulberries, cherries and medlars were grown for the table, as well as apricots and peaches whose fruit was encouraged to ripen early by setting the trees against double walls, the hollow in between heated by stoves. Examples of such walls can be seen at Packwood House and at Berrington Hall. Herbs were used in great quantity, strewn on the floors to sweeten the house, and in food and drink to add flavour.

Topiary at Levens Hall that was once an early seventeenth-century parterre.

There were raspberries, gooseberries and strawberries, and orange trees made their appearance (albeit only for decorative purposes). What was to become an indispensable part of our diet — the potato — was introduced in 1569, from South America.

Secure and confident, the landowner lavished his wealth on his property, and the rise in foreign trade and our success as a seafaring nation meant that there was no lack of new and exciting goods to buy. Fruit trees and plants collected in Europe, America and the Canary Islands by our first professional planthunters — the Tradescants, father and son — were much desired and large sums were invested in them. Not many books were owned by even the richest of men, but more than likely one of them would be a herbal, because this period saw the birth of botanical science and the spread of knowledge. John Gerard's *Herball*, published in 1597, though not always accurate and plagiarising from other books, was written in a lively and digestible style and listed over one thousand plants.

The moat surrounding the walled Elizabethan garden at Helmingham Hall.

The many advantages of peace established gardens as a well-loved feature. They continued to fulfil a practical purpose as a source of food and medicine, but had evolved into a status symbol, a necessary adjunct to a gracious dwelling, a place of entertainment and a superb medium to display man's increasing dominance over nature and his burgeoning artistic talents. Plants were grown for their beauty and not for purely practical reasons, and by the time of the Stuarts the yeoman had joined the wealthy landowner as a lover of gardens. Gardens which date from this time and contain period features can be seen at Helmingham Hall, Hatfield House, Cranborne Manor, Montacute House, Haddon Hall and Hardwick Hall.

THE FORMAL SEVENTEENTH-CENTURY GARDEN

Travel, learning and politics began to exercise an enormous influence on gardens during the seventeenth century, and those belonging to the rich and noble began to show foreign influences. They grew greatly in size and their design became increasingly grand and formal, reflecting the style of the Italian Renaissance, the flamboyantly grand French, and the more domestic but horticulturally-advanced Dutch gardens. In the Jacobean and Stuart periods the garden was linked more harmoniously to the architectural style of the house; symmetry and perspective were taken into account and the growing enthusiasm for garden-making gave birth to the botanist, the nurseryman, the garden designer, the garden writer and the collector of exotics.

Initially, although the garden grew in size it did not throw off entirely its well-defined divisions between the cultivated and the wild. Architectural taste was changing: Inigo Jones (1573–1652) was inspired by the work of Palladio in Italy, and became England's first classical architect. Architectural and horticultural features were made to blend and link a series of formal gardens in harmony with the house. The colourful painted statues and heraldic beasts gave way to increasingly formal features — long canals, fanciful waterworks and statuary.

As more plants came into this country and the choice widened, there was no longer any need to mix decorative with practical subjects. Fruit trees were still planted against walls, but culinary and medicinal plants joined fruit bushes and vegetables in the new, quite separate, kitchen gardens. The ornamental gardens were still over-looked by the house, but the small Elizabethan knot evolved into a parterre with a more free-flowing design, decorated with coloured minerals, gravel or dust, as well as flowers. The former turfed pattern of the maze was replaced by the tall evergreen hedges of the labyrinth, which masked the symbolic design of paths. Avenues and *allées* were laid out to form the grid of a garden which resembled a vast, embroidered geometric pattern. Nature was being put firmly under the thumb of man and even though concessions were made in the form of Wilderness gardens, the symmetry of their design and the manner of their planting was so artificial that they were no more than vague nods in the direction of the natural.

It might be imagined that the Civil War and the Commonwealth of the seventeenth century would have had a dire effect on garden-making, but quite the contrary. The Royalists returned to their estates and concentrated on their improvement, and those exiled to Holland or to France had an opportunity to study the sophisticated gardens of those countries. By the time they returned home, they were impatient to recreate the controlled and geometrical style of these foreign gardens, particularly those laid out by the French gardening genius, Le Nôtre, who had made such awesome and splendid gardens for his master, Louis XIV, at Versailles, St Cloud and Fontainebleau. Their design had been inspired by the Italian Renaissance garden, but was different in that it was laid out on level rather than on sloping ground, terraces, if they existed at all, were gently graded, and the glorious extent of the gardens, which seemed to stretch to infinity in all directions, could be seen at a glance. Few could fail to be overwhelmed by the power and wealth of one who owned such a creation — which was the object of the exercise for the Sun King; he had not only to impress visiting dignitaries, but to house, entertain and hold sway over a vast court.

The principles of design were a central axis aligned on the grand façade of the house or palace, with many cross axes forming a cat's-cradle of walks, rides, *allées* and avenues which would slice through woodland in the far reaches

The Carolean garden at Packwood.

of the garden. These created a series of grand vistas to architectural, sculptural or water features, the whole forming a precisely composed picture of great depth with an immediate visual impact. Matching parterres were placed on either side of a central walk to the house, and long canals and elaborate fountains were important decorative elements in this highly-cultivated part of the garden. Beyond lay blocks of 'boskage' or woodland, its rides lined with avenues of trees such as limes or chestnuts; the layout of these often resembled the bone structure of a goose's foot, a *patte-d'oie*, or the radiating spokes of a wheel. It had a more 'natural', even romantic, character and an exploration of its rides revealed a series of surprise features, focal points set in circular openings where paths intersected.

The Englishman did his best to emulate this grand style, though he had to cope with rolling countryside and had considerably less to spend than the King of France. Le Nôtre never came to this country, but his influence was overwhelming and French gardeners or those who had trained in France were much in demand. Though the formal English seventeenth-century garden was not on the scale of the French and the parterres were considered pale copies, the overall picture was similar in its unembarrassed grandeur and revelation of man's autocratic domination over nature, a contrast with and not altogether surprising backlash to the austerity of

The seventeenth-century terrace gardens at Powis Castle.

the Commonwealth years. On his return in 1660, Charles II was determined to change the English way of life and to promote learning and the arts; his subjects were not slow to follow in his footsteps. A leader of fashion, he promoted the new style of garden-making — by improving the gardens of St James's Palace and Hampton Court, where he planted avenues and made canals.

Tree planting was much encouraged, particularly by the virtuoso garden-designer and writer John Evelyn. As a member of the Royal Society, he had investigated the lack of timber for ship-

building when stocks had been used up during the Commonwealth. In 1664 he published his *Sylva or Discourse on Forest Trees*, which encouraged the planting of trees and described the way they could be used in the garden in addition to being a source of timber. Like many of his contemporaries, he wrote extensively about the gardens he had visited, commenting on their design, the newly-introduced plants they contained, and how they were being cultivated. Books were published which gave detailed advice on design and took a more scientific approach to horticulture, and the serious study of plants was advanced by the establishment of the Botanic Garden in Oxford in 1621 and the Physic Garden in Chelsea in 1673; both of them exchanged knowledge and plants with established botanical gardens in Europe.

The Lebanon cedar and holm oak enriched the landscape, and over twenty-one different varieties of rose and several hundred of tulip were being grown. Over twenty varieties of apple and pear were available and even more of peaches and plums. Exotic fare was being raised, too: melons, figs, pomegranates and orange and lemon trees were widely grown, not so much for their fruit as for their decorative value. These sought-after evergreens and other exotics were sent back by missionaries in faraway places such as North America, and were also brought by plant-collectors such as John Tradescant the Younger, and by refugees and seamen. Being tender, exotics and some evergreen plants could not be left out during the winter and their cultivation and care prompted the building of orangeries and greenhouses (so-called because they housed what were known as 'greens'). They were crudely heated at first with open fires, and because it had not been realised that such plants needed maximum light to thrive, their roofs were not glazed. The 'Hot Bed', formed of a thick layer of warm dung covered by a further layer of tanner's bark, was also used to raise tender plants, the much-prized pineapple in particular.

The Dutch were the most horticulturally sophisticated nation at the time and with the accession to the throne of William and Mary in 1688 English gardens were introduced to a wealth of new plants from the Mediterranean countries and from the East and West Indies. Evergreens were more popular than ever and the yew came to be considered a good subject for hedging and topiary. Aloes, myrtles, phillyreas and laurustinus were set around the garden in pots and boxes, together with the orange and lemon trees, and these and deciduous shrubs were clipped to form architectural and fanciful shapes like sailing ships and imaginary animals. Naturally, bulbs were planted in great quantities and intricate flower beds were bright with pinks and polyanthus. Topiary, water and statuary created highly artificial and overcrowded pictures which were soon to meet with disapproval from influential writers like Alexander Pope and Joseph Addison.

By the time Queen Anne ascended the throne in 1702, nurseries could offer a wide-ranging stock of plants and trees, the most famous of these being London and Wise of Kensington. Both George London and Henry Wise, as well as running a successful nursery, became royal gardeners, their combined names synonymous with all that was most desirable when it came to designing a garden in the grand French style. The queen employed them to design and stock the gardens at Blenheim Palace for her victorious general, the Duke of Marlborough, but these were to have a short life and today only London and Wise's walled vegetable garden survives. The gardens of Blenheim, designed to offset Sir John Vanbrugh's superb baroque palace, were, like many others, swept away in the mid-eighteenth century to make way for that radical innovation, the landscape garden.

Only a handful of formal gardens from this period now exist, though an idea of their grandeur can be gained from studying the bird's-eye view engravings by Leonard Knyff and Jan Kip of scores of estates. Laid out to a strict pattern, designed with a ruler rather than freehand, they resemble giant chessboards of geometric formal gardens and woodland, or cats-cradles of cross-cutting avenues, *allées* and gravel paths. The cost of planting and maintaining such massive, precise and work-intensive gardens was immense and contributed to their downfall; their scale and formality would never be rivalled. Intellectual and emotional forces, as well as practical considerations, were gathering momentum at the beginning of the eighteenth century and a revolution in garden-making was about to take place. Pope's wish for a greater appreciation of the 'amiable simplicity of unadorned nature' was to be granted and a style unique to this country was to make its appearance.

Gardens illustrating features of the seventeenth-century formal garden can be seen at Ham House, Wrest Park, Melbourne Hall, Chatsworth, Hampton Court and St Paul's Walden Bury.

The tulip, one of the most highly prized seventeenth-century flowers.

THE EIGHTEENTH-CENTURY LANDSCAPE GARDEN

It was the writers of the time who first began to rebel against the extreme formality of the late-seventeenth-century garden, to mock its artificiality and its often absurd features. The gentlemen of 'taste' who read books and articles written by Joseph Addison and Alexander Pope, or who knew them personally, were quick to feel the change in the climate. Various practical and financial elements, joining with this new mood, brought about the birth of Le Jardin Anglais. This new and natural style of garden worked with nature instead of seeking to dominate it, and had been advocated by Francis Bacon in 1625, in his essay *Of Gardens*, but it took a century for his ideas to be endorsed.

The rich landowner had long since ceased to shield himself from the countryside surrounding his grounds, and now welcomed a fine prospect of his property to nourish his feelings of power and wealth and make them obvious to others. Garden-visiting is far from being a twentieth-century innovation; strangers as well as guests were given conducted tours of a gentleman's garden by the head gardener, or by the owner himself, who was far from shy of showing off his new status symbol. The landscape garden was not designed to be viewed solely from the house, but was meant to be explored by a prescribed route so that its various features could make their full impact. Whether on foot or in a carriage, visitors were constantly on the move, the sight of a distant feature or a surprise vista beckoning them onward.

A long time had passed since it was thought desirable to live hugger-mugger under one roof with those of lesser birth, and gradually, as servants were given their separate living quarters within the house, the landowner also wished to distance himself from the community life of the village. This involved finding a suitably commanding site for a new house, or altering the old while sometimes even uprooting and transplanting an entire village. During the eighteenth century the move towards enclosure made such extravagant ideas possible. The Enclosure Acts fenced in waste and common land and smallholdings, which were then put to more profitable agricultural use. Turnips and swedes were introduced from abroad, and the practice of crop rotation by enterprising landlords like 'Turnip' Townsend of Norfolk, made it no longer necessary to leave land fallow every third year. The crop not only nourished the soil but was used to feed the cattle and sheep in winter, which meant they could be slaughtered for meat throughout the year. The advantages to the landowner were considerable — not only was his income swelled but his table was supplied with a constant source of fresh meat. The disadvantages, inevitably, were suffered by the small farmer who, deprived of his land, was driven to find employment in the city. This, in its turn, would influence the garden-making style of the Victorian era.

The new vogue for travel, simply for pleasure, was to play a most important role in the birth of the landscape movement. The Grand Tour was considered necessary to a young gentleman's education. The notion that 'travel broadens the mind' still holds good today — the young hitch-hiker, like his earlier counterpart, still returns home with that easily portable commodity, ideas; but he cannot transport an impressive collection of works of art and scientific curiosities as his predecessor did in the eighteenth century. The paintings of Claude Gellée of Lorraine, who came to be known simply as Claude, and his French compatriots Nicholas and Gaspard Poussin, were particularly sought after. They depicted idyllic views of the Italian countryside where classical ruins, woodland, soft glowing light and mythical figures create an Arcadian scene. The works of Salvator Rosa of the Neapolitan school, which showed wilder and more dramatic scenes of cascades and satanic rock formations, were also popular despite the fact that these artists had all completed their work by 1682, well before they became a cult in Britain. They inspired travellers to attempt similar sublime and romantic scenes at home; well-lined purses, enthusiasm and newly-acquired artistic tastes gave them the courage to fashion a new style of garden which, though influenced by the art and architecture of Europe, was to be uniquely English.

The Royal Gardener, Charles Bridgeman, was the first to sense a change in the air at the beginning of the century. He was still laying out vast gardens with formal beds and straight avenues, but he broke the mould by introducing the odd curved path to the wooded and less formal areas of the garden. He created lakes rather than long canals and was the first to use that uniquely useful device, the ha-ha, which was to prove an indispensable, though invisible, feature of the 'landskip' garden. It banished the harsh division between the garden proper and the countryside, the sight of which was now welcomed. Although Bridgeman struck the spark, William Kent lit the torch of the landscape movement and carried it nobly. He was to follow and 'improve' on Bridgeman's work at Stowe, Claremont and Rousham, sweeping away all vestiges of formality.

Chiswick House gardens, one of William Kent's early creations.

In 1719 Kent returned from Italy, where he had been sent to study painting by wealthy patrons. Originally a coach-painter's apprentice, Kent embarked on a career as a landscape designer and architect which was to mark him out as a genius. During his stay in Italy he had the good fortune to meet the foremost patron of the arts of his day, Lord Burlington, who offered not only his friendship but his backing. Kent was exceptionally talented, but without the financial support and patronage of Burlington his rise could not have been so meteoric. Both men had great admiration for the work of the sixteenth-century Italian architect, Andrea Palladio, which reflected the 'regular' principles of Roman architecture and of all things classical; he was to be a strong influence on Kent's landscape gardens. These were 'prospects to excite not only the eye but the imagination', — classical temples, specially-constructed ruins and other architectural features set around a 'natural' landscape to provoke a series of emotions, or even make political or philosophical statements (it was the Whig fraternity who most favoured the new, freer style). The garden would melt into the countryside; clumps rather than blocks of trees, and sheets of water would play important roles. It took time for Kent to develop his own style, and his early work (such as that at Lord Burlington's villa in Chiswick), though decorated with architectural features in the classical style and the odd winding path, retained its formal lines. But it was not long before 'he leapt the fence and saw that all nature was a garden', as Horace Walpole wrote. An artist rather than a gardener, Kent saw the overall design as more important than the plant content, and he was even known, on occasion, to use a dead tree to 'set a scene' effectively.

Kent's popularity as a garden designer contributed to the rise and eventual glory of a young gardener from Northumberland called Lancelot Brown. Originally employed as head kitchen gardener at Stowe, at a time when Kent was involved in creating his glorious landscape, Brown inevitably learnt much from working with him. Kent's commissions elsewhere meant that Brown was put in charge of executing his designs, and he may well have added ideas of his own.

Brown undoubtedly benefited, particularly when it came to overseeing the construction of architectural features; unlike Kent, he was an experienced gardener and knew the habits of trees and plants, but he had been given no opportunity to gain any architectural skills. His talent as a landscape designer was soon recognised and he was soon being consulted by other landowners around Stowe and farther afield.

This gave him the confidence to leave the security of his job in 1751 and set himself up as a landscape gardener. He became known as 'Capability' rather than Lancelot Brown, because of his habit of extolling the capabilities or potential of any property he surveyed, though he could as well have earned it for his skilful organisation of a workforce. He was the first to subcontract workmen, who would then be overseen by one of his own men. Portraits of Brown depict him as engaging, with a twinkly eye, and, though something of a social climber, his honesty and astonishing capacity for work, interrupted only by bouts of asthma, ensured that he never crossed or lost a client — a considerable achievement when one considers the scale and radical nature of his work. His powers of persuasion must have been considerable, for his treatment of landscape often involved much more drastic 'improvement' than that of Kent. It could not have been easy to persuade scores of landowners to destroy completely their expensively built and extensive formal gardens and replace them with a landscape they would never see mature. Doubtless he argued that when the costly destruction, earth-moving and planting were complete, their fashionable young landscape would enhance their standing and suit their pockets, being productive and cheap to run. 'Weeder-women' would no longer have to be employed and stock could be increased because new grazing land was available.

Apart from being criticised for his wholesale destruction of so many formal gardens, Brown is often accused of having worked to a formula. This is true to some extent, but it underrates his extraordinary skill in converting unpromising sites into noble landscapes. He insisted that landscape ran up to the very walls of the house, usually set on high ground, where it played a major role in the design and enjoyed a fine prospect. A belt of trees, broken to open up views of the countryside beyond, surrounded the landscape and further clumps were planted at strategic points to create vistas and soften or emphasise the vast open spaces. Man-made lakes, formed by swelling the banks or altering the course of a river, were linked by ornamental bridges or cascades, and temples backed by trees made focal points on lakeside banks or islands. He used beech, oak, Scots pine and sweet chestnut in great quantity and with consummate skill to create scenes which took into account the changing seasons and the light. His genius in being able to visualise what the landscape would look like when it was mature has resulted in his work being mistaken for that of nature itself. Like any great art, his work appears effortless.

Brown's purist treatment was followed by the

An Arcadian landscape garden by William Kent peopled with nymphs and satyrs.

more human and pliable stance of Humphry Repton. In 1778, due to lack of funds, this young gentleman from Norfolk was forced to decide what career he should pursue to sustain his young family. A quick assessment of his talents pointed to his becoming a landscape gardener. Well educated, a fine artist, mathematician and knowledgeable plantsman, he embarked on a highly-successful occupation. Perhaps he did not share Brown's flair for business, but his ability to design a garden which suited clients' needs — dedicated followers of fashion were tiring of unrelieved landscapes — guaranteed his success. His work is the stepping-stone between the 'natural' landscape and a return to the often ostentatious formality of the Victorian era.

The landscapes on which he was consulted (unlike Brown he did not oversee the work) were shrinking in size — which emphasised the importance of the house. He believed it should be more harmoniously linked to the landscape by means of terraces, paths and eventually flower beds or areas devoted to specific collections, such as American plants, which would make the surrounds of the house more human. This frequently involved advising on improvements to the house as well as the garden, and the Red Books, where he illustrated his ideas for clients, show the changes to be made to the landscape and to the outward appearance of the house. One page showed the property as it stood, and an overlay illustrated how the scene might be improved. These Red Books were ingenious and display admirably his fertile imagination and 'eye' for transforming an unremarkable house and garden into one of style and beauty. He was as adept at turning his hand to different architectural styles — Gothic, and even Indianesque — as he was at masking defects in the landscape. He made the boundaries of smaller properties seem much larger than they were, and he could visualise how any scene would look at different times of the day or year.

Despite his artistic talents, he was not seduced into joining Richard Payne Knight and Sir Uvedale Price, who were making wild and rustic rather than romantic 'picturesque' landscapes. He did not want to create a static picture but a living garden, and he never forgot the havoc the changing seasons and light could bring. He used rustic or fanciful features, but only if it suited the situation and contributed to the whole.

Not all the fine landscapes of the eighteenth century were designed by professionals such as Kent, Brown or Repton. As is often the case in garden-making in this country, the work of the talented amateur is the most inspiring. Henry Hoare's landscape at Stourhead, John Aislabie's at Studley Royal and Charles Hamilton's at Painshill (in the throes of being renovated) stand out. The grotto at Painshill represents the vogue for melancholy-inducing features which also housed a collection of minerals. Collections of scientific and other artefacts were all the rage at the beginning of the century, and the collectors, who would often go to great length to collect absurd oddities, came to be known as 'virtuosos'.

The landscape garden has weathered the test of time better than any other style. It took a considerable time to mature, but even when it turned the corner and began to decay its romance was intensified rather than blighted. The temples which sprout weeds from crumbling pediments, the now-genuine ruins and twisted and decaying trees seen in these old landscapes now resemble those Arcadian scenes painted by Claude and Poussin more nearly than when they were first laid out. Ours is probably the last generation to see Brown's landscapes as he intended them; his clumps and belts of trees are nearing their end and their placing was so precise that newly planted groups do not produce the same skilfully-composed series of vistas.

Only a limited collection of plants was used in the landscape, apart from trees and evergreens such as laurel and yew, but the botanical world was fizzing with life and those who had the money were making extraordinary collections of exotics. The Swedish botanist Linnaeus became renowned for his classification of plants and the respected curator of the Chelsea Physic Garden, Philip Miller, published his *Gardener's Dictionary* in 1731. The professional planthunter made his début and those such as the King's Botanist, John Bartram of Philadelphia, were able to turn a hobby into a full-time occupation. In 1768 Sir Joseph Banks sailed with Cook to Australia aboard *The Endeavour*, frequently risking his life in his efforts to find new botanical treasures. He encouraged many others to do the same and it was due to his efforts that Kew, then a royal garden, became the most obvious place to send new botanical finds. Plants were sent by Jesuit priests from China, pelargoniums, heathers and proteas from South Africa, the West Indies and Azores, and orchids and rhododendrons were introduced. So great was the interest in plants and garden-making by the end of the century that seven men (one of whom was Banks) met at Hatchard's bookshop in Piccadilly on 7 March 1804 and formed what was to become the Royal Horticultural Society.

The work of William Kent can be seen at Rousham, Claremont, Chiswick House and Stowe. There are too many examples of 'Capability' Brown's work to list, but good examples can be seen at Blenheim Palace, Harewood House, and at Bowood and Longleat in Wiltshire. Humphry Repton's work can be seen at Attingham Park and at Sheringham Hall.

THE VICTORIAN GARDEN

The diverse collection of styles and the use of intricate detail in gardens during the nineteenth century, though gradually introduced, were in complete contrast to the restraint of the eighteenth-century landscape, whose 'natural' beauty relied on the discipline of their designers. Had they lived a century later, Kent, Brown and Repton would not have allowed their clients to muddy the picture by insisting on features often used only for ostentation or novelty. It is not difficult to understand the re-awakened desire at this time for a garden rather than a landscape, but many gardens of this period show a lack of decision or eye for harmony, which resulted in a hotch-potch of styles rather than a well balanced overall design.

That great nineteenth-century invention, the steam engine, epitomised the pace and energy of the Victorian era. It heralded a new prosperity and confidence. Progress in one area triggered off advances in others; so fast did one innovation follow another that discrimination was not always exercised. The 'workaholic' is not a twentieth-century invention; the scientists and inventors of Victorian times did not spare themselves in pursuing new discoveries and ideas. When they were not researching or constructing, they were putting pen to paper so that others could benefit by reading their books and magazine articles. The impact and spread of knowledge was consequently greater and quicker than ever.

The Chinese garden at Biddulph Grange, a unique Victorian theme garden.

As industry and commerce prospered, a wealthy middle class emerged who wished to live conveniently near their source of income but set themselves apart from the squalor and overcrowding they had helped to create in the cities. Improved transport and roads contributed to the building of villas on the outskirts of towns, where there was fresh air and an opportunity to display new-found wealth.

The evolution of the villa garden owes much to John Claudius Loudon, who worked himself to a standstill, dying on his feet while he dictated another book to his wife. He wrote extensively about the design, content and care of villa and

The Egyptian garden at Biddulph Grange.

other gardens in books like *The Suburban Gardener and Villa Companion*, published in 1823. As Brown took on the mantle of Kent, and Repton that of Brown, Loudon was an enthusiastic advocate of his forerunners' work though he, like Repton, was to develop a style of his own: the 'gardenesque'. He described this as 'that kind of scenery which is best calculated to display the individual beauty of trees, shrubs and plants in a state of nature; the smoothness and greenness of lawns; and the smooth surfaces, curved directions, dryness and firmness of gravel walks; in short, it is calculated for displaying the art of the gardener.' Loudon took into account the needs of those who used the garden; this, rather than aesthetic principles, dictated its design, and he also took much more interest in the choice, care and use of plants. Better known for his books and for publishing *The Gardener's Magazine* than for the private gardens he designed, he influenced the layout and planting of many of the public parks which were beginning to appear.

Mindful of how they appeared to the world at large, the wealthy Victorians — whether suffering from guilt, a genuine philanthropic feeling or simply a desire to make their cities more splendid — were energetic in creating such welcome public spaces. Urban life today would be sadly impoverished without them, and many still reflect the fashions of those times, though the scale of bedding-out of tender and half-hardy plants typical of the period can no longer be afforded. Loudon was responsible for encouraging the planting of more broad-leaved flowering trees and shrubs in these parks, relieving the gloom produced by the popular evergreens. His taste in design and plants was lighter, more practical and altogether less ostentatious than that of Sir Joseph Paxton, who was to overtake him and oversee the development of the high Victorian garden.

An archetypal Victorian, Paxton was able to pursue several successful careers on top of administering the Duke of Devonshire's garden at Chatsworth. An architect, engineer, railway director and Member of Parliament, his inventive skills in designing and constructing stoves and greenhouses — including that king of glasshouses, the Crystal Palace — was unmatched.

His work influenced the fashionable gardens of the time in a dramatic way. He built a stove house for the Duke's collection of exotics which covered an acre. He succeeded in bringing to flower *Victoria amazonica*, the giant water lily whose leaves were big enough to support a small child, and this prompted a further glass house, the design of which inspired that of the Crystal Palace. Soon no garden was complete without its greenhouses for raising thousands of tender and half-hardy bedding-out plants and growing early-ripening fruit, but also one devoted to a collection of exotics. Whether it was due to the wealth of his employer or to personal taste, whatever Paxton created was larger than life. He was not an innovative garden designer, favouring styles already popularised by Loudon and Barry, but everything he touched was bigger, more colourful and more richly embellished.

The Victorian villa garden, though on a considerably smaller scale, was evolving in much the same way as that of the aristocratic mansion. An Italianate terrace was considered a suitable platform for both a noble and a middle-class dwelling, an architectural device which linked the garden to the house. Much used by the architect Sir Charles Barry, who had been impressed by them in the Renaissance gardens of Italy, they were usually balustraded and decorated with fountains, urns and vases, grandiose flights of steps, and parterres.

Both Sir Charles and the designer William Nesfield did much to promote intricate and disciplined parterres composed of swirling patterns or 'arabesques' of low box hedging, which were filled with bright contrasting flowers or coloured gravels and minerals. As the plants used were frequently tender or half-hardy (geraniums, calceolaria, and lobelia being popular) and varied from year to year (even from season to season), these gaudy features were an ideal vehicle to display an owner's financial good health and show off the gardener's talents. The cost of raising these in heated greenhouses was considerable, due to the quantities of fuel needed for the system of hot water pipes.

There was a more scientific approach to the cultivation of plants, because enthusiasts pooled their talents to further the cause of horticulture.

Victorian grandeur at Waddesdon.

At the top of the scale was the Horticultural Society, which received its Royal prefix in 1861; lower down there were the more modest but no less serious gardening clubs set up by artisans. The clubs concentrated on raising what were called 'Florist's flowers' — auriculas, primulas, carnations and pinks. A dramatic increase in the number of nurseries also brought about a higher standard of plant cultivation and knowledge. Wealthy societies could afford to commission artists to make botanical drawings and then lay out their own ornamental or botanic gardens; most, whether large or small, held flower shows.

Thanks to the encouragement and example of Sir Joseph Banks, the introductions of plant-collectors were doing more to change the face of nineteenth-century gardens and the English landscape than any other factor. The Victorians were hungry for anything new, a plant's novelty value often taking precedence over its beauty or usefulness. Large sums were paid for these novelties, which enabled nurseries like Veitch and Sons, as well as botanic gardens and horticultural societies, to finance further plant-hunting expeditions. The dour and intrepid David Douglas faced scalping by Indians and starvation in north-west America in his determination to return with an unrivalled bag of new introductions, which included the Monterey pine, the Douglas fir and other, now familiar, conifers.

These trees prompted the gentleman of the day to enhance his property with an arboretum. No one had any idea of how these novelties would fare in our climate or to what size they would grow, but their availability was good enough reason to start a collection. Touring the countryside today, it is not hard to spot where some fine country mansion lies: it may well be tucked out of sight, but the towering spires of conifers, a little ragged with age, soon give its position away. The modest but decorous proportions of nineteenth-century villas are now made ridiculous by giant firs lowering over them; the misguided habit of planting monkey puzzles right outside the front door, which intriguingly persists today, reveals the botanical ignorance of those who originally planted them.

A London doctor working in the East End, Dr Nathaniel Ward, invented a miniature glasshouse or terraria, called a Wardian Box. This gave the planthunters a much greater chance of success. Until 1834, if plants were lucky enough to survive the journey across wild terrain to a port, they were stored on deck, exposed to salt winds and spray, or starved of light and air and eaten by rats in the ship's hold. Dr Ward's boxes offered protection, light and moisture. Joseph Hooker, the son of the administrator of Kew, Sir William Hooker, benefited from it, and planthunted successfully in South America, India and Africa. Two brothers, William and Thomas Lobb, commissioned by Veitch and Sons, also scoured South America and the East Indies, and another Scotsman, Robert Fortune, benefited from the opening up of China and Japan. Orchids became all the rage, as did variegated and other evergreens such as mahonia. Tuberous begonias were added to the list of bedding plants, and azaleas, rhododendrons, tree peonies and chrysanthemums became available.

As the choice of plant material widened and knowledge of their care expanded, the gardener's load was eased by the invention of the lawnmower in 1832. An important and powerful figure on the estate payroll, despite no longer having to hand-scythe the lawns, the head gardener still had to oversee a large staff, keep the town house and the country house well stocked with fruit and flowers, stoke the greenhouse boilers and raise and plant out the formal beds two or three times a year. The manufacture of artificial stone during this time enabled many people to add fountains, statues and vases to gardens already sagging under the weight of rustic and other fashionable features — thatched summerhouses, root houses, iron and trellis work. In the 1840s James Pulham invented a

cement which could be poured over rocks to form vast boulders, which were then fashioned into naturalistic rock formations. Ferneries under glass or in the open were popular, as were Japanese gardens with bridges and tea-houses. Mixed borders were planted with lines of flowers of contrasting colours, forming gaudy 'ribbons' and, while the gentleman of the house was busy planning his arboretum, his wife was tending her conservatory, now as much a part of the house as the morning room or the smoking room. She would see that her recently acquired house plants were kept watered, enter competitions for table and other floral decorations of 'refined taste' and did not feel it beneath her dignity to take an interest in the garden itself. Gardening began to be considered a ladylike pastime and books on the subject such as *Gardening for Ladies*, *The Ladies Flower Garden*, and *The Lady's Country Companion* written by John Loudon's widow, Jane, were well received.

At a time when refined people were covering the legs of their pianos, the Victorian garden reached a pitch of vulgarity and unembarrassed ostentation. By the 1880s it had gone as far as it could go and a backlash was about to be felt. The spotlight was being turned on to the forgotten and uncontrived contents of the simple cottage garden and hedgerow, which was to inspire, yet again, a return to a quite different but again 'natural' garden-making style.

Gardens containing Victorian features are numerous; good examples can be seen at Ascott, Cliveden, Waddesdon Manor, Chatsworth, Tatton Park, Chester Zoo, Peckover House and at Alton Towers. Two gardens much talked about and considered unique in their time are at Elvaston Castle and at Biddulph Grange.

FROM ROBINSON'S NATURAL GARDEN TO JOHNSTON'S HIDCOTE

The dramatic action of a young Irishman was to sound the death knell of what he would later call the 'pastry-cook' style of gardening. Whether it was in a fit of pique or an accumulation of fury

Lupins at Jenkyn Place, where the borders have an Edwardian generosity.

is not known, but in 1861 William Robinson threw open the doors of his employers' hot-houses, exposing the tender plants to the cold, and fled. The deed was symbolic and character-istic, for Robinson spent the rest of his life waging war on the artificial and tortured style of Victorian gardens and their worship of tender plants. He advocated instead the making of wild or natural gardens, a new ecological view which would warm the hearts of today's conservationists.

Naturally, Robinson's gesture was not the sole cause of the ensuing garden revolution. It happened to coincide with other influential el-ements. Hardy plants were beginning to flood in from China and Japan; increasing numbers of the well-to-do were building small country houses in the home counties and elsewhere; labour and fuel costs had risen, which caused the disappearance of hordes of gardeners and extensive hot-houses; and the new Arts and Crafts Movement led by Morris and Ruskin, which promoted the craftsman-made, essentially

English article as opposed to the machine-made; all these elements created the conditions for a new attitude to garden-making. Robinson's message suited the needs and the tastes of a new generation of garden-owners.

His work in the Royal Botanic Gardens in Regent's Park, where he was responsible for hardy herbaceous plants and building a collec-tion of English wild flowers, inevitably led him down country lanes, past hedgerows and cottage gardens. These expeditions and those he made later to France, Switzerland and America must have influenced him, and it was not long before he, like former innovators, gave up regular em-ployment and devoted himself to writing books and publishing magazines which would most effectively transmit his message. In *The Wild Garden* he says: 'The idea of the wild garden is placing plants of other countries, as hardy as our hardiest wild flowers, in places where they flourish without further care or cost.' Shrubs should be planted to display their individual qualities (an idea which Loudon, whom

Robinson admired, had held before him); hardy herbaceous plants should be allowed to grow in a wild situation, bulbs should be scattered in the rough grass around shrubberies, and the walls of the house should be draped with clematis and roses.

Robinson tolerated a degree of formality around the house, but recommended that the garden should become increasingly wild the farther it stretched for, as he wrote in his *The English Flower Garden* '. . . the best kind of garden grows out of the situation, as the primrose grows out of a cool bank.' Many of his ideas are now so well absorbed that it is easy to forget the impact they had when first put forward. Some of his ideas, as is often the case when a cause is championed by a dogmatic and eccentric character, proved to be impractical and a little absurd: peonies in rough grass and delphiniums in hedgerows were examples. Robinson did not always follow his own dictates; despite the fact that he inveighed against a garden made of straight lines and regimented beds, his own at Gravetye in Sussex contained its fair share of these, and he was not above growing a few tender and exotic plants.

In 1871 he launched *The Garden*, 'an illustrated weekly journal of horticulture in all its branches', to which he invited his gardening friends to contribute articles. Among these were churchmen like Dean Hole and Canon Ellacombe who typified a new breed of garden enthusiast. Sufficiently wealthy, with time on their hands to collect, cultivate and experiment with plants, they eloquently and often entertainingly informed their readers of their gardening experiences and botanical observations. These enthusiastic amateurs exerted considerable influence and the dean's passion for and knowledge of roses was to lead to his involvement in the foundation of the National Rose Society.

From 1899 to 1902 Miss Gertrude Jekyll edited the magazine, a woman whose education, artistic talents and practical attitude to gardening had already earned her a reputation as a designer. Miss Jekyll was in full agreement with Robinson's message, and was much more adept at putting it into practice. She inspired where he exaggerated and dismayed, and her garden-

making ideas and principles are as applicable today as in her lifetime. She loved the artless beauty of the cottage gardens near her home in Surrey, which were filled with old-fashioned plants overlooked for so long. Her use of these, with the improved varieties of herbaceous plants such as delphiniums, peonies and an avalanche of newly-introduced hardy plants, was innovative and skilled and gave birth to the herbaceous border as we know it today. Although failing eyesight prevented her from pursuing a career as an artist, her artistic talents were not wasted: her understanding of the effects of light, and her feeling for colour, texture and form were focused on gardens rather than canvases. Garish constrasts of warm and cold colours were replaced by blending and progressions, climaxes of hot reds and oranges and purples and blues being gradually built up. Roses, such as 'The Garland', were planted to cascade over holly trees, and plants such as hostas, bergenias and silver-leafed subjects created subtle foliage effects. Gertrude Jekyll was not averse to including the tender plants or formal elements of design from an earlier era, but only if they suited the situation. In *Wood and Garden* she said: 'The main purpose of a garden is to give its owner the best and highest kind of earthly pleasures', but she was impatient with those who imagined they could enjoy these without putting in a great deal of hard work. She always wrote from experience and her books, far from being simply airy-fairy sources of inspiration, were packed with practical information and good sense.

The host of rhododendrons, azaleas and other shrubs and specimen trees then becoming available were used to link the garden to its natural, often woodland, surroundings. Woodland gardens, first developed during the Victorian era, became popular, and began to be enriched by this flood of accommodating plants; those blessed by the Gulf Stream were able to grow a number of surprisingly tender varieties. The choice of plants was widened further by enthusiasts who produced their own hybrids. The gardens where plants, shrubs and trees displayed their natural beauty instead of being straitjacketed by rigid, formal design, were cheaper to create and easier to maintain. They suited and

Rhododendrons at Bodnant, one of the finest twentieth-century gardens.

were most readily taken up by the prosperous middle class who were building their modest country houses, and by those who chose to enjoy the best of both worlds and made their homes in one of the new garden suburbs. Miss Jekyll's own garden at Munstead Wood was a perfect example; as she was uncrowned queen of what came to be known as the Surrey School of Gardeners, it helped to engineer the change. The acid, sandy Surrey soil of Munstead Wood was particularly friendly to the flood of new hardy plants like rhododendrons and azaleas, which flourished in the dappled shade of the pine and birch woodland, the 'wild' part of the garden.

Architecture and garden design have always been inextricably linked but the turn of the century saw an extraordinarily successful collaboration between the two; Reginald Blomfield and Edwin Lutyens were the foremost architects of the turn-of-the-century country house. To own a Lutyens house and a Jekyll garden was considered the height of fashion. Edwin Lutyens was considerably younger than Gertrude Jekyll, but the enthusiastic young man and formidable, rotund old woman struck up a fruitful friendship. Both were admirers of fine craftsmanship, and together they produced over a hundred gardens designed as harmonious extensions to houses. Lutyens designed an architectural frame — symmetrical stone or herringbone brick paths, terraces, circular steps, rills and ponds, pergolas

and tranquil walks. Miss Jekyll complimented his design with suitable and imaginative plants. Blomfield also laid out gardens with a strong architectural base, so strong in fact that their symmetry and stonework dominated the plant content, forcing it to play second fiddle. William Robinson railed against what he considered Blomfield's abominable treatment of nature, and Blomfield responded by defending his principles in his book *The Formal Garden in England*, illustrated by F. Inigo Thomas who had designed the gardens at Athelhampton in Dorset.

Harold Peto was also demonstrating his skill as an architect-cum-garden-designer. He had a greater knowledge and love of plants than Blomfield and his attachment to Italian gardens was revealed in his use of classical antique and other sculptural and architectural features in his garden at Iford Manor in Wiltshire and in the garden at Buscot Park. Those at Dyffryn, in Glamorgan, and The Hill in Hampstead, designed by Thomas Mawson, are further examples of the vogue for gardens with a strong architectural base.

Gertrude Jekyll was far from being the only woman to put pen to paper and get down to gardening. Mrs Theresa Earle, though a relative lightweight, advocated its joys and passed on

Scented Loderi rhododendron at Ramster.

gardening tips (in a cosy and often amusing way) to readers of her books such as *Pot Pourri from a Surrey garden*. The beautiful and wealthy Ellen Willmott was compiling *The Genus Rosa* and filling her garden with a large and expensive collection of unusual plants. In 1902 Viscountess Wolseley set up her College for Lady Gardeners at Glynde and a few years later wrote *Gardening for Ladies*. Even though women had not won the vote, they were making themselves felt in the horticultural world.

One section of the botanical world which remained male-dominated was that of plant-hunting, which had once again helped to bring about a change of fashion. The hardy plants which became available at the end of the century did not rely on an ever-open purse and an army of gardeners for successful cultivation, so they appealed to those of relatively modest means. Missionaries in China discovered hardy herbaceous and alpine plants as well as hardy shrubs, all of which were popular with the increasing band of plantsmen in this country. Botanical and commercial organisations like Veitch and Sons sent out professional plant-hunters to find accommodating beauties in a systematic and thorough manner; the amateur planthunter's day was over.

Ernest Henry Wilson, whose ability to get on with the Chinese must have contributed greatly to his success as a planthunter, discovered several thousand new species. He introduced the Regale Lily, the yellow Himalayan poppy *Meconopsis integrifolia*, *Rosa moyesii* and rhododendrons and azaleas. George Forrest planthunted in the Yunnan for A. K. Bulley, the founder of Bees Seeds, and discovered thousands of new rhododendron species, camellias and other plants such as the *Pieris formosa Forrestii*, introduced in 1910, which has remained a firm favourite ever since. Frank Kingdon Ward, also sent to China by Arthur Bulley, returned with new rhododendrons, primulas and the blue Himalayan poppy *Meconopsis betonicifolia*. A list of all they introduced would make a book, and their feats of daring and courage in the field make exciting reading. Their introductions were particularly welcomed by those who were inspired to make the newly popular woodland gardens

— magnolias, azaleas, rhododendrons, camellias, primulas and other acid- and shade-tolerant plants were ideal candidates.

Alpines were welcomed by those building the status symbol of the times, the rock garden. Reginald Farrer, planthunter, intellectual and writer was to mock the more pretentious features of this sort in his books, calling them 'Drunkard's Dreams, Almond Puddings or Devils' Lapfuls'. An experienced gardener, he did for rock gardens what Gertrude Jekyll did for herbaceous borders, giving good practical and aesthetic advice on their design and cultivation. Farrer collected plants in the Alps, Japan and Burma and introduced 'The Threepenny-bit Rose' (*R. farreri*) and *Buddleia alternifolia*. He was much enamoured of Japan, as were many others at the time, and Japanese gardens with authentic tea-houses, bridges, stone lanterns and bronze ornaments began to make their appearance. They were attractive but lacked the restraint and serenity of the genuine article. Like some wines, they did not travel.

At the beginning of the twentieth century, a few years before World War I was to harvest the youth of this country and transform the nation's way of life, an American called Lawrence Johnston began to turn into a garden the fields which surrounded his Cotswold manor. Hidcote has been a singular source of inspiration to garden-makers and, typical of our greatest gardens, it was the work of an amateur. It is a sublime marriage between the profuse and informal planting of the cottage garden and the strict lines of the formal garden; a natural charm and strict geometry being enjoined in a series of enclosed areas, linked to one another by vistas and symmetrical walks set on an axis. The enclosed areas or individual rooms, which vary in decoration and character, are set within hedges; pleached limes, serene pools, stylish gazebos and well-laid paths and steps all play their part without producing a confused or overdone picture. The effect Hidcote had on those lucky enough to see it in Johnston's lifetime was dramatic because he perfected it without ever putting pen to paper to publicise it or himself. Others did it for him by using his ideas in their own gardens: Vita Sackville-West and Harold

Nicolson at Sissinghurst were a perfect example. Hidcote was the first important garden to come under the care of the National Trust, which had been formed in 1895 to preserve properties of historic importance. Its establishment shows that there was an awareness of and desire to protect fine houses and gardens which might otherwise be lost to the nation.

During World War I few could afford to indulge in imaginative garden-making and growing vegetables, rather than making an ornamental garden, absorbed gardeners' energies. No one style was to dominate the scene again; just as Lawrence Johnston used the best ingredients from humble and grand gardens to produce an harmonious whole, so did those who followed. Practical considerations, availability of space and personal taste were to dictate design.

Apart from those mentioned, gardens which illustrate this period can be seen at Barrington Hall, Hestercombe, Great Dixter, Emmetts and Godinton Park; at Nymans, Wakehurst, Heaselands, High Beeches, Sheffield Park and Leonardslee; at Standen, the Savill and Valley gardens, and Folly Farm; Knightshayes, Castle Drogo, Muncaster Castle and Lingholme; Glendurgan, Trelissick, Trengwainton; Harrington Hall, Newby Hall and Parcevall Hall; Arley Hall, Rodmarton Manor, Sandringham, Spetchley Park and many others.

WORLD WAR I TO THE PRESENT DAY

The speed with which all aspects of life were to change (a single new discovery or invention generating a host of others) and the more diverse sociological spread of the nation's population who owned and took pride in their gardens, brought about a new attitude to garden-making. Until this time those who could afford to do so created gardens which reflected the current 'fashionable' style, but from now on the individual was far more inclined to follow his own taste, convenience and pocket. Gardens might contain scaled-down versions of period features, but purist attitudes were no longer struck. The

diversity of style of the exhibition gardens to be seen at the annual Chelsea Flower Show illustrate this fact admirably. A number display a re-awakened interest in wild flowers or formal geometric and architectural creations, but the majority reflect an evergreen enthusiasm for features from earlier eras, such as colourful bedding-out and rockeries.

The period between the two World Wars did not see widespread changes. In the 1920s and 1930s the architect Christopher Tunnard laid out gardens to suit the severe lines of his houses; they still seem ultra-modern today. His work, including his book *Gardens in a Modern Landscape*, received attention but did not have widespread appeal. Garden designer Percy Cane was very much more popular, less radical and perhaps better suited to the conservative English nature and terrain. The long-lasting qualities of his work can be admired at Dartington Hall, where characteristic features, such as vistas channelled through areas enclosed by trees and shrubs or hedges, abound.

The National Gardens Scheme was established in 1927 as a memorial to Queen Alexandra; it was and is an almost infinite source of inspiration and guidance to the amateur. Scores of private gardens were opened to the public, boosting that now incredibly popular pastime — garden-visiting. The National Trust formed its Gardens Committee in 1948, and talented garden-makers like Vita Sackville-West and Lord Aberconway were involved in the choice of and treatment of an increasing number of historic and important gardens. In 1929 the Institute of Landscape Architects was born; their aims were 'the advancement of the art of landscape architecture; the theory and practice of garden, landscape and civic design; the promotion of research and education therein; and the creation and maintenance of a high standard of professional qualifications'. The Institute brought about a more enlightened attitude and less haphazard treatment of public and private spaces. A number of architects still seem reluctant to think deeply about the surroundings of a new building and are often apt to plant the most unsuitable plants and trees due to horticultural ignorance. Happily, more and more architectural practices now have resident landscape architects, whose technical and artistic talents are allied with a knowledge of plants.

This age has certainly seen the emergence of the professional, particularly after World War II, when there was a strong desire to build anew, not only houses but life itself: the Festival of Britain in 1951 heralded an optimistic new beginning. The Festival gardens at Battersea were designed by Russell Page who promoted a greater awareness of the shape and texture of massed plants and the importance of the design of the garden in relation to features beyond its confines. His book, *The Education of a Gardener*,

Candelabra primulas in the Beth Chatto garden.

which described his theories and the gardens he had designed here and abroad, is as widely read now as when it was first published in 1962. The skills of landscape architects such as Sylvia Crowe, Geoffrey Jellicoe and Preben Jakobsen were increasingly in demand to transform neglected urban and rural public spaces. The surrounds of reservoirs and factories, and the proliferating number of new housing estates (the Span estates built by Eric Lyons being good examples), with towns such as Harlow New Town and Milton Keynes, were given attractive and human faces, softened by imaginatively chosen and placed plant material.

The private garden, now very much smaller, began to be treated as an extension of the house: an outside living-room which had to accommodate different functional and recreational features depending on the lifestyle of its owner — children's swings, climbing frames and slides, greenhouse, compost heap, vegetable plot and, latterly, the barbecue and swimming pool. The patio (a relation of the terrace) made its appearance; it suited ideally the modest proportions of town and suburban gardens. In the 1950s and 1960s horticulture began to grow into what is now a hugely prosperous industry, and a large number of its man-made and botanical products were produced to cater for the army of amateurs wanting an 'easy care' garden. Mechanical tools, chemical weedkillers and fertilisers, and accommodating new varieties of plants transformed the work of the gardener and gave instant results. All these, (though the range of plants on offer was limited because only reliable and easily raised varieties were stocked) could now be purchased from garden centres, trips to the nursery and hardware shop being things of the past. The hybridisation of roses which began at the turn of the century resulted in floribundas and hybrid teas blooming throughout the summer; new dwarf varieties of hardy perennials precluded the need to stake and tie; F1 and F2 hybrids of annuals produced stronger and disease-free plants; pelleted seeds, mechanically-heated propagators, and, especially, mixed and sterilised composts all combined to help the weekend gardener achieve quick and easy results.

Gardening programmes on television and radio did much to popularise the hobby, together with an ever-widening range of books and magazines giving easily digestible advice on design and gardening methods. Broadcasters such as Percy Thrower demonstrated with such ease the propagating of fuchsias or the digging of a border that many were seduced into imagining they would enjoy equal success with similar effortlessness. Island beds were a feature of his garden, a new and still popular vehicle for displaying herbaceous and other plants, promoted by the nurseryman, Alan Bloom. Lanning Roper and, later, John Brookes also influenced the design of the small garden. Brookes has written many well-illustrated books, in which his sensitive use of architectural and other plants is complemented by the suitability of the design.

Gardens displaying a collection of unusual plants, with individual specimens taking precedence over the overall design, are increasingly popular today. Through television the botanist and plant collector, Roy Lancaster, among others, has broadened gardeners' knowledge and appreciation of such plants, by describing entertainingly their natural habitats and special qualities. The enthusiast has always sought after the rare but today, thanks to a large number of specialist plant societies such as the Hardy Plant and Alpine Societies, the unusual is more readily available. Those of modest means can now contribute to plant-collecting expeditions and, in turn, with typical generosity, they share their 'finds' with fellow enthusiasts.

The flower arranger has helped to expand the range of plants being grown — variegated, architectural and colourful foliage is now as much in demand as flowers. Nurseries, neglected for a time by those who favoured the garden centre, are propagating a much wider range of plants, their customers having become more demanding. Their lists, and those of seed companies, advertise nothing like the quantity of varieties of one plant offered by their Victorian forebears,

but, together with proliferating small specialist nurseries, they are breaking new ground by introducing new plants and propagating many old favourites. Old-fashioned shrub roses have made a comeback, gardeners happily sacrificing a bush which flowers throughout the summer for a shrub which produces delicate, or fragrant blooms for only a few weeks a year. Violas and double primroses are as much sought after as new hybrid rhododendrons and oddities such as pink delphiniums and blue roses. Unfortunately, the plantsman's garden is particularly vulnerable to decay; once the collector has ceased to tend it, much irretrievable material is lost. The individual 'personality' of any garden, painstakingly designed and planted by its owner, is an equally fragile quality. Even though faithfully tended in its habitual way, without its creator's magic touch it often has a lacklustre air.

The continuing 'life' of a garden is a problem of our age. A number of the most beautiful were created during the twentieth century (Bodnant and Sissinghurst being good examples), but a large proportion were not planted for posterity. Perhaps their owners felt that they would soon be moving on, be wiped out by The Bomb or were reluctant to invest in plants and trees they mistakenly thought they would never see mature. Owners of large estates, as well as those of more slender means, have failed to plant or replace trees. The dire results on the countryside of Dutch elm disease failed to alert them to the danger of shortsightedness. The garden's protective overcoats — shelter belts, and the superb collections of native and specimen trees in landscape, woodland and other gardens — are now reaching the end of their lives and it is only now, thirty years too late, that owners are beginning to cater for the future. It is odd that when so much is being done to preserve the environment one of its most lasting elements comes so low on the list of priorities.

Fortunately, our rich heritage of plants is now protected by the National Council for the Conservation of Plants and Gardens in Britain. Run on a voluntary basis, branches of the NCCPG all over the country are responsible for various collections of plants, some varieties of which might otherwise have been lost. A number

Barbara Hepworth modern sculpture garden.

of these National Collections can be seen in private and other gardens open to the public. It could be said that certain insignificant varieties are not worth the trouble of conserving and propagating but who is to decide what is and what isn't? On balance, it is better to do a thorough job.

The current interest in ecology and natural good health has seen the emergence of the wild and the organic garden. Gardeners are now aware of the dangers of liberal doses of chemicals and that 'easy care' gardening methods, speed and convenience are a two-edged sword. These have banished wild life from the garden — ladybirds, which formerly kept down pests, have been killed off, and bees, which aided fertilisation, have been frightened away, together with other welcome visitors such as butterflies and birds. Today's wild gardens, whose purpose is to attract and provide cover, food and a safe habitat for such insects and animals, are not like those advocated by William Robinson a century ago. Instead of marrying cultivated plants to a 'wild' environment they try to recreate the well-balanced genuine article — pond, meadow, hedgerow and woodpile being the essentials. The uninitiated might think that a wild garden will simply evolve if you leave an area of cultivated ground to revert to a jungle. This is not the case; it is as man-made as the eighteenth-century landscape garden. Its owner has to know the needs of the fauna he wants to attract, and be willing and able to provide them; time also has to be spent preventing some more robust elements from swamping others. Contrary to what some people suppose, it is not simply an excuse for the presence of nettles.

Meadows, orchards and banks of rough grass are increasingly being enhanced by wild flowers. The cowslip is now as highly valued as the hybrid rhododendron and has its place in the garden with other protected wild flowers; primroses, fritillaries and violets. The garden writer Margery Fish did much to popularise common and unusual varieties of these plants during the 1950s and 1960s, rescuing a large number from extinction. It is not easy to naturalise such plants, since spreading mixed grass and wild-flower seed is not enough. The ground must be cleared of docks and thistles, grass must be sown and the flowers, raised from seed, introduced individually. Those delightful meadows spotted with ox-eye daisies and other wild flowers, seen in gardens such as Cranborne Manor, are deceptively natural. They take time and energy to establish.

The organic garden, where no chemicals or artificial fertilisers are used, relies on predatory insects doing their job and on the beneficial properties of manure and 'home-grown' compost. The flower garden flourishes, the growing medium being friable and fruity, and fruit and vegetables grown in this way, though uneven and marginally less productive, are full of flavour and free of that bogey man of the age, 'artificial additives'. The energetic pursuit of good health which has become almost a new religion, will increase the popularity of this method of gardening, particularly in the vegetable garden.

Enthusiasm for conservation in the botanical world is matched in other related areas. The Garden History Society was formed in 1965, and has worked ever since to promote an interest in all aspects of garden history from architectural and garden design to the propagation of plants. It has listed and advised on the restoration of historic gardens, Claremont Landscape Garden being an example. We have a rich heritage of historic gardens, a good number of which have been simplified or neglected due to lack of funds or labour. Interest in these period pieces, and the insatiable appetite for garden-visiting mean that many of these are rising like phoenixes. Period features, such as work-intensive parterres, are being faithfully reinstated; architectural and man-made features are being repaired. When restoring an historic garden overlaid with distinctive features from a later period, it is not always easy to decide what should take precedence. The opinions of the historian, architect, landscape designer and gardener are often in conflict and a compromise has to be made. At least it is well-informed.

Gardens today are so diverse in character that it is difficult to pinpoint a unifying factor. One might be that in the private sector they are invariably designed and tended by the owners. Another is their reduced size and the tendency to include a variety of scaled-down period and modern features — knot gardens, double herbaceous borders, *allées* of pleached limes, island beds, arboreta and wild gardens. These can produce a busy rather than restful picture if the importance of including serene open spaces is ignored. The modern town garden, if not romantic and wild, is becoming increasingly formal and purist. Geometric beds, gravelled or paved paths, elegant gazebos, clipped evergreens and, often, only white flowers, produce a stylish plot, easy to tend and reminiscent of an ancient courtyard or seventeenth-century formal garden. The Victorian and Edwardian cottage garden, so romantically portrayed in the paintings of Helen Allingham, is also popular with gardenmakers. Many strive for that profuse, fragrant, rustic effect, which is much harder to engineer than might be imagined and even harder to tend.

Unfortunately, there will always be a faction which classifies gardens into U and non-U categories, the words 'good or bad taste' being liberally used. Plants fall in and out of fashion as do garden-making styles. What, in a former age, was considered the height of fashion is now unjustly thought of as vulgar or ugly, instead of being valued as historically interesting. The ribbon planting so beloved by wealthy Victorians now decorates the small cottage or suburban garden and, in turn, the style of the humble Victorian cottage garden has been transported to the country house. Though certain periods have seen the introduction of clearly defined styles, it was only a small minority of the population who could afford to follow fashion in the past. The majority changed their gardens only gradually and were always one or several steps behind the times. Thankfully, the rich landowning classes who might have changed their gardens consistently to reflect current taste, were sometimes prevented from doing so by periods of financial hardship. Accordingly, many untouched period gardens have survived and been restored. We have an extraordinarily rich heritage of gardens in this country, and an army of experts and enthusiasts to guarantee its safety.

Japanese effect created by conifers and large scale scree.

The Japanese Garden at Tatton Park

The Gardens

ABBOTSBURY SUB-TROPICAL GARDENS

MAP I

Abbotsbury, near Weymouth
9m (14½km) west of Weymouth on B3157
Owner: Strangways Estate
Tel: Abbotsbury (0305) 871387
Open daily mid-March to mid-October

The climate of this garden is unique in Britain. A combination of warmth and low rainfall, the result of its position on the seaward side of the coastal range of hills, renders it capable of growing tender plants that need protection in other places. It is in an area of outstanding natural beauty and placed where a loamy-acid soil allows lime-hating plants to grow in a region of chalk downs.

Abbotsbury Castle, the Georgian house from which the garden was separated by a quarter-mile of drives, no longer exists, but the gardens are still owned by the Fox-Strangways family, one of whose ancestors, the 4th Earl of Ilchester, was a renowned botanist, whose original introductions of the nineteenth century still thrive at Abbotsbury.

The gardens are now fully restored after a period of neglect during the first half of this century, and recent expansion to twenty acres has fulfilled the plans of the nineteenth-century designers. The garden is in a constant state of evolution horticulturally as well, with new introductions from all over the world proliferating each year as Abbotsbury becomes more and more to be a test bed for hardiness as well as a sumptuously beautiful garden.

There are some magnificent specimen trees, a Chinese wing nut which is considered the finest in Europe, magnolias, and superb cornus. Tree ferns, azaleas, rhododendrons, camellias, osmanthus and hydrangeas present a lush and colourful picture. The rose garden has old-fashioned varieties, chosen specifically for their fragrance and delicate blooms, and the banks of ponds and the stream that winds down the valley are decorated with moisture-loving primulas, rodgersias, lysichitums and gunneras. The outsize architectural foliage of the gunneras adds a touch of drama to this botanically fascinating garden.

ACORN BANK

MAP A

Temple Sowerby, near Penrith
On the A66 just north of Temple Sowerby, 6m (9½km) east of Penrith
Owner: The National Trust
Tel: Ambleside (053 94) 33883
Open regularly from Easter to end October
(peak seasons spring and summer)

The most interesting feature of the two-and-a-half acres at Acorn Bank is an attractive herb garden set within the old walled kitchen garden. It has one of the finest collections of medicinal and culinary plants to be seen in the country: common and unusual varieties which were used to cure, flavour and scent are here in abundance, many as popular today as in centuries past. The Knights Templar inhabited the site in the twelfth century and were followed by the Knights Hospitallers, whose home it was until the Dissolution of the monasteries. Mixed borders where clematis and roses abound surround a rectangular area containing orchards divided by hedged paths. As the name suggests, there is a steep bank shaded by oaks which runs down to Crowdundle Beck, carpeted with daffodils in the spring. A large number of these were planted by Mrs McGrigor Phillips who gave what was then called Temple Sowerby Manor to the National Trust in 1950. The wheel has now turned full circle and the red sandstone house is let to the Sue Ryder Foundation.

ALTON TOWERS

MAP F

Alton
4½m (7¼km) east of Cheadle on B5032, turn
north. Clearly signposted from the M1 and M6
Owner: J. L. Broome
Tel: Oakamoor (0538) 702200
Gardens open daily throughout the year
(peak months May and June)

The former home of the Earls of Shrewsbury, Alton Towers is better known as a fun park than for its Victorian gardens. Its various attractions are spread over several hundred acres and resemble, in parts, a film set, and in others a funfair. The vast Victorian Gothic house, like a sinister mansion in a horror film, surveys a scene not altogether alien to its past.

Alton has been a showpiece since Charles, the fifteenth Earl of Shrewsbury, enlarged the house and developed the gardens between 1814 and 1827. His nephew, the sixteenth earl, planted a great number of what are now dramatically large conifers. No expense was spared and the garden was packed with fantastic architectural and other features. The Victorian garden writer, John Loudon, described it as 'the work of morbid imagination joined to the command of unlimited resources'. It was — and is — a slice of eccentric garden history, a nineteenth-century period piece. The character of the unusual pleasure

gardens remains, and a number of the original architectural features have been restored, with the 'entertainments' firmly placed beyond its boundaries.

A ride in the cable car gives an exciting bird's eye view of the gardens high over the dark spires of the conifers and the Chinese pagoda, designed by Robert Abrahams, which has a seventy-foot-high jet of water. The gardens in the steep-sided valley can then be explored on foot: the conservatories which look over to the Swiss Cottage on the far side, the many flowering shrubs and dwarf conifers in the rockery, the Italian garden and the Dutch garden with its yew arches, the Roman bath and colonnade, corkscrew fountain, the canal, ponds and lake. In true Victorian style, the formal flower beds are filled with brightly-coloured bedding plants and, in spring, the rockery is a waterfall of brilliant azaleas. A number of the listed features take time to find. Note the fine trees and the period feel of this unusual garden.

ANGLESEY ABBEY

MAP G

Lode, near Cambridge
In the village of Lode, 6m (9½km) north-east of
Cambridge on B1102
Owner: The National Trust
Tel: Cambridge (0223) 811200
Open several days a week from Easter to late June
and daily from end of June to mid-October
(peak season spring)

In 1926 the first Lord Fairhaven transformed what was formerly flat and windswept farmland into the impressively mature and composed garden to be seen today. The scale is awesome and the style, a mixture of French seventeenth-century formality and eighteenth-century landscape, even more so. Money apart, it took courage and vision to lay out such a garden in the twentieth century. A major element is the quantity of classical and other statuary and ornaments, collected by Lord Fairhaven, distributed throughout the garden. These decorate majestic walks, act as focal points and strengthen the atmosphere of various areas. Avenues of trees, some over half a mile in length, rolling lawns and mature specimen trees, together with hidden formal gardens, present a varied but cohesive picture.

The emperors' walk, recently replanted with Norway spruces (Anglesey suffered bitterly from the loss of elms), is lined with twelve busts of Roman emperors. At present, because the spruces are young, the statuary and ornaments (such as the magnificent porphyry urn) over-power the scene, but time will restore the balance and the spruces will become an effective back-cloth to this imperial walk. Formal compositions like this are constant surprises: ten Corinthian columns rise out of a dark circle of yew, a copy of Bernini's statue of David stands centre stage on the enclosed lawn, the whole set against a glowing background of golden privet and elders, and silvery willows.

A short distance from the Tudor house is a pool with a statue of Narcissus gazing at his reflection, his back turned to the hyacinth garden hidden nearby. In spring the scent from the geometric beds of blue and white hyacinths is caught within the enclosure of yew, and in summer the metallic shine of the bronze dahlia foliage echoes the vases set around. On the far side of the house, dahlias are massed in a half-moon border against a beech hedge. A ribbon of colour in a crescent-shaped corridor, the dahlia garden is designed to be admired on the move, because one can never see its full extent. But the beauty of the D-shaped herbaceous garden, designed by the late Major Vernon Daniell, is immediately apparent. Once again brilliant herbaceous plants such as delphiniums, lupins and large sprays of the delicate white blooms of *Crambe cordifolia* are set against a beech hedge.

Beyond these formal gardens, the treatment becomes increasingly natural; avenues of trees and winding walks lead to a varied collection of features. The mood changes constantly. The natural woodland charm of the surroundings of the quarry pool, the banks of the Lode millstream and swathes of daffodils and wild flowers give way to features more obviously man-made, elegant and formal. Anglesey Abbey garden is a wonderfully successful blend of symmetry and natural beauty.

ARLEY HALL AND GARDENS

MAP B

near Northwich
5m (8km) north of Northwich near Great Budworth
Owner: Hon M. L. W. Flower (HHA)
Tel: Arley (056 585) 353
Open regularly from Easter to end of September
Plants for sale

A series of gardens, rather than a single set piece, Arley covers sixteen acres. Justly famous, their variety, wealth of interesting plants, colour and fragrance appeal as much to the plants-man and garden lover as to those interested in design. The Warburton family have lived at Arley since the fifteenth century, but the present Jacobean-style Victorian house was built in 1840. Commissioned by the present owner's great-great-grandfather, Rowland Egerton-Warburton, the mansion is set apart from the gardens and overlooks the park; the intricate detail of its architecture being left to speak for itself.

The gardens have seen two major periods of development: the first in the mid-eighteenth century under the direction of Rowland and Mary Egerton-Warburton and the second in the nineteen sixties when the present owner's mother, Lady Ashbrook, made important changes and enriched them with a fine collection of plants. They continue to evolve; a peaceful grove was recently planted with specimen trees and shrubs such as rhododendrons, azaleas and spring bulbs.

I can describe here only a fraction of all Arley has to offer, and suggest that you follow the excellent guide. There are many hidden areas and more than one entrance to some gardens, so your steps may easily be deflected by the sight of the 'room' next door and you may miss some attractive areas. Because there is a well-balanced mixture of formality and naturalness, follow-ing the correct sequence is more rewarding than haphazard exploration. A walk lined with pleached limes leads up to the clock tower which links an ancient tithe to a Tudor barn. Beyond lies a courtyard, and an archway in one of its walls is the entrance to the gardens. The visitor is greeted with the mingled scent of roses and lavender in the intimate flag garden, where clematis clambers up poles. House and park can be admired from the furlong walk, which forms a boundary to the garden. The glorious double herbaceous borders are backed on one side by a wall and on the other by a yew hedge; they are divided into sections by ornamental buttresses of yew which frame a series of pictures.

Early in the season the colours are soft yellows, blues and white; the colouring becomes more exuberant as the season advances. An elegant summerhouse or alcove stands at the far end and at right angles to it there is an avenue of large, cylindrical ilex, which leads to a circular lawn, decorated with a sundial and beds of shrubs and roses. What was once a nineteenth-century rockery is shady and lush with unusual willows, maples, shrubs, and moisture-loving plants around a small pond. The old kitchen garden is now a formal walled garden with a central pond surrounded by Dawyk beeches and heraldic beasts. Borders around the perimeter have felicitous collections of shrubs and plants, many with unusual foliage. Greenhouses in another walled kitchen garden have figs, vines and exotic plants for the house, and beyond lie two intimate 'rooms' — a herb garden and one, enclosed by yew, filled with scented plants.

ARTHINGTON HALL

MAP B

Arthington, near Otley
5m (8km) east of Otley on A659
Owners: Mr and Mrs C. E. W. Sheepshanks
Tel: Leeds (0532) 842 115
Open one day a year for charity and by
appointment
(peak months May and July)

Built in 1801, the sandstone mansion has a splendid view down over the river Wharfe to an eyecatching, multi-arched, railway viaduct to the east. The garden is to the west, protected from the bitterly cold east winds which race up the river valley.

A handsome south-facing conservatory acts as an entrance to the house, and is decorated with tender subjects, oleanders, a trumpet vine and mimosa. Lawns, large beds of heathers and fine trees add interest immediately around the house, the garden proper being at a distance behind a belt of conifers. The conifers shelter an informal area liberally planted with unusual shrubs and specimen trees. Rhododendrons, azaleas, magnolias, a snowdrop tree, *styrax japonica*, and the seldom seen white poplar 'Richardii', with its gold and silver foliage, all flourish here. The fascinating bark and autumn colour of over forty different maples prolong the season of interest. Exuberant borders of annuals, perennials and dahlias form a swathe of colour below the long wall which divides the informal garden from the kitchen gardens. Here you must decide whether to explore the half-mile-long beech walk, bounded on either side by a ha-ha, or go into the kitchen gardens.

Opportunities to see a kitchen garden run on traditional lines are rarely offered and should not be neglected. Arthington displays a good range of fruit, vegetables and flowers, both in box-edged beds and in greenhouses. The problems of maintaining such a garden to its original high standard are many but, although not in peak condition, it is still wonderfully productive. Espalier fruit trees, soft fruit, flowers for the house, roses and a splendid bed of delphiniums grow in the open together with neat rows of vegetables. A number of the greenhouses are devoted to growing a specific fruit or flower, such as melons or camellias, but there are also figs, nectarines, peaches, muscat grapes on a ninety-year-old vine and, surprisingly, strawberries. An early crop of these is grown in large pots, where the fruit ripens without being spoiled by rain or eaten by pests. Sweetly scented foliage plants, carnations and chrysanthemums also bloom under glass, completing a period picture of a working kitchen garden.

ASCOTT

Wing, near Leighton Buzzard
On south side of A418, ½m (1km) east of Wing,
2m (3km) south-west of Leighton Buzzard
Owner: The National Trust
Tel: Aylesbury (0296) 688242
Open a varying number of days a week
between Easter and September
(peak seasons spring and summer)

Ascott, though not as grand or extensive as other properties once owned by the Rothschild family, is no less rewarding to visit. It woos rather than awes and the atmosphere is of a happy and loved home. Used as a hunting box by Leopold de Rothschild from 1874, the half-timbered and gabled house is surrounded by a garden which combines Victorian formality with the natural style of garden becoming fashionable at the turn of the century. Ascott is unusual in that the formal gardens are hidden and stand at a distance from the house, which is surrounded by rolling lawns, studded with mature specimen and other trees. The immediate impression is of space and stature, enhanced by fine views over the Vale of Aylesbury to the Chilterns.

Veitch and Sons of Chelsea were involved in the original planning and planting. The house was lived in by the family only from autumn to spring, so shrubs and trees gave good colour and structure over that period: weeping copper and cut-leafed beeches, evergreens such as junipers, variegated hollies and a large quantity of golden yews. The glowing colour of the yews prevent the overall effect from being dark and heavy. Quantities of spring bulbs decorate natural areas, borders of summer flowers, good autumn colour and the garden's evergreen bone structure now give it all-year-round interest.

A unique feature is the evergreen sundial of box and yew on one of the higher lawns, which is set against a dark semi-circle of hedge. The low-clipped evergreens form Roman numerals and gnomon and spell out the words of the inscription, 'Light and shade by turn but love always'. Evergreen topiary and hedges abound and decorate and enclose the formal gardens below the grass terraces. A hedge of golden yew is an ideal backcloth to the blue, purple and lavender colouring of the herbaceous borders along the Madeira walk. Nearby, but hidden behind hedges, is a garden with a central ornamental pool and fountain in the form of a statue of Venus in her chariot, by Thomas Waldo Story. He was also responsible for the tiered fountain in the Dutch garden, which has circular beds of annuals and standard roses. To the far side of the house, a recently-planted hornbeam avenue runs down to a large lake, its surface quilted with waterlilies.

ASHRIDGE HOUSE

Berkhampstead
4m (6½km) north of Berkhamsted on B4506
Owners: Governors of Ashridge
Management College (HHA)
Tel: Little Gaddesden (044 284) 3491
Open most weekends from April to October
(peak month May)

There is so much to see in the gardens at Ashridge that visitors should leave ample time to explore its ninety acres. The setting alone is spectacular because the garden is set high and overlooks a vast acreage of wood and heathland. The first impression is of majesty: massive banks of rhododendrons, fine old trees, clipped yews and flowing lawns. These larger-than-life features are skilfully placed; the dense and dark clipped yews and evergreen mounds of rhododendrons form a contrast to the graceful foliage of spreading trees.

Ashridge has a rich history. A monastery in the eleventh century, it then became a royal residence, where Princess Elizabeth was arrested in 1554. The Bridgewater family bought it and rebuilt the house in its present Gothic style in 1808. The landscape gardener Humphry Repton was commissioned to re-plan the garden and it is a particularly interesting example of his work, for it broke with the tradition of creating pure landscape. At the Earl of Bridgewater's request, he designed formal and hidden gardens and so provided a stepping-stone to the more intensely worked gardens of the Victorian age. By that time, Repton was an invalid due to a carriage accident, and he was unable to oversee the work himself. His plans were altered and the surviving features are the mount garden and the rosary. Since Repton's time many individual gardens and features have been added, the formal Victorian terrace garden and arboretum, the heather garden, conservatory and the sunken rose garden which was once a skating and boating pool.

Be sure to seek out the twin beech treehouses to the east of the sunken rose garden; they are most unusual and intriguingly formed. The incense cedars encircling the Bible garden at the end of a stately avenue of Wellingtonias should also be seen. Throughout the season one or other of the well-tended gardens is at its peak, the massed and brilliant colours of the rhododendrons being particularly popular in May.

The three main attractions of the garden are its unspoilt setting, its well-designed landscape and the diverse collection of individual gardens. Each enhances the beauty of the other and the individual impact of each is unimpaired.

ATHELHAMPTON

MAP I

Puddletown, near Dorchester
On A35 lm (2km) east of Puddletown
Owners: Cooke family (HHA)
Tel: Puddletown (030 584) 363
Open several days a week from Easter to
mid-October

There has been a house at Athelhampton since the Middle Ages, though the present building is essentially early Tudor. The design of the formal gardens seems to be in perfect sympathy with the house, so it is surprising to find that they were begun only in 1891. Formal and strongly architectural, they are composed of a series of

Yew obelisks on the Great Terrace at Athelhampton.

interlinking 'rooms' in which stone, topiary and water play an important part. When they were designed, battle was raging between the architect and garden designer, Reginald Blomfield, who favoured formality, and William Robinson, who initiated the fashion for 'natural' gardens. Blomfield expounded his views in his book *The Formal Gardens of England* and the garden's designer, Inigo Thomas, contributed drawings.

Blomfield and Thomas were swimming against an adverse tide, but fortunately the gardens at Athelhampton stand witness to Thomas's skill and discernment. He designed the great court, terrace, corona, private garden and the lion's mouth. Obelisks decorate the Ham stone walls of the central corona and their design is echoed by the twelve, twenty-four-foot-high obelisks of yew around the pool by the great terrace. Two garden houses stand at either end, decorated with stone faces which smile with joy for summer in the west and scowl for winter in the east. Fountains, statues, lime, apple and laburnum walks create focal points at the end of vistas, and act as links or divisions between the various parts. Individual areas have been designed by the present owners, who have also contributed a collection of trees, plants and shrubs which suit the period feel of the garden. Informal walks can be enjoyed through woodland, beside the river and beyond a terrace and recently constructed canal where young trees will soon form a vista across the meadow.

ATTINGHAM PARK

MAP D

Shrewsbury
4m (6½km) south-east of Shrewsbury on A5
Owner: The National Trust
Tel: Upton Magna (074 377) 203
Open daily throughout the year

When, in 1797, Humphry Repton was commissioned by the second Lord Berwick to improve the grounds at Attingham, he was faced with a small park set on flat ground. As practical as he was imaginative, Repton realised he had to make the surrounds of the fine Palladian house appear larger and more impressive than they were and he produced one of his famous Red Books to illustrate his suggestions. He lengthened the drive by altering its alignment, planted shelter belts and clumps of trees, and created a graceful sheet of water by swelling the river Tern. He also created the illusion of a park that was limitless, by masking from view the road which ran a short distance from the front of the mansion.

Attingham is still a park and not a garden and the bones of Repton's work can be seen today, features such as a handsome grove of cedars, surviving from that time. Behind the house a walk underplanted with rhododendrons leads to an avenue of *Gleditsia triacanthos* or honey locusts and to a nut walk bordering the lawn by the old kitchen garden. A bee-house with old-fashioned straw bee-skeps stands at the far end of the lawn, its design echoed in the ornamental white seats set against the long kitchen-garden wall which supports espaliered fruit trees.

BARBARA HEPWORTH SCULPTURE GARDEN

MAP H

Barnoon Hill, St Ives
200 yards (180m) from parish church and harbour in old part of the town
Owner: Trustees of the Tate Gallery
Tel: Penzance (0736) 796226
Open regularly throughout the year
(peak months May and June)

In the heart of the old part of St Ives, this small walled garden enjoys a view of the sea over nearby rooftops. It is unusual in that it contains a collection of modern sculpture that appears quite at home in a domestic garden.

Miss Hepworth understood the landscape and our relation to it, so it is appropriate that her work is displayed in her own small landscape. Trewyn Studio was her home from 1949 until she died in 1975 and her workshops, to one side of the garden, are much as she left them, with two unfinished works on display. Many so-called architectural or sculptural plants find a home here: yuccas, phormiums, palms and bergenias, their stylish foliage forming a background or frame for the many abstract pieces, whose size is easy to relate to and may provide inspiration to those who want to include a modern, rather than a traditional, feature in their gardens.

Sculptures by the late Barbara Hepworth in her garden at St Ives.

BARNSLEY HOUSE

MAP F

Barnsley, near Cirencester
On A433 4m (6½km) north-east of Cirencester
Owner: Mrs Rosemary Verey (HHA)
Tel: Bibury (028 574) 281
Open from Monday to Friday throughout the
year and on the first Sunday in May, June and
July
(peak months April to September)
Plants for sale

Mrs Verey has contributed much to the popularity and enjoyment of country-house gardens. Her articles and books and her own garden are sources of inspiration to the professional and amateur gardener alike. Much influenced by garden writers of the past, from ancient herbalists to the books of Gertrude Jekyll and Russell Page, she uses in the garden at Barnsley design and botanical features of former ages, as well as a rich collection of well-associated plants.

In front of the seventeenth-century Cotswold stone house, mature trees shade lawns planted with spring bulbs, the more formal and intensely-

The temple in the garden at Barnsley Manor.

planted areas lying on the far side. A knot garden of dwarf box, flanked by variegated topiary hollies, is to one side of a stone terrace softened by a green haze of *Alchemilla mollis* or lady's mantle. Striking away from this is a path lined with cylindrical yews, whose dark green emphasises the frivolity of the rock roses dancing along its length. Borders of strikingly well-associated plants provide scent and colour near the house, and a pool stands in front of a classical-style temple, to the far side of an elegant wrought-iron gateway.

Vistas to various features cross and link, producing a symmetrical design which is cohesive and flowing, rather than fragmentary and diverse. A pleached lime walk becomes a laburnum arch underplanted with alliums, the sundial at the far end providing a focal point and an axis. A path leads to the fountain, roses and a delicate Gothic summerhouse a short distance from a small wilderness garden planted with ornamental trees.

A *potager* or ornamental vegetable garden lies beyond the boundary wall, a seldom-seen feature which originated in France. Box-edged geometric beds, divided by brick paths for ease of maintenance, contain an attractive collection of unusual varieties of vegetables and fruit; red chard, cabbages and lettuces, kale, alpine strawberries and standard gooseberry bushes. Arbours of golden hop, trained and dwarf fruit trees and standard 'Little White Pet' roses further enhance this area. It is a fascinating addition to a garden which manages to encompass a wide range of botanical, design and historical garden delights in a surprisingly small space.

BARRINGTON COURT

MAP I

near Ilminster
At the east end of Barrington village, 2m (3km)
north of A303 between Ilchester and Ilminster
Owner: The National Trust
Tel: South Petherton (0460) 41480
Open several days a week from Easter to late
September
(peak months May to September)

A scene of unassuming charm greets the visitor to Barrington court in the spring — a sea of daffodils colours an orchard to one side of the walk to the house. Built of Ham stone, the moated sixteenth-century building and seventeenth-century stables now converted into a house rise above walls which conceal the formal gardens, a series of enclosed 'rooms'. These were added after 1920, when Colonel Lyle, who had leased the property, embarked on its restoration and development. He consulted Gertrude Jekyll on layout, the planting of borders and beds and the pattern and construction of paths.

Each garden has a distinctive character, is set on different levels and in some cases bounded by the walls of old buildings. Miss Jekyll's influence can be seen in the imaginative design of the brick paths, the use of shapely foliage plants and in the softly blended colour, — the blues and purples of lavender, iris and clematis in the iris garden being a good example. A rose garden with geometric beds, which recently suffered from rose sickness, has had to be replanted with less vulnerable subjects, and the lily garden beyond contains large, generously planted borders of shrubs, perennials and annuals. Intimate, colourful and often fragrant, these intensely planted 'rooms' contrast with the simplicity of other features: the large expanse of lawn that stretches from the house to a ha-ha dividing the garden from the park, and arboretum and lime walk on the far side of a gateway in the wall to one end of the lawn.

A large walled kitchen garden, divided into four sections, displays espaliered fruit trees, vegetables and flowers. The whole is beautifully kept and imaginatively planted, maximum use being made of the diverse areas and available wall-space.

BARTON MANOR

MAP I

Whippingham, Isle of Wight
Next to Osborne House, near Whippingham off
A3021 East Cowes to Newport and Ryde road
Owners: Mr and Mrs A. H. Goddard (HHA)
Tel: Isle of Wight (0983) 292835
Open daily from April to mid-October
(peak seasons spring and summer)
Plants for sale

As historically interesting as they are attractive, these gardens enjoy a long season of interest.
Spring bulbs are followed by azaleas and rhododendrons, and the baton is taken up by roses
and herbaceous plants in the summer. Between
1845 and 1922 the ancient manor house, mentioned in the Domesday Book, was the property
of the crown. It was part of the Osborne House
estate, used as an overflow to Queen Victoria's
home on the island, where staff and European
royalty could stay and from which the royal
family could distance themselves politely. Prince
Albert laid out the gardens and planted many of
the fine trees which can be seen today.

The gardens of the stone-built manor cover
twenty acres and contain a satisfyingly wide
range of plants and trees and a diverse collection
of features: a fragrant secret garden, a vast lake
covered with waterlilies, a water garden with
meandering stream and waterfall, woodland
bright with rhododendrons and azaleas, a grove
of young cork oaks and the six-acre vineyard
which produces prize-winning wines. Originally
planted in 1928, there are now vast drifts of
naturalised daffodils, and borders on the terraces
near the house are generously planted with roses
and herbaceous plants. The National Collection
of watsonias and kniphofias or red-hot pokers
can also be seen here.

BATEMAN'S

Burwash, Etchingham
Off the A265 ½m (¾km) south of Burwash
Owner: The National Trust
Tel: Burwash (0435) 882302
Open regularly from Easter to end of October
(peak seasons spring and summer)

'That's her! The Only She! Make an honest
woman of her — quick!' exclaimed Rudyard
Kipling when he saw Bateman's for the first
time. Famous houses are constantly being re-
ferred to as so-and-so's 'home' but few, like
Bateman's, reflect the true meaning of the
word. Secure and welcoming, the unpretentious
Jacobean house lies, seemingly cut off from the
rest of the world, in the embrace of low Sussex
hills. While it was Kipling's home from 1902
until 1936, the gardens were altered to create a
series of different areas. They accommodated
some pre-existing features — the pleached limes
and mature trees — and were designed to suit
the character of the house. Now the ten-acre
garden is a blend of formality and naturalness
which, neither designed by a 'name' nor having
an outstanding collection of unusual plants and
trees, forms a delightful frame for the house. The
happy atmosphere is seductive and the scale and
design of the gardens easy to absorb.

The layout of the garden is essentially formal.
Symmetrical honey-coloured stone paths, walls
and yew hedges form divisions between a series
of small and large 'rooms'. Box-edged borders of
shrubs and perennials decorate the more intimate of these, and a magnolia, wisteria, *Campsis
grandiflora* and *Actinidia kolomikta* grow against
the house. To the south, on the lawns running
down to the river, is a rectangular pool. A stone
seat backed by yew is at one end, and a rose
garden, edged with London pride, at the other.
Kipling fans should note the sundial which he
had inscribed with the words 'It is later than
you think', and the stone that formerly marked
Kipling's grave in Westminster Abbey.

The walk to the mill house by the river has
cherry trees, wild flowers and spring bulbs

growing in areas of rough grass; the giant foliage of gunnera and skunk cabbage decorate the banks of the river. To the north of the house is a tunnel of fruit trees interwoven with clematis, the walk lined with beds of shade-tolerant plants such as violets, lilies-of-the-valley, perennial geraniums and Solomon's seal. On the hill beyond is an orchard, a small vegetable garden and a simple wooden pergola which, like the old fruit tree beside it, is almost smothered by the sweetly-scented rose, 'Wedding Day'. The long bed below the boundary wall is planted with herbs.

BATSFORD PARK ARBORETUM

MAP F

Moreton-in-Marsh
On A44, 1½m (2½km) north-west of Moreton-in-Marsh
Owner: Batsford Foundation (HHA)
Tel: Moreton-in-Marsh (0608) 50722 or Blockley (0386) 700409
Open daily April to October
(peak months May, June and October)
Plants for sale

First developed in 1880, this fifty-acre arboretum stands on a south-facing limestone slope. Paths and streams weave through woodland and glades which display an exceptionally wide collection of specimen trees as well as intriguing oriental features. When the architect Ernest George completed the building of the house in 1880, the first Lord Redesdale, a former British Ambassador to Japan, laid out what he called his 'wild garden'. He planted unusual trees and shrubs and embellished it with objects from the Orient: a pair of Japanese deer, a rest house, a Chinese bronze lion and Buddha, still to be seen today.

The Dulverton family bought Batsford and the second Lord Dulverton, who inherited it in 1960, decided to create an arboretum. The original garden was by then in a sorry state, but offered a promising foundation on which to build. Much has been achieved and the arboretum is now beautiful as well as botanically fascinating. Magnolias and maples are particularly well represented, and groups of evergreen and deciduous trees create a lush picture. A grove of blue cedars shimmers mistily, and the characteristic bark, foliage and flowers of other specimens is highlighted by shafts of sunlight.

Batsford will disappoint neither the specialist nor those who simply seek an energetic and attractive walk.

BEARES

MAP G

Saxtead, near Framlingham
Off A1120 between Saxtead Green and Dennington
Owners: Mr and Mrs S. A. Notcutt
Tel: Framlingham (0728) 723232
Open occasionally for charity and by appointment (peak months June, July, and autumn)

The name of the owners, the same as that of the famous East Anglian nursery, should alert the plantsman to the wealth of interest to be found in this three-acre garden. Developed over the last twenty-five years, the layout is informal, existing ditches and ponds having been skilfully incorporated into the design. The overall picture has much in common with the classic cottage garden. A water garden is lush with moisture-loving and bog plants; borders, set against a dark evergreen background, are filled with flowering shrubs and perennials. Well-labelled specimen trees are here aplenty, planted in groves and shading flower beds. A garden of this type demands constant attention and though this is not always available the wide range of material used and the relaxed atmosphere of Beares more than makes up for its uneven condition.

BEDGEBURY NATIONAL PINETUM

MAP J

Goudhurst
7m (11km) east of Tunbridge Wells on A21 turn
north on to B2079 for 1m (2km)
Owner: Forestry Commission, Research Division
Tel: Goudhurst (0580) 211044
Open all year round

In 1925 the Royal Botanic Gardens at Kew and the Forestry Commission joined forces to gather and administer a comprehensive collection of conifers. The Bedgebury estate, part of an existing forest which contained conifers planted in the last century, was acquired for the purpose. Now administered solely by the Forestry Commission, it covers one hundred acres. High ground runs down to two valleys, each of which has a stream, the two ultimately joining to form Marshall's Lake. Now the most comprehensive collection in Europe, the magnificent proportions and nature of these conifers create a pocket of Kentish countryside quite different to that familiar in the county known as England's Orchard.

The natural drama of the site and the scale of the trees make Bedgebury an exciting place to visit. Although they have been planted mostly in family groups, the irregular placing and the inclusion of a large number of deciduous specimens, such as oaks and maples, make the picture anything but artificial or monotone. The conifer expert, Walter Dallimore, was responsible for the design and created vistas with informal

Autumn in the arboretum at Batsford.

avenues of trees. One of the more regular of these is of Leyland cypress, whose awesome size should deter anyone from planting them as hedging material ever again.

There is something for everyone here, young and old, expert or amateur. Some will marvel at the mighty proportions of the hundreds of trees, even attempt to measure their girth, while others will see how many different sorts of cones they can spot or admire the subtle differences of colour, shape and texture within one family. Some may seek out specimens which might suit their own gardens, the collection of dwarf conifers near the information centre being of particular interest. The expert will thrill to the rare and unusual.

The seasons engineer subtle changes: the fresh green of new growth, flowers of rhododendrons and unusual cornus and the brilliant autumn colours giving the pinetum year-round interest. It is hard to believe, surveying such a robust scene, that the pinetum is vulnerable to frosts throughout the year, and that the soil is inhospitably sandy. It has to be rigorously prepared before anything can be planted.

23 BEECH CROFT ROAD

MAP F

Oxford
Beech Croft Road runs east-west between the
Banbury and Woodstock roads
Owner: Mrs Anne Dexter
Tel: Oxford (0865) 56020
Open by appointment only

The tiny garden at Beech Croft Road bears out the truth of 'Small is Beautiful'. Once having seen the ingenuity with which the owner has transformed such an unpromising site into a charming and richly planted garden, no one will dare to complain of lack of space again. Those who are about to make their first garden can learn a great deal from it.

The design of this tiny plot — 23 by 7 yards (20 by 6 metres) — a central path, surrounded on three sides by raised beds, is not dissimilar to

a sentrybox, but the similarity ends there. By making different levels with dry-stone walls and rocks, and raising the height of the boundary walls with trellis, Mrs Dexter can grow a staggeringly wide range of plants. She is a keen and talented plantswoman, so few of these are run-of-the-mill. The choice of plant material and the way it has been layered and disciplined is masterly. Standard prunus, *Eleagnus ebbingei* and other shrubs have been used as a backcloth to climbing roses and a collection of about thirty clematis. Smaller shrubs and herbaceous plants form the next layer and bulbs, dwarf varieties of plants and alpines grow to the front of the beds and in stone sinks near the house. Ferns, ivies, hellebores, hydrangeas and bamboo thrive in the shady passage which runs down the side of the house. Not an inch of space is wasted.

BELGRAVE HALL

MAP F

Belgrave, Leicester
Off Thurcaston road, in Belgrave, 2m (3km) from
city centre on the Loughborough road, A6
Owner: Leicestershire Museums Service
Tel: Leicester (0533) 554100 or 666590
Open regularly throughout the year
(peak season summer)
Plants for sale

A pocket of period charm, the early eighteenth-century house stands in a quiet backwater, surrounded by the bustling suburban sprawl of Leicester. The walled gardens are secluded and peaceful and, though not in tip-top order, should interest the plantsman and dendrologist and please those who enjoy discovering hidden places. The old-fashioned style of the layout — a series of walled 'rooms' is appealing, box-edged beds and gravel paths being much in evidence. A satisfying collection of unusual plants is on display, apart from borders and lawns. One area has botanical order beds and another contains glasshouses of exotics and other tender plants. There are a good number of mature specimen trees, a swamp cypress, arbutus, gingko, cercidiphyllum, nothofagus, sorbus and handsome cornus.

BELL COTTAGE

MAP B

Vale Royal, Whitegate, Northwich
Turn off A556 to Whitegate, opposite church
follow drive for ¾m (5−6km). Bell cottage to
rear of Vale Royal Abbey
Owners: Mr J. W. Ellis and Mr G. K.
Armitstead
Tel: Sandiway (0606) 883495
Open by appointment
(peak months May, June and July)

This three-acre plantsman's garden has two
quite separate parts. The smaller lies to the front
of the cottage where a lawn, rockery and alpine
garden stand between the house and the woodland below. The soil is acid, so rhododendrons
and azaleas thrive on the wooded slope, together
with other shade- and acid-loving plants. Hostas
are planted in generous groups, and perennial
geraniums, primulas, maples and a cercidiphyllum have all been used to best advantage.

Behind the cottage is the walled garden which
was once the kitchen garden to Lord Delamere's
home, Vale Royal Abbey. The cottage, originally the gardeners' bothy, looks on to an area
filled with unusual plants of all kinds. The walls
are thickly clad with climbers; borders and a
snake-like design of informal beds set in the
lawn contain old-fashioned shrub roses, herbaceous plants and shrubs such as the yellow
flowering weigela and *Ribes odoratum* or 'buffalo
currant'. A small arboretum adds interest to a
far corner of the garden.

BELSAY HALL

MAP A

Belsay
Off the A696 14m (22½km) north-west of
Newcastle upon Tyne
Owner: Sir Stephen Middleton
Tel: Belsay (066 181) 636
Open daily from April to September
(peak months May, June and July)

A twelfth-century castle, seventeenth-century
manor house and an early nineteenth-century
hall are surrounded by thirty acres of grounds.
Historically fascinating in themselves, these contain a number of period garden features, one of
them unique. The architectural style, period
and surrounding terrain of a house inevitably
influence the design of its garden. At Belsay, it
was the actual building of these which triggered
the creation of the extraordinary quarry garden.

In 1804 Sir Charles Monck and his young
bride embarked on a two-year honeymoon tour
of Europe, the whole of the second year being
spent in Athens. A keen classicist and talented
draughtsman, Sir Charles was much struck by
the ancient and neo-classical buildings he saw.
He determined, on his return, to build himself
an equally well-proportioned and noble house at
Belsay. One hundred foot square exactly, the
austere, symmetrical hall was built of stone
quarried from the grounds.

Sir Charles saw the potential this quarry might
have as a garden and, being an enthusiastic
plant-collector, he introduced many fine specimens. Successive generations have extended the
quarry and enriched its contents and it now
resembles an exotically decorated gorge which it
is an adventure to explore. A path weaves between sheer rock faces whose height is exaggerated by being topped with dark yews. The
brilliant huge species rhododendrons are shafted
by sunlight or, spied around a corner, constantly
beckoning you forward. Glossy and feathery
ferns revel in the gloom and plants grow out of
the rock at extraordinary angles. The scale and
treatment of the quarry puts it in a class of its
own. Sombre and secret enough, but too richly
decorated with plants, it cannot be classed as an
eighteenth-century grotto, and its giant proportions rule out its being compared to a Victorian-
style rockery.

Terraces at the front of the hall are decorated
with beds of lilies, roses and lavender, a ha-ha
dividing this formal area from the woodland
and rhododendron garden. The latter areas are
not open to the public. A winter garden, bounded
by high walls and the ha-ha, lies to the west, its
beautifully-kept lawn offset by fine heathers and
conifers. These gardens are gradually being restored to their former glory, having suffered from
neglect since World War II.

BELTON HOUSE

MAP G

Grantham
3m (5km) north-east of Grantham on the A607
Grantham-Lincoln road, signposted from A1
Owner: The National Trust
Tel: Grantham (0476) 66116
Open several days a week from Easter to end of
October

The symmetry of Belton House, one of the finest examples of Restoration architecture in this country, is admirably offset by the formality of its Italian and Dutch gardens. Built in the 1680s, the honey-coloured stone house was formerly thought to be the work of Wren but was, in fact, designed by William Winde for Sir John Brownlow, the son of a successful Elizabethan lawyer. It once boasted extensive seventeenth-century formal gardens, but the scene which greets the eye today dates from the early nineteenth century. It was then that Sir Jeffry Wyatville was commissioned to build the handsome orangery and lay out the Italian gardens for the first Earl Brownlow.

Sundial in the formal gardens at Belton House.

Terraced lawns decorated with box parterres stand in front of the orangery, which is filled with camellias and other shrubs. They overlook an immaculately-tended expanse of lawn, at the centre of which stands an ornamental pool and fountain, surrounded by topiary and flower-filled urns. These stone urns, together with the Italian statuary, are stylish features of the gardens, the unusually large cisterns in the Dutch garden being as eyecatching as the beds of roses. Beyond the gardens lies the landscaped park in which somewhat derelict but soon to be restored eighteenth-century features can be seen: the Belmount tower, which was once an observatory, and the wilderness, with its cascade and ruins. Woodland and other walks can also be explored.

BENINGBROUGH HALL

MAP C

Shipton-by-Beningbrough
8m (13km) north-west of York, 2m (3km) west of
Shipton, 2m (3km) south-east of Linton-on-Ouse
(A19)
Owner: The National Trust
Tel: York (0904) 470666
Open at weekends in April and regularly from
May to end of November
(peak months June and July)

Settled and elegant, the English baroque house stands at the far end of a double avenue of limes. It is built of unusually small, locally made, red bricks, and flanked by pavilions with cupola roofs, the scene little changed since the house was built in the early eighteenth century. The same cannot be said of the garden at the back of the house. Like many dating from the period, it originally boasted a parterre which was swept away later in the century and replaced by landscaping, then fashionable.

Today the seven acres of gardens stretching from the south front of the house contain a mix of period and other features. The old kitchen garden to the east, no longer used in the traditional manner and grassed over, still displays some interesting features. Its surrounding walls are hollow, which enabled the heat generated by four boilers to circulate, warm the walls and so ripen the fruit. The pitted appearance of the bricks, particularly near the entrance, is the work of masonry bees who doubtless still pollinate the pear trees that shade a central path.

The informal American Garden nearby is not devoted to plants from that part of the world, but planted with an attractive collection of spring and flowering shrubs, shaded by mature trees. Despite the limy soil, rhododendrons and azaleas grow here, with briar roses in hummocks of soft pink. Snowdrops, daffodils and fritillarias have been naturalised in the rough grass and a seldom seen coxcomb beech is an intriguing sight near the outer boundary. A bed of surprisingly tender shrubs — veronicas and other New Zealand plants — is on the far side of the kitchen garden wall, and a fragrant and luxuriant double border lines a corridor between a hedge and a wall; especially planted for the blind, this border will delight everyone. A further border near the house, where initially hot colouring fades to softer tones, was planned by the National Trust's former garden adviser, Graham Stuart Thomas. Shrub roses, peonies and a noteworthy collection of viticella clematis dominate both double and single borders.

Two yew-hedged, formal gardens, recently re-designed by Paul Miles, are on the south front of the house. One is planted with cool lemon and white flowers and the other with brilliant red roses, verbena and plants with golden foliage. A *Carpenteria californica* is against the walls of the house, where a dainty Banksian rose climbs. A nineteenth-century conservatory contains a collection of tender and other plants which create a colourful show well suited to its period character. Expansive lawns run down to the ha-ha, and the view over the water meadows beyond is uninterrupted by hedge or fence.

BENINGTON LORDSHIP

MAP G

Benington, near Stevenage
In village of Benington, 3m (5km) south-east of
Stevenage on A602 turn north to Aston
Owners: Mr and Mrs C. H. A. Bott (HHA)
Tel: Benington (043 885) 668
Open one weekend early in March, Easter
Monday; two days a week from May to July; Bank
Holidays and a few days in August; also by
appointment throughout the year
(peak months May to July)
Plants for sale

It is hard to believe that the garden surrounding the redbrick, eighteenth-century house was made only at the beginning of the present century, because it has a timeless air characteristic of an English country garden at its best. Views to the Saxon church nearby and the presence, beside the house, of a flint folly reinforce the illusion. The folly was constructed on the ruins of an ancient castle and the dry moat which once surrounded it is a marvellous sight in March, a sea of snowdrops.

When the present owner's grandfather bought the estate in 1906, very little existed of what we see today. A bowling green which lay to the south of the house has been transformed into a sunken rose garden, its geometric beds filled with varieties especially chosen for their colour and scent. To the west the garden falls away, in a series of grassed terraces, to the two ponds and the old park beyond. The condition of these lawns is as near perfection as you will ever see, quite an achievement on heavy clay soil. To the north lie a series of gardens that differ widely in character; an Edwardian rockery planted with subjects which add colour throughout the season and the yew-enclosed Shylock garden which shelters a statue of the Shakespearean miser. Restrained and peaceful, the cool dark green of the hedges rest the eye before it strikes the long herbaceous borders beyond. Profuse with old-fashioned plants of subtle colouring, these run down either side of a sloping path. It is questionable whether they are better viewed from above or below, but do not bypass the entrance to the walled kitchen garden halfway down. Well-kept and productive, it provides fruit and vegetables for the family, and its central path is flanked by beds of unusual plants and shrubs.

Benington Lordship has great charm: no feature of its garden seems out of place, over-contrived or pretentious, and there is much to interest the plantsman. The owners' love and enjoyment of the garden is well transmitted.

BENTHALL HALL

MAP D

Broseley
1m (2km) north-west of Broseley (B4375). 4m
(6½km) north-east of Much Wenlock
Owner: The National Trust
Tel: Telford (0952) 882159
Open a few days a week from Easter to end
September
(peak months May to July)

In the late nineteenth century, Benthall Hall was the home of the author of *The Genus Crocus*, George Maw. The gardens of the lovely Elizabethan house were filled with rare and unusual bulbs and alpines from Europe and North America. Only a few still exist, but there is no lack of interest thanks to the efforts of Benthall's subsequent owners. The Benthall family, who originally built the house, returned to it in 1934; they and Mr and Mrs Robert Bateman, who lived there before their return, are to be thanked for what we see today.

The rose or pixy garden, a complex series of small stone terraces with a pond and scree bed, is beside the house, and is planted with roses, Chinese tree peonies, bog myrtle and potentilla. Neat topiary cones and balls of yew decorate the top of a hedge and create an individual and stylish entrance. Either side of the lawn which runs away from the front of the house rise banks of trees and shrubs, the Japanese angelica tree, *Aralia elata*, being much in evidence. It, like the intriguing mouse plant, *Arisarum proboscideum*, and varieties of perennial geranium and Balkan acanthus, happily propagate themselves at

Benthall. To one side of the lawn, a rustic summerhouse stands beneath a lime tree, a charming period feature which adds to the garden's friendly and unpretentious nature.

BERKELEY CASTLE

MAP E

Berkeley
On B4066 at Berkeley
Owner: Mr R. J. E. Berkeley (HHA)
Tel: Dursley (0453) 810332
Open regularly from April to October
(peak months May to September)

The awesome battlements of this twelfth-century castle overlook eight acres of south-facing terraces, which have superb views over the water meadows of Doverte Brook and the surrounding countryside. A fortification decorated with plants rather than a garden, the castle's warm stone walls are a sympathetic home and backcloth to roses, wisteria, self-seeded valerian and evergreen magnolias. A swimming pool on one of the terraces has been turned into a lily pond and beds of shrubs and perennials lie in the shelter of the terraced walls. There is a small woodland garden to the north of the castle, where young specimen trees and shrubs have been planted, and the walls of the car park have been generously decorated with roses — an appropriate introduction to the garden of the great-nephew of Ellen Willmott, plantswoman and author of *The Genus Rosa*.

BERRINGTON HALL

MAP E

near Leominster
On A49 3m (5km) north of Leominster
Owner: The National Trust
Tel: Leominster (0568) 5721
Open a varying number of days a week depending
on the season from Easter to October

Berrington Hall gardens have two quite distinct attractions. The largest and most obvious is the

Berkeley Castle rising above its terraced gardens.

landscape laid out by 'Capability' Brown, which surrounds the Palladian-style mansion designed by Brown's son-in-law, Henry Holland, for the Honourable Thomas Harley, MP. The handsome house, the outer skin of which is built from locally-quarried pink sandstone, commands a fine view over a fourteen-acre lake (a classic Brownian feature) to the Black Mountains, Brecon Beacons and Radnor Forest beyond. The ha-ha, a vital ingredient of any eighteenth-century landscape, is in the throes of being excavated, and will once again create an illusion of the countryside running up to the very walls of the house. In autumn, the lawns immediately around the house are carpets of Neapolitan cyclamen and ladies' tresses orchids.

In contrast to the 'natural' landscape, the more highly cultivated gardens on the far side of the house display a good collection of tender and unusual plants. Azaleas and rhododendrons are sheltered by woodland, and fifteen different varieties of holly, a mature variegated sycamore, cut-leaf elder, handkerchief tree and snake bark maple provide colour and interest. Camellias flourish in the walled 'drying ground', where the household laundry used to be hung out of sight to dry. Tender plants grow against a sunbaked outer wall of the old kitchen garden: a *Rosa bracteata*, *campsis* 'Madame Galen', abutilon, tamarisk, piptanthus, and an intriguing and vigorous member of the marrow family, *Thladiantha oliveri*. The long path from the mansion to the gatehouse is edged with balls of golden yew, spaced apart and clipped to shape with military precision.

THE BETH CHATTO GARDENS

MAP G

**Elmstead Market, near Colchester
5m (8km) east of Colchester on A133 road to
Clacton, beyond Elmstead market on the right
Owner: Mrs Beth Chatto
Tel: Wivenhoe (020 622) 2007
Open regularly throughout the year
Plants for sale**

Beth Chatto has done a superb job of promoting interest in, and greater use of, unusual plant material. Her prize-winning exhibits at flower shows, such as Chelsea, magnetise the plantsman and the flower arranger, and her garden is one of the most fascinating plantsman's gardens to be seen in the country. Her books are invaluable handbooks and the nursery, begun in 1960, is an obvious success. Anyone grappling with the difficulties of cultivating extra dry and sunny, wet or shady areas, will find much to interest them here and a choice of solutions to their problems.

The garden is informal in design and covers a four-acre site which was a gravel slope running down to level, shady ground. The gravel slope was sunbaked and dry, and the shady ground waterlogged. Working with the existing conditions, Mrs Chatto transformed an unpromising site into a garden as vigorous and healthy as it is attractive. On and around lawns, beside paths and water and shaded by woodland, are island beds and borders containing a 'living catalogue' of unusual subjects. Many of these have been obtained from botanical gardens and specialists over twenty-two years.

Aromatic and succulent Mediterranean and other plants thrive on the dry slope, which has been terraced. Set around the pools below are bold compositions of moisture-loving plants, shaded by handsome specimen trees such as dawn redwood, swamp cypress and a *Paulownia imperialis* or foxglove tree. There are areas of dry as well as damp shade which, thanks to a thick layer of mulch, are lush with hellebores and *Arum italicum* 'Pictum'. The thick layer of mulch helps to retain moisture and suppress weeds,

and stands witness to hard work as well as an informed and imaginative use of plants. Interesting foliage abounds, from the umbrella-sized leaves of gunnera to the tiny silver filigree of an artemisia, the diverse size, shape and colour of unusual foliage being used to create a myriad of striking associations.

Every sort of plant — specimen trees, shrubs, perennials, ground coverers, herbs, grasses, alpines, bulbs — has been used and the enthusiast is recommended to leave plenty of time to explore. Opportunities to see noteworthy collections of unusual plants are less rare than they were, but they sometimes resemble a museum of plants rather than a visually pleasing picture. Mrs Chatto's garden is a delightful exception.

BICTON

MAP H

**East Budleigh, Budleigh Salterton
On A376 3m (5km) north of Budleigh Salterton
Owner: Bicton Park Trust
Tel: Colaton Raleigh (0395) 68889
Open from March to end December
(peak months May to July)
Plants for sale**

Despite the fact that the great French garden designer André Le Nôtre died in 1700, it was once thought that he had laid out the formal gardens at Bicton, which date only from 1735. They certainly show his influence, however, being Italianate, symmetrical and grand. Set a considerable distance away from the mansion, now an agricultural college, they are the heart of a large garden which contains a noteworthy pinetum and other features. Grassed terraces, instead of offsetting the façade of the house, flow away from a classical-style temple flanked by orangeries, a palm house and other glasshouses.

The first of the three terraces is decorated with formal beds generously filled with bulbs or annuals. Well-filled borders beneath the boundary walls are covered with the glossy foliage of *Magnolia grandiflora* 'Exmouth'. Urns and a line of small cherubs set on low pillars introduce the square pond on the lower terrace, which is enclosed on three sides by a canal. At each corner of the pond a statue represents one of the four seasons and in the centre there is a five-tiered fountain. The water for these elegant features comes from a spring which rises on Woodbury Common; the pressure never flags and no pump is needed, even in the driest of summers. There is a fine vista from the temple, the focal point being an obelisk high on a ridge the far side of a distant valley. Great cedars, dark yews and other mature trees frame and cast dramatic shadows over this disciplined scene.

An unusual nineteenth-century palm house, designated a Grade I building, stands to the west of the temple. High-domed and constructed of thousands of overlapping, scallop-shaped pieces of glass, this period building contains a miniature rain forest of tropical, sub-tropical and aquatic plants. The glasshouses on the top terrace have dazzling collections of geraniums and fuchsias, and temperate and tropical houses nearby are luxuriant with exotics. A variety of period and other features are beyond the walled formal gardens — a shell house and a small Victorian garden which was originally the 1984 Chelsea Flower Show *Amateur Gardening* exhibit, a long pergola draped with a variety of climbers and an oriental garden with a summerhouse, bamboo screens, rocks, water and carefully raked gravel. Camellias, azaleas, maples and peonies add colour to this soothing picture.

The magnificent pinetum, begun in the nineteenth century when so many new varieties were being introduced, is on the other side of the

A composition of moisture-loving plants in the Beth Chatto gardens.

formal gardens. Honey fungus has caused some damage, but new specimens have been planted and it is hoped that the recent loss of a shelter belt of trees will not slow down their growth. The house can be glimpsed on the far side of a large lake, dwarf conifers interplanted with heathers running down to its banks. This richly textured carpet is overlooked by the hermitage summerhouse, with its roof made of oak tiles and floor of deers' knuckle bones.

Apart from the many historically and botanically interesting features at Bicton there are exhibitions and children's play parks, which are well placed and designed not to disturb the peace or detract from the beauty of these well-kept gardens.

BIDDULPH GRANGE

MAP B

Grange Road, Biddulph
North of Stoke-on-Trent at Biddulph, turn east off A527
Owner: The National Trust
Tel: Stoke-on-Trent (0782) 513149
Open by appointment only, until further notice
(peak months May to July)

The gardens of Biddulph Grange, as yet little known, are an exciting and unique example of Victorian garden-making. Exploring its eccentric and frequently hidden and theatrical features offers an unforgettable experience. At the time of writing, The National Trust is trying to raise funds to restore these unusual gardens which, although not radically altered or added to since their heyday, have become sadly dilapidated. Some of the buildings have been vandalised and an outstanding collection of unusual plants lost.

Covering twenty acres and begun in 1842, Biddulph Grange was developed on what was then bleak and swampy moorland by James Bateman, son of a wealthy industrialist. An enthusiastic and distinguished plantsman, he determined to adorn it with an exceptional range of plants. He was helped in this ambitious task by his wife, Maria Warburton, and the versatile

landscape designer, artist, botantist and geologist, Edward Cooke. Their combined talents produced a creation way ahead of its time, a cleverly linked and highly original collection of gardens varying widely in character. It was recognised as unique and *The Gardener's Chronicle* ran seven consecutive articles describing its design and contents.

The brilliantly engineered series of surprise elements capture the imagination at Biddulph. Ground formerly flat and uninteresting was transformed by earth mounded to make high banks and hillocks, and tons of local stone were fashioned to form seemingly natural dark tunnels, rugged banks and a rocky glen. These banks and mounds not only created divisions between one area and another and, topped by trees, added stature to the overall picture, but they also provided superb stages where Bateman could arrange particular collections of plants. There is a hidden gem at the centre of the garden known as China, which is reached through a secret passage moulded from huge pieces of stone. Pitch dark, with niches for storing ice, the curve of the tunnel known as the 'living rock' preserves the impact of what lies beyond. You step out from the darkness into bright light, and a magical oriental scene is before you. A Chinese bridge spans an area of water surrounded by a joss house, temple, willows, maples and bamboos, the whole surrounded by what is

Ornamental bridge in the Chinese garden at Biddulph Grange.

Rhododendrons and azaleas in the Victorian garden at Biddulph Grange.

known as the Great Wall of China. Another feature known as Egypt is equally exciting. Clipped yews and sphinxes flank the entrance to a large stone tomb, its darkness intensified by the presence of a crouching, scowling, stone ape, the Messenger God. Emerge from the exit of the tomb and glance back: you will see you have come not from a sinister tomb but a replica of a cosy Cheshire cottage.

There is a pinetum of towering and unusual conifers, particularly monkey puzzles and, viewed from a distance, a walk set on a gently rising slope has been fashioned to resemble an obelisk. The garden behind the house — terraces falling to a pond surrounded by evergreen trees and shrubs such as rhododendrons — gives no hint of the surprises which lie beyond. The corridor-like paths running between banks of earth and rock must be explored and features discovered. This garden once contained a myriad of unusual

botanical and man-made features, and a number still survive. When fully restored, Biddulph will stand as one of this country's most important period gardens.

BLAENGWRFACH ISAF

MAP E

Bancyffordd, near Llandyssul
In Bancyffordd, 2m (3km) west of Llandyssul
Owner: Mrs Gail Farmer
Tel: Llandyssul (055 932) 2604
Open for charity daily May to July and by
appointment April, August and September
Plants for sale

The one-acre garden is set into a steep hill overlooking the Teifi valley. Falling away from the Welsh longhouse and down to a stream, it has an unsophisticated, cottage-garden character which suits both the old house and the surrounding, unspoilt countryside. The owner's interest in natural history, wildlife and old-fashioned plants means that the garden is filled with plants which will not only interest the enthusiast but attract butterflies, bees and moths. No harmful chemicals are used and birds are tempted into the garden by numerous nesting-boxes. Clematis clamber through some of the one-hundred-odd shrub roses, ramblers scramble into trees and specimen trees, such as an hoheria, magnolia, parrotia persica, cercidiphyllum, quince and several different cornus and maples, provide year-round interest. Perennial geraniums and dianthus thrive here, stone sinks are filled with alpines and one bed grows flowers for drying. This well-kept, sheltered garden is a sanctuary where the owner has worked hand-in-hand with nature.

BLENHEIM PALACE

MAP F

Woodstock
9m (14½km) north-west of Oxford on A34
Owner: The Duke of Marlborough (HHA)
Tel: Woodstock (0993) 811325
Open daily from mid-March to end October
(peak season summer)
Plants for sale

Paid for by the nation, Blenheim Palace must be one of the greatest examples of a country's gratitude to a conquering hero. Designed by Vanbrugh, the dramatist turned architect, the Baroque palace was built for the first Duke of Marlborough between 1705 and 1772. Queen Anne's gardener, the renowned nurseryman Henry Wise, was employed to lay out the original gardens. An exceptional example of seventeenth-century formality and symmetry, their vast proportions and the intricacy of their design matched the grandeur of Vanbrugh's architecture. All that survives of Wise's work is the eight-acre walled kitchen garden; the ornamental gardens lasted only fifty years before being obliterated to make way for a landscape, then highly

fashionable. Designed by 'Capability' Brown, this noble, man-made but seemingly natural landscape greets the visitor today. It runs up to the walls of the palace and superbly offsets its grandeur.

The palace is situated on high ground, above the river Glyne, so the lie of the land was well-suited to Brown's formula of damming rivers to make lakes and give an impression of space. Vanbrugh's bridge across the river is now the most striking feature in the landscape, Brown having emphasised its heroic design by swelling the river on either side of it to create lakes. Brown was ingenious in forming views to architectural and other features by the visionary placing of belts and clumps and trees, and laid out a landscape which continuously reveals glorious and unexpected vistas. Brilliantly thought out but appearing uncultivated, the everchanging scene is never dull. The trees planted by Brown are coming to the end of their lives, but recent replanting has seen to it that future generations will enjoy a mature landscape. Brown built the picturesque cascade at the western end of the lakes and it is well worthwhile making the effort to see this. The sight from the narrow bridge over the river, of the water frothing over glistening black rocks, is a dramatic one.

In the 1920s the ninth Duke of Marlborough wanted to re-create a formal garden to complement Vanbrugh's baroque masterpiece and break Brown's purist landscape, and he asked the Frenchman, Achille Duchêne, to design the present Italianate water gardens which overlook the lake. Intensely formal and confident, the two terrace gardens are decorated with fountains, statuary and box parterre, and the sound of falling water adds a soothing note. To the east front of the palace, bounded by the orangery, Duchêne placed an intricate parterre of scrolls and arabesques. The dark green patterns of dwarf box are offset by hedges of glowing golden yew and topiary clipped in the shape of charmingly dumpy birds and other animals. Evocative of an earlier age, autocratic and flamboyant, it is hard to believe that these formal gardens were created only during the present century.

There are numerous other botanical and architectural features to be seen in the park and

Blenheim Palace viewed from the far side of 'Capability' Brown's lake.

garden, but the overall impression of Blenheim is one of lavish grandeur, an heroic monument to a victorious general.

BLICKLING HALL

MAP G

Blickling
On B1354, 1½m (2½km) north-west of Aylsham
on A140
Owner: The National Trust
Tel: Aylsham (0263) 733084
Open several days a week from Easter to end
October
(peak months May to August)

You alight suddenly upon this Jacobean house, set back from the road. Its simple forecourt is edged with four-hundred-year-old yews. The gardens and park behind this confident stage-set show the patina of having been developed and altered to suit current fashion over several centuries. Seventeenth-century formality blends into an eighteenth-century landscape and features from later ages, architectural and botanical, meld into a harmonious picture.

A formal garden which was originally an intricate French-style parterre designed by W. A. Nesfield stands to the east of the house. Modified in 1930 by Norah Lindsay, this now contains four large beds which mix polyantha roses and herbaceous plants. The colouring of those nearest the house is cool blue, pink and white, those the far side of the central pool and fountain being filled with warm yellows and oranges. Sentinel yews, shaped like medieval hats, stand at the corners of each bed, adding stature, and a border to one side is massed with penstemon. The generosity of the planting is typical of this beautifully kept garden.

Steps rise out of this sunken area up to a

turfed avenue, bounded by woodland and edged with azaleas and rhododendrons, which leads to a Doric temple. You can admire the view of the house from here and note that the parterre garden is completely masked from view, not to detract from the grandeur of the architecture. Explore the far side of the temple and the garden suddenly becomes the park, a raised gravel walk creating a division between the two and offering an informal walk with soothing views. The famous landscape designer, Humphry Repton, who is buried nearby in Aylsham churchyard, did much to improve this park and was possibly responsible for making the mile-long curved lake. Either side of the central avenue is a seventeenth-century formal wilderness garden of straight *allées*. These radiate from clearings and cut through oak, beech and sycamore woodland underplanted with yew and carpeted with bluebells in spring. Many of the trees are reaching the end of their lives, but recently planted specimens are striving to reach the light. The preservation of a period feature like this poses problems: the young trees need the light, but if the over-mature specimens are cut down the beauty of the design is lost.

An orangery, possibly built by Repton's son, the architect John Adey Repton, stands on the boundary of the garden overlooking the park. It still contains orange trees, as well as other, glossy-leafed evergreen subjects such as fatshedera, ivy, camellias, and ferns. A secret garden, designed by Norah Lindsay, hides behind a beech hedge — a peaceful oasis, with a summerhouse and beds of scented plants. A striking feature of the gardens is the vigorous and ancient oriental planes on the lawn. Their layered, serpentine branches produce a cool explosion of lime green foliage wonderfully offset against a background of lush green grass and the foliage of cut-leaf limes.

BODNANT

Tal-y-Cafn, near Colwyn Bay
8m (13km) south of Llandudno and Colwyn Bay
on A470, entrance 1½m (1km) along the
Eglywysbach road
Owner: The National Trust
Tel: Tyn-y-Groes (0492) 650460
Open daily from mid-March to end October
(peak months mid-April to end September)
Plants for sale

If Bodnant is not the most beautiful garden in Great Britain, it is certainly the most exciting to visit. Exploring its eighty acres is an adventure, with unexpected and glorious sights around each corner, an endless series of surprises and views. It begs to be painted or photographed, and requires several reels of film to do it justice.

Since 1874, the gardens have been developed by succeeding generations of the Aberconway family, which should alert the enthusiast to what lies in store. Two members of the family were past presidents of the Royal Horticultural Society and three were awarded the Society's highest award, the Victoria Medal of Honour. Three generations of the Puddle family have also overseen the development of the garden, two having been awarded the Victoria Medal and the third, like his grandfather and father before him, holds the post of head gardener today.

Full use has been made of the natural beauty of the site, which slopes in a south-westerly direction down to the River Conway, with Snowdonia as a dramatic backcloth. The decision to work with nature, planting in profusion specimens which flourished in the mild, wet and acid conditions, has produced a vigorous and luxuriant picture of bold proportions. The garden could be divided into two parts. The first flows away from the gabled house, with informal lawns and Italianate terraces whose heroic scale suits the lie of the land. The second — the pinetum, wild and dell gardens — lie in the steep-sided valley of the River Hiraethlyn, a tributary of the River Conway. Its upper part is predominantly formal; the lower is natural and dramatic. There is a rarely seen richness of plant material — rhododendrons, camellias, azaleas and magnolias, and magnificent specimens of unusual and native trees.

The terraces were added at the beginning of the present century by the second Lord Aberconway. They took several years to complete and single Bodnant out as an exceptional twentieth-century garden: treated in different ways and varying in size, they could stand as individual gardens. The flagged rose terrace, with beds of roses and low-growing subjects and a huge arbutus tree near the house, competes with the glorious views to the mountains. The lawned croquet terrace is overlooked by the two flights of steps which run down either side of a baroque fountain framed by two varieties of white wisteria. A rectangular lily pool with a semi-circular bay dominates the lily terrace. Bounded on one side by a yew hedge which echoes the shape of the pool, this terrace also supports an Atlas and a Lebanon cedar which pre-date the building of the terraces. Below lies the rose terrace and pergola, where the trellis work is eyecatchingly decorated with skilfully turned, wooden urns.

Azaleas shaded by beech trees in the gardens at Bodnant.

The canal terrace is the grand finale. At one end, mirrored in the long ribbon of water, stands Pin Mill, an Elizabethan garden house of stucco and stone which originally came from Gloucestershire. An open-air stage provides interest at the far end, its wings of tightly clipped yew providing a background to a classical-style garden seat. Plants of all kinds abound in borders and beds on these terraces, clamber up walls and jewel the surface of the water, their colouring as carefully considered as their placing. The strong presence of evergreens, vast inky conifers, huge shrubs and tightly clipped yew hedges highlight the soft or brilliant colours of flowering subjects and create strong, architectural shapes, on the terraces and in the dell.

Below the terraces the atmosphere changes. Excitement is generated by the sound of water gushing over waterfalls and tumbling over rocks. Shafts of sunlight fall through the canopy trees highlighting pools of brilliant colour and accentuating the size of the many unusual conifers. Paths vein the steep sides of the valley, cross bridges and offer a new picture at each turn: an area of exposed natural rock studded with dwarf rhododendrons and azaleas; the fern and moss-covered roof of the Old Mill, its walls underplanted with the outsize glossy foliage of skunk cabbage; rainbow swathes of deciduous azaleas, and moisture-loving plants on the riverbanks.

Bodnant is famous for its rhododendrons, not only its own hybrids but the number of species grown from seed collected by planthunters such as E. H. Wilson, George Forrest, Frank Kingdon Ward and Dr J. F. Rock. These can be seen throughout the garden, in shrub borders, set around the lawns and in the woodland, their flowering season extending over many months. In borders above the dell and on lawns near the house handsome shrubs and specimen trees produce both flowers and foliage colour — pieris, kalmias, berberis, sorbus, cherries, embothrium, maples and fine eucryphias. Channelled between banks of large shrubs and across a lawn near the house, there is a fine vista over the park. Divided from the front lawn by a ha-ha, it blends with the garden, its rough grass embroidered with spring bulbs and bluebells.

It will take more than one visit to explore this

The woodland garden at Bodnant in spring.

splendid garden and take advantage of its thoughtfully placed seats to drink in the beauty all around. A short distance from the exit is the laburnum arch, a wide curved walk dripping with sulphur blooms, a memorable sight which typifies the beauty and high standards of this exceptional garden.

BORDE HILL GARDEN

MAP J

Haywards Heath
1½m (2½km) north of Haywards Heath on the Balcombe road
Owner: Borde Hill Garden Ltd
Tel: Haywards Heath (0444) 450326
Open several days a week from end March to end October
(peak months April and May)
Plants for sale

This large, informal woodland garden contains an exceptional collection of ericaceous and other plants fascinating to the plantsman. The imposing stone house is set on a ridge and looks over the valley of the River Ouse to the north and across a large lawn and park to the south. Spreading to the east and west from the house are dells, glades and woodland richly planted with unusual shrubs and trees, many of these, especially conifers, being the largest of their kind in this country. In relatively formal areas like the tiny walled gardens on the site of the old potting-sheds are herbaceous borders, and around bride's pool are sun-loving, tender and perennial plants. A walled garden near the house contains rare subjects from China and Japan and in spring the azalea ring is brilliant with deciduous (Knaphill strain) azaleas, evergreen varieties being massed to the west of the south lawn. Large-leafed loderi and other rhododendrons are here in abundance, a good number sheltering in Warren and Little Bentley Wood.

Horticulture was on the brink of one of its most exciting periods of development when the late owner's grandfather, Colonel Stephenson Clarke, bought Borde Hill in 1893. Over the next fifty years planthunters such as E. H. Wilson, Reginald Farrer, George Forrest and Frank Kingdon Ward were to alter radically the gardens of this country by introducing a wealth of new hardy plants. Colonel Stephenson Clarke subscribed to a number of these expeditions and received a share of the seeds they brought back from China, Japan and the Himalayas. The mature plants grown from these, as well as a large number he raised himself, now adorn the garden and woodland at Borde Hill, together with many more recent additions. It would be impossible to attach a label to each tree and shrub giving its name, where and when it was found and by whom, but it would make fascinating reading. A now widely-popular shrub raised by the Colonel is the free-flowering pink camellia 'Donation'. This is a cross between *C. japonica* 'Donckelarii' and *C. saluenensis* and a group of these can be seen near the walled garden. The rhododendrons and azaleas are the stars of Borde Hill, but there is also an impressive collection of magnolias and maples. The vast acreage and nature of the gardens inevitably pose problems of maintenance, and some areas have been allowed to become wilder than others. But the Trust formed to administer Borde Hill is energetic in its efforts to preserve not only the well-established collection of rare and unusual plants, but constantly to add to it, so that the gardens will continue to evolve.

BOUGHTON HOUSE

MAP G

Kettering
On A43 between Weekley and Geddington, 3m (5km) north of Kettering
Owners: The Duke of Buccleuch and The Living Landscape Trust (HHA)
Tel: Kettering (0536) 82248
Open one day a year for charity, daily during August and by appointment for parties
Plants for sale

The country of Northamptonshire is richly blessed with fine houses, and Boughton must stand as one of the most impressive. Set around seven courtyards, it was transformed from a fifteenth-century monastery to a great mansion between 1530 and 1695. Its appearance, particularly that of the north front, resembles a seventeenth-century French château rather than an English stately home. The architecture dominates the scene, with simple gravel walks, terrace and lawns linking it to its surroundings.

In the stable court to the north front, a mixed border faces the house, with large-leafed plants such as *crambe cordifolia*; the shrub roses and perennials are various shades of yellow, blue and white. At one time, a great parterre stood to the west of the house on what is now the broad walk. In times of drought the outlines of an intricate pattern of beds still reveal themselves. Today a vast expanse of lawn runs down to the lake known as broad water. Avenues of limes, seven deep in places, bound it, stretch far into the distance and create a superb and uninterrupted vista across the park. Dark yew hedges either side of the lawn back statues, and behind these are planted willows to one side, cherries and walnuts to the other. Wisteria and roses climb against the west front of the house and handsome urns, planted with pink and white flowers, stand on the terrace. To the south is a circular rose garden, its beds set around a sundial. These are filled with a mixture of modern and old-fashioned shrub roses, underplanted with *Stachys lanata*, peonies and rock roses. Specimen trees, the catalpas being particularly fine, stand nearby. Steps lead up to the old monastery pond, covered with waterlilies, and a further flight leads to an avenue of limes. This is delightful in spring, when the rough grass either side is jewelled with daffodils, narcissi and snakeshead fritillarias.

The walled kitchen garden beyond continues to produce fruit, vegetables and flowers for the house and shelters a nursery raising a range of plants, some unusual, for sale. A further garden, fish court, can be admired from the windows of the great hall in the house. A pool is surrounded with hostas and irises and clematis; roses and other white-flowering plants fill the beds beneath the walls.

BOWOOD HOUSE

MAP I

Calne
1m (2km) west of Calne on A4 turn south to Derry Hill
Owner: The Earl of Shelburne (HHA)
Tel: Calne (0249) 812102
Open daily April to October
(peak months April to September)
Plants for sale

The beautifully maintained grounds of Bowood House are noble and elegant: within the ninety acres are an arboretum, landscape, formal terraces and woodland, which are individually rewarding. Together, they are a rare collection of period and botanical features.

The arboretum, set a distance from the house, is an impressive introduction to the gardens and contains a large number of the four hundred species of different trees to be found at Bowood. The first of these were planted early in the eighteenth century, and the collection grew as new species were introduced by planthunters such as David Douglas and Robert Fortune. In 1848 a pinetum was begun, the trees being planted in their correct geographical sequence. A number of these, having reached the end of their lives, have been replaced by the present earl who has also added new species. Giant cedars, pines, redwoods, cut-leaf horse chestnut and tulip trees are spaced well apart over smooth lawns. The effect is soothing and humbling, a preparation for 'Capability' Brown's heroic landscape beyond. He created the forty-acre lake set against a backcloth of trees, which lies below the house, extensive lawns sloping down from the terraces to its banks. The Doric temple, a note of romance on the far bank, and the dramatic cascade nearby were added at a later date.

In contrast to the spaciousness and natural character of the landscape, the terraces are formal and highly embellished. Built in 1818 in front of the Adam orangery, they are bounded by balustraded stone walls decorated with urns. The terraces are patterned with gravel paths, lawns and geometric flowerbeds, and are planted in a restrained manner. Red geraniums and roses, mixed with the grey foliage of helichrysum, decorate the urns and flower beds, and their brilliant colour is emphasised by lines of dark sentinel yews. Intriguingly, these trees, uniform in size, all lean slightly to the east.

The fifty-acre woodland garden, set on a ridge of greensand, shelters rhododendrons, azaleas and other acid-loving plants. Carpets of bluebells, spring bulbs and the scent of *Rhododendron loderi* enhance this and other parts of the garden in spring. An adventure playground, imaginatively constructed of timber, blends into the woodland — a tempting stop for younger visitors. The design of this playground, the nursery and shop, and the excellence of the guide book testify to the high standards of everything on offer at Bowood.

BRAMDEAN

MAP I

Bramdean, near Alresford
On A272 in Bramdean Village
Owners: Mr and Mrs H. Wakefield
Tel: Bramdean (096 279) 214
Open several days a year for charity and by appointment
(peak months June and July)

This immaculately-kept country-house garden, set on chalk, covers four acres and is divided into three sections. The first, nearest the house, contains superb borders, lawns and mature trees; the second is the walled kitchen garden; and the third, an orchard. Striking out from the mid-eighteenth-century house and ornamental lily pond are wide and luxuriantly-filled borders set against green walls of clipped box. Foliage shapes and colour have been carefully considered: tall, striking *Crambe cordifolia* and onopordums take centre stage, and the whole is a well-blended composition of pale and dark purples, blues and yellows. A grass path between these borders leads up to wrought iron gates, and a mass of voluptuous peonies introduces us to the walled kitchen garden, planted in the traditional manner with flowers, vegetables and fruit. At its

centre stands a sundial, either side of which are flower beds. Clipped yew hedges provide a dark backcloth, but do not interrupt the glorious vista from the house up to the orchard.

In contrast to the formal, highly-cultivated character of the rest of the garden, this is shaded by fruit trees garlanded with honeysuckle, roses and clematis. Underneath, aconites, snowdrops and daffodils thrive and multiply. In winter, when the trees are bare, the focal point of the vista from the house is the old apple store with its clocktower and weathervane, the brilliant blue of the clock face matched by the door to the store. The view from the orchard, through the kitchen garden, down between the borders and to the house, the hills rising behind, is a delightful finale.

BRESSINGHAM HALL GARDENS

MAP G

near Diss
2½m (4km) west of Diss on A1066
Owner: Alan Bloom
Tel: Bressingham (037 988) 386
Open in conjunction with the Bressingham Steam Museum on Sundays from May until September, Thursdays from June until mid-September and Wednesdays in August
(peak months June to August)
Plants for sale

The name Bressingham is synonymous with hardy perennial plants, and the nursery adjoining the garden enjoys an international reputation. Owned by the Bloom family, it raises over five thousand varieties of perennial and other plants. Both garden and nursery were developed by Alan Bloom and the garden is remarkable not only for the rich variety of its plants but for its design. Dictated by the shape and lie of the land, the five-acre dell is an informal scene of island beds, ponds and lawns set in a shelter belt of trees.

Once a meadow, the garden could be called the home of the island bed, as Alan Bloom did much to popularise this now familiar garden feature. It suited perfectly the informal character of the garden he created from rough ground and proved an ideal vehicle for displaying a wide range of plants. It is easier to tend than a wide herbaceous border and offers a series of pictures, rather than a single view. Hardy herbaceous plants obviously feature widely, because Alan Bloom has raised and named over one hundred of these since 1926. These associate well with alpines, heathers, dwarf shrubs, moisture-loving and aquatic plants and specimen trees, and the picture changes constantly as new varieties are added. Plantsmen will thrill to such a feast of unusual varieties, many of which have been saved from extinction, and the amateur will be inspired to strive for similarly attractive effects.

During one weekend in early September it is possible to see Foggy Bottom, the garden of Alan Bloom's son, Adrian. Adrian is a skilled plantsman like his father (both have been awarded the Victoria Medal of Honour by the Royal Horticultural Society). Foggy Bottom has been developed over the last twenty-two years and contains a comprehensive collection of conifers from all over the world. Planted in island beds in conjunction with heathers, dwarf shrubs and other suitable plants and trees, the colouring and varied texture of imaginatively associated groups presents a rich and fascinating picture. Before leaving, note the mature elms near the entrance to the Steam Museum — few of their age still survive in the country.

BRIDGEMERE GARDEN WORLD

MAP B

Bridgemere, near Nantwich
On the A51 between Woore and Nantwich
Owner: Bridgemere Nurseries Ltd
Tel: Bridgemere (09365) 381/382
Open daily throughout the year
Plants for sale

The imaginative manner in which living and other features are displayed mark Bridgemere as a model and innovative garden centre, as attractive as it is comprehensive. Instead of serried rows, the trees, shrubs and plants for sale are put around raised island beds housing sympathetically arranged collections, each bed containing plants for different situations. You can see the eventual size of any plant you may wish to buy, the conditions in which it might thrive and other subjects it might associate with successfully. A large informally-designed display garden is a further source of inspiration, and conservatories, greenhouses and other garden features are appropriately set.

BROADLEAS

MAP I

Devizes
Off A360 south of Devizes
Owner: Lady Anne Cowdray,
Broadleas Gardens Ltd (HHA)
Tel: Devizes (0380) 2035
Open several days a week from April to end October
(peak seasons spring and autumn)
Plants for sale

Hidden from sight, the beautiful Dell Garden at Broadleas lies down a steep slope which falls away from the terrace near the house. When Lady Anne Cowdray first arrived in 1946, the valley, with its oaks and pines, offered a perfect chance to make a woodland garden. It is embraced by steep slopes and sheltered from the wind; the frost rolls away to the countryside below. The garden lay on greensand, so it was an obvious home for tender and other shrubs such as rhododendrons and camellias. The wide collection of these, plus fine ornamental trees such as a *Nyssa sylvatica*, handkerchief tree, *Cercidiphyllum japonicum* and over twenty different varieties of magnolia can be found here, a number underplanted with primroses, anemones, mecanopsis and spring bulbs.

A formal note has been struck at the bottom of the woodland garden, where an elegant stone urn fronts a clipped beech hedge. A path winds back up the valley and past the cool, pale green spread of a catalpa, eyecatching drifts of wild cyclamen, autumn crocus and shade-loving plants such as hellebores and daphnes add colour and scent along the route. Other, smaller gardens to one side of the terrace come into view at the top of the slope: the sunken, walled, rose garden to the east, and a border of rock and herbaceous plants, and an intimate area hedged with prunus which shelters maples, dwarf bulbs and unusual shrubs. An ornamental herb garden near the entrance gate is another pocket of interest.

BROOK COTTAGE

MAP F

Alkerton, near Banbury
6m (9½km) west of Banbury on A422. In Alkerton
take lane opposite War Memorial then right fork
Owners: Mr and Mrs David Hodges
Tel: Edge Hill (029 587) 303 or 590
Open several days a year for charity and from
April to end October by appointment

Set on a steep west-facing slope, this private four-acre garden surrounds an L-shaped cottage built of Hornton stone. The slope has been divided into a series of well-designed interlinking areas using terracing, stone walls and hedges to create the framework, and it is abundantly filled with unusual plants. There are intimate and enclosed 'rooms' of varying degrees of formality immediately around the cottage. These give privacy and protection from the weather, and are preludes to the informal parts of the garden which blend into the surrounding countryside. It is hard to believe that this well-established garden was begun twenty-three years ago on what was originally a field.

David Hodges is an architect and his feeling for material and design are much in evidence. The proportions of the small enclosed gardens suit those of the house and features such as the wide stone steps with rills running down either side, the water garden, and a sundial set on rings of stone divided by a water course, are attractive and original in design. Mrs Hodges is a skilful plantswoman, who has used a wealth of interesting and beautiful plant material. Her eye for sympathetic associations and choice of subjects is excellent, whether to suit waterside, steeply sloping ground, walled and hedged 'rooms' or areas of scree.

Lush mounds of hostas and other shade-loving plants fill the small courtyard and large shrub roses have been planted on lawns, well spaced to display their blooms and hips. These are normally difficult to stake unobtrusively, but the Hodges have devised an ingenious way of controlling them without detracting from their beauty. A large collection of *Sorbus* and unusual varieties of willow and birch can be seen at the far end of the garden. A curved avenue of *Prunus* 'Shirotae' near the cottage creates a cool tunnel of white blossom in spring, and a copper beech hedge divides the formal and the natural parts of the garden. This immaculate garden is planted to give year-round interest and boasts an underground watering system. Black plastic sheeting has been laid under the stone paving and rocky banks, retaining the moisture and cutting down weeding. This garden is a prime example of how, with energy and imagination, a field can be transformed into a delightful picture.

BROUGHTON CASTLE

MAP F

Broughton, near Banbury
2½m (4km) south-west of Banbury on B4035
Owner: Lord Saye and Sele (HHA)
Tel: Banbury (0295) 62624
Open a few days a week from mid-May to
mid-September
(peak months June to August)
Plants for sale

The beautiful setting and secure and happy atmosphere of this ancient castle is seductive; those interested in period garden design and the skilful use of colour will find much to please them here.

Surrounded by a moat which divides the garden from the park, the Hornton stone walls dividing one area from another have influenced the colouring and positioning of the beds. A long border set against a battlemented wall has blue, yellow, grey and white plants; another, a cleverly-blended mix of pinks. The lady's garden, intimate and walled, contains a period knot, with a *fleur de lys* design which is best viewed from the windows above. Its box-edged beds are filled with roses and lavender, and their scent is delightfully trapped in the enclosed garden 'room'. Old photographs, taken in the late nineteenth century, show Broughton's gardens lavishly decorated with ornate garden features. These no longer exist, because the gardens have been replanted in the last eighteen years in a style far more suited to the castle.

BROUGHTON HALL

MAP B

Skipton
3½m (5½km) west of Skipton on A59
Owner: Mr Henry Tempest
Tel: Skipton (0756) 2267
Open occasionally for charity and by
appointment for parties
Plants for sale

Here is one of the few remaining examples of the work of the Victorian garden designer, William Andrew Nesfield. He was famed for his imaginative parterres, and at Broughton he created what is known as a *tapis vert*, an intricate scroll-and-feather design of golden and common green dwarf box. Set on a slope which runs down to the south front of the house, this period feature has an Italianate stone gazebo at the top east corner, a superb point from which to admire the garden and the park.

Nesfield also designed the dolphin fountain with its steps and balustrading, the parterre beds next to the handsome conservatory, and he directed the imaginative placing of the stone statues of pastoral and other figures throughout the garden. It is richly planted with clipped and other evergreens which add a touch of formality and create dense, evergreen skirts around shrubberies and shape woodland and other walks. The garden has a Victorian air and a strong framework: well-kept lawns, spring bulbs and numerous flowering trees rise above the evergreens and prevent heaviness. The uniformly good condition of the many mature trees, the fine views and delightful walk beside Broughton Beck, make the garden at Broughton Hall as

Herbaceous border at Broughton Castle.

pleasurable as it is historically interesting to visit.

BRYNHYFRYD

MAP D

Corris, near Machynlleth
6m (9½km) north of Machynlleth, 10m (16km)
south of Dolgellau, turn off A487 at Corris on to
the old Corris road
Owner: Mrs David Paish
Tel: Corris (065 473) 278
Open by appointment throughout the year
for charity
(peak month May)

Few would contemplate making a garden on the steep slopes of a bare and rocky mountainside, but in 1961 Mrs Paish and her late husband did just that. The garden at Brynhyfryd is a unique example of what can be achieved on inhospitable terrain, and should be a source of inspiration to those in a similarly 'impossible' situation.

Now in her eighties, Mrs Paish cares for the garden single-handed, climbing the paths which snake up through the four acres of mountainside to tend her collection of hybrid and other azaleas and rhododendrons. These, together with other acid-loving plants, are shaded by native and specimen trees such as magnolias, umbrella pines, *Styrax* and eucryphias. The tropical-looking blooms and handsome foliage of large-leafed rhododendrons and many other flowering shrubs are underplanted with heather and wild bilberries, and the garden is a successful mixture of the wild and dramatic and the highly cultivated and tender.

BURFORD HOUSE GARDENS

MAP E

Tenbury Wells
On A456 ½m (1km) west of Tenbury Wells
Owner: Mr John Treasure
Tel: Tenbury Wells (0584) 810777
Open daily from Easter to October
Plants for sale

Adjoining the famous nursery, Treasure's, the gardens of Burford House are outstanding for the richness and variety of their contents, imaginative design and immaculate upkeep. It is worth driving a considerable distance to see and learn from this splendid plantsman's garden.

When John Treasure came to the Georgian brick house in 1954, he was faced with a four-acre wilderness boasting only a handful of mature trees. The soil was fertile because the River Teme runs along the end of the garden, occasionally flooding, and leaves a thick layer of alluvial silt when the water recedes. As an architect, John Treasure knew the importance of linking the garden design with that of the house. This, and his good eye for textures and shapes and meticulous execution of the work, influenced its development.

Island beds were laid out on the lawns and planted to create vistas and surprises, the whole melting happily into the surrounding country-side and flattering the house. A twentieth-century innovation, island beds are not to everyone's taste, but here they are planted with such skill that they seem an entirely appropriate way to display a wide range of trees, plants and shrubs. Formal touches have been added: a long and serenely simple pool to the front of the house, and the stone terraces and enclosed gardens to the back and side.

The garden is rich in rare and unusual plants of immense interest to the plantsman. Compositions of evergreen trees form flattering backcloths to variegated foliage and autumn colour, and their often tall and solid shapes act as a foil to shrubs and trees of a more delicate and lax habit. The nursery nearby is famous for its clematis (it holds the National Collection) and a superb range of these can be seen growing through, along, up and under living subjects as diverse as trees and tiny violas. The garden evolves constantly as new plants are introduced and associations experimented with; no opportunity is missed to interlace one plant sympathetically with another. A stream garden, beds of alpines and heathers, shrub roses and herbaceous borders come suddenly into view, all plants well labelled and not a weed to be seen. Burford House warrants repeated visiting — with a camera or notebook and pencil to hand.

Effective mix of shapes and textures in the garden at Burford House.

BURNBY HALL GARDENS

MAP C

Pocklington
On the B1247, 13m (21km) east of York
Owner: Stewart's (Burnby Hall) Gardens and
Museum Trust
Tel: Pocklington (0759) 302068
Open daily from Easter to mid-October
(peak months August and September)

Waterlilies have a romantic and exotic quality which, like the outsize blooms of magnolia, never fails to please. At Burnby Hall, spread across the surface of two large lakes, thousands of these lovely flowers can be seen, their heads rising above shiny, platelike leaves. This splendid collection of waterlilies, the garden and lakes were created by Major P. M. Stewart, who came to gardening in his middle years. When he bought Ivy Hall (which he renamed Burnby Hall) in 1904, apart from building a large concrete lake and filling it with fish, he did not bother to develop the grounds further, preferring to pursue his interest in fishing, hunting and travel.

After World War I, having satisfied his and his wife's passion for travel, he began to develop the garden, building a second lake and enlarging the first. He planted these with waterlilies, gradually building up a collection of scores of hybrids and different varieties, the majority of which survived the harsh climate. Today, thanks to the major, the lakes look entirely natural and display over forty different types of waterlily.

The larger of the lakes is set on slightly higher ground, and a cascade which tumbles through and over a rock garden to link the two. The banks are softened with plants, shrubs and trees which form a backdrop to a picture reminiscent of the much-loved painting of waterlilies by Monet.

BURTON CONSTABLE

MAP C

Burton Constable, near Hull
1½m (2½km) north of Sproatley, 7½m (12km)
north-east of Hull
Owner: Mr J. Chichester Constable (HHA)
Tel: Skirlaugh (0401) 62400
Open regularly from Easter to end
September and by appointment for parties
(peak month July)

Garden historians will be interested to see, within this redbrick Elizabethan house, Lancelot 'Capability' Brown's original plans for the landscape. The work was carried out in the 1770s and the twenty acres of lakes, spanned by a handsome, arched and balustraded stone bridge, still exist, but Brown's characteristic clumps of trees have been eroded by age and battered by harsh winds. New clumps have been planted but it will take time for these to enhance the landscape.

The four-acre garden immediately around the house contains a handsome eighteenth-century orangery by Thomas Atkinson of York, ancient yews and crumbling statuary. Though there are beds of herbaceous and other plants, the design has been kept simple, so as not to detract from the architecture of the house.

BUSCOT PARK

MAP F

Faringdon
Between Lechlade and Faringdon, on A417
Owner: The National Trust
Tel: Faringdon (0367) 20786
Open several days a week from Easter to end
September
(peak periods Easter and June to August)
Plants for sale

Much restoration work has been done on the five acres of the walled garden at Buscot and it now possesses a fine landscaped garden and an attractive formal garden. Successive owners of the late eighteenth-century house have contributed to the development of the park either by planting trees, creating new vistas or building dramatic features such as the water garden. The restoration of the formal gardens is but the latest in a line of enterprising additions.

They are designed as a series of symmetrical gardens within walls, and trees such as pleached hornbeams and standard false acacias have been used to decorate and divide them into sections, with the axial paths focusing on a central ornamental pool. A large area has been divided into four parts representing the four seasons. Borders designed by Peter Coates and edged with box contain flowers of shades of blue and yellow, and the use of lime-green foliage is effective here and elsewhere.

Three *allées* radiate from the terrace east of the house, and cut through woodland. The two to the right are wide avenues, one lined with fastigiate beech and the other with limes; prostrate junipers, planted to simulate a pool of water, are the focal point at the far end of one of these. The *allée* to the left of the picture is channelled down the formal water garden. Water flows, falls and tumbles over and under a manmade assault course of rills, ponds, waterfalls and bridges, until it reaches a lake overlooked by a temple. The journey is a masterpiece of restrained design and invention by the early twentieth-century architect and landscape designer, Harold Peto. A great admirer of the Italian Renaissance garden, Peto's cool and entrancing water garden at Buscot reveals this influence.

CAERHAYS CASTLE

MAP H

Gorran, near St Austell
10m (16km) South of St Austell. On coast by
Porthluney Cove, between Dodman Point and
Nare Head
Owner: Mr F. J. Williams
Tel: Truro (0872) 501310
Open a few days a year for charity and by
appointment for coach parties only
(peak season spring)
Plants for sale

This sixty-acre woodland garden has been developed by the Williams family since 1880 and is remarkable for its superb collection of plants. It was the birthplace of the *Camellia x williamsii* and numerous other hybrids, and the home of some magnificent magnolias, rhododendrons and specimen trees which were the first of their kind to be grown in this country. The garden stands one hundred feet above sea level and above the early nineteenth-century castle set into the side of the hill, a buffer between the woodland and the fields which run down to the sea. Paths vein the concave slope where the rich collection of species and hybrid shrubs and trees grow beneath a canopy of beeches, conifers and specimen trees, laurel hedges providing shelter and forming rough terraces.

At the beginning of the century, the family invested in plant-collecting expeditions made by E. H. Wilson and later by George Forrest, whose finds were to transform the gardens of this country. The original specimens grown from seed of *Magnolia sprengeri diva* and *M. campbellii mollicomata* can still be seen today, towering over more recent introductions. Other mature specimens dating from that time were purchased from the famous nursery of Veitch, who sponsored so many expeditions but were forced to close down in 1914.

There is a fine collection of rare and unusual oaks, many being early introductions; others, such as the Korean and Californian oaks, have been added more recently. Rhododendrons and camellias abound, many raised by the Williams family, and the original specimens of *Camellia saluenensis* and *C. japonica*, crossed by J. C. Williams in the 1920s to produce the first *williamsii* hybrid, can still be seen near the front door of the house.

No one had any idea how large or how well the new introductions would grow, so the garden evolved rather than being planned. The original specimens of cherries and small rhododendrons have reached the end of their lives; others are now overmature, but are constantly being replaced. New introductions and hybrids are also raised, areas of half an acre being cleared and replanted on a regular basis. One of the latest hybrids is a semi-deciduous rhododendron with pale purple flowers called 'Emma'; it is very hardy and should interest northern gardeners.

Be prepared to climb steep paths as many of the finest shrubs and trees grow to the top of the woodland. Gumboots are recommended, and I suggest you admire the magnificent blooms of the Asiatic tree magnolias and gigantic rhododendrons from higher ground, rather than strain your neck.

CAMBRIDGE UNIVERSITY BOTANIC GARDEN

MAP G

Cambridge
¾m (½km) south of city centre. Entrances in Trumpington Road, Bateman Street, Hills Road and Brooklands Avenue
Owner: University of Cambridge
Tel: Cambridge (0223) 336265
Open regularly throughout the year

Many of the world's most accomplished gardeners, botanists and planthunters have worked or been trained in these forty-acre botanic gardens. Their primary function is to educate and facilitate research, but they are as aesthetically pleasing as they are botanically fascinating. This is no dry and indigestible 'museum' of plants; the garden lover and amateur will derive as much pleasure from the grounds as the expert.

Informal in design, the gardens have an open and spacious feeling, the spires of Cambridge being barely visible beyond clumps and belts of mature trees. Lawns, a large rockery, natural areas of rough grass and dry paths form divisions and create ideal conditions for the display of an outstandingly wide range of plants of all kinds. Individual areas are devoted to a single family or group of plants which thrive in specially prepared conditions. This offers an opportunity to observe and compare growing habits, learn where they came from, how they evolved and their uses. Great efforts are made to see that the overall beauty of an area is more than the sum of its attractive contents. The informal shape of the

systematic or order beds, which house eighty different families of flowering plants, are as decorative as they are instructive.

The rockery surrounding and rising steeply from the lake is a fine sight, richly studded with alpine and other suitable subjects planted geographically. The National Collection of tulip species and *Lonicera* find a home here, together with special collections of perennial geraniums and European *Saxifrage*. The rose garden's beds are designed by Graham Stuart Thomas and show the development of the modern rose. Island beds, designed by Alan Bloom, are filled with herbaceous plants and shrubs. A winter garden demonstrates how the use of plants with interesting foliage, bark and winter flowers can create a pleasantly textured and lively picture. Scented plants are placed in sheltered spots and in raised beds, which lets you enjoy their fragrance at close quarters. A long curved bed displays, in chronological order, plants which have been introduced to this country from abroad over the centuries from the *Acanthus mollis* brought by the Romans to the *Euphorbia griffithii* recently introduced from the Himalayas. A large mound, of ecological interest, is covered with native, endangered and East Anglian wild plants, and areas of rough grass are planted with wild flowers and spring bulbs.

More exotic fare can be seen in the many greenhouses: the temperate house is filled with Mediterranean and other tender plants; the decoratively-filled conservatory, the alpine house, the stove and palm house, lush with tropical plants; the tropical fern, orchid, carnivorous plant and succulent houses all contain rewarding and imaginatively displayed collections. Low rainfall and the cold winds of this part of the country prevent trees from growing as fast or as large as elsewhere, but mature and unusual specimens abound here. There is a good collection of maples, oaks and limes and a young pinetum, planted on relatively wet ground, is making good progress. The pinetum is an example of how these botanic gardens have been encouraged to evolve and display new-found knowledge and plants as well as meeting current ecological and garden-making demands and taste.

CANONS ASHBY

near Daventry
On B4525 Northampton to Banbury Road
Owner: The National Trust
Tel: Blakesley (0327) 860 044
Open several days a week from Easter to end
October
(peak seasons spring and summer)

The National Trust has done a marvellous job of restoring these period gardens to their original 1710 layout. Opened to the public only in 1984, their formal design reflects the style of the seventeenth-century designers, London and Wise, and was almost completely hidden from view until a short while ago. The gardens stand on two sides of a modest house built of ironstone and dating from the sixteenth century. Their period design, plant content and peaceful and romantic atmosphere create a stylish picture. There are architectural and decorative features to interest the garden historian, and the often unusual and effective choice of plant material, will interest the gardener.

The gardens have two separate parts, enclosed and divided by walls. The terraces descend from the south front and the more intimate green court stands to the west. Overlooking countryside which was once a landscaped park, the descending terraces are of formal design but are planted in an increasingly natural way. Symmetrical gravel paths, borders and smooth lawns give way to mown grass paths and areas of turf planted with fruit trees and wild flowers, autumn crocus, fritillarias and scillas. Yew topiary, like the pair of 'cake stands' decorating the top two terraces, and young cedars planted to replace the original ones, stand either side of a central flight of stone steps. Old varieties of fruit trees and lines of Irish yews and flowering shrubs decorate the lower terraces, which resemble an ordered orchard and a wild garden. The blocks of turf on the lower terraces have been cut to different lengths to create subtle divisions between one area and another.

The vast cedar on the far west of the top terrace adds a touch of nobility, and elegant stone gateways and a canopied oak garden seat dating from 1712 fortify the period feeling. Borders near the house and on the terraces have a range of plants in keeping with the style of the garden. The nursery owned by London and Wise was famed for the range of fruit it stocked, and it is appropriate that fruit trees such as apples and plums, a black mulberry, currants and standard gooseberries are as much at home here as flowers. Roses, herbs, pinks and spring bulbs form a ribbon of colour below the house and a mixture of fruit, herbs and flowers — an unusual and successful one being rhubarb interspersed with London pride — stand beneath the boundary walls. Plants with large, architectural foliage like rhubarb, acanthus and cardoon have been used to great effect throughout.

A charming lead statue of a shepherd boy playing a pipe stands on the lawn of the green court. Framed by a stone gateway with finials shaped like obelisks, he looks down a double line of topiary yews to the elegant doorway of the house. The architectural character of this walled garden is not spoiled by colourful flower beds, because the perimeter borders are filled with restrained foliage and white-flowering plants. Cherries and pears are trained against the walls.

CAPEL MANOR

Bullsmoor Lane, Waltham Cross
3m (5km) north of Enfield on A10 at junction with
M25
Owner: London Borough of Enfield Education
Committee
Tel: Lea Valley (0992) 763849
Open regularly from April to end October
Plants for sale

Anyone beginning to make a garden or seeking new ideas should visit Capel Manor. Now an educational establishment for the vocational and non-vocational horticulturist, the eighteenth-century house is surrounded by thirty-six acres of gardens. These contain an extraordinarily

Graceful racemes of standard and climbing wisterias in spring.

diverse collection of period and other features and demonstrate scores of ways in which a modestly sized garden can be laid out or made more attractive. Guidance on the cultivation of problem and other areas is given — sunny walls, scree, waterside and dry and damp shade. There are plant collections of botanical interest, a garden for the disabled, theme and period gardens, glasshouses and examples of how paths, terraces and pergolas can be constructed to suit a particular situation. Herb, knot, walled, rock, water, woodland and spring gardens can all be seen, together with a collection of old roses and a number of fine trees: a two-hundred-year-old copper beech is outstanding.

The individual gardens are as attractive as they are instructive. The theme gardens which lie hidden behind yew hedges display well-associated choice white-flowering subjects, foliage plants or hardy geraniums. Their subtle colouring is highlighted against the dark yew. A seventeenth-century garden is also surrounded by a yew hedge, and the wrought-iron well at its centre is surrounded by an immaculately tended knot of box-edged beds filled with low-growing foliage and other plants. Plants clamber up a gazebo built of trellis, and beds of herbs dating from the time of Parkinson and Culpeper surround a stone sundial. Stone troughs of alpines and dwarf conifers are near the alpine display house, and in the tropical house a succulent collection of subjects thrive in the warm humidity.

Each garden is on a relatively small scale, so no contortions of the imagination are required to relate their design and contents to the needs of the average gardener. A source of inspiration and guidance throughout the season, these gardens are a happy example of how knowledge can be imparted in an agreeable and highly effective manner. More than one visit is recommended.

CAREBY MANOR GARDENS

MAP G

Careby, near Stamford
In Careby, 6m (9½km) north of Stamford.
From A6121 Stamford to Bourne road turn
west at Rhyall on to B1176, after 3m (5km)
cross railway bridge into Careby
Owners: Mr and Mrs Nigel Colborn
Tel: Castle Bytham (078 081) 220 or 729
Open Sundays and Bank Holidays from
Easter to end September
(peak months June and July)
Plants for sale

The weather conditions of this area would discourage most gardeners: the bitterly cold winds, frequent droughts and late frosts. Not the Colborns, who began to develop this small farmhouse garden in 1977. It now covers over two and a half acres and contains over 3500 species.

Composed of a series of gardens, each with an individual theme, these display a prodigious number of unusual plants that thrive on the alkaline soil. A large number have also been planted especially to encourage wild life — which is not to say that they have simply been allowed to 'evolve' or go wild. They are a model of orderliness and an example of how a garden can be hospitable as well as highly cultivated.

Set around the limestone manor is a terrace garden, a sizeable part of it on scree. Bulbs and alpines are set in beds on low walls, and beds of foliage plants contain fifteen varieties of *Pulmonaria*. A gravelled courtyard with raised beds, sheltered by the barn and house, displays old-fashioned roses specifically chosen to give colour over a long period. More gravel to the front of the house is devoted to late winter- and spring-flowering subjects and a huge stone sink by the front door has been planted with a dwarf *Ilex*, *Salix helvetica* and sweetly-scented *Daphne collina*. The formal, rectangular Elizabethan garden is planted with herbs, columbines and *Auriculas*, some of which are the owner's seedlings. Wild cyclamen, snowdrops and aconites form a bright pool beneath a huge old lime tree. Unusual

81

shrubs and plants with interesting foliage, texture and shape cluster around the small lawn of the town garden, and old-fashioned annuals and perennials, double primroses and wild strawberries colour the cottage garden.

No opportunity has been missed to suit the growing conditions to a particular range of plants; the skilful colouring of borders is enhanced by these being set against walls and hedges; an area of boggy ground is planted with *Ligularias*, *Rheum* and *astilbes*, and a long screen dividing one area from another is covered with *Akebia*, golden hop and everlasting pea. Between these defined areas are unusual shrubs and specimen trees. Keen plantsmen should take pencil and paper on repeated visits to Careby to keep up with its development and contents. The boundaries of the garden are by no means fixed — new features and plants are continually being added.

CARROG

MAP E

Llanddeiniol, near Aberystwyth
In Llanddeiniol, off the A487, 6m (9½km) south
of Aberystwyth
Owners: Mr and Mrs Geoffrey Williams
Tel: Llanon (097 48) 369
Open by appointment for charity
(peak months April to June)

Wales is less well endowed with fine gardens than other parts of Great Britain, but those which are privately owned and open to the public usually belong to talented plantsmen. Carrog is one of these. Its development began eighteen years ago when Mr and Mrs Williams decided to transform two fields near the house into a garden of trees and shrubs. They were determined that it would be labour-saving and would satisfy their ever-growing interest in plants. It now covers five acres, and the acid soil nourishes a surprising range of plants, kept in order with the help of a sit-on mower and the judicious use of weedkillers.

Sheltered by mature beeches and oaks, large island beds house an impressive collection of shrubs and trees. Many have grown to a great size considering their youth, and the garden gives the impression of being in its prime. Specimen trees such as magnolias, maples, *Cornus* and *Styrax japonica* are underplanted with hellebores, hostas and peonies; the always fresh, lime-green foliage of *Robinia pseudoacacia* 'Aureus', the false acacia, and *Gleditsia triacanthos* stand out against darker subjects and form an arresting contrast. Shrub roses proliferate as do seldom-seen shrubs such as *Rhus trichocarpa* and the light and feathery elder, *Sambucus tenuifolia*. Evergreen trees have not been neglected: an *Abies koreana*, Brewer's weeping spruce and Atlantic cedars are handsome and distinctive. The bog garden by the pond and the peat bed nearby are colourful with moisture-loving and ericaceous plants, both warranting inspection. Carrog is predominantly a tree and shrub garden, but herbaceous plants can be seen in the walled garden near the house, which also accommodates a vegetable garden and a greenhouse. The greenhouse shelters a collection of carnivorous plants like sundews and Venus flytraps, a fascinating addition to a garden full of surprises for the plantsman.

THE CASTLE

MAP I

St Helens, near Ryde, Isle of Wight
House to east end of St Helens
Owners: Mr and Mrs D. H. Bacon
Tel: Isle of Wight (0983) 872164
Open one day a year for charity and by
appointment
(peak season spring)

Falling down to the sea, away from the early nineteenth-century house, are formal and informal gardens, lawns and ornamental trees, covering five acres. Wonderfully private, they enjoy a superb sunbaked position, and their layout and contents will be of particular interest to the plantsman and those with seaside gardens. The plant material, much of it unusual, has obviously proved itself 'seaworthy', though shelter has been provided in the shape of hedges and groups of shrubs and trees. The generosity with which spring bulbs of all kinds have been planted is noteworthy; the scillas that form pools of blue beneath some cherry trees are a memorable sight. Plants of one colour such as deep red, almost black, polyanthus have been massed spectacularly and there is also a charming white garden. Near the house is a Victorian greenhouse of generous proportions, scented by jasmine and freesias, and richly filled with plants like *Cineraria cruenta* of every hue.

CASTLE ASHBY

MAP G

near Northampton
6m (9½km) east of Northampton, off the A428
between Denton and Yardley Hastings
Owner: The Marquess of Northampton
(HHA)
Tel: Yardley Hastings (060 129) 234
Gardens open regularly throughout the year
(peak season summer)

The gardens belonging to this splendid Tudor house will be of particular interest to the garden historian. They boast a number of large period features which have been added over several centuries, touches of seventeenth-century formality, an eighteenth-century landscape, and a nineteenth-century parterre and Italian garden.

When William of Orange visited Castle Ashby in 1695 he suggested that four impressive avenues should be planted to the north, south, east and west of the house. This was done, but today only one of these can be seen because 'Capability' Brown was commissioned to 'improve' the gardens in the following century. With characteristic élan he scrapped two of the avenues and divided the one running to the east into clumps, but mercifully left intact the one running south. Once planted with four rows of trees either side, limes now form a magnificent vista to the countryside from the elegant south front of the house, a later addition by Inigo Jones. Brown, always a purist, scrapped the formal Elizabethan gardens, extended the ornamental lakes to form large, natural ponds, set a temple on a far bank and planted the park with clumps of trees. The ponds, temple and a number of his original chestnuts and Lebanon cedars can be admired today.

A century later, in the 1860s, Matthew Digby Wyatt and J. B. Blashfield were commissioned to design the vast terraces east of the house. Now simplified, they are still an impressive sight. Fountains are surrounded by a grass parterre which resembles the subtle pattern on a damask tablecloth; on the lower level box-edged beds are filled with brightly coloured flowering plants. A unique feature is the balustrading composed of letters spelling out biblical quotations, similar to those which decorate the parapet of the house. The fountains and flower-filled urns are, surprisingly, not made of stone but of terracotta.

Wyatt also built the handsome orangery and the triumphal arch which links the greenhouses in the walled Italian garden. There was a vogue for formal features of this kind at the time, but few were successful in evoking a genuine Italian scene and atmosphere. The romantic and secluded garden at Castle Ashby is an exception. On a warm summer's afternoon, when the sun is low and gilding the stonework and the many stately evergreens cast shadows over lawns and wide gravel paths, England seems a million miles away. The condition of the gardens is patchy, but this does not detract from their interest.

CASTLE DROGO

MAP H

Drewsteignton
4m (6½km) south of A30 Exeter to Oakehampton
road via Crockernwell
Owner: The National Trust
Tel: Chagford (064 73) 3306
Open regularly from Easter to end October
(peak seasons spring and summer)

The granite castle, designed by Edwin Lutyens, stands nine hundred feet above the Teign gorge — a dramatic and unexpected sight which provokes widely differing reactions. One cannot feel lukewarm about the architectural style of the castle, but it is impossible not to be bowled over by its spectacular outlook over the moors and valley.

A small hidden garden stands beneath its walls: the chapel garden, planted as was originally intended with lavender, miniature roses and box. The main part of the twelve-acre gardens are some distance from the castle, not attempting to soften its austerity. Below the castle's terrace wall is a valley planted with acid-loving shrubs such as hybrid and species rhododendrons and camellias. In spring further colour is added to this sloping woodland by magnolias, cherries and maples.

Lutyens designed the flower gardens on the formal terraces above. They have a strong architectural character, yew hedges and stone work forming the framework. His great friend and collaborator, Gertrude Jekyll, is known to have been consulted but, though she influenced their design, George Dillestone was commissioned by Julius Drewe, the owner of Drogo, to design their planting. Elegant steps lead up to a series of yew-hedged terraces sheltered by beech trees. Borders of white flowering plants and beds of roses decorate the first of these; modern shrub varieties have been chosen because old-fashioned roses are vulnerable to disease in the wet climate. Above the clean-cut, box-shaped yews, trained umbrellas of *Parrotia persica* rise at each corner, their burning autumn colour creating a warm and lively contrast to the darkness of the hedges. Herbaceous borders of old-fashioned plants — hollyhocks, lupins, red-hot pokers and campanulas are set against the retaining wall dripping with wisteria. Yuccas, always a Jekyll favourite, stand on the terrace above, and beds of herbs with distinctive foliage such as sage and rue. Shrubs provide interest on the final terrace which leads to the circular, yew-hedged croquet lawn. Elegant garden seats designed by Lutyens are the only decoration in this restrained and tranquil pool of green, apart from the shadows playing on the smooth lawn.

CASTLE HOWARD

MAP C

near York
15m (24km) north-east of York; 3m (5km) off the A64; 6m (9½km) west of Malton
Owner: Honourable Simon Howard (HHA)
Tel: Coneysthorpe (065 384) 333
Open daily from late March to end October
Plants for sale

A five-mile-long avenue of trees is a suitably impressive introduction to Vanbrugh's first and major masterpiece. But had this been twice the length and planted eight lines deep, it is doubtful whether it would prepare visitors for their first sight of the grand Baroque palace. The gardens of Castle Howard are remarkable for their range, period features and the richness of their plant content. Leave plenty of time to explore the landscape, wander through the woodland and formal gardens and discover the walled gardens.

Set on an east-west ridge overlooking the vale of York, the landscape running to the east is noteworthy for being ahead of its time. When Lord Carlisle employed Vanbrugh and Nicholas Hawksmoor to design this in the last days of the seventeenth century, the landscape movement was not even a glint in the eye of either Lord Burlington or William Kent. Bold in size and concept, the scale of its architectural features is so grand that those decorating landscapes made in following centuries seem to lack bite in comparison. A winding walk — formerly the main street through the deliberately destroyed village of Henderskelfe — leads to Vanbrugh's heroic Temple of the Four Winds, from which you can see the handsome Roman bridge spanning the serpentine river which splashes from the south lake down a series of cascades to the vale below. In the distance stands Hawksmoor's mausoleum where Lord Carlisle is buried. Dramatically placed and appropriately sombre, its dome is supported by pillars on a large stone base. Horace Walpole wrote that it 'would tempt one to be buried alive'.

Ray Wood, which lies on the high ridge east of the house has been developed as a woodland ingly planted shrubs, herbaceous, foliage and scented plants and a fine collection of modern and old-fashioned roses. Formal in design, beds are edged with box, lavender, red berberis and veronica. Arbours, pergolas, silver weeping pears and cupressus add points of height and interest. Silverleafed plants and the crisp foliage of hostas flatter other more strident subjects or create a textured skirt to evergreens; the borders, massed with delphiniums, are radiant rivers of blue.

Statue shaded by yew in the landscape garden at Rousham.

CASTLE TOR

MAP H

Oxlea Road, Torquay
From Higher Lincombe Road turn east into Oxlea Road; 200 yards (180 metres) on right
Owner: Mr Leonard Stocks
Tel: Torquay (0803) 214858
Open several days a year for charity and by appointment
(peak months July and August)

garden since 1975. Once embellished with statues and fountains, walks now weave through the woodland replanted since World War II. Ferns and wild flowers like bluebells, primroses, bugle, garlic and foxgloves colour the mossy floor. A great number of specimen trees and a collection of over seven hundred varieties of hybrid and species rhododendrons are maturing beneath the canopy of trees.

The famous nursery-men and garden designers London and Wise were commissioned to make the formal gardens at the south front. In 1850, these were transformed into an intricate parterre garden by the Victorian designer, William Nesfield. All that survives is the dominant Atlas fountain, acquired from the 1851 Great Exhibition. This is surrounded by a restrained and symmetrical pattern of paths, lawns and clipped yew hedges, a wonderfully ordered picture which offsets the architecture of the house.

An eleven-acre walled garden shelters a series of flower gardens — Venus, sundial, fountain and Lady Cecilia. These 'rooms' have charm-

These steeply terraced gardens will ring a bell for those familiar with the work of Edwin Lutyens. They were designed in the 1930s by one of his former students, Frederick Harrild, for the son of Edward VII's bookmaker, Horace Pickersgill. No expense was spared. A complete quarry of Somerset limestone was exhausted to build the high terrace walls, well-proportioned flights of steps and the long lily pond, tower, orangery, pillars and portcullised gatehouse.

The garden is a marvellous folly, verging on the vulgar, the stonework being relieved by yew topiary and brilliant splashes of colour. A long flight of steps, with sea views glimpsed through stone roundels, leads down to the top terrace and the modest 1920s house. No one could fail to be seduced by the uninterrupted views, between wooded hills, over Tor Bay and from the circular terrace garden, over Babbacombe Bay.

The lower terraces were recently under threat from speculative builders but it is hoped that this fantasy period garden will soon be restored to its former glory and saved for posterity as a unique feature of Torquay.

CEFN BERE

MAP D

Cae Deintur, Dolgellau
Turn left at top of main bridge on Bala to
Barmouth Road, 20 yards (18 metres) on turn
right, then right again behind school and up hill
Owners: Mr and Mrs Maldwyn Thomas
Tel: Dolgellau (0341) 422768
Open by appointment for charity during spring
and summer
(peak months February to October)

This fascinating plantsman's garden on a south-facing slope enjoys a fine view over the town of Dolgellau to the Cader Idris mountains. The view is matched by the diverse and thoughtfully associated contents of the garden. Although only a quarter of an acre in size, it manages to display, rather than cram together, an admirable collection of seldom-seen plants. The beauty and suitability of each has been assessed before being given valuable space, and the owner's eye for colour has ensured that the shades of one area do not clash with another — no mean achievement when, apart from being planted to give all year round interest, the whole garden can be seen at a glance.

The soil is acid, so azaleas and rhododendrons of suitable proportions can be accommodated, the compact *Rhododendron yakushimanum* being an ideal subject. Unusual, ornamental trees like small maples and birches have been planted, and the ground under and around shrubs supports woodland and unusual wild flowers, particularly daphnes. Grasses and ferns are well represented and there are stone troughs of alpines and an alpine house. One side of this is used as a propagating bench; in the other is an immaculately kept tuffa bed studded with an intriguing collection of these miniature plants. The garden warrants close inspection by plantsmen, but a seat has thoughtfully been placed at the top as a resting place to enjoy the sympathetic surroundings and a fine view.

THE CHAIN GARDEN

MAP E

Chapel Road, near Abergavenny
Top of Chapel Road, off A40 1m (2km) north of
Abergavenny
Tel: Abergavenny (0873) 3825
Open by appointment from April to October for
charity
(peak periods May, June and autumn)

Once garden to the Victorian house, the Chain Garden now accommodates two more recently-built houses, but these additions have not caused it to be divided up or become fragmented. On the contrary, it has been revitalised with plants of all kinds.

High above the town and covering two acres, the changing levels and different departments flow naturally one into the other. Original features still exist, such as an ancient and twisted mulberry tree, an old medlar and the walled kitchen garden, which retains its period air thanks to the high standard of its upkeep. The productive asparagus bed, carefully-trained fruit trees against the walls and the neat lines of vegetables are a picture of order and fruitfulness. Apples and apricots thrive here, and peaches are interestingly protected from peach leaf curl by a two-foot canopy attached to the wall, to keep out the wet. A mature Turkey oak and substantial shrubs such as rhododendrons thrive on the acid soil, which also satisfies more recently-planted subjects. There are several *Stuartias*, an *Halesia*, *Magnolia sinensis* and *Carpenteria* as well as several daphne and carpets of cyclamen. *Agapanthus*, a *Rosa banksiae* 'Lutea' and vigorous wisteria surround a swimming pool; evergreen azaleas are banked beside the drive and the stream running through the garden is richly planted with astilbes and other moisture-loving plants. Peonies, penstemon and clematis are here in plenty and a rock garden near the house is planted with unusual dwarf and alpine plants.

CHARLECOTE PARK

MAP F

Wellesbourne, near Warwick
On west side of B4086, 1m (2km) west of
Wellesbourne, 5m (8km) east of Stratford-upon-
Avon, 6m (9½km) south of Warwick
Owner: The National Trust
Tel: Stratford-upon-Avon (0789) 840277
Open several days a week from Easter to
October

The Lucy family has lived at Charlecote since the mid-thirteenth century and the park and gardens which surround the present nineteenth-century, neo-Jacobean house have seen many changes. Shakespeare was caught poaching here by Sir Thomas Lucy and, though he was *persona non grata* in those days, his 'association' with Charlecote is now celebrated in the garden with flowers he wrote about: violets, columbine, aconites, hyssop, sweet majoram and rue. Fallow and red deer and a flock of Jacob sheep still graze in the park and there is an Elizabethan brick gatehouse at the far end of an avenue of Turkey oaks. The formal forecourt is decorated with large cones of yew, with borders of roses, lilacs and perennials against the perimeter walls.

The Turkey oaks, planted to replace ancient elms, stand witness that 'Capability' Brown was not always given a free hand to transform an intensely formal garden into a picturesque landscape. He linked the River Hele to the River Avon which flows through the park and built the inevitable ha-ha, but was forbidden to touch the avenue. The river now runs below a terrace at the back of the house, the elegant steps down to the water being reminiscent of a Venetian more than an English scene. During the Victorian era Mary Elizabeth Lucy altered the house and gardens to reflect the fashions of the day and much of what can be seen today dates from that time. The Victorians loved brightly-coloured flower beds, so an impressive number of bedding-out plants were raised each year. Features dating from this period are the balustraded walls and terraces decorated with urns, balls of box and beds of lavender and catmint, the stately cedars

and the orangery. At the bottom of the steps to the orangery stand two lead statues by John van Nost — a charming shepherd and shepherdess. A woodland garden of wild and cultivated plants such as campion, columbine, Solomon's seal, box and variegated elder lies behind the orangery and the thatched cottage.

Since Charlecote was given to the Trust in 1946, they have restored many of the architectural features and rescued or replanted neglected areas, leaving intact its peaceful and romantic air.

CHATSWORTH

MAP B

Edensor, near Bakewell
2m (3km) south of Baslow on B6012
Owner: Chatsworth House Trust Limited
Tel: Baslow (024 688) 2204
Open daily from late March to end October
(peak month May)
Plants for sale

Set into the side of a hill overlooking the house, park and unspoilt countryside, the gardens of Chatsworth have one of the most beautiful settings in the country and are of unrivalled splen-

The serpentine beech hedge at Chatsworth.

dour. Generations of the Devonshire family have added to and improved the richly-decorated canvas; the present Duke and Duchess have contributed several features, and some of the most famous names in garden-making history have worked here, so there are many fascinating garden-making styles and period features.

The hand of nurserymen London and Wise can be seen in Flora's temple and the sea-horse fountain which once adorned the intensely formal seventeenth-century garden. During the same period, Grillet, a pupil of Le Nôtre, created the magnificent cascade, a giant, deeply treaded staircase of smooth water which is a magnetic focal point on the slope behind the house. Gravity fed, the water comes from man-made lakes on the hill above, flows from the temple high on the hill, down the cascade over the twenty-four steps which are twenty-four feet wide and then, intriguingly, disappears underground, to rise again in the sea-horse fountain.

Following the fashion of the day, the fourth duke commissioned 'Capability' Brown to improve the landscape. He banished London and Wise's parterres, planted clumps and belts of trees and with characteristic boldness widened the banks of the Derwent so that its scale would be in keeping with the grandeur of the whole. In 1826, a young man of twenty-three called Joseph Paxton was employed as head gardener and embarked on a career which revealed his many and varied talents. His work here made his name as famous as that of the gardens he tended.

Paxton's engineering skills were harnessed to construct the emperor fountain, the exciting and powerful spout of water which rises out of an unadorned canal and shoots more than two hundred feet into the air. He had huge stone boulders moved to form a humbling world of crags, rock faces and waterfalls, planted a pinetum and an arboretum filled with specimens unusual even today and designed the wallcases resembling narrow greenhouses, which shelter tender shrubs and fruit trees. An immaculately-kept maze, overlooked by towering Wellingtonias, stands on the site of his great conservatory. This was famous not only for its size (a carriage could pass down its centre) and magnificence, but for triggering off the fashion — soon to become a

rage during the Victorian era — for growing exotics under glass. The first Amazonian water-lily in this country, *Victoria amazonica*, produced a flower in this conservatory. So rapidly did it grow and to such an amazing size (it is now grown from seed each year as an annual) that Paxton built the lily house to accommodate it. This glasshouse inspired the design of his masterpiece — the Crystal Palace. Like the great conservatory, the lily house was demolished after World War I, but the model village of Edensor on the estate still stands witness to his architectural skills. His energy and achievements mark him out as a true Victorian, but his work at Chatsworth does not reflect the pomposity of some gardens of the period.

The beech-hedged walk, of an inspired serpentine design, was planted by the Duke and Duchess in 1953. They also built the new, ultra-modern greenhouse, a startling contrast to the period building in the rose garden nearby. It is divided into three sections to accommodate temperate, Mediterranean and tropical plants and boasts ingenious watering, heating and ventilating systems. A cool and shady terrace nearby is made of stone which was originally part of Paxton's lily house, the snake which features in the Cavendish family crest being incorporated into the design.

I have described only a selection of what can be seen at Chatsworth. Wander over the vast expanses of lawns shaded by handsome trees, explore the woodland and upper reaches of the gardens and you will discover many other features, for example, the unique willow-tree fountain, gravity fed and made of copper; it has a sense of humour and the visitor should beware of a minor soaking. These are sublimely confident and beautiful gardens.

Rock and water garden at Chatsworth.

CHELSEA PHYSIC GARDEN

MAP J

66 Royal Hospital Road, London SW3
Entrance via Swan Walk between Chelsea
Embankment and Royal Hospital Road
Owner: Trustees of the Chelsea Physic Garden
Tel: (01) 352 5646
Open on Wednesday and Sunday afternoons from
mid-April to mid-October
Plants for sale

The second oldest botanic garden in England, Chelsea Physic Garden is of historical interest as well as being botanically fascinating. It is hidden in a peaceful oasis behind a high wall, and the four acres run from the handsome brick house towards the river. Though attractive, the gardens have not been laid out to present a series of pictures. Despite its name, the *raison d'être* of the Physic Garden is not simply to further the cause of medicine but to encourage the study of plants and promote research into their related uses, conservation and environment. The orderly lay-out of beds and paths was designed to aid the student rather than entertain the visitor, who has only recently been allowed to view this treasure-chest of botanic specimens. Rectangular order beds have been filled with individual plant families, to ease the observation of their different characteristics. Other beds display variegated rock, woodland or shade-loving plants, shrubs, herbs and Mediterranean varieties. One contains the National Collection of Cistus and others are devoted to plants used for dyeing or grown for their scent.

The garden's fortunes have varied since its foundation in 1683. Some curators, like Philip Miller who directed its development from 1722 to 1770, were outstandingly successful in furthering its interests. He was recommended for the job by the garden's great benefactor, Sir Hans Sloane, and he not only wrote the first modern gardening dictionary but introduced and distributed a wealth of new plants from abroad. This established the Physic Garden's reputation, and an area has now been laid out with the many plants he and other curators introduced — an historical walk. Some of the most famous names in the botanical world enriched these gardens: Sir Joseph Banks, William Forsyth (of forsythia fame), Robert Fortune and Dr John Lindley.

Though the garden was designed as a research and educational aid, it is not indigestible or dry, and can be enjoyed on several different levels.

Statue of Sir Hans Sloane surveying Chelsea Physic Garden.

Its back to the fine old Curator's house, the white marble statue of Sir Hans Sloane is well placed to enjoy an outlook embracing the ancient mulberry, olive, holm and cork oak and the fine Chinese willow pattern tree, *Koelreuteria paniculata.* These shade some beds and cast shadows over the lawns; the constant roar of traffic on the far side of the wall is the only reminder of the city all around.

CHENIES MANOR HOUSE

MAP J

Chenies, near Amersham
In Chenies, off the A404 between Amersham and
Rickmansworth; 2m (3km) Exit 18 off M25
Owners: Lieutenant-Colonel and Mrs MacLeod
Matthews (HHA)
Tel: Little Chalfont (024 04) 2888
Open Wednesdays and Thursdays from April to
October and by appointment
Herbs for sale

Mentioned in the Domesday book, visited by Henry VIII (Catherine Howard conducted her adulterous affair with Thomas Culpeper here) and Elizabeth I, this redbrick Tudor manor was once the principal residence of the Earls of Bedford. Since the present owners came here in the 1950s they have worked hard to create surroundings in keeping with the manor's architecture and past, and their efforts have been highly successful.

Chenies has a collection of small gardens laid out in formal period style, which contain a delightful selection of plants. Offset by domes and hedges of yew and box are generously-filled beds of modern and old-fashioned plants — standard honeysuckles and buddleias, spring bulbs, herbaceous and edging plants such as the hazy green ribbons of *Alchemilla mollis*. There is a sunken garden, a small topiary, a white garden, and an intriguing physic garden planted with herbs. The formal beds of the physic garden display three hundred species, each bed containing a different group of plants such as poisonous, culinary or medicinal subjects.

The garden also boasts some interesting period features: an old skittle alley, an octagonal tiled building which shelters a medieval well, and a rarely-seen grass maze. The forerunner of the hedged labyrinth, this was laid out to resemble that featured in a sixteenth-century picture at Woburn Abbey, the present home of the Dukes of Bedford. There is also an exhibition of the history of English pleasure gardens and a display of dried flowers grown and arranged by Mrs MacLeod Matthews.

CHESTER ZOOLOGICAL GARDENS

MAP B

Chester
Off A41 at Upton on northern outskirts of Chester
Owner: North of England Zoological Society
Tel: Chester (0244) 380280
Open throughout the year
(peak seasons spring and summer)

This splendid zoo is now as well known for its superb floral displays as for its collection of animals. Victorian in character, the gardens are a must for those seeking inspiration for new bedding-out combinations or who simply enjoy seeing beautifully-maintained and exuberantly-filled beds of annuals, roses and shrubs. Many of the beds, backed by hedges to improve display, reflect the Victorian 'gardenesque' style of planting, but the imaginative use of unusual plants and the sensitive way in which they have been mixed also reflects modern taste and illustrates the wider choice available today. Over eighty thousand plants are raised in the greenhouses annually and the beds are replanted three times a year. Apart from the brilliant colours of thousands of roses, fuchsias and begonias, there is a butterfly garden planted with buddleias, stocks and verbena, a rock and water garden and an area devoted to South American trees and shrubs.

The animal cages are surrounded with carefully-chosen shrubs, trees and climbers. These soften the severe and unnatural habitat of the animals and subtly but firmly prevent visitors going too close to less friendly or vulnerable inhabitants. The tropical house is a *pièce de résistance*, some of the zoological inmates being as exotic as the botanical. Luxuriant shrubs and climbers stretch high into the roof, creating a jungle-like effect. Near the exit is the jubilee garden, in which a fountain by Sean Rice depicts Noah and the Four Winds. Set in a pool and surrounded by moisture-loving plants and beds of shrubs and ferns, this science-fiction-style sculpture is a modernistic contrast to that classic feature of Victorian parks — a floral clock. It displays a tightly-planted and brightly-coloured embroidery of succulent and other subjects.

CHIDMERE HOUSE

MAP I

Chidham, near Chichester
In Chidham, 6m (9½km) west of Chichester
Owner: Mr Thomas Baxendale
Tel: Bosham (0243) 573095
Open severals days in spring for charity and
by appointment for parties
(peak seasons early spring and early summer)

Laid out on what was, in 1930, the site of an old farmyard, orchard and fields with limy soil, walls and neatly-clipped hornbeam hedges enclose a series of 'rooms' linked by corridors; these corridors not only create long and delightful vistas but enhance the garden's many surprise elements. Openings in the hedges reveal hidden 'rooms' decorated with handsome ornaments: an urn or a statue. These were acquired by the owner's great-grandfather at the Paris Exhibition of 1867 and add greatly to the stylish formality of the garden.

Colour is provided by flowering shrubs and specimen trees such as a *Cornus kousa chinensis*, a magnolia and a handkerchief tree. In spring, daffodils gild the orchard and in late summer the herbaceous border comes into its own. Complementing the soft colour of the charming Tudor house with its stables and gatehouse is the conservatory, set against a fifteen-foot-high wall. Geraniums have been trained against it and orchids and a bottle brush plant add further interest and colour. The five-acre lake nearby, Chidmere pond, is a private nature reserve.

CHILCOMBE HOUSE

MAP I

Chilcombe, near Bridport
Turn south from A35 4m (6½km) east of Bridport
Owners: Mr and Mrs John Hubbard
Tel: Long Bredy (03083) 234
Open occasionally for charity and by
appointment from June to September
(peak months June to September)

The setting, design and plant content of this two-acre hillside garden are a trinity of beauty, charm and interest well worth making a detour to see. Unspoilt countryside rolls away from the seventeenth-century stone house and the small chapel which nestles beside it. The garden was begun by the present owners in 1969; it is skilfully divided into different areas by walls, hedges, pergolas and arches, and comprises a formal courtyard, a wild meadow, and a series of interlinking 'rooms' which contain generous and appealing groups of plants.

John Hubbard is an artist and his exceptional eye for colour and form is reflected everywhere. The basic design is formal, but the planting is relaxed and the colouring subtle; the garden gives the impression of having been painted rather than planted. It has a cottage garden nature and there are many alluring associations as well as unusual plants. Climbing, rambling and shrub roses, perennial geraniums, violas and alliums abound and two beeches — common and copper — yew and holly have been used to make a tapestry hedge. The bank above the house is overhung with trees and filled with shade-loving plants. Decorative bantams range freely here and add to the charm of this away-from-it-all garden.

CHILLINGHAM CASTLE

MAP A

Chillingham, near Alnwick
5m (8km) east of Wooler, turn south at Chatton
to Chillingham
Owner: Sir Humphrey Wakefield
Tel: Chatton (066 85) 390
Open regularly from May to September, weekends
only April and October
(peak month June)

This is the age of period garden restoration. Owners of historic houses who welcome visitors have stopped trying to simplify historical and work-intensive features and are hard at work restoring them. Chillingham Castle is a fascinating case: it has risen like a phoenix from the ashes. When Sir Humphrey Wakefield bought the castle in 1982, it was a ruin. The garden was invisible and the courtyard a forest of saplings. It is hard today to visualise their former unruly state, because, since being restored, they have a disarming, time-warp atmosphere. Over the centuries, successive generations have scrapped or added various features to the castle and garden as fashions changed. No doubt new 'finds' will be made as the work of restoration continues.

The Italian garden, with its topiary and geometric, box-edged flower beds is within the battlemented walls to the west of the castle. Sweetpeas romp over the ramparts and towering Wellingtonias cast their shade across a well-ordered scene which was smothered under a blanket of brambles and willow herb a short while ago. Woodland walks have been opened up, and seats placed where the lake and rhododendrons can be admired.

CHILWORTH MANOR

MAP J

Chilworth, near Guildford
3½m (5½km) south-east of Guildford on A248; in centre of Chilworth turn left up Blacksmith Lane
Owner: Lady Heald
Tel: Guildford (0483) 61414
Open several days a week for charity and by appointment
(peak months April to August)
Plants for sale occasionally

Sarah, Duchess of Marlborough, must have found the natural charm of her new home at Chilworth a relief after the grandeur of Blenheim. Once the site of an ancient monastery mentioned in the Domesday Book, the handsome house is surrounded by gardens set on terraces and around expansive lawns. These run down to a woodland and an attractive water garden developed around the ancient stew ponds. An elegant country home rather than a showpiece, the Duchess's original walled garden, at one side of the house, is saved from aggressive formality by being planted with fruit trees and decorated with borders whose contents spill over the retaining walls. Note the *clair-voie* in the top wall.

In the ten acres, there are striking ornamental trees such as a Judas, snowdrop, catalpa and dawn redwood, and the borders, rockery, and woodland have been planted with discernment. The walls of the house sport climbing plants, chosen for their summer and autumn colour. Seek out one of the well-placed seats and enjoy the happy mixture of history, design and content in this garden admirably tended by only one gardener.

CHIRK CASTLE

MAP D

Chirk
½m (1km) west of Chirk village off A5
Owner: The National Trust
Tel: Chirk (0691) 777701
Open regularly from Easter until end September
(peak season spring)
Plants for sale

This fourteenth-century border castle stands high on a hill, formidable and stark against the skyline. It is hard to believe that a garden exists at all. Drawing nearer, you can see cones of yew on the far side of a wall, and this topiary and the hedge on the high terrace, beautifully clipped into cones and wedges, are a dramatic introduction to the extensive and diverse gardens at Chirk. The large hedge and the topiary, shaped like high-crowned medieval hats, give the impression of having been there for centuries, but they were only planted towards the end of the nineteenth century.

In 1764 formal gardens were destroyed to make way for a fashionable landscape designed by William Eames. However, he did not sweep away the terraces and on one of them, beneath the castle walls, are borders and a reinstated sunken rose garden. These are not so surprising as the garden lying beyond an opening in the hedge, with huge wedges of yew and a pair of bronze nymphs guarding the entrance. A seemingly endless vista down a grass walk stretches over the park and countryside spreading below. Either side of the grass walk are informal twentieth-century gardens. Mature conifers stand to one side in rough grass where spring bulbs have been naturalised; on the other side are mixed borders and cherries. The walk leads to Hawk House, thatched and partially surrounded by a rocky bank planted with low-growing subjects. Walks strike out to either side of the wide lawn and wind to beds of shrubs and trees and a pool garden. There is a particularly good example of a mature *Cornus nuttallii* and other unusual ornamental trees, rhododendrons and azaleas.

CHISWICK HOUSE

MAP J

Burlington Lane, Chiswick, London W4
Entrance off Burlington Lane, Chiswick
Owner: English Heritage
Tel: (01) 994 3299
Open daily dawn to dusk

Now a public park, Chiswick House is a place of pilgrimage for lovers of Palladian architecture and garden historians. The villa, modelled

The sphinx at Chiswick House.

on Palladio's Villa Capra, was built by Lord Burlington to house an art collection. The garden, quite unlike what would normally have surrounded a classical Italian villa, is an early example of the innovative talent of the landscape designer, William Kent. Lord Burlington's patronage of Kent began when they met in Italy, Burlington on a Grand Tour and Kent studying to be a painter. Inspired by the villas of Andrea Palladio and the paintings of Arcadian scenes by Claude and Salvator Rosa, these two determined to recreate similar romantic scenes on their return to England — a classical architectural style was popularised and the eighteenth-century landscape movement born.

The garden is far from being a full-blooded 'natural' landscape, that revolutionary style being then only in its infancy. The formal axial paths, the walk flanked by dark spreading cedars and stone sphinxes, clipped yew hedges and vaguely serpentine canal hark back to the earlier, seventeenth-century French style; the later nineteenth-century additions, such as the conservatory filled with camellias and the formal bedding of the Italian garden, are more Paxtonian than Kentian. The hand of Kent is more obviously seen in the irregular, winding paths which thread through the Wilderness, past the dark yews and neo-classical architectural and other features which create the romantic atmosphere and feeling of expectation. They may not be inhabited by nymphs, pagan gods and heroes, but the presence of neo-classical busts, temples and obelisks give the gardens an ancient and Italianate feel. Irrespective of the time of year (to see it under a blanket of snow is an experience), its serenity and distinctive character hold a fascination which the presence of dogwalkers and cycling children cannot diminish.

CHOLMONDELEY CASTLE GARDENS

MAP B

Malpas, Cheshire
8m (13km) north of Whitchurch off the A49
Owner: The Marquess of Cholmondeley (HHA)
Tel: Cholmondeley (082 922) 202/3
Open Sundays and Bank Holidays from Easter to end September
(peak months May to July)
Plants for sale

The neo-Gothic castle, built between 1801 and 1804, stands on Fir Hill, with a fine view over the park and surrounding countryside. There is an old chapel, near which two earlier Cholmondeley homes once stood. The younger of these was surrounded by a formal seventeenth-century garden designed by London and Wise and some remaining features add elegant, period touches to the garden which surrounds the castle today: a wrought-iron gate by Tijou, another by the blacksmith Robert Bakewell, a lead statue by van Nost and a temple.

The present owner has developed the gardens considerably since he inherited the property in 1950. Then there were handsome and mature trees such as cedars, limes and beeches and some of the more common varieties of rhododendron, but the immaculately-kept gardens are now filled with unusual trees and plants chosen and associated to give as much interest in autumn as in spring and summer.

A curving cherry walk is underplanted with blue anemones, and fuchsias. Shrubs lie beneath a terrace wall and the vibrant blue of *Agapanthus* is a fine sight in summer. The glade, cleared in 1966, is now planted with rhododendrons, azaleas, maples and a good selection of shrubs. Next to the tennis court are raised beds of roses edged with lavender, and arches smothered in ramblers such as 'New Dawn' and 'The Garland'. The colouring here and along the herbaceous borders, backed by silver weeping pears, is softened by the presence of silver-foliaged plants. The temple garden, too, is carefully planted: flowering shrubs, roses and, moisture-loving plants all play a role. The temple stands on an island in the lake jewelled with waterlilies, and another, with a domed wrought-iron roof which shades the van Nost figure, stands above the waterfall and impressive rockery. The banks of the stream which feeds the lake are planted with *Gunnera manicata*, and trees chosen for their fiery autumn colour or fascinating bark. The walk along the drive or up Tower Hill above the castle will not be time wasted, because the planting here reflects the uniformly high standards of this garden.

CHYVERTON

MAP H

Zelah, near Truro
3¼m (5km) south-west of Zelah on A30
Owners: Mr and Mrs N. T. Holman
Tel: Zelah (087 254) 324
Open by appointment on weekdays only,
March to May
(peak months April and May)

Chyverton gardens are a happy marriage between an eighteenth-century landscape and twentieth-century woodland. Quite different in character, each enhances the beauty of the other. The mature woodland acts as a frame for the landscape, which sweeps away from the house and down to the lake, spanned at one end by an elegant stone bridge. The tranquil scene of spacious lawns, water and trees which rise above a vast wall of rhododendrons gives no clue to what lies beyond, but a closer look brings into focus the exotically large blooms of magnolias and other unusual and beautiful subjects.

The shrub and woodland gardens contain an extraordinarily fascinating range of plants collected over the last sixty years. A number were grown from seed collected in China by the plant-hunter Frank Kingdon Ward, and others originated in Australasia and South America. Magnolias, some raised at Chyverton, are an important feature, together with camellias and seldom-seen rhododendrons such as the *Rhododendron macabeanum* which bears huge soft, prim-

rose-yellow flowers. Ornamental trees with splendid autumn foliage or flowers (like *Nyssas* and *Styrax*, maples and handkerchief trees, colour the woodland, and there are a number of rare conifers.

At ground level there is a rewarding collection of smaller plants — an example being a primula recently introduced from China, — white- and yellow-flowering skunk cabbage and small carpets of the mouse plant, *Arisarum proboscideum*, which, though usually found beneath willows, flourishes under oaks at Chyverton. Despite the rich collection of rare and unusual plants, the woodland glades and banks of pools and streams have retained their natural character. A twenty-acre garden like this could pose problems of upkeep, but the plants look after themselves and the only work involved is regular mowing of the grass paths.

Those with gardens afflicted by honey fungus should note how successfully it is kept at bay here. A dose of copper carbonate powder is administered to the soil before a new subject is planted.

Irises, ferns and foxgloves in the woodland garden at Clapton Court.

Overlooking the haha which divides the park from the garden at Clapton Court.

CLAPTON COURT

MAP I

near Crewkerne
3m (5km) south of Crewkerne, on B3165 turn east
Owner: Captain S. Loder
Tel: Crewkerne (0460) 73220/72200
Open regularly throughout the year
(peak months April to September)
Plants for sale

Justly popular with the garden-visiting public, and immaculately kept, the ten-acre gardens of Clapton Court are part formal, part woodland. They were first developed in 1950 when Louis Martineau bought the late-Georgian house and began to make a garden around it and in the five acres of woodland beyond the ha-ha. Captain Loder bought the property in 1978, when Louis Martineau's ill health and death had allowed much of his work to fall into decline and disrepair. The name Loder is synonymous with that of a number of great gardens, various members of the family having created those at Wakehurst, Leonardslee, and High Beeches in Sussex. Within a year, the gardens at Clapton had been restored, many parts replanted, others extended and a garden centre established. If that were not enough, a nursery raising fuchsias and pelargoniums was also begun and the garden was opened to the public.

A series of different gardens, creating an attractive and cohesive whole, now stand around the house, on the terraces to the north and around the lawns running down to the ha-ha. On the terraces, which support a number of garden 'rooms', well-associated plants in a silver-and-white garden are offset by the matt green walls of a cupressus hedge. Hybrid tea, shrub and other roses scent and colour the formal rose garden and the top terrace has a selection of variegated, yellow-foliaged shrubs and flowers. A summerhouse overlooks a croquet lawn and Chinese pots planted with bulbs or geraniums decorate the surrounds of an ornamental lily pool. On the terraces the compact, white-flowering *Hebe subalpina* has been used as an effective and unusual edging plant; the garden seats are

set against an imaginative variety of hedging materials.

Clapton boasts some fine and unusual trees; a majestic fern-leafed beech can be seen to one side of the drive, a young sweet buckeye chestnut near the house, an eighty-foot Norway maple next to the water garden and, in the woodland, the biggest ash tree in the country. It is over two hundred years old. A good collection of unusual and other rhododendrons, camellias, maples and eucryphias flourish in the woodland garden. In front of the house is a string of eight pools, their banks generously planted with moisture-loving plants like hostas, primulas and astilbes, whose foliage is as effective as their colour. In the old kitchen garden, near the exit, are the glasshouses which contain the dazzling collection of several hundred different varieties of fuschias and pelargoniums.

CLARE COLLEGE FELLOWS GARDEN

MAP G

Cambridge
On the Backs in Cambridge, across the river from Clare College
Owner: Clare College
Tel: Cambridge (0223) 333200
Open a few days a week throughout the year
(peak months June, July and October)

The Cambridge 'Backs' are famed for their beauty and are an important feature of the city. Well positioned along these stand the two-acre gardens of Clare College, an area of peace but a stone's throw from the hustle and bustle of town-and-gown life on the far side of a bridge leading into the college.

Dark yews and conifers form a boundary to one end of the garden, sheltering it from the bitter winds and providing a dark background to its well-blended contents. Once a kitchen garden and orchard, it was redesigned in 1946 by a group of Clare College Fellows and now contains formal and informal features, both lively and restrained in design and colour, and providing all-year-round interest.

Generously-filled borders, their colouring a skilfully achieved progression from yellow through gold to blue, or confined to interesting foliage and white-flowering plants, are set against dark yew or groups of shrubs with distinctive variegated and golden foliage. The colouring throughout is noteworthy, and the choice of plants and their association is original and effective. Smooth lawns give the garden a feeling of space and are a foil to the more brightly-coloured island beds, which are filled with hot red and orange flowers and autumn tints. At the centre of the garden, hidden behind immaculately clipped yew hedges, is the peaceful pond garden, where narrow beds of low-growing plants form a rectangle of colour around a sunken lawn. A small lily pond stands at its centre, and the conical cypresses at each corner give the 'room' an Italian air. Two apple trees are all that is left of the old orchard.

A further secret 'room', the scented garden, lies at the far end of a tunnel of yew. This is planted not only with sweet-smelling annuals like heliotrope or 'Cherry Pie', stocks and tobacco plants but with deliciously-scented winter-flowering shrubs, *Chimonanthus praecox* and *Viburnum bodnantense* and spring bulbs. Fragrant and decorative herbs have been used to great effect throughout the garden, and there are some handsome and unusual trees — a *Metasequoia glyptostroboides*, swamp cypress, Ohio buckeye, Judas tree and weeping lime.

CLAREMONT LANDSCAPE GARDEN

MAP J

Esher
On south edge of Esher on the east side of the A307
Owner: The National Trust
Open daily throughout the year, except Christmas and New Year's Day

Once described as 'the noblest in Europe', the recently-restored landscape garden at Claremont is a perfect example of the eighteenth-century landscape movement. Set at a considerable distance from the mansion, its purpose was to tempt guests to discover a series of delights in a deceptively natural setting. The lake and its island are the focal point; the walks cut through woodland and evergreens on steeply-sloping and level ground, and lead to a number of fascinating period features: a formal bowling green, belvedere (set at the far end of a formal walk, this can be admired but not entered), grotto, and a unique turf amphitheatre which overlooks the lake.

When they were developed, the autocratic formality and intense detail of the French-style seventeenth-century garden was being rejected for more natural and romantic garden-making. Punctuated by classical temples, lakes and other features, this fashionable landscape garden was laid out to blend into the surrounding countryside. In 1711 the Duke of Newcastle bought the property from Vanbrugh and then commissioned him and the garden designer, Charles Bridgeman, to build a new mansion and create an impressive garden.

They were the first to eradicate the artificial barriers of a garden, do away with walls and hedges, and throw it open to the countryside beyond. Vanbrugh built the belvedere on a mount, a romantic copy of a medieval tower from which the gardens and surrounding countryside could be admired. Bridgeman designed the four-in-hand avenues and the impressive amphitheatre — a series of vast semi-circular turf steps — overlooking the 'stage' and the lake. It was, however, still relatively formal and it was not until the 1730s that William Kent transformed these pleasure gardens into a true landscape garden. He softened the lines of the lake, extended it, and made an island where he placed the now-restored pavilion.

In 1768 Clive of India became the owner of Claremont and commissioned 'Capability' Brown to build him a new mansion and, yet again, improve the landscape. The property was smaller in size than many others he had laid out, so Brown refrained from destroying features such as the grotto, the bowling green or the amphitheatre, but he planted more trees and evergreens and re-routed the road which ran near the lake. In such a way, over several decades, its 'genius'

Herbaceous border and island bed of red flowering plants at Clare College.

or natural character was enhanced. Subsequent owners of Claremont, like Prince Leopold of Saxe-Coburg, left their mark on the landscape. The present camellia terrace stands on the site of the camellia house he built in 1824 and retains the iron railings with the initial L.

Before 1975, when restoration work began, the design of the landscape was masked by dense woodland; architectural and other features which had not been demolished were in a sorry state. By 1980 restoration was complete and the garden layout and many of its features were once again revealed. The comon laurel, much in evidence throughout and though not to everyone's taste today, is historically correct. Its effect on the landscape is better appreciated from afar. A good number of reproduction period garden seats, humanises and adds to the beauty of this important landscape garden.

CLAVERTON MANOR

MAP I

Claverton, near Bath
Off the A36 2½m (4km) south-east of Bath
Owner: Trustees of the American Museum
Tel: Bath (0225) 60503
Open every day except Monday from end March to end October
(peak months April and June)
Herbs for sale

Claverton Manor, high above the Avon valley, has a particularly beautiful setting. Mature trees, like evergreen holm oaks, form a strong and protective background to the garden and to the classical villa of Bath stone designed by Sir Jeffry Wyatville. The manor became the home of the American Museum in 1961 and since then period and botanical features have been added to the fifteen acres, to reflect the gardening history of America. A small, box-hedged herb garden, a gift from a Long Island garden club, is filled with fragrant, culinary and medicinal plants, a number of which are unusual in this country. There is also a replica of part of George Washington's garden at Mount Vernon, laid out with beds of roses and other plants. A mixed border near the house was the work of the American-born garden designer, Lanning Roper, and an arboretum displays American trees. The dark, spreading skirts of cedars throw shadows across the peaceful lawns and stylish white garden seats, and a model of a Red Indian tepee adds style and interest.

CLEVEDON COURT

MAP E

Clevedon, near Bristol
1½m (2½km) east of Clevedon on B3130 Bristol road
Owner: The National Trust
Tel: Clevedon (0272) 872257
Open a few days a week from Easter to end September

Once a popular and elegant watering place, the town of Clevedon is now somewhat cut off from the rest of the world by the M5. Not long ago the fourteenth-century house had an unspoilt view over the wide plain to the east, and it must have been painful to see this cut through by a wide and noisy ribbon of traffic. The garden behind the house literally and aesthetically rises well above this outlook, its most striking feature being the high-walled terraces, sheltered and backed by a wall of trees such as holm oaks. A Gothic summerhouse stands at one end of the terraces and a charming eighteenth-century garden house at the other.

When Gertrude Jekyll visited Clevedon she said that full advantage had not been taken of the sunbaked walls and walks of the terraces. Today these are richly planted with a wide range of plants, of subtle colouring and imagin-

atively associated. Many tender species flourish here — ornamental trees such as a Judas and a strawberry tree, Chusan and seldom-seen dwarf palms, and splendid magnolias. The fragrant, saucer-shaped blooms of a *Magnolia watsonii* are captivating, as are those of a scented white wisteria, the vivid blue skirts of *Ceanothus repens* and intriguing weigela-like flowers of the rare Chinese shrub *Dipelta floribunda*. Monterey pines and *Thuja plicata* (grown from the original seed introduced to this country) are much in evidence in the lower garden, and provide shelter and privacy. Having been loved and tended by the Elton family for generations, the garden has an individual and charming air, even though it is now tended by only a fraction of its former staff.

CLIVEDEN

MAP J

Taplow, near Maidenhead
2m (3km) north of Taplow on B476 from A4
Owner: The National Trust
Tel: Burnham (062 86) 5069
Open daily March to end December

The elegant mid-nineteenth-century mansion stands on high ground, a dominant feature above the River Thames, snaking below. Glimpses of it can be snatched between the belts of trees, the terraces behind the house and over the formal and pleasure gardens, where it is an important feature. There is much to discover in the 130 acres developed over several centuries by Cliveden's various owners, from the second Duke of Buckingham who lived here in 1699, to the American millionaire Astor family who gave Cliveden to The National Trust in 1942. The visitor must be energetic and curious.

The present Italianate house was built for the Duke of Sutherland by Sir Charles Barry in 1850 and acquired by William Waldorf Astor in 1893. It was Astor who embellished the gardens with classical and other statuary and stonework: the Roman sarcophagi in the forecourt and the stone and brick balustrade from the Villa Borghese in Rome, which decorates the lower terrace. Below the impressive terraces stretches the parterre, redesigned by the head gardener, J. Fleming, in 1852.

The pattern of triangular beds planted with santolina and senecio and interspersed with sentinel yews are a restrained and disciplined introduction to the glorious views and pleasure gardens beyond. If you explore the walks striking away from this formal feature and from the avenue to the mansion, through woodland underplanted with rhododendrons, you will come upon a host of period and botanical features — the eighteenth-century Octagon Temple and Blenheim Pavilion, designed by Giacomo Leoni; the oval-shaped and tufa-walled War Memorial Garden to the memory of those who died in the military hospital at Cliveden during World War I; the seventeenth-century grass amphitheatre designed by Charles Bridgeman, where Thomas Arne's 'Rule Britannia' was first heard in 1740; the Long Garden with its topiary, Italian statuary and serpentine parterre of box-edged beds filled with variegated euonymus.

A delicate rose garden set in a woodland glade was designed by Geoffrey Jellicoe and there is a delightful water garden a short distance from the old walled kitchen garden. Planted with moisture-loving subjects and azaleas, rhododendrons, magnolias, maples, bamboos and spring bulbs, this is the most colourful and richly planted part of the gardens. A pagoda with a delicately painted ceiling, made for the 1867 Paris Exhibition, stands near a pond alive with carp and golden orfe. Other hidden features, vistas and fleeting views of the Thames can be enjoyed in the far reaches of the garden, but a 'must' is the marble fountain of love (the work of Thomas Waldo Story) at the end of the main drive to the house. Lifesize stone figures and cupids disport themselves on a scallop shell so vast that one wonders how it was transported to its present site without mishap. The National Trust continues to restore these gardens, replanting tired or neglected areas and preserving the grandeur of the whole. Appropriately, the house is now a glamorous hotel.

COATES MANOR

MAP J

Fittleworth ¼m (½km) south of Fittleworth turn off B2138 at Sign 'Coates'
Owner: Mrs G. H. Thorp
Tel: Fittleworth (079 882) 356
Open for charity a few days in June and by appointment for parties
(peak months May to October)
Plants for sale

It is difficult to pinpoint the most appealing component in this delightful garden, for it is a marriage of so many attractive elements. It is one acre in size, so it is easy for the amateur gardener to relate to; it was designed for minimum care and to give year-round interest — scent as well as colour; it contains a collection of plants which will satisfy the keen plantsman and the flower arranger. It is not a museum of unusual plants but a well-associated and subtly-blended series of pictures. A further attraction is the owner's willingness to share the knowledge gained from creating her garden.

The design complements the style of the Elizabethan manor, built of stone. The 'bone structure' is formal, the planting generous and relaxed. Hedges and walls divide the areas and supply a 'hook' on which to hang climbers. A mixed border is a skilful composition of blue and yellow foliage and flowers; the outsize, cool lime-green leaves of a golden catalpa and the foliage of a blue spruce play as important a role as the brilliant blue mop-head flowers of hardy agapanthus. The contrasting textures and shapes, especially of a wealth of foliage plants, have been as carefully considered as colour, and ornamental trees such as a *Prunus 'Tsubame'*, paperbark birch and standard wisteria are particularly eyecatching. The scent of lilies, philadelphus and honeysuckle is deliciously trapped within the walls of a small garden at the back of the house and there is a fine view of the surrounding countryside through a *clair-voie* cut in a conifer hedge.

COBBLERS

MAP J

Mount Pleasant, Jarvis Brook, Crowborough
Turn off A26 at Crowborough Cross taking B2100
to Crowborough Station, at second cross-road turn
into Tollwood road for ¼m (½km)
Owners: Mr and Mrs Martin Furniss
Tel: Crowborough (089 26) 5969
Open most Sundays during the summer for
charity and by appointment
(peak months June and July)

Transformed from rough fields over twenty years ago, Cobblers has a charming cottage-garden air. It is abundantly planted with colourful perennials and the garden almost completely encircles the old, tile-hung farmhouse and barn which stand on a south-facing slope. Well-sheltered by beech woodland, the garden has two natural water sources — a well and a stream of which full advantage are taken.

Informal, but designed with precision and care, the garden must be explored in the right way if all its features are to be enjoyed fully. Once you are set on the right path, there is no doubt where your footsteps should take you as vistas and features gradually come into view. The owner being an architect might be a reason for the success of the layout: the design of the paths, flights of steps of brick and stone, and the skilful placing of white-painted seats, made and designed by Martin Furniss, have been as carefully considered as the compositions of plants.

Below the house, a rock garden and the banks of a long pool fed by the well are luxuriantly planted with moisture-loving plants — rodgersias, ligularias, hostas and Asiatic primulas. The primulas are one of this garden's star turns and the brilliance of their colour is emphasised by the variegated foliage of irises. A second pool, this time fed by a stream, is lush with water and bog plants. Behind and around both pools are beds of rhododendrons and azaleas, astilbes, lilies and perennial geraniums which form a long-lasting backcloth of interest. Beside the steps leading away from this pool are beds of irises stylishly edged with brick, and a white-painted, circular seat beneath a handsome ash

catches the eye before drawing it to the long vista down the north lawn. Against a background of conifers, a wide, curving border is planted with well-blended groups of both warm- and cool-coloured flowers and foliage. On the far side of the north lawn there is an island bed of tall shrubs. Consistent with the rest of the garden, it is generously-planted, vigorous and healthy, and kept weed-free by a thick mulch of leaf-mould.

COLETON FISHACRE GARDEN

MAP H

Coleton, Kingswear
2m (3km) from Kingswear, take Lower Ferry road
and turn off at tollhouse
Owner: The National Trust
Tel: (080 425) 466
Open a few days a week from Easter to end
October
(peak seasons spring and summer)
Plants for sale

Coleton Fishacre lies near the mouth of the Dart, enfolded in a sheltered combe running down to the sea. A twentieth-century 'Manderley' but with a sunny atmosphere, it evokes pictures of 'bright young things' dashing down to the sea for a bathe. The large, well-built and unpretentious stone house was designed by a pupil of Edwin Lutyens, Oswald Milne, for the D'Oyly Carte family, famous for their Gilbert and Sullivan productions.

Pines and holm oaks, so typical of this part of Devon, were planted to shelter the garden from salt winds, but the humid and gentle climate enabled these and a range of tender and unusual shrubs and trees to grow to great size. The eighteen acres of garden lie on acid Dartmouth shale. They are threaded with streams and paths, exploration of which reveals an interesting collection of rhododendrons, camellias, mimosas, handkerchief and snowdrop trees, Chilean myrtles, fire and lantern trees. Tender, sun-loving plants decorate the terraces and walls of the house. A formal walled garden contains a rill, and pools on the terraces are bright with moisture-loving plants. Climbers and beds of perennials provide interest nearby. A gazebo hangs dramatically above the quarry from which the stone for the house was taken. The view from here to the sea and Mewstone is spectacular, especially in spring when the garden is vivid with flowering shrubs, trees and spring bulbs.

When The National Trust acquired the property in 1982 the garden had been left to its own devices for a considerable time. After Rupert D'Oyly Carte's death in 1949, the property was sold to Mr Rowland Smith who lived here until his death in 1979. He maintained but did not alter, thin or add to the garden so imaginatively planted by Lady Dorothy D'Oyly Carte; due to its rapid rate of growth, by 1982 it had become overgrown and misshapen. The Trust had to embark on a radical thinning, pruning and re-planting programme, but the design and mature contents should soon recover.

COMPTON ACRES

MAP I

Canford Cliffs Road, Poole
2m (3km) west of Bournemouth on A35 turn
south to Canford Cliffs
Owner: Lionel Green
Tel: Canford Cliffs (0202) 708036
Open daily from 1st April to end October
Plants for sale

Compton Acres is on a cliff top overlooking Poole harbour, with a magnificent position and view. The house was built in 1914 and after World War I Thomas William Simpson began to transform the rough, steep ground into a sophisticated garden. It deteriorated drastically during World War II due to lack of staff, but was rescued and restored by J. S. Beard, who bought the property in 1950 after Thomas Simpson's death. It has been open to the public since 1952, and must today be one of the most popular features of this holiday resort. Several changes have had to be made to accommodate the visitors: paths have been redesigned, stone

being replaced by tarmacadam in places, and vulnerable peat banks have been replaced by stone walls.

Compton Acres boasts a series of gardens: a circular Roman garden, an Italian garden with a rectangular lily pool, and the palm court, all three essentially architectural and formal. Stone work and statuary abound, together with colourful beds of annuals and roses backed by a high clipped hedge of *Rhododendron ponticum*. The informal rock and water garden above steeply-sloping ground is richly planted with shrubs and moisture-loving subjects, and king carp swim lazily around the pool's aquatic plants. Work is in progress to make the woodland and sub-tropical glen below this area more accessible to all those who want to see the tender species which grow in the sheltered valley. Paths weave around the top of the cliff, past the café, to the Japanese garden decorated with a temple, summerhouse, bronze torre gate and other oriental ornaments. Designed and built by Japanese workmen brought to England for the purpose, it contains Japanese varieties of azaleas, maples and cherries.

Maximum use has been made of every inch of flower bed at Compton Acres to produce a colourful and welcoming effect. Whether Mr Simpson or Mr Beard would approve of the way their garden had been altered since their deaths is questionable, but it clearly delights its innumerable visitors.

Sympathetic mix of bamboo and aquilegia in the Beth Chatto garden.

CORNWELL MANOR

MAP F

Kingham, near Chipping Norton.
Turn south off A44, 2m (3km) west of Chipping
Norton
Owner: Hon Peter and Mrs Ward
Tel: Kingham (060 871) 671
Open a few days a year for charity and by
appointment for parties in June
(peak months June and July)
Plants for sale

Blending into the charming village of Cornwell
(where certain buildings show the hand of Clough
Williams-Ellis of Portmeirion fame), the nine-
acre gardens of Cornwell Manor are a mixture
of the formal with the informal. Old-fashioned
shrub roses and herbaceous plants are as much
at home here as unusual ornamental trees and
shrubs.

The elegant house overlooks lawns which run
down to canals fed by the stream running
through the village of honey-coloured Cotswold
stone. These canals link formal and natural
features like the ornamental pool, aligned to the
façade of the house, which stands below a flight
of stone steps punctuating grass terraces. They
flow between banks lined with silver weeping
pears, cascade through a rock garden and splash
into the water garden. This part of the garden is
at its best in spring when the countless species
and other bulbs reveal themselves, but throughout the year the design and varied plant content
are pleasing.

A formal terrace garden in tune with the period
architecture, stands beside the house, supporting
geometric box-edged beds of peonies and
standard Portugal laurels and wisterias. Other
highly-cultivated garden 'rooms' are west of the
house. An avenue of cherries, set in a wide
corridor of yew hedges, supplies serene contrast
to the interest and colour of the walled
swimming-pool garden and the secret garden,
which shelters a collection of unusual plants.
The immaculately tended organic kitchen garden
is kept in peak condition by liberal doses of
compost, manure and rye grass. It is only one

instance of the craftsmanship practised in this
beautiful country-house garden.

COTEHELE HOUSE

MAP H

St Dominick, near Saltash
On the west bank of the River Tamar, 2m (3km)
east of St Dominick, 4m (6½km) from Gunnislake
(turn at St Anne's Chapel); 8m (13km) south-west
of Tavistock; 14m (22½km) from Plymouth via
Tamar Bridge
Owner: The National Trust
Tel: Liskeard (0579) 50434
Open daily throughout the year
(peak seasons spring and summer)
Plants for sale

The position of the medieval granite house, high
above an unspoilt stretch of the Tamar, and its
great age give an impression of peace and permanence — a time capsule unspoilt by twentieth-
century additions. The garden has gathered
period features over the centuries, but has never
suffered radical redevelopment.

Venerable sycamores shade the sloping lawns
and the drive to the house, and old-fashioned
roses, wisteria, camellias and the welcome mid-
winter-flowering *Iris stylosa* colour the ancient
cobbled and lawned courtyards. North-west of
the house lies the meadow, planted with Judas
trees and medlars, and the rough grass beneath
these trees is a riot of daffodils in spring. A
doorway in the wall to one side leads to the
sheltered upper garden, with borders of peonies
and fuchsias, ornamental trees rising above neat
beds of shrubs and a square lily pond fed by a
rill. Formal nineteenth-century terraces planted
with roses or magnolias are to the east of the
house, whose walls support a handsome *Magnolia
grandiflora* and *Rosa bracteata*. The informal valley
garden runs down to the river; planted with
rhododendrons and other acid- and moisture-
loving plants, this is very much more typical of a
Cornish garden. A medieval stew pond and
dovecote stand on the higher, more cultivated,
reaches of this glen. Eucryphias, maples,

magnolias, camellias, gunnera and ferns gently give way to spruces, hemlocks and larches as the winding paths descend to the water, sparkling through the trees below. These well-kept gardens contain many unusual and tender trees, shrubs and plants, but the contentment and period atmosphere of the place are the abiding memories.

COTON MANOR GARDENS

MAP F

Ravensthorpe, near Northampton
10m (16km) north of Northampton, from A428 or
A50 follow tourist signs
Owners: Commander and Mrs H. Pasley-Tyler
Tel: Northampton (0604) 740219
Open on Sundays and Bank Holidays from Easter
to end September and parties at other times by
appointment
Plants for sale

These six-and-a-half-acre gardens, developed in 1926, are remarkable not only for their beauty and rewarding plants, but for providing a home for many exotic waterfowl. Flamingoes, cranes, ornamental geese and ducks and pheasants, as well as parrots and macaws, are as much at home here as specimen trees, flowering shrubs, moisture-loving and herbaceous plants. Many of the birds range freely, but the imaginative way others have been caged or penned does not give the slightest impression of a zoo or aviary.

Originally a seventeenth-century farmhouse, now a mellow stone manor, Coton stands on high ground overlooking the garden, which is on different levels. Hedges, walls and water play a strong role. A focal point is a spring-fed pond overhung by a Japanese flowering cherry, and pools and streams punctuated with waterfalls offer an interesting habitat for the birds and ideal conditions for woodland, moisture- and shade-loving plants. Between the house and the large pond are lawned and paved terraces, with a series of different gardens bounded by walls and neatly-clipped hedges. Near the stone loggia and paved terrace, embroidered with self-seeded, low-growing plants, is a rose garden, its circular

pattern of beds planted with shrub roses, peonies and silver-foliaged plants. The terrace below has a border, simple, well-kept yew hedges and lawns which highlight the liveliness of intensely-planted areas such as these.

The colouring of the borders at Coton is noteworthy: one composed of blues and purples — euphorbias, unusual thistles and white foxgloves — is used to great effect. The woodland garden is beyond an arch in a hedge, and is shaded by a vast tulip tree. Shade-lovers, spring bulbs and wild flowers proliferate, and ferns, azaleas and moisture-loving plants like skunk cabbage and astilbes colour the banks of the streams and pools in the nearby water garden. A long dry bank beside the old orchard and aviaries has been planted with varieties of tender plants from Australia and New Zealand. A short distance on, philadelphus and lilacs scent the air, and rugosa roses are underplanted with an outstanding array of hostas.

There are a number of charming features: an arbour of holly which shelters a seat, honesty which has seeded itself freely, white campion and valerian. The unpretentious beauty of these matches that of the unusual and more sophisticated plants. A tropical house, for tender plants in winter, contains palms, abutilons, a mimosa and plumbago.

THE COURTS

MAP I

Holt, near Trowbridge. 3m (5km) south-west of
Melksham, 3m (5km) north of Trowbridge, on
B3107 turn south at Holt
Owner: The National Trust
Tel: Trowbridge (0225) 782340
Open several days a week from Easter to end
October and by written appointment

In the middle of Holt hidden behind high walls, the house and garden of The Courts once played a role in the prosperity of the small town. Until 1888 a woollen mill stood near the house and certain features in the garden date from those days: the pools in which fleeces were washed, and the eight stone pillars, linked by chains, which acted as washing-lines where the newly-woven cloth was dried. A gate in the garden wall leads to a path, between pleached limes, up to the house, whose early eighteenth-century facade is so elegant that it is hard to imagine such humble work being carried out within its view.

The design of the garden is unusual in that the formal areas, a series of surprise enclosures divided by topiary and hedges, are not set around the house but divided from it by lawns. Though the basic garden was laid out by Sir George Hastings at the beginning of the century, it was The Courts' subsequent owner, Lady Goff, who decorated these 'rooms' with a profusion of attractive and interesting material and gave the garden its surprise elements. An arboretum takes up a good half of the garden, displaying many unusual trees and sheltering a wildflower reserve, a popular and much-loved feature of gardens to day. This reserve contains fritillarias and other protected wild flowers and provides a safe home for wildlife. The murmur of traffic can be heard and the church tower and roofs of Holt can be espied over the walls of this secluded and peaceful garden. Another ancient industry — tanning — is carried out in the town today, and visitors may detect a whiff of this in the garden.

CRAGSIDE

MAP A

Rothbury, near Morpeth
1m (2km) north of Rothbury on B6341
Owner: The National Trust
Tel: Rothbury (0669) 20333
Open daily from end March to end September and a few days a week from November to March (peak month June)

As the name suggests, this is no ordered country-house garden, but a dramatic and seemingly untamed landscape. The fact that Lord Armstrong chose this site, then bare and craggy moorland, to build himself a retreat, marks him out as a man of strong character and energy. A successful inventor, industrialist, scientist and arms magnate, he was not short of funds and he used these and his scientific and innovative

talents, to create an exciting landscape. He formed lakes, generated his own electricity from a waterfall, and planted over seven million trees which, in time, brought about a change of climate in the area. He lived in a relatively modest house when he bought the estate in 1863, but in the following year he commissioned the architect, Norman Shaw, to design the present impressive gabled mansion commanding a view over the Debdon Beck and the gorge. This house was the first in the country to be lit by electricity generated by water power.

There is nothing mean or twee at Cragside. The dramatic terrain is covered with a dense jungle of massive trees, thickly underplanted with *rhododendron ponticum* and the common yellow azalea. Conifers predominate and some of the North American species are the largest in the country. Inevitably, some are coming to the end of their lives, but a programme of replacement planting and general restoration will ensure the garden's future.

The beautiful stretches of water, huge rocky outcrops and boulders, waterfalls, views of the surrounding hills and down over the giant trees, are a grand sight. In spring, the scent of the yellow azaleas adds another pleasing dimension. Children will enjoy exploring about here and will hardly notice the amount of ground they cover; those less energetic should be warned that over forty miles of walks thread through the nine hundred acres of Cragside.

CRANBORNE MANOR GARDENS

MAP I

Cranborne 10m (16km) north of Wimborne Minster on the B3078
Owner: Viscount Cranborne
Tel: Cranborne (072 54) 248
Open every Wednesday from April to September (peak months June and July)
Plants for sale

The garden of Cranborne Manor is one of the loveliest in England. It is not only cleverly designed — genuine period features inter-

Pinks lining a walk at Cranborne Manor.

mingling happily with later additions, and richly planted to flatter the character of individual areas — it also has a potent atmosphere of period romance. Part formal, part natural it is homely and secure rather than grand, despite its illustrious history. A series of different gardens, with doorways in walls and hedges leading to sheltered courtyards, and walled and yew-hedged 'rooms' initially hidden from view.

Cranborne was given to the Cecil family by James I early in the seventeenth century and Mounten Jennings and the king's gardener, John Tradescant, laid out the original gardens, parts of which survive today: the mount, with its

clipped yew and beds of lavender, originally constructed to give a fine view over the surrounding countryside and the garden, and the Jacobean yew bowling alley, are examples.

The period character of the original garden has influenced recent additions, and the various courts which surround the house contain sweet-smelling and old-fashioned plants. An Elizabethan knot garden is planted with pinks, crown imperials and double primroses, which grew in this country during the sixteenth and seventeenth centuries. The north court is a subtle composition of white flowering plants and the church walk and kitchen garden show a happy mix of fruit, vegetables and flowers. Beds lining a pergola walk are planted with London pride, irises, lilies and pinks, and wisteria, climbing roses and clematis cling to the long wall nearby. Climbers also clamber up the walls of the sheltered south court and the charming twin gatehouses set at the entrance. The arch between them faces the double avenue of beeches, with copper beeches on the outer edge. Aligned, but striding away from the north gate, is another, more recent avenue of plane trees and poplars, which replaced the original Cornish elms. A short distance from the house is the enclosed chalk wall garden filled with shrubs and herbaceous plants, a handsome Judas tree at either end, and the herb garden. Beds edged with santolina are filled with fascinating culinary and other herbs, with standard honeysuckles adding height.

There is a further dimension to these gardens, which is now immensely popular with enthusiasts and conservationists. Wild gardens have been an important feature of Cranborne for some time, their unassuming but charming nature ideally suiting its period feeling and providing a contrast to the more disciplined parts. The crab-apple orchard and river garden are jewelled with wild flowers and liberally-scattered spring bulbs, autumn crocus and cyclamen. These areas of rough grass, dotted with ox-eye daisies in early summer, are left unmown until July, by which time the wildflower seed has set.

The plantsman will enjoy many things, from tiny unusual violas to ornamental trees; all garden-lovers will revel in the generous and artistic planting, the way in which roses are entwined with clematis or interlaced with honeysuckle, and the subtle colouring of features like the green garden of foliage plants within a box-edged knot.

THE CROSSING HOUSE

Meldreth Road, Shepreth, near Cambridge
½m (1km) west of A10, 8m (13km) south-west of Cambridge
Owners: Mr and Mrs Douglas Fuller
Tel: Royston (0763) 61071
Open throughout the year for charity
(peak months May to September)

The main line to King's Cross runs beside this quarter-acre garden and many travellers must have caught a fleeting glimpse of the flowers planted along the railway banks. Only an inspired and talented plantsman could have transformed such an unpromising site into a fascinating garden. Not an inch has been wasted, and you will certainly notice the skilful way in which a surprisingly wide-ranging collection of plants — carefully chosen to give year-round interest — has been accommodated in such a small space.

Informal beds, a number of which are scree or rock to prevent their becoming work intensive, are planted with alpines, perennials, trees and shrubs. Paths weave around them and lead to the two hexagonal greenhouses, whose exterior has been softened by trellis screens, laced with delicate climbers. A small lawn, partially encircled by a mixed border, cools the eye, and an arbour of yew is trained stylishly over strong metal hoops usually used to reinforce concrete. Every plant must pay its way — either by flowering repeatedly through the season, having evergreen or interesting foliage, bearing berries, or boasting distinctive bark or fine autumn colour. Most important, it must not grow too big; the owners admit that when anything does become too bullish it is taken out and replaced by a newer and perhaps more docile 'find'. Mrs Fuller is as generous with her knowledge of plants and in her welcome as the garden is full of good ideas.

DALEMAIN

Ullswater near Penrith
On A592 3m (5km) south of Penrith and the M6
(junction 40)
Owners: Mr and Mrs Bryce McCosh (HHA)
Tel: Pooley Bridge (08536) 450
Open regularly from Easter to mid-October
Plants for sale

Originating as a modest herb garden in the twelfth century, the gardens, like the house, have expanded and gathered a variety of period features over many centuries. The Georgian façade of the house now masks the original Norman pele tower, the old ramparts of which support a seventeenth-century terrace overlooking the park and northern fringes of Ullswater.

The terrace is decorated with urns; old-fashioned and blush China roses, thought to be over a hundred years old, grow against the walls of the house. Beyond lies the long walk, edged with an herbaceous border set against a sun-baked wall. A towering silver fir stands sentinel between this and the ancient enclosed garden above. Here, around a small ornamental pool, is a knot garden patterned with box-edged beds filled with herbs and spring and summer flowers. Borders here and in the higher garden are planted with Himalayan blue poppies (*Meconopsis betonicifolia*), peonies, alstromeria and rogersias, together with old-fashioned shrub roses. There are also old and now rare varieties of pleached fruit trees and a pergola, and two architectural period features: the Georgian summerhouse containing a Chippendale-style seat made of oak from the estate, and a Tudor gazebo with a pointed roof. The gazebo stands in the far corner of the garden with a view over Dacre Beck and what was once the old coach road running through the park, and was used to act as a look-out. Shaded beds nearby display the large, pleated foliage of *Veratrum album* and primulas, hellebores and ligularia. The low or wild garden is planted with fruit and ornamental trees. The rough grass here is threaded by mown paths and bright with aconites in winter,

bulbs in spring and self-seeded martagon or Turk's cap lilies in summer. A grove of specimen trees beside the drive to the house shade more aconites and Turk's cap lilies.

DARTINGTON HALL

Dartington, Totnes
2m (3km) north-west of Totnes off the A384
Owner: Dartington Hall Trust
Tel: Totnes (0803) 862367
Open daily dawn to dusk
(peak months March to July and October to end of November, April to October)
Plants for sale

When Dorothy and Leonard Elmhirst purchased the Dartington Hall estate in 1925 they were faced with restoring a derelict fourteenth-century hall and outbuildings and a grossly overgrown garden, which had been the home of the Champernowne family for nearly four hundred years. The garden had some magnificent trees and period features such as a fourteenth-century tiltyard, a bowling alley and line of clipped yews known as the Twelve Apostles. These features, the great age of the buildings and the natural beauty of the landscape influenced the design and planting of the whole.

The Elmhirsts commissioned two garden designers to advise them, the American Beatrix Farrand, who (prevented from coming to England during World War II) was replaced by the then popular landscape designer, Percy Cane. The work of these two, allied to the sure eye of Dorothy Elmhirst, transformed an overgrown wilderness into what is today a surprisingly little known but outstanding example of twentieth-century garden-making.

The tiltyard is at the heart of the gardens, one of the few areas of level ground and a focal point from which other features flow or are aligned. The architectural Apostle yews and the long sunny border composed of blue, yellow and white flowers are on one side, and on the other giant turf steps climb a hill topped by centuries-old sweet chestnuts. Wings of yew hedge form boundaries to the ends of the tiltyard and emphasise the garden's central vista — from the swan fountain by Willi Souko, through the tiltyard and down over the valley field to the open countryside beyond. Woodland walks, an azalea dell, a small water garden and glades and lawns shaded by mighty plane trees rise away from the fountain. Surprises are constant: the statue of Flora at the far end of a hydrangea walk; a meadow garden planted with *Hupehensis* crabapple trees, stewartias and cercidiphyllum; a glade with a neo-classical temple which slopes down to the serene Henry Moore figure high above the tiltyard; and the magnificently wide flight of steps, lined with magnolias, which runs to the valley field and is overlooked by a bank of autumn colour.

The texture and varying shades of green of trees and shrubs rising above masonry-like yew hedges are remarkable: the silvery *Eleagnus umbellata* 'Parvifolia' near the fountain which rises out of a circle of dark green sweet box; the curving path below the tiltyard which does not interfere with the central vista; and the inky Monterey pine bearing away from the fresh green turf terraces. In winter you should seek out the grove of witch-hazels, the thickly planted hellebores along woodland walks scented with sweet box, and note how skilfully evergreens have been used to sustain the strong design of the garden. In spring bulbs proliferate — vast lakes of crocus stand beneath huge oaks and other trees, and swathes of daffodils, narcissi and wild flowers colour grass banks and lawns. Camellias, rhododendrons, a handkerchief tree, various cornus and a splendid collection of magnolias decorate the woodland and other walks. In summer the rose and sunny borders come into their own, as does the brightly coloured flower garden by the gardener's thatched office below a peat bank planted with heathers and conifers. At the end of the gardening year maples, euonymus, spindles, nyssas and parrotias produce brilliant autumn colour; there is a wide ribbon of nerines near the bowling alley and autumn crocus beside the curving drive. The warm caramel scent of the rotting leaves of *Cercidiphyllum japonicum* heralds winter in this exceptional garden that warrants visiting throughout the year.

DEENE PARK

MAP G

near Corby
On A43 Kettering to Stamford road, 8m (13km) north-west of Oundle, 6m (9½km) north-east of Corby
Owner: Edmund Brudenell (HHA)
Tel: Bulwick (078 085) 278
Open on Bank Holidays and on Sundays in June, July and August
(peak months June and July)

From a low mansion of mellow Northamptonshire stone, wide grass terraces and sloping lawns descend to a canal spanned by an arched and balustraded bridge. Deene Park has been the home of the Brudenell family for over four hundred and fifty years, and the garden, like the Tudor and Georgian house, has evolved over that time.

The first impression is of a landscaped park, with the more highly cultivated parts hidden from sight. Borders of roses, perennial geraniums and lavender are next to the house and others below the terrace wall, are planted with shrubs and perennials. A handsome golden-leafed maple is a glowing focal point and prostrate junipers, like huge dark-green cushions, decorate the bank of the canal. The terrace near the house stretches to an octagonal summerhouse built into the corner of the boundary wall, and double borders line this terrace walk. There is a hidden 'room' planted with foliage and white flowering plants like rugosa roses, philadelphus and lilac. Another is set behind a circular hedge of hornbeam. The serenity of this second hidden garden is enhanced by its formality: narrow beds of lavender and statues of the four seasons surround the circular lawn, at whose centre stands a low stone vase. A stone seat, in an arbour of hornbeam, is well placed to enjoy the view, through a break in the hedge, over stone steps and lawn, to the canal — an effective composition. Beyond the terrace lies a 'natural' area laced with mown grass paths, which weave around islands of rough grass, shoulder-high cow parsley and unusual shrubs and trees. A

Magnolias flanking the long flight of steps at Dartington Hall garden.

cascade can be admired from one of the Chinese-style bridges, and a peaceful walk on the far side of the canal, shaded by ancient yews and beech trees, offers fine views of the house and its setting. There are some good specimens of unusual trees, such as the cut-leaf beech near the arched stone bridge and the gleditsia which almost obscures the octagonal summerhouse.

DENMANS

MAP J

Denmans Lane, Fontwell, near Arundel
5m (8km) from Arundel and Chichester. Turn
south on A27 at Denmans Lane, west of Fontwell
Racecourse
Owner: Mrs J. H. Robinson
Tel: Eastergate (024 368) 2313/2808
Open regularly from end March to end October
and by appointment
(peak months May, June and September)
Plants for sale

John Brookes, the landscape designer and plantsman, runs this important three-and-a-half-acre garden, as part of a school of garden design. The originality of its layout and skilful use of a huge range of plants hold lessons for both the student and the amateur gardener. The overall design is harmonious and cohesive, but any one section could stand on its own merits. Each is a lesson in how a plot of modest proportions can be laid out and planted.

Developed since 1946, the immaculately-maintained gardens are the creation of Mrs Robinson. They are informal and luxuriantly planted and stand on what was once a market garden around Westergate house. Its gardener's cottage was converted to become the Robinsons' home. Cool areas of lawn and wide, winding gravel paths show off the bold plantings of shrubs and trees, grouped to form memorable blends of texture and colour. Plants have been allowed to seed themselves in the large expanse of gravel, being removed only if they spoil the total effect. Two walled gardens are treated in much the same way, though one is filled with flowers and the other with trees and shrubs. All sorts of climbers decorate the walls, including a fremontodendron, old-fashioned shrub roses, wisteria and a wide selection of clematis. Tender and grey-leafed plants thrive on the sunbaked terrace next to the cottage. A dry gravel stream swirls across what was once a meadow, now planted with specimen trees, its bed embroidered with foliage plants. An unheated conservatory is filled with half-hardy plants from Australasia and the Mediterranean.

THE DINGLE

MAP D

Frochas, near Welshpool
3m (5km) north of Welshpool follow A490
towards Llanfyllin for 1m (2km); turn left for
Groespluan; after 1½m(2½km) fork left to garden
on left
Owners: Mr and Mrs D. R. Joseph
Tel: Welshpool (0938) 5145
Open daily (except Tuesdays) throughout the year
for charity
(peak months June and October)
Plants for sale

This garden is full of interesting and unusual plants and year-round ideas. Facing south on the side of a hill, it exhibits a wide range of plants on sale in the adjoining nursery and imaginative associations. Being south-facing, the garden is apt to dry out, especially the steep bank which runs down to the pond in the valley, but the soil is neutral medium loam, able to support peat- and lime-loving plants.

Conifers and unusual trees, with good summer and autumn foliage, are mingled with shrubs, perennials, ground-coverers and rock and alpine plants. No one bed is devoted to a single type of plant, so you will find plenty of planting ideas for your own garden. The lawn next to the house is surrounded by informal, mixed beds which illustrate the Josephs' good eye for colour combinations. The bank running down to the pond is more intensely planted, a zig-zag network of paths dividing one bed from another; each warrants close inspection. The trees and shrubs around the pond, though still young, are making their presence felt, particularly in autumn and winter when the warm foliage colours, bare bark and coloured twigs of shrubs such as cornus are reflected in the still water. The ultimate satisfaction of a visit to a garden like this is the availability of especially-noted plants in the adjoining nursery.

DODDINGTON HALL

MAP C

near Lincoln
5m (8km) west of Lincoln on B1190
Owner: Mr Anthony Jarvis, (HHA)
Tel: Doddington (0522) 694 308
Open a few days a week from May to end
September and by appointment for parties
(peak months May to July)

Laid out at the beginning of this century, the five-acre gardens of the Elizabethan house suit its architecture perfectly. They are not reproductions of sixteenth-century gardens, but the scale and design of formal areas has a period character. The symmetrical brick house was designed by Robert Smythson of Hardwick Hall fame, and has not been altered since 1600. It is topped by three cupola turrets, and its windows overlook the formal walled gardens to back and front. The forecourt lies to the east and is entered through a gabled gatehouse. Gravel paths lead up to the front door and around smooth lawns. The old cedars which once stood here have been replaced by weeping cherries, now being formed into arbours; the restrained treatment of the enclosed area emphasises the symmetry of the house.

The three gently-graded terraces of the walled garden to the west are lively with parterre and other beds divided by gravel paths. Matching box-edged beds are filled with irises, their sword-like foliage rising above the dense, neat hedges — an effective mix of textures. The pattern of this parterre is echoed by the geometric beds on the lawn of the lower terrace, and borders beneath the walls complement the whole. The lines are formal, but the planting delightfully relaxed: soft colouring, the scent of old-fashioned pinks,

shrub roses and lavender, herbaceous plants and strong foliage shapes. Wrought-iron gates in the wall at the far end of the terraces look down a yew-hedged walk and a recently replanted avenue of poplars which strikes out across the flat surrounding countryside.

Beyond the walled garden formality gives way to an increasingly 'wild' scene: a croquet lawn with its pleached hornbeams and Victorian arbour of veronica, the huge skirts of old suckering sweet chestnuts, a small herb garden and a walk of cherries leading to an ornamental stone seat. Flowering trees, shrubs in rough grass, spring bulbs and frothy mounds of rambling roses decorate the wild garden, together with rhododendrons grown from seed collected by Frank Kingdon Ward. There is a temple and a maze authentically created of turf not hedges, and the banks of a boundary ditch are planted with moisture-loving rogersia and skunk cabbage.

A surprising number and variety of period and botanical features decorate this garden, but it is the way in which they have been laid out and planted which makes it such a pleasure to visit.

DOROTHY CLIVE GARDEN

MAP F

Willoughbridge, Market Drayton
On A51 9m (14½km) south-east of Nantwich
Owner: Willoughbridge Garden Trust
Tel: Pipegate (063081) 237
Open regularly from beginning March to end
November
(peak months May, June and autumn)

Set on the side of a hill, with some steepish paths, this well-stocked plantsman's garden is divided into two distinct parts. Above the house it has a 'natural' character; below, it is open and more highly cultivated. The upper, original part was created by Colonel Harry Clive in 1939 for his wife. Due to ill health, her daily exercise was restricted to dull turns about a lawn. Colonel Clive determined to transform a wooded and defunct quarry nearby into what is now a superb woodland garden. Bowl-shaped, it is filled with hybrid and unusual rhododendrons and deciduous and evergreen azaleas. Paths weave through and around the top of the steep-sided dell, which is a theatre of colour in spring. There are blood red *Rhododendron thomsonii*, pale yellow *R. campylocarpum elatum* and large groups of yellow, pink, orange and red Exbury and Knaphill azaleas. Native and specimen trees shelter tender and unusual shrubs and produce good autumn colour. These, in turn, are underplanted with spring bulbs, primroses, cyclamen, lilies and willow gentians.

Following his wife's death in 1942 the colonel built a bungalow below the dell and turned his attention to cultivating the field which sloped away below. He did not live to see this part of the garden completed, but a trust was formed, work continued and the garden's future was assured. This beautiful, informal slope overlooks the Shropshire hills. Ornamental and unusual trees — maples, cornus, nyssas, cherries, swamp cypress and catalpa — shade island beds, scree, rock and pool gardens which display a fascinating collection of plants of all kinds — flowering shrubs; roses, conifers, grasses, herbaceous and moisture-loving plants; *Lithospermum diffusum*, seldom seen white-flowering *Arisarum proboscideum* or mouse plant, penstemons, dahlias and perennial geraniums and hydrangeas. The plant material is thoughtfully associated and a lesson in how to lay out a rewarding but 'laboursaving' garden.

DUDMASTON

MAP F

Quatt, near Bridgnorth
4m (6½km) south-east of Bridgnorth on A442
Owner: The National Trust
Tel: Quatt (0746) 780866
Open a few days a week from Easter to end
September

Mature cedars and other venerable trees offset the handsome seventeenth-century mansion and add nobility to the eight-acre gardens landscaped

and developed nearly two hundred years later. The lake, or big pool, formed by joining several small pools, is overlooked and linked to the south-facing house by a grass terraced slope. Woodland rises away on the far side of the lake, Clee Hill being glimpsed beyond.

In a valley to the west lies the dingle, an important period feature laid out in the eighteenth-century and said to resemble The Leasowes, the famous garden owned by the eighteenth-century poet and landscape gardener, William Shenstone. The National Trust hopes to restore the walks, cascades and ornamental features of this romantic area, and an American garden planted with magnolias, snowdrop tree, kalmias and other ornamental trees and shrubs is also being restored.

There is a rose called 'Gava' in the bed by the Brew House that Lady Labouchere, the present inhabitant, brought back from Madrid, and modern sculptures can be seen by the pool and on the terrace. There is a fine collection of botanical pictures in the house.

DUNCOMBE PARK

MAP C

Helmsley
On minor road south of the Castle, 1m (2km)
south-west of Helmsley
Owner: Lord Feversham
Tel: Helmsley (0439) 70217 or 70213
Open one day a week from May to end August
(Pass card from Tourist Information Office in
town square)

The terrace is the most important and wonderfully dramatic feature of these gardens. It is a turfed walk of majestic dimensions, which follows the curving line of an escarpment hanging over a ravine. No less exciting than that at nearby Rievaulx, it is an integral part of the gardens surrounding an architecturally-splendid house. Both were created by members of the Duncombe family and it is thought that Rievaulx, built around 1758, was intended to link up with Duncombe by means of a viaduct. Three miles divide the terraces so it would have

115

been surprising if this had been achieved. The same intention gave birth to the terrace at Farnborough Hall in Warwickshire and met with similar lack of success.

Commissioned by Thomas Duncombe in 1713 and completed in 1730, the terrace forms a crescent-shaped boundary to the formal and pleasure gardens spreading away from the house. The whole is an interesting marriage of seventeenth-century formality and eighteenth-century 'naturalness'. Level lawns, on which a green parterre stood, run from the house to the terrace, dividing two large areas of woodland. A straight walk runs the length of the garden, cutting through the woodland and passing in front of the house. Others form vistas and induce increasing expectation.

The terrace is a magnificent and dramatic sight which cannot fail to impress. An immensely wide and long grass walk follows the clean, curving line of the escarpment which runs from north to south. Its purposeful air is emphasised by the height of the woodland trees on its inner edge. The view over Ryedale which the terrace must once have had is now obscured by trees and shrubs, but the drama is intact. At the northern end is a rotunda with Ionic columns on a bastion, set against a backcloth of trees. Attributed to Vanbrugh, it strongly resembles the rotunda at Stowe in Buckinghamshire. At the southern end, standing out against the skyline, is a Tuscan temple also set on a bastion, thought to have been designed by Sir Thomas Robinson. Nothing has been allowed to interfere or detract from the clean lines and dramatic effect of the terrace and its architectural features.

DUXFORD MILL

near Duxford
On the B1379 close to Duxford village, 9m
(14½km) south of Cambridge and 1½m (2½km)
from Junction 10 of M11 (Cambridge bypass)
Owners: Mr and Mrs Robert Lea
Tel: Cambridge (0223) 832325
Open several days a year for charity and by
appointment for parties
(peak months late June and July)
Plants for sale

The flowing lines of this garden follow those of the stream which gushes from the mill-race. This lively and magnetic feature stands centre stage and is surrounded by level lawns with groups of shrubs and trees. Irregularly shaped borders and island beds create vistas to architectural and sculptural features: the Regency stone temple and a group of angels. Framed by a belt of trees to protect the gardens from the bitterly cold winds, the picture is uncluttered and serene.

In 1948, the owners embarked on transforming an area of wasteland into a garden, determined that it should be easy to care for, and there are a number of lessons to be learnt here. The proportions of the level lawns and the way in which one flows into another, the curling shape of the long border and island beds, and the absence of intricate features all facilitate the use of modern machinery for mowing and spraying.

Approximately two thousand modern roses colour the long border — a superb river of colour from June to October, and the garden's major feature. Many are hybrids which Robert Lea has raised over the last twenty years. Groups of shrubs, chosen for their autumn, winter or spring foliage, a grove of unusual birches planted to display their striking bark, and an herbaceous border are positioned to give all-year-round interest. Behind the mill, the garden becomes increasingly natural: spring bulbs and specimen trees are set around a pen of exotic wildfowl, stream and pool. You can see a *Koelreuteria paniculata* and a *Metasequoia glyptostroboides*, grown from cuttings from the original tree sent to the Arnold Arboretum in 1948. There is also a

High summer in Eastgrove Cottage Garden.

small water garden, lush with hostas, kingcups, primulas and irises.

The surroundings of Duxford Mill are much altered since Charles Kingsley fished here with his friend the miller, but there is still an abundance of trout, which churn the surface of the water when they are fed.

DYFFRYN GARDENS

MAP E

St Nicholas, Cardiff
1½m (2½km) south of St Nicholas on the A48
west of Cardiff
Owners: Mid and South Glamorgan County
Council
Tel No: Cardiff (0222) 593328
Open daily from April to September
Plants for sale

The fifty-five acres of garden seem to hold the splendid Edwardian mansion in a gentle embrace. Formal gardens, ornamental features and flower beds of bulbs and bedding-out plants give the surrounds of the house a well-kept, period feel. Enclosed 'rooms', each with a theme, lie hidden to one side and the outer edges of these large gardens are planted with a rewarding collection of trees and shrubs.

One of the best-known gardens in Wales, Dyffryn was designed at the beginning of the century by the landscape architect, Thomas Mawson. Few changes have been made since; some of his characteristic stonework has had to be replaced, but the style of the garden is little altered. Sir John Cory commissioned Mawson to design the garden, but his son Reginald Cory supervised the main part of the work. Mawson described Cory as being 'a typical example of the English enthusiast for horticulture and arboriculture at its best', and the two combined their talents to create a beautifully-balanced picture. Cory was a keen collector of the new plants which were being introduced in the 1920s and 1930s and contributed to and joined plant-hunting expeditions. Dyffryn was thus filled with unusual and rare specimens from China and Japan. The maples, particularly the mature

specimens of *Acer griseum*, are outstanding, as is the collection of magnolias and rare oaks. The gardens are justly famous for these trees, some being the largest of their kind in the country and worth seeking out.

There were no views from the south front of the house, so Mawson laid out an extensive lawn with a canal and a lily pond running down its centre. The grandeur of this area, decorated with topiary and formal flower beds, with a bank of mature trees rising away to the east, matches that of the house. West of the lawn, hidden behind yew hedges and walls, is a network of interlinking architectural gardens. Flights of steps, yew alleys and archways lead from one garden 'room' to another: a rose garden, where a glasshouse contains exotic orchids; an herbaceous walk; the pleasingly restrained Pompeian garden with its fountain and classical temple: the theatre garden where Reginald Cory placed his Japanese plants in pots; the rotunda or yew-hedged circular garden with beds of brilliant fuchsias and other intimate areas.

Wide grass paths weave around groups of unusual shrubs and trees, eventually leading to more formal features: the heart-shaped hedge and pattern of beds planted with fibrous-rooted begonias; a pergola, planted with several varieties of vines, running across the far end of the south lawn, dividing the more intensely-planted areas from the arboretum. Wild flowers and handsome and unusual trees flourish in the arboretum. A rockery east of the house has a true alpine look — recently stripped of its intricate flower beds and paths, the natural rock has been exposed. A heather garden and a palm house are a short distance from the entrance gate.

EASTGROVE COTTAGE GARDEN

MAP F

Sankyns Green, Shrawley, near Little Witley
1m (2km) north-west of Worcester on road
between Shrawley (on B4196) and Great Witley
(on A443).
Owners: Mr and Mrs J. Malcolm Skinner
Tel: Great Witley (029 921) 389
Open regularly mid-April to end October; closed
in August
(peak months late June and October)
Plants for sale

The term 'cottage garden' is now so loosely used to describe anything filled with old-fashioned plants that one is tempted to use superlatives when faced with the real thing. This seventeenth-century half-timbered farmhouse and its three-quarter-acre garden are the real thing. The old yeoman's cottage nestles in the embrace of a bower of flowers. It is set in unspoilt, rolling countryside, and is reminiscent of a Helen Allingham painting. Nothing looks out of place: rustic arches and benches, arbours and herring-bone brick paths contribute to the charm of the whole. Although unpretentious in style, the garden contains a wealth of unusual plants, chosen and positioned with care.

Divided into different sections by paths, hedges and small lawns, old-fashioned borders of lupins, daisies and poppies lead to intimate corners such as one planted with foliage plants. The association of golden box, marjoram and euonymous, euphorbia, hostas and pale maple is particularly successful. Beds devoted to colour combinations — lime and white, hot oranges and pink, silver and white foliage and flowers — are spaced well apart so as not to spoil one another's effect. Beside the cottage is a bed of mixed plants which is at its best in autumn. Heathers form a pool of colour beneath a laburnum and 'The Great Wall of China' (a small, walled area of scree) contains a host of tiny saxafraga and other alpines. Perennials abound; so do old-fashioned favourites like auriculas, violas, and rock roses. There are herbs and wonderful gnarled apple trees.

Beyond the hedge which divides the more intensely-planted areas from the surrounding farmland is a paddock of rough grass, with ornamental trees, and a bog garden of pale pink and other primulas, ligularia and irises. Beautifully maintained by the owners, the free-draining sandstone soil can sustain an extraordinarily wide variety of plants, a large number of which are on sale in the adjoining nursery.

EAST LAMBROOK MANOR

MAP I

East Lambrook, South Petherton
7m (11km) east of Ilminster on A303, turn north
to South Petherton and East Lambrook
Owners: Mr and Mrs Andrew Norton
Tel: South Petherton (0460) 40328
Open Mondays to Saturdays and on Bank Holiday
weekends throughout the year
(peak months March and late June)
Plants for sale

Peonies, tulips and perennial geraniums at East Lambrook.

East Lambrook Manor will be of particular interest to those who have read some of the books by the late Margery Fish. Her enthusiasm and talent saved many cottage-garden plants from extinction and her interest in these and ground-cover and foliage plants were an inspiration and an education to her readers. Mrs Fish's ideals are being followed by the new owners, and her garden restored with the help of one of her original gardeners. Unusual varieties which she gave to friends, and many which she herself raised, are finding their way back to the garden: *Hebe* 'Margery Fish', *Artemisia* 'Lambrook Silver' and *Santolina* 'Lambrook variety'.

This intimate, plantswoman's cottage garden has several areas, divided one from another by paths, lawns and hedges, making maximum use of the space available. A double row of cypress trees, clipped into soft cone shapes, line a path; her readers will recognise these as the 'pudding trees'. A large number of the plants she wrote about are here — hellebores, violets, pinks, artemisias, euphorbias, pulmonarias and lamiums, colour banks and flower beds. Her favourite was the primrose, and double and unusual varieties of these abound.

The walk lined with 'pudding trees' at East Lambrook Manor.

EDNASTON MANOR GARDENS

MAP F

Brailsford, near Derby
On A52 Derby to Ashbourne Road, 1m (2km)
from Brailsford
Owner: Mr L. W. Pickering
Tel: Brailsford (033 528) 325
Open one day a week from Easter to end of
September
(peak months May and June)
Plants for sale

Conditions are harsh in this part of the country, where Ednaston offers a rare opportunity to see a well-designed garden which contains a rewarding collection of plants, trees and shrubs. The manor, at the heart of the garden, was built between 1913 and 1919 to a design by Edwin Lutyens; symmetrical and built of brick and stone, it is Queen Anne rather than 'Surrey' in style.

Terraces around the house, patterned with herringbone brick paths, are planted with roses and clematis, low-growing and aromatic shrubs and plants. A series of different gardens is at the back of the house. Their framework is formal, their planting generous. There are borders devoted to varying shades of one colour, a rose walk, a tapestry hedge, a rockery and a sheltered orchard which has been planted with specimen trees. In complete contrast, a woodland garden is to the north-west of the house, richly planted with acid-loving shrubs and unusual trees. Paths weave around beds of hybrid and other rhododendrons such as the scented *R. loderi*, and open into peaceful glades decorated with a pond or bright with azaleas, past magnolias, cherries and climbing and rambling roses cascading out of trees. The garden is kept in excellent order, and there is a small nursery selling plants propagated from specimens in the garden. Many of these are raised in the greenhouses, one of which contains a mist propagating unit.

ELVASTON CASTLE

Borrowash Road, Elvaston
6m (9½km) south-east of Derby. Main entrance
off B5010 Borrowash to Thulston road, north of
Elvaston Village. Road signs from A6 and A52
Owner: Derbyshire County Council
Tel: Derby (0332) 571342
Open daily throughout the year
(peak seasons spring, summer and autumn)

This vast and important Victorian garden is now a country park. It was formerly the home of the Stanhope family, Earls of Harrington, and the neo-Gothic castle stands on the flat, rather than the dramatic, terrain of the county. On being asked to submit a design for a landscape by the third Earl, 'Capability' Brown turned down the commission, deeming the land devoid of any 'capability' at all. But he did offer the Earl six cedars of Lebanon, which have now grown to a mighty size.

In 1835, the fourth Earl, undefeated by this harsh judgement, embarked on making a two-hundred-acre garden which was one of the most remarkable of the Victorian era. He had shocked society by living openly with his mistress, albeit reclusively, and created these gardens to celebrate their romantic love. He employed William Barron, a gardener from the Botanic Gardens at Edinburgh, to assist him and, together with ninety men, Barron completed the task within a decade. Highly skilled and inventive, Barron planted the gardens with a mass of already mature trees, evergreens and newly introduced and increasingly popular conifers such as monkey puzzles. He laid out formal and topiary gardens, formed vistas, planted eleven miles of evergreen hedges, and made a huge lake with a backcloth of dramatic artificial rockwork.

Although it suffered a period of neglect before becoming a country park in 1969, the major features survive: the topiary gardens with their geometric patterns, scrolls and balls of golden and common yew; the Moorish temple in what was once the Alhambra garden, and the melancholy labyrinthine gloom of the rockwork around the lake, which the Duke of Wellington described as 'the only natural artificial rock work I have ever seen'. The walled kitchen garden now contains an Old English garden admirably laid out and planted. There are huge double herbaceous borders, lavender-edged rose beds, informal beds of shrubs and a paved area — planted with herbs and other scented plants for the blind. Colourful and fragrant, these intimate gardens are a contrast to the serious grandeur beyond.

EMMETTS

Ide Hill, Sevenoaks, Kent
On the Sundridge to Ide Hill road, 1½m (2½km)
South of A25
Owner: The National Trust
Tel: Lamberhurst (0892) 890651
Open regularly from Easter to end October
(peak seasons spring and summer)

High on a greensand ridge, the six-and-a-half-acre gardens overlooking the woodland of the Weald are remarkable for their large and beautiful specimen trees and unusual shrubs. Towards the end of the last century when Frederick Lubbock came to live at Emmetts, he planted these 'exotics' in the natural wildness which sloped away from the house. He was inspired to plant them informally by his friend William Robinson who was an enthusiastic advocate of the new 'natural' style of garden-making.

Spaced well apart, the mature shape and loveliness of handkerchief trees, magnolias, eucryphias, castor oil trees, maples and cornus — a *C. controversa* being an outstanding example of its kind — are perfectly displayed. A number had been purchased from Veitch and Son before they closed down their premises in Kingston in 1914; they were large specimens then, so their present size can be imagined.

The shrubs are no less interesting: unusual rhododendrons, a huge *R. ferrugineum* 'Alpine Rose', possibly the largest in the country, pieris, variegated syringa or Himalayan lilac, heathers, conifers and roses such as 'The Threepenny-bit

Rose', *R. farreri persetosa*. It is worth paying a visit in spring to admire the bluebells carpeting the woodland floor. A formal rose garden and a rockery stand on the level ground near the house.

ENGLEFIELD HOUSE

MAP I

Theale, near Reading
Entrance on the A430; 6m (9½km) west of
Reading off M4 (junction 12)
Owners: Mr and Mrs W. R. Benyon
Tel: Reading (0734) 302 221
Open every Monday and one Sunday in April and
May for charity
(peak seasons spring and summer)
Plants for sale

At first glance, Englefield House seems to be a highly decorated and impressive nineteenth-century mansion. In fact, it is an E-shaped Elizabethan house which was re-faced and embellished in both the eighteenth and nineteenth centuries. It is set into the side of a hill and commands a superb view over the deer park and Berkshire countryside. A woodland garden spreading across the hillside rises away behind the house, and below lie wide terraces. These were built by Italian craftsmen in 1860, and their generous proportions and decoration create a suitably grand platform for the house. Their balustrading is decorated with urns, and their great length punctuated with large bays and flights of steps.

In its Victorian heyday the terrace was ornamented with a complex network of beds containing roses and annuals. Roses still have a place, but they are now grown in the mixed border running beneath a terrace wall. The garden designer, Lanning Roper, suggested the simplification of this area, which now has a more informal nature. Beds curve into the long sweep of lawn, gently dividing one area from another. Much new planting has been done by the present owners and young trees, when mature, will strengthen the divisions.

The woodland garden above was laid out in the 1930s by the Tunbridge Wells firm of R.

Wallace and Company, and the trees and shrubs, such as rhododendrons and azaleas, are now in their prime. There is no sudden and dramatic change of character above the terraces; large groups of rhododendrons and mature trees decorate lawns which gradually give way to the woodland garden. The higher the garden climbs the wilder it becomes. The colour and scent of deciduous azaleas and unusual flowering shrubs and specimen trees decorate the glades shaded by oaks and conifers. The banks of a stream garden are thickly planted with magenta, candelabra primulas, and carpets of naturalised bulbs and bluebells colour the garden and woodland in spring. At a distance from the garden proper, an avenue of standard wisterias leads up to the gate of the walled kitchen garden, beside the church remodelled by Gilbert Scott.

ERDDIG

MAP D

near Wrexham
2m (3km) south of Wrexham, off A525
Whitchurch road or A483/A5152 road
Owner: The National Trust
Tel: Wrexham (0978) 355314
Open regularly from Easter to mid-October
(peak seasons spring and summer)

Although these gardens reflect the taste of three centuries, it is the formal early eighteenth-century garden that is of most interest. Derelict ten years ago, it has been saved and painstakingly restored by the Trust. Created by John Meller, it stands to the east of the house with its eighteenth-century façade, and the proportions, style and warm brick of both are well matched. Despite being enclosed by walls, it has a great feeling of space and an uncluttered character, being divided into sections by symmetrical walks, hedges, water and lawns.

Fruit trees are an important feature, and a great number of old-fashioned varieties have been planted in a formal orchard or immaculately trained against the walls. Beneath the espaliered or fan-trained apples, peaches and apricots are clumps of old-fashioned narcissi, daffodils and herbaceous plants. Two yew hedges, at the far end of a large rectangular pond, are clipped to form a series of bays in which bee skeps were kept. The pond supplied fish and the bees produced honey and pollinated the fruit trees. A screen and a handsome pair of eighteenth-century wrought-iron gates at the far end give an illusion of a garden that stretches to infinity.

The view from these to the house follows the backbone of the garden, the long canal and walk decorated with 'Versie' boxes of Portuguese laurels. This vista is initially channelled down an avenue of mature limes which were originally thought to have been pleached. The young pleached limes flanking the central walk nearer the house will not be allowed such freedom and in time will form an effective division between the areas and emphasise the vista. Narcissi and wild flowers like fritillarias have been encouraged to decorate the banks of the canal and other areas of rough grass.

In the walled garden are a number of Victorian features: the shady moss walk spinney contains many varieties of holly, and part of the National Collection of ivy grows against a nearby wall. The Victorian garden beyond the spinney is lively with standard, rambling and bush roses associated with clematis, thrift, London pride and variegated box elder. Ornamental, stone-edged flower beds are edged with catmint, which complements the rose 'Reine des Violettes'. Its branches are pegged down early in the season to encourage a vigorous cushion of growth. Clipped box and Irish yews line a path leading back to the house, in front of which there is a Victorian parterre with stalagmitic fountains by Blashfield.

In the old drying area beyond the walled garden are medlars and damsons. Three different varieties of cherry shade the car park. A long bed of herbs and a fig tree, trained against the wall, are near an old dovecote. The landscape, a further period feature, rolls away from the front of the house, and in a hollow below lies the 'Cup and Saucer' — a circular basin with a hole at its centre down which flows water from a brook. By means of an hydraulic ram, the 'Cup and Saucer' supplied water to the fountains and the house.

ETAL MANOR

MAP A

Ford, near Wooler
On B6354 10m (16km) north of Wooler
Owners: Lord and Lady Joicey
Tel: Crookham (089 082) 205
Open for charity several Sundays in early summer
and autumn
(peak seasons spring and autumn)

Obviously loved and cherished, this woodland garden has a peaceful and intensely private air. Few gardens in the country are so easy to relate to because the majority open to the public are on a much grander scale.

In early summer the woodland is bright with rhododendrons and the flowers and foliage of unusual and other shrubs. In September the autumn crocus spreads sheets of pink and white beneath spreading beech trees and, as it gets colder, the burning foliage colours of specimen trees and shrubs come into their own. The lawn is immaculate, an important feature of any garden but one apt to come low on the list of priorities.

EXBURY GARDENS

MAP I

Exbury, near Southampton
In Exbury village, 3m (5km) south of Beaulieu,
15m (24km) south-west of Southampton
Owner: Mr E. L. de Rothschild (HHA)
Tel: Fawley (0703) 891203
Open regularly from March to mid-July and for
six weeks in September/October
(peak month May)
Plants for sale

The name Rothschild conjures up a picture of a superb collection of rhododendrons and azaleas and the colourful gardens of Exbury. Over twelve hundred new hybrids have been raised at Exbury over the last seventy years and these, and much else, can be seen in the two-hundred-acre woodland garden.

Japanese maple shading a pond in the woodland garden at Exbury.

Lionel de Rothschild purchased the estate by the Beaulieu river in 1919 and began to transform what had been part of the New Forest into what is now one of the best-known and richly-planted woodland gardens in the country. One hundred and fifty men were employed for ten years clearing parts of the oak, beech and pine woodland, preparing and planting beds, making paths, ponds and bridges and laying down a vast underground watering system. Lionel de Rothschild not only raised a spectacular number of hybrids himself, but joined and contributed to plant-hunting expeditions to China, Japan and the Himalayas. On his death, in 1942, his son Edmund continued to develop the gardens and increase the collection.

Visitors should be prepared to spend several hours, if not a day, if they want to explore the whole garden, three separate walks being colour-coded and signposted. Running away from the Regency-style house, its lawns shaded by cedars, is the main path which leads to Home Wood; this shelters the majority of the Exbury hybrids. The now famous Exbury hybrid deciduous azaleas form huge swathes of orange, apricot and gold and further colour is added by the moisture-loving plants which edge the pools. The winter garden is at its best in April and May when the early rhododendrons and azaleas are in flower, later varieties being concentrated in Yard Wood. There is also a recently restored, two-acre rock garden planted with dwarf azaleas and other suitable subjects. The central walk leads to Witcher's Wood, where a winding path is planted generously with the rhododendron 'Lady Chamberlain'. Its waxy, bell-like apricot flowers, form a glowing corridor. Specimen trees such as magnolias and Japanese maples, and a constantly growing collection of acid-loving and other plants, extend the dazzling display in this beautifully-tended garden.

The woodland garden at Exbury.

FAIRFIELD HOUSE

MAP I

Hambledon
10m (16km) south-west of Petersfield, on B2150 in Hambledon village
Owners: Mr and Mrs Peter Wake
Tel: Hambledon (070 132) 431
Open by appointment for charity
(peak period end of June and beginning of July)
Plants for sale

Redesigned and developed since 1970, this beautifully kept four-acre garden belongs to a Regency house set on a south-facing slope. It lies beneath a chalk down, sheltered by mighty cedars, hedges and walls, and contains a glorious collection of bush, shrub and climbing roses. These clamber up garden walls, up the charming house, over pergolas and netting and grow freely in rough grass. Where necessary, they are supported by an almost invisible and extendable network of five stakes — a clever device invented by the owner. The fragrance from flowers in the borders and from climbing plants is trapped in a walled garden, where there is also a fruitful vine house.

The design is largely informal, lawns giving way to rough grass threaded with mown paths. These wind up the slope above the house and around vast hummocks of shrub roses, spring bulbs and flowering trees. Mixed borders add further interest, and below lie the swimming pool and tennis court, which blend into the overall picture. An excellent plan of the garden, showing which roses grow where, is available, and should be of great use to those seeking varieties for their own gardens. A final unusual feature, and one characteristic of the standards of upkeep at Fairfield, is the toolshed, its contents immaculately cleaned and oiled. An opportunity to see the 'back room' of a good garden is seldom on offer, and should not be missed.

FARNBOROUGH HALL

MAP F

near Banbury
6m (9½km) north of Banbury, ½m (1km) off A423
Owner: The National Trust
Tel: (029 589) 202
Open several days a week from Easter to end September
(peak season spring)

On his return from his Grand Tour in the middle of the eighteenth century William Holbech, like many others, was inspired to improve his property. With the help of his friend, the architect Sanderson Miller, he refashioned the now elegant Hornton-stone house and created an unusual landscape feature — a spectacular terrace walk, remarkable not only in itself, but for having survived unchanged for so long.

It was designed to link with his brother's property at nearby Mollington, and runs for three-quarters of a mile along a curved ridge which hangs, like a theatre's dress circle, over the Warwickshire plain. The view is superb: Edge Hill, the site of the Civil War battlefield, stands out across the valley, and on a fine day the Malvern hills can be seen in the distance. Another, more recently fought — and sadly lost — battle was waged against the planners of the M40, which will soon cut through this magnificent outlook. The wide grass walk of the terrace is bounded on one side by old yews and belts of trees (the loss of the elms and the great age of some of these has necessitated much new planting). Along the outer edge is a low hedge of laurels, with bays shaped like balconies. The focal point of the walk is an impressive obelisk, an exclamation mark at its far end.

A temple with Ionic pillars and a charming oval summerhouse with a pillared loggia are eyecatchers and viewing points along the way. Note the delicate plasterwork on the domed ceiling and walls of the summerhouse's upstairs room — a fine example of rococo work, thought to be by the *stuccadore*, William Perritt, who decorated the interior of the Hall. A game larder, more robust in design, stands the far side of the belt of trees. Hexagonal, with Tuscan columns, it looks over stew ponds and lakes, one of which runs under the drive to the hall; the change in level is engineered by a falling spiral of water. The small rose garden, a later and more formal addition to the gardens, lies on the far side of the house, where the pink of 'The Fairy' rose is echoed by the painted interior of an alcove seat in the brick wall.

FELBRIGG HALL

Felbrigg, near Cromer
Near Felbrigg village, 2m (3km) south-west of Cromer off A148
Owner: The National Trust
Tel: West Runton (026 375) 444
Open several days a week from Easter to end October

The gardens of Felbrigg stand at a distance from the house, hidden behind the walls of the old kitchen garden. These are still tended in the traditional manner and are as productive as they are ornamental; they have retained the framework of their original period design, and house a pleasing collection of herbaceous and other plants as well as fruit. The fine seventeenth-century house is surrounded by a spacious park and sheltered by a woodland of the same date.

The path to the gardens runs behind the house and past the early eighteenth-century orangery, luxuriant with camellias and ferns. The design is symmetrically divided into three rectangular sections by walls. Gravel paths, flanked by hedges of dwarf box, create subsections on which stand orchards, lawns and flower beds. Borders of phlox, peonies, roses, herbs and dahlias lie beneath the perimeter walls and edge areas are planted with thorn trees, medlars, apples and plums — a colourful scene, wonderfully disciplined and well kept. A dovecote is the focal point at one end, which now houses only a fraction of the original one thousand birds so important then as a source of food. Inevitably, the fantail doves still devour whatever they fancy, and the succulent buds of pinks are particularly vulnerable. The doves, the wind, and lack of moisture, which encourages mildew, are the garden's major enemies.

There is an ornamental pond, surrounded by a circle of the deep purple lavender 'Hidcote'. Its brilliant colour is offset by a frothy cushion of lime-green alchemilla mollis, which has been planted on the small central island. Espaliered fruit trees are trained against the perimeter and dividing walls, one sunbaked stretch supporting fig trees above a long bed of herbs. There are borders of flowers for cutting and, in autumn, wide ribbons of autumn crocus are a delightful sight.

FERN COTTAGE

MAP B

Holme, near Carnforth
5m (8km) north of Carnforth off A6070, beside canal bridge on south side of Holme
Owners: Mr and Mrs Clive Jones
Tel: Carnforth (0524) 781700
Open several days a year for charity and by appointment
(peak season summer)
Plants for sale

A fascinating plantsmen's garden, created by the present owners, it is of as much interest to the professional as to the amateur. Maximum use has been made of three-quarters of an acre, which attractively accommodates a large and noteworthy collection of plants. The house was once a canal-keeper's cottage and the garden is sheltered and private.

Lawns divide island beds which display ideally the wide range of unusual trees, plants and shrubs. To give all-year-round interest, berries, catkins, bark and variegated and textured foliage are as much in evidence as flowers, but no area is crammed or haphazardly filled. There are some impressive collections: over sixty different maples, some rare; seventy varieties of hosta including American hybrids, and osteospermum and Solomon's seal. There is also a collection of ivies and one of bonsai, some raised by the owner, whose love for and skill with plants is obvious.

FLINTHAM HALL

MAP F

Flintham, near Newark
6m (9½km) south-west of Newark on the A46
Owner: Mr Myles Thoroton Hildyard
Tel: Newark (0636) 85214
Open a few days a year for charity and by written appointment

Flintham Hall has seen many changes since its medieval beginnings. It has now come to rest and stands as a striking example of Victorian Italianate architecture of palatial proportions. The garden and park, too, have evolved and display a number of period features, such as the Victorian conservatory attached to the house, a remarkable example of its kind. The majority of glasshouses built at that time fell into disrepair and were done away with decades ago, only vast ones like those at Kew standing the test of time. That at Flintham is a delightful period piece, recently restored. Designed by T. C. Hine, it is long and narrow with an unusually high barrel-shaped glass roof and tall arched windows. Architecturally romantic and botanically jungle-like, the style of the design is reminiscent of an Italian cloister, a pillared balcony evoking memories of *Romeo and Juliet*. Exotic plants entwine themselves around pillars, flow out of hanging baskets and grow out of beds set around a central pool and cake-stand fountain.

A short walk over lawns decorated with classical-style statuary brings you to Georgian walled gardens with box-edged beds and es-paliered fruit trees. Huge mounds of species roses grow in the rough grass of the shrubbery with flowering trees and shrubs. In the spring woodland, snowdrops and daffodils are shaded by native and unusual trees such as four Luccombe oaks.

FOLLY FARM

MAP I

Sulhamstead, near Reading
7m (11km) south-west of Reading on A4 between Reading and Newbury, take road marked Sulhamstead at Jack's Booth 1m (2km) after Theale roundabout. Entrance 1m (2km) on right through brown gates marked Folly Farm Gardens
Tel: Reading (0734) 303098
Open several days a year for charity and by appointment for parties only
(peak months April to September)
Plants for sale on occasion

This is a fine and beautifully-maintained example of a garden created by the partnership of Edwin Lutyens and Gertrude Jekyll. The

The Victorian conservatory at Flintham.

Dutch-style house is also interesting for being the only one that Lutyens both designed and lived in for a time and Jekyll also stayed there during that period.

Despite recent modification, the gardens have retained their strong architectural framework, the various 'rooms' and paved areas acting as an extension and platform for the house. Note the characteristic use and mixture of stone and brick to form paths, steps and walls, divisions between one 'room' and another being effected by changes in level. The planting is characteristically Jekyll with subtle blends of colour, generosity of planting and foliage shapes and colour softening the picture. Fuchsias, shrub roses, peonies and other herbaceous plants and her favourite bergenias can all be seen here. There is a yew-hedged sunken garden, parterre, courtyard garden and ornamental canal. An avenue of limes lead to a white garden made by the present owners, and landscaped lawns planted with spring bulbs, shrubs and trees flow to the boundaries.

seen: the monks' stew ponds, for example, which were reshaped and incorporated into a formal garden in the eighteenth century. The Victorian era saw the introduction of fine evergreen trees such as redwoods, cedars and firs, and the now-towering specimens planted then play a dominant role in parts of the garden today. Beneath them are groups of acid-loving shrubs, and trees and plants such as rhododendrons, magnolias and pieris. Beside a lake known as the great pond stands an exceptional bog garden. Wonderfully lush and well planted, it displays Asiatic primulas and water-loving plants with dramatic foliage and vivid flowers, such as gunnera, lilies and ferns. Overlooking the four-acre pond is a small house constructed of beech, an unusual and attractive feature. An arboretum of rare and unusual trees lies to the north-east; developed by the owner's father in 1947, it well rewards those energetic enough to seek it out. The kitchen garden behind the abbey is still tended in the traditional way, but now also shelters a good nursery and plant centre.

FORDE ABBEY

MAP I

near Chard
4m (6½km) south-east of Chard, 7m (11km) west of Crewkerne, signs from A30
Owner: Mr M. Roper (HHA)
Tel: South Chard (0460) 20231
Open daily throughout the season
(peak months April to September)
Plants for sale

The ancient abbey is surrounded by twenty-five acres of essentially informal gardens which contain herbaceous borders, shrubberies, rock and bog gardens, and an arboretum, all with an open and mature air. A Cistercian abbey from 1140 until the Dissolution of the monasteries in 1539, the house and its surroundings have seen many changes, particularly between 1500 and 1700. The house, built of Hamdon Hill stone, is now a mixture of English Baroque and Gothic architecture; the gardens reflect the styles of a wider spectrum of time.

Traces of the abbey's ancient history can be

THE FOX-ROSEHILL GARDEN

MAP II

Melvill Road, Falmouth
On B3290, main road through centre of Falmouth
Owner: Carrick District Council
Tel: Truro (0872) 78131
Open daily throughout the year
(peak season spring)

Now a public park in the middle of Falmouth, this garden is one of many in this part of Cornwall created by the Fox family during the last century. It covers two acres and contains a large number of sub-tropical plants from New Zealand, Australia and Chile, which the plantsman will find particularly rewarding: embothriums, acacias, eucalyptus, *Jovellana violacea*, and tree ferns. Shaded by pines, palms and other mature trees are cestrum, a banana tree, cordylines, echiums, phormiums and rhododendrons, camellias and magnolias. Vast griselinias add to the densely planted and exotic picture which is a far cry from most municipal gardens. There is a good collection of euphorbias and perennial plants which take the place of annuals and contribute to the garden's private character. Do not be put off by the unprepossessing appearance of the entrance; it misrepresents totally what lies beyond.

FRIARS WELL

MAP F

Wartnaby, near Melton Mowbray
In Wartnaby, 4m (6½km) north-west of Melton Mowbray. From A606 turn west in Ab Kettley; from A46 at Durham Ox turn east on A676
Owners: Lord and Lady King
Open several days a year for charity and by appointment
(peak months May to July)
Plants for sale

The four-acre garden at Friars Well contains the best elements of an English country-house garden. Stylish but never pretentious, it has been laid out to harmonise with the house and with the surrounding countryside. Initially hidden from view, and protected from the wind by hedges, are terraces, with sunken, paved and lawned gardens. The framework of these intimate 'rooms', some of which have a colour theme, is formal; the planting is relaxed and far from run-of-the-mill.

Foliage is as important as flowers and, though herbaceous plants, shrubs and old-fashioned roses are much in evidence, bulbs, ground-coverers, herbs and specimen trees form well-associated pictures. Doorways in the hedges provide vistas down an avenue of limes to a distant urn, and across the main lawn to the back of the house. Bounded by a ha-ha, the lawn melts imperceptibly into a continuous view over fields, the only decoration being the serpentine border immediately below the terrace. This peaceful view rests the eye before it is again surprised by the bog garden, set in a dip.

A young arboretum — an increasingly popular addition to plantsmen's gardens — has been developed in the old orchard to one side of

the drive. This is lined with a beech hedge planted in a Grecian key pattern. The young lime trees planted in its bays are making good progress towards a handsome avenue. Against the walls of the brick and stone house, built in 1934, grow an autilon, loquat and yellow banksian rose. A greenhouse has a vine and a colourful array of plants raised for the house.

FULHAM PALACE GARDENS

MAP J

Bishop's Avenue, London SW6
End of Bishop's Avenue, off Fulham Palace Road
Owner: The Church Commissioners, leased to London Borough of Hammersmith and Fulham
Tel: London (01) 736 7181
Open regularly throughout the year

This secluded and peaceful walled garden stands on an ancient site beside the Thames. The marauding Danes were thought to have over-wintered here, and it was later the official residence of the Bishops of London, one of whom was famous during the seventeenth century for his newly-introduced plants. Henry Compton, a mercenary soldier turned cleric, encouraged his missionaries and clergymen in North America not only to tend their flocks of colonists and Indians but to collect and send him plants. He built up one of the finest collections of exotics and North American trees in the country, employing the young George London (who set up the famous nursery London and Wise) as his gardener. Sadly, these treasures were of no interest to Compton's successor, who sold the contents of his stove-houses and garden to local nurseries. Fortunately, later bishops were interested in the garden, and the eleven acres now contain some venerable and unusual trees and interesting plants.

There are several walled sections. Holm oaks and chestnuts line a path to the courtyard in front of the house, which has a central ornamental pool and fountain and perimeter beds filled with shade-loving plants like euphorbias.

To the back of the palace are lawns shaded by handsome trees: cedars, tulip and magnolia, a black walnut and groups of shrubs and spring bulbs. A small doorway, surrounded by a bold brick arch, leads to another walled garden, with a lozenge-shaped, box-edged parterre, planted with herbs, bounded by old greenhouses and a long curve of wisteria. The lawns were partly laid out as a botanic garden, and order beds are filled with either a family of plants or those with an historical significance, such as woad. A myrtle grows against the back of the house, which has a fine view of the church tower beyond the lawns and high wall.

FURZEY GARDENS

MAP I

Minstead, near Lyndhurst
In Minstead 3½m (5½km) north-west of
Lyndhurst, 1m (2km) south of A31, 2m (3km) west
of Cadnam and end of M27
Owner: Furzey Garden Charitable Trust
Tel: Southampton (0703) 812464
Open daily throughout the year
(peak months April and May)

Laid out in the 1920s by Hew Dalrymple, the eight-acre garden is on an open, south-facing slope, with views over the New Forest to the Isle of Wight. Once rough pastureland covered in gorse, lawns now sweep away from a tiny sixteenth-century thatched cottage down to large island beds, luxuriant with evergreen azaleas, rhododendrons, woodland plants and ornamental and unusual trees. Planted in bold groups with an eye to sympathetic and harmonious colours, and scented by common yellow azaleas in spring, magnificent eucryphias in summer and witch-hazels in winter, the gardens are open and informal. The planting becomes denser as the garden descends.

Huge mounds of brilliantly coloured azaleas, rhododendrons and primulas form spring islands of colour in a cool sea of lawn; bulbs, wild flowers, cherries and amelanchiers deepen the interest. The generosity of some of the planting is striking: wide streams of astilbes and the crisp foliage of scores of hostas form neat bands of colour and texture; thickly planted heathers carpet the banks of a long, sloping walk. Specimen trees give the garden year-round interest; the barks of unusual birches, foliage and berries of sorbus, creamy flowers of cornus, unusual flowers of tender subjects such as Chilean fire bushes, leptospermums, bottle brush trees from New Zealand and the fiery autumn foliage of parrotias, enkianthus and liquid ambers all come into their own at different times. In the shady water garden at the bottom of the garden there are a number of ferns, once again popular with plantsmen, skunk cabbage and carpets of pink primulas.

THE GARDEN HOUSE

MAP H

Buckland Monachorum, near Yelverton
1m (2km) west of A386 between Buckland
Monachorum and Crapstone
Owner: Fortescue Garden Trust
Tel: Yelverton (0822) 854 769
Open regularly from April to end September
(peak months May and July)
Plants for sale

Created since 1945 on the site of an ancient monastery, this garden will inspire and fascinate both the plantsman and the garden lover. It is on a north-facing slope which runs down to the River Tavy west of Dartmoor, and has two distinct parts. The upper is set on acid soil, informal in design and devoted to a superb range of spring-flowering subjects like rhododendrons, camellias, magnolias, pieris and azaleas, many of which are unusually large. The lower part lies within an old walled garden, cut with steep terraces, and is a series of cottage-garden-type areas set in limy soil. Summer-flowering herbaceous and other plants, unusual shrubs and trees predominate here.

From 1945 until his death in 1982, Lionel Fortescue was single-minded in his determination to create an outstandingly beautiful garden, filled with the loveliest varieties of often rare plants. The inhospitable site involved a massive clearing job, the planting of a shelter belt of Leyland cypress (some of the first planted in this country) and the renovation of a thirteenth-century tower and barn in the walled garden. Endless time and care was taken to form sympathetic plant associations and superb colour effects. Thanks to the skill of the present head gardener, these continue to be a feature of the gardens.

A brilliant blue haze of chionodoxa rises from a carpet of variegated ivy, blue meconopsis cluster under a huge *Magnolia salicifolia*, and the layered branches of a variegated aralia are underplanted with hostas. There are many tender plants and specimen trees — eucryphias thrive, as do hoherias, magnolias and cornus — a *C. controversa* 'Variegata' and *C. alternifolia* are fine examples of their kind. You can enjoy a view of the beds, divided by hedges, walls and cool grass paths, from the top of the tower at the centre of the walled garden — an ideal spot to admire the subtle changes of colour and features like the amusingly grouped and clipped conifers. The garden has continued to evolve, extending the season of interest. The adjoining nursery sells a superb range of unusual plants, the majority of which have been propagated from the garden.

THE GARDENS OF THE ROSE

MAP J

Chiswell Green Lane, St Albans
2m (3km) south-west of St Albans off B4630
Owner: Royal National Rose Society
Tel: St Albans (0727) 50461
Open every day from mid-June to end October
Miniature roses for sale

The home of the Royal National Rose Society since 1960, The Gardens of the Rose display over 30,000 varieties of this most loved of garden flowers. Imaginatively laid out and much more diverse than you might imagine, they are an ideal place to choose varieties to suit individual tastes. The gardens cover twelve acres of high and exposed ground (a shelter belt of elms having

been lost) which consists of a thick layer of loam covering gravel subsoil; they should encourage those who feel they do not have ideal rose-growing conditions. Hard work and quantities of organic matter have proved that the most inhospitable conditions can be overcome and roses of exceptional quality grown.

Roses and poppies in the Gardens of the Rose.

Climbers, ramblers, miniatures, old and new shrub roses, species roses and the popular hybrid teas and flouribundas present a dazzling and fragrant show. Different areas are devoted to different types of rose or model rose gardens, conifers and balls and cones of yew adding touches of formality and dense shape. But few gardens contain only roses, so other plants which associate well have been admitted. The Alpine Society has mixed a selection of small subjects with miniature roses, and a pergola supports climbing roses and numerous clematis. How certain types can be grown and displayed — in trees, over banks or as ground-coverers — can also be seen. There are trial grounds where the new varieties, raised by growers all over the world, are put through their paces prior to being integrated into the garden or given the accolade of a gold medal.

The British Rose Festival is held here early in

July, and on the last weekend in February the gardens are open to those who want to attend pruning and planting demonstrations or consult the experts on rose-growing problems.

GAULDEN MANOR

MAP H

Tolland, near Taunton
9m (14½km) north-west of Taunton near Lydeard
St Lawrence, 1m (2km) east of Tolland Church
Owners: Mr and Mrs James Le Gendre
Starkie (HHA)
Tel: Lydeard St Lawrence (09847) 213
Open a few days a week from May to
mid-September
(peak months June and July)
Plants for sale

Those who enjoy motoring through gloriously unspoilt countryside and feeling that they have made a 'discovery' are recommended to make the journey to Gaulden Manor. Dating from the twelfth century and once the home of Thomas Hardy's d'Urberville and Wolcot families, the manor nestles in a valley between the Brendon and the Quantock hills. The fine views and the rich red soil contribute greatly to the garden's charm and fertility.

Since 1967, the present owners have developed a series of different gardens from farmland and cider orchards. They surround the ancient house and enhance its character. What is known as the duck garden is planted with shade-tolerant hellebores and fragrant mahonia; there are sweet-smelling rose and scented gardens, a herb garden with a camomile seat, a shaded secret garden luminous with white-flowering shrubs, and a bog garden lush with bold groups of primulas, hostas, arum lilies and rogersias. The presence of water, spring-fed, in ponds and channels and a good collection of old-fashioned shrub roses are important features of these private and peaceful gardens.

GLAZENWOOD

MAP G

Bradwell, Braintree
4m (6½km) east of Braintree, ½m (1km) south of
A120
Owners: Mr and Mrs D. Baer
Tel: Silver End (0376) 83172
Open for charity most Sundays from mid-May to
mid-July.
Plants for sale

The pendulum of fortune has swung wildly for the garden of Glazenwood. In the early nineteenth century it was the home of Samuel Curtis, the publisher of *The Botanical Magazine*. The garden was planted with thousands of fruit trees and unusual flowering shrubs and plants. The next hundred years were chequered and by 1964, the present owners were faced with bulldozing the debris of a huge commercial nursery and tackling the gingko tree, planted by Curtis, which had grown through the roof of the house.

The present seven-acre garden is informal and set on level ground, a particular advantage for disabled visitors. The skilfully-planned network of paths through the more intensely-planted areas give an impression of a garden of great size. From the terrace near the house, paths weave away around groups of shrubs, trees and plants and alight upon individual gardens such as those around the swimming pool and tennis court. The kitchen and woodland gardens are gradually revealed, and rambling roses, cascading from the trees, provide a grand finale. The way a not particularly unusual range of plants has been grouped — a single variety often massed or associated with others — is worth noting.

On the far side of the lawn is a bed planted for winter interest, the twigs of cornus and other suitable subjects creating a colourful feature at a dull time of the year. Another unusual, and possibly unique, feature is the semi-circular avenue of limes around the drive — a happy legacy from a former owner.

The laurel-hedged maze at Glendurgan.

GLENDURGAN

MAP H

Helford, Mawnan Smith, near Falmouth
4m (6½km) south-west of Falmouth, ½m (1km)
south-west of Mawnan Smith on road to Helford
Passage
Owner: The National Trust
Tel: Bodmin (0208) 4281
Open a few days a week from March to October
(peak months April and May)

The Fox family are renowned for the gardens they created in this part of Cornwall. They not only had the 'eye' for a superb position but, being shipping agents, were ideally placed to built up collections of newly-introduced plants.

First developed in the 1820s and 1830s by Alfred Fox, Glendurgan stands protected by woodland at the top of a steep-sided valley which runs down to the Helford River and the unspoilt former fishing village of Durgan. Thanks to the kindly Cornish climate and its age, Glendurgan displays unusual specimens of exceptional size. But, though informal in design, it is not predominantly a woodland garden; rolling lawns, meadows and glades form welcome open spaces. They also accentuate the beauty of mighty trees, groups of flowering shrubs and

features such as the laurel-hedged maze halfway down the valley.

The balance and beauty of the overall picture has not been sacrificed to a slavish accumulation of rare or unusual plants. Wild flowers — sheets of primroses, violets and bluebells on the banks of rough grass, in the meadow and along woodland paths — are as pleasing as the mounds of colour produced by camellias, Asiatic rhododendrons, hydrangeas and flowering specimen trees: magnolias, cornus, styrax and eucryphias. Vast cedars, weeping spruce, Chusan palms, a gnarled and moss-encrusted plane, tulip trees over one hundred and fifty years old, cherries and unusual conifers all display their beauty alongside the architectural foliage of gunneras, bamboos, aloes and tree and other ferns.

The less energetic can admire the many fine views over the garden and down to the river, from the garden's upper reaches. Those with more puff can explore the winding paths in the eastern valley, admire the river from the beach at Durgan and return via the woodland walk and the western valley garden. They will pass a forerunner of the playground whirligig, the Giant's Stride, and eventually land up in the walled garden beside the house, where, sheltered and sunbaked, there are tender and other climbers, shrubs and roses, and old fruit trees.

The Helford estuary viewed from the gardens at Glendurgan.

Due to the great age of a large number of trees and shrubs and their exceptional rate of growth, certain specimens are coming to the end of their lives, but The National Trust's programme of replanting ensures that Glendurgan will continue to be one of Cornwall's most charming gardens.

GODINTON PARK

MAP J

Ashford
On A20 1½m (2½km) west of Ashford at Potter's Corner
Owner: Mr Alan Wyndham Green (HHA)
Tel: Ashford (0233) 20773
Open over Easter and Sundays and Bank Holidays or by appointment from June to end of September
(peak season spring)

The garden to the Stuart house is one of the few designed by Sir Reginald Blomfield which is open to the public. It was originally laid out in the eighteenth century, but was improved and altered by Sir Reginald in 1904. Characteristically architectural in style, certain areas reflect the period design of the house and give the impression of being as old as the redbrick house itself.

A yew-hedged topiary garden is at one side of the mansion: the shape of the tightly clipped, immensely broad yew hedges echoes the Dutch-style gables of the house. Within this enclosure are a series of geometric box-hedged and other patterns which create a multi-textured weave of varying shades of green. The foliage of an *Acer pseudoplatanus* 'Brilliantissimum' and of silver weeping pears shine in this area, their colours and graceful shapes emphasized by the masonry-like evergreen topiary and hedges. There is a formal lily pool garden and herbaceous borders and an Italian garden. Quite different in character but equally formal, this is decorated with classical-style stonework, statuary, a long narrow pool and a pillared loggia and screen draped with wisteria. In contrast to the formality around the house there is a wild garden, shaded by trees and carpeted with bulbs in spring and cyclamen in autumn.

GOLDNEY HOUSE

MAP I

Lower Clifton Hill, Bristol
At top of Constitution Hill, Clifton
Owner: University of Bristol
Tel: Bristol (0272) 265698
Open several days a year from spring to autumn and by appointment for parties
(peak season summer)

Those interested in garden history will relish an exploration of the grotto in this nine-acre garden. It was first developed by a prosperous Quaker merchant, Thomas Goldney, in the mid-eighteenth century; now very much smaller in extent, it still has some interesting (and one uniquely well-preserved) period features.

A box-edged parterre has recently been restored and the orangery, no longer used to overwinter tender evergreens, is generously draped with wisteria. An avenue of unclipped yews, which may well be overgrown topiary, runs from the house to the terrace — beneath which lies the grotto. This cavernous structure, arched and pillared, and composed of several different chambers, is covered with shells, minerals and fossils. It was the custom of the time for owners of grottoes to exchange gifts of these decorative materials and Thomas Goldney was in a good position to obtain them. At the far end of the grotto, in a shaft of light, sits the figure of Neptune. He is leaning on an urn from which water originally gushed and fell into a pool, via giant clam shells.

The terrace above hangs high over the floating dock: the bastion and colonnaded rotunda were built as viewpoints for the superb views over the city. Handsome chestnuts and cedars and statues decorate this area and to the west end of the terrace is a tower built to house what Goldney called 'my fire engine': a steam-powered pump which supplied water to the grotto, small canal and fountains.

GOODNESTONE PARK

MAP J

near Wingham, Canterbury
South of the B2046 2m (3km) from Wingham
Owners: Lord and Lady FitzWalter (HHA)
Open several days a week from April to July and
September and by appointment
(peak months April to June)

The elegant eighteenth-century façade and out-look of what is pronounced 'Gunston' have dic-tated the treatment of the gardens to the front of the mansion. The unspoilt outlook, over a patch-work of fields to a backcloth of trees and rising ground, and the spacious feel of the surrounding park, are accentuated by the simple treatment of the grass terraces. Originally features of the eighteenth-century garden, these have been planted with shrub roses such as 'Nevada' and 'Maigold' which form vast mounds of white and yellow in early summer. Handsome cedars, holm oaks and conifers planted during the Victorian era provide shelter from the north-east winds, and add stature to the surroundings. There are many fine trees — one of the oldest Spanish chestnuts in the country, Dawyck beeches and a cut-leaf alder planted at the beginning of this century.

These period and botanical features are satisfying, but it is the gardens developed by the present owners since 1960 that make Goodnestone such a joy to visit. Covering several acres, they lie a short distance from the house and are hidden behind the walls of the old kitchen garden. Over three hundred varieties of shrub rose can be seen here, wonderfully exuberant, colourful and fragrant. A series of different gardens divided by walls and grass paths, these have been as-sociated with pinks, lavender, silver-foliage and other sympathetic plants. The focal point of a long vista is the church tower rising above the far boundary wall, which presents a picture intensely English and evocative of a kinder age. Not a foot of wall space is wasted, and her-baceous plants and shrubs ensure continuation of colour and interest to the end of the season.

A woodland garden is being developed north-west of the house on an area of greensand, (the rest of the garden has limy soil). Magnolias, rhododendrons and camellias grow beneath native trees, and young oriental planes, decidu-ous azaleas, cornus, maples, hellebores and hy-drangeas colour the wood threaded with winding paths. In a clearing lies a rock and water garden lush with hostas, waterlilies, conifers and ever-green shrubs.

GRAYTHWAITE HALL

MAP B

Graythwaite, near Ulverston
Midway between Newby Bridge and Hawkshead,
west of Lake Windermere
Owner: Mr M. C. R. Sandys (HHA)
Tel: Newby Bridge (0448) 31333
Open daily during April to June
(peak months May and June)

The gardens at Graythwaite are at their best in spring, when the bulbs in the wild garden planted beneath young specimen trees, and the rhodo-dendrons and azaleas nearer the house come into their own. Late-flowering species have been chosen, because the garden is vulnerable to sur-prise frosts, but the historian will find the layout of the six acres around the mansion interesting at any time of the year. This was the first major commission undertaken by the garden designer Thomas Mawson in the Lake District in 1889. His brief was to create a labour-saving garden which accommodated the existing mature trees, and the success of his design is manifest. Some of the old conifers are past their prime, but other mature trees and his balustraded stone terrace give it a stylish, purposeful look.

The design is a happy and unpretentious blend of the formal and natural. Lawns spread away from the stone terrace, the scene becoming pro-gressively wilder until it melts into a backcloth of woodland. A rose garden and borders decorate the terrace and yew hedges, clipped to resemble battlements, edge the drive. A restrained circle of yew also hides a dogs' cemetery or 'happy hunting ground'. More clipped yew hedges en-close a Dutch garden at the side of the house, on

The churchtower rising beyond the gardens at Goodnestone Park.

the site of the old stables. This has formal box-edged beds and lines of wonderfully uniform yew topiary around a sundial set on a tall stone pillar. A handsome cut-leaf beech stands near the entrance and an unusual weeping elm a short walk down the gravel path.

GREAT COMP GARDEN

MAP J

Borough Green, Sevenoaks
Between Sevenoaks and Maidstone, 2m (3km) east
of Borough Green; A20 at Wrotham Heath, take
Seven Mile Lane, B2016; at crossroads turn right,
½m (1km) on left
Owner: Great Comp Charitable Trust
Tel: Borough Green (0732) 882669
Open daily from April to end October
Plants for sale

Packed with interest for the plantsman and amateur gardener alike, the seven-acre gardens at Great Comp display a wealth of plant material and an attractive layout. Various parts of it would translate happily to a smaller private garden, and it was also designed to be 'easy care'. Mr and Mrs R. Cameron, who created it, tended it without help for many years.

In 1957, when they came, Great Comp was a tired Edwardian-style garden, with limes, woodland and paddock surrounding the seventeenth-century house. The paddock is now part of the informal garden, which is surrounded and sheltered by a thick belt of trees and shrubs. The main part of the garden is laid out with large island beds filled with well-associated groups of ornamental and other trees, and shrubs and plants; it resembles highly-cultivated woodland with a seldom-seen richness. Over one thousand varieties of shrubs and trees, as well as azaleas and roses, can be seen, extending the season of interest. There are conifers and witch-hazels which give shape, fragrance and colour in midwinter; magnolias, cornus, rhododendrons and azaleas in spring; viburnums, eucryphias, lilies, perennials and roses in the summer, and in autumn a glorious bonfire of colour is produced by scores of unusual maples, sorbus and hea-

thers. So many and various are the grass paths that weave around these beds and through glades, it would take several visits to ensure that all the lovely plant compositions had been inspected. The paths also ensure that the garden never appears crowded, no matter how many visitors there are.

South of the house, beds displaying a mass of heathers flank a vista down a wide river of lawn. Their varied textures and colours are highlighted against a background of dark conifers. Apart from the garden containing two hundred different varieties of heather, there is a fine collection of small specimen trees, and shade-loving and ground-cover plants are well represented. Each bed is a layer cake of interest though the plants are never crammed or thoughtlessly placed. There are formal gardens near the house — the yew garden, planted with hybrid tea roses, and the square, with its borders of herbaceous plants which do not need staking. Urns, seats and a temple are focal points or delightful surprises at the far end of walks and lawns.

GREAT DIXTER

MAP J

Northiam, near Hastings
12m (19½km) north of Hastings on A28 turn west
to Northiam
Owners: Lloyd family (HHA)
Tel: Northiam (07974) 3160
Open every afternoon except Mondays from April
to October
(peak months June and September)
Plants for sale

Those who have enjoyed the many gardening books and articles written by Christopher Lloyd will find particularly absorbing the garden he so entertainingly writes about. Only a handful of experts have the courage to open their plots to the public and reveal whether they have had success with the features and methods of work they have so enthusiastically described. Great Dixter was originally laid out by his parents at the beginning of the century, and has been allowed to evolve ever since, with new plants and ideas consistently added by Christopher Lloyd and his mother before him. The gardens have accordingly retained their individuality — a personality preserved only in a garden still tended by those who created it.

It stands one hundred and eighty feet above sea level on a south-west-facing slope of the High Weald. The soil is clay, and receives constant doses of mulch and manure. The half-timbered, gabled house with tall chimneys is at the heart of the garden, the oldest part dating from the fifteenth century and the youngest from 1910. In that year Nathaniel Lloyd bought the property and employed Edwin Lutyens to enlarge and renovate it. Apart from some old farm buildings and orchards, little surrounded the house and Lutyens was required to lay out the bones of a garden as well. Typical of his style, the framework is architectural rather than botanical, incorporating the old outbuildings. The walls, terraces and steps are an extension of the house and suit its period character.

There is a series of different areas, some formal and enclosed and others open and 'natural'. Apart from the pool garden designed by Nathaniel Lloyd, the formal features were designed by Lutyens, the informal planting being added by the Lloyd family. Walls, arches, steps, paths, yew hedges and different levels have been used to create divisions and links between the areas. Each has an individual character, and all contain well-associated and interesting collections of plants. A topiary garden has huge birds perching on cones of yew; there is a formal rose garden, a sunken pool garden with raised borders, and a seventy-foot-long border of shrubs, perennials and annuals, which is at its best in summer. A meadow is delicately embroidered with wild flowers and the orchard is lively with naturalised bulbs in spring. To describe in detail the plant content of each area would be a mistake, for changes are constantly being made and experiments carried out on new and successful plant associations.

Mixed borders abound, plants of all kinds being used to create layers of interest which reveal themselves gradually throughout the season: annuals used in borders to offset more permanent specimens, in a relaxed rather than 'municipal' manner, and the way in which clematis have been incorporated are well worth noting. There are many varieties of clematis and they, together with unusual and other plants seen in the garden, are on sale in the adjoining nursery.

GREATHAM MILL

MAP I

Greatham, near Liss
5m (8km) north of Petersfield. From A325, at Greatham turn on
to B3006 towards Alton; after 600yds (550m) fork left into 'No through road' lane to garden
Owner: Mrs E. N. Pumphrey
Tel: Blackmoor (042 07) 219
Open every Sunday and Bank Holiday from mid-April to end September and on other days by appointment
Plants for sale

When Mr and Mrs Pumphrey came to the seventeenth-century mill in 1949, all that existed was an old orchard, rough land, the all-important River Rother and the mill waterways. The one-and-three-quarter-acre garden is now one of the loveliest cottage-style gardens in the country, outstanding for its wide-ranging collection of plants. The enthusiast should be prepared for a long visit or, even better, should visit the garden throughout the season. Colours and shapes change from month to month and new-found plants are constantly added. Planted to give year-round interest, the garden is on alluvial clay soil on the acid side of neutral, and is well mulched and fed.

You approach it over a small bridge spanning the river. The redbrick house, draped with wisteria and the single yellow rose 'Helen Knight', nestles into the garden. At its front lies a water garden, and to the back the larger informal garden, which follows the line of the river. The extent and colours of the front garden can be admired from above on the far side of the boundary parapet wall, or inspected at close quarters. The banks of the millstream are lush with moisture-loving plants, and herbaceous borders stand around a small lawn. Island, scree and rockery beds of imaginatively composed groups tempt you down the garden to the back, where there is an abundance of alpines, specimen bulbs, grasses, ground-coverers, herbs, herbaceous plants, flowering shrubs, specimen trees and all important foliage plants.

Shrub roses feature widely and beds devoted to subtle colour combinations decorate the long lawn and the converted tennis court. A young arboretum makes good headway at the far end of the garden, which becomes increasingly natural the further it strays from the house. A list of even a fraction of the unusual varieties to be found at Greatham Mill would make tedious reading; suffice it to say that the admirable standards of upkeep are matched by the plant content. Many can be bought from the adjoining nursery garden.

GREAT THURLOW HALL

MAP G

Great Thurlow, near Haverhill
2m (3km) north-east of Haverhill on A143 turn
north-west on to B1061
Owner: Mr Ronald A. Vestey
Tel: Thurlow (044083) 240
Open for charity during the spring and summer,
write for details
Peak season spring

In 1942, when Mr Vestey bought the property, very little of the present gardens existed around the neo-Georgian house. They now cover twenty acres, are immaculately maintained and have a peaceful and spacious air. They are also obviously much loved and enjoyed, not simply a showpiece.

Formal gardens surround the house, terraces giving on to rose and pool gardens. Shrub roses, heathers and herbaceous borders flank grass walks and link formal and natural areas. Brightly-coloured beds decorate the intensely-cultivated parts of the garden near the house, the scene gradually giving way to lawns, flowering shrubs and trees. These run down to and

edge the banks of a canal which almost completely encircles the garden, and carpets of aconites, snowdrops, bluebells and spring bulbs add to the unpretentious charm of the scene.

There are some surprise features, like the stone pavilion which is the focal point at the far end of a walk; flanked by borders, it is reached by a bridge thickly entwined with wisteria. A walled kitchen garden, one of the original features, is run on traditional lines, with espaliered fruit trees spread along the sunbaked walls and trim lines of vegetables and fruit in the box-edged beds.

GREY'S COURT

MAP I

Rotherfield Greys, near Henley-on-Thames
3m (5km) west of Henley-on-Thames on road to
Peppard, A423
Owner: The National Trust
Tel: Rotherfield Greys (049 17) 529
Open regularly from Easter to end September
(peak season summer)

The most interesting and highly-cultivated part of the garden lies a short walk from the Jacobean manor. Within the ruined walls of a fourteenth-century fortified house is a series of roofless 'rooms' whose design and plant content emphasise the colour and texture of the flint walls. The plant colouring is soft and one variety of rose, shrub or tree is massed rather than dotted around formal beds.

One 'room' is filled with old-fashioned roses; another, circular in shape, with *Wisteria floribunda*, their twisting stems dripping with long, pale and dark lavender racemes of flowers. The kitchen garden has a central octagonal tank, the focal point of two walks; one is lined with cherries, the other with espaliered apples and beds of peonies. The tower garden is filled with white flowering shrubs and flowers in beds around a lily pond, and a little knot garden provides a surprise near the tea-room. An intriguing feature beyond the walled gardens is the brick-pathed archbishop's maze, laid out in 1980, with an armillary sundial, on a base of Westmorland stone carved in the shape of a Byzantine cross, at its centre.

On the lawns around the house are some fine trees such as a weeping ash, a tulip tree and strawberry trees and behind the house a Chinese-style bridge and moon gate span the ha-ha.

A striking use of evergreens and flowering plants.

GUNBY HALL

MAP C

Gunby, near Spilsby
7m (11 km) west of Skegness on A518
Owner: The National Trust
Tel: Scremby (075 485) 212
Open a few days a week from Easter to end
September and by written appointment
(peak months June and July)
Plants for sale

There is a homeliness about the seventeenth-century hall and its gardens which makes them easy to relate to and enjoy. Given to the Trust by the Massingberd family in 1944, Gunby's personal and private air has been preserved and the garden kept up to good old-fashioned standards. It covers seven acres and contains a well-balanced mixture of intensely planted, formal and informal areas; the proportions and design of house and garden suit each other very well.

Lawns spread away from the house, shaded by an old cedar, silver lime, mulberry and quince, and bounded by informal beds of shrubs and roses. Beneath the walls of the house, box-edged beds of the rose 'Mrs Oakley Fisher' add a dash of colour, and in front of the house yew hedges frame beds set around a sundial. These are planted with topiary yellow privet, lavender and catmint. Wild flowers and spring bulbs thrive in areas of rough grass, and down what is known as the ghost walk low-growing plants spill on to the path between a hedge and a long pond, backed by trees and shrubs.

All these features are attractive enough, but the walled gardens of fruit, vegetables and flowers have even greater charm. Roses feature widely throughout the garden at Gunby but in these sheltered 'rooms' there is a fine collection of old-fashioned varieties, in beds and against the walls. There are also mixed borders, the colouring of which alters as the season advances, from blues to yellows to purples and pinks. Geometric beds contain over one hundred herbs, and espaliered and standard fruit trees, as well as an apple walk lined with irises, ensure that the garden is productive as well as decorative.

'Mind your own business' creeps over the floors of the greenhouses against the end wall. Bright with pelargoniums and climbing geraniums, they also contain a black Hamburg grape, lemon tree and collection of ferns. A domed summerhouse snuggles against the dovecote; a small corridor of yew leads to a walled orchard overlooked by the brick dovecote draped with the rose 'Alberic Barbier'. The paths, edged with roses, fruit trees and herbaceous plants, divide this into four sections, and espaliered fruit trees and more roses decorate the walls. A medlar is underplanted with Japanese anemones, an apple with chives and rue, banks of hydrangeas, flowers for picking, and vegetables and soft fruit cages create a rare picture of old-fashioned fruitfulness and beauty.

HADDON HALL

MAP B

Bakewell
2½m (4km) south-east of Bakewell on A6
Owner: The Duke of Rutland (HHA)
Tel: Bakewell (062 981) 2855
Open regularly from April to end September
(peak months June and July)

Secure and intimate, the gardens are an integral part of the superb medieval fortified house. Laid out in the seventeenth century, they stand on steep walled terraces which slope down to the River Wye and are varied in treatment and character. Not an inch of wall space has been wasted, and climbers including that most rampant of roses, 'Kiftsgate', tumble over and down high terraced walls; even the nooks and crannies of the large stone buttresses have been used, making an original resting place for alpines. Small but wide-spreading 'Scarlet Haw' thorn trees, *Crataegus pedicellata*, can be seen on the top terrace, and borders on the terrace below are filled with perennials and roses. Edging the lawn are small cones of yew surrounded by autumn crocus, like medieval headresses encircled with amethysts. Wide stone steps lead down to the peaceful fountain lawn patterned with beds of roses. The secluded lower garden lies beside the river. There are some good views of the unspoilt countryside and river valley and spring bulbs of all kinds can be seen throughout.

by a wooded hill; many tender plants can thus be grown, such as the superb Paulownia or 'foxglove' tree, and a range of Australasian plants. The character of the garden is sunny as well. Seats in intimate and fragrant areas invite you to rest and admire your surroundings or views over the countryside and garden.

The 'bones' were laid out in the last century, but because it was neglected over a long period much of what can be seen today dates from 1967. It was then that the well-known garden writer, Penelope Hobhouse, went to live at Hadspen, and began to reclaim and replant the garden, a task which involved her for well over ten years. Many unusual trees were planted: an oriental plane, a Chinese wing nut and *Cornus controversa* 'Variegata', whose delicate, tutu-like layers of foliage have become a striking feature of the lower, more informal part of the gardens. An exceptional range of hostas can be seen in the old walled kitchen garden, and the alkaline clay of Hadspen also suits the National Collection of rodgersias.

Mown grass paths weave through a meadow of wild flowers and around groups of shrubs planted for their foliage effects in the lower part of the garden, and shrub roses, tender climbers and silver-foliage plants scent the cottage and sunbacked lily pond gardens set into the side of the hill. The work involved in tending the garden and raising plants for the nursery is considerable, so the former sometimes suffers but it still has much to offer the garden lover and plantsman.

HADSPEN HOUSE

MAP I

Castle Cary
2m (3km) south of Castle Cary on A371
Owner: Trustees of the late Sir Arthur Hobhouse
Tel: Castle Cary (0963) 50939
Open every day from April to October and by
appointment
Plants for sale

Hadspen has a particularly favoured position. The eight-acre garden faces south and is sheltered

HAM HOUSE

MAP J

Sandy Lane, Ham, Richmond-on-Thames
On the south bank of the Thames, west of A307 at
Petersham
Owner: The National Trust/Victoria and Albert
Museum
Tel: (01) 940 1950
Open regularly throughout the year

On one of the most attractive stretches of the Thames, opposite Marble Hill, this fine Stuart house enjoys surprisingly secluded and unspoilt surroundings. The design and scale of the house and gardens are elegant and formal but never overbearingly grand, and are not difficult to relate to. The gardens are among the few from the seventeenth century to be seen in this country, most having been swept away by the eighteenth-century vogue for landscapes. Painstakingly restored by the Trust to their original 1676 layout, the gardens are bounded by walls, are predominantly formal and symmetrical, and cover twenty acres.

The layout was drawn up by a military engineer and surveyor, John Slezer, for the Countess of Dysart, who was then chatelaine of Ham House. No major additions or changes were made from about 1680, but their restoration involved a massive clearing job, the whole garden to the south of the house having to be ploughed up. The wilderness, a popular and (despite its name) formal feature of seventeenth-century gardens, had become truly wild and was a dense thicket of common rhododendrons and undergrowth.

The forecourt to the north is restrained, dignified only by a Coade stone statue of a river god who faces the gates and Thames beyond. Busts are set in oval bays of the walls, little but evergreens being allowed to detract from the impressive facade of the house. The cherry garden to the east is enclosed by yew hedges and laid out with a pattern of box-edged beds filled with santolina and lavender. Arbours of hornbeam and cherries (fruit trees were important features of gardens of this period) have been planted against the wall. The whole of the south front is filled with plants that would have been used during the seventeenth century. The main part of the gardens is a formal arrangement of eight large grass squares, divided by gravel paths, which are decorated with Versailles tubs of evergreens. A wide central path leads up to and through the wilderness, creating a vista from the house, through the south gates in the boundary wall and down an avenue to Ham Common. The design of the wilderness is a *patte-d'oie* of grass paths radiating from the central clearing; the wedges of ground produced are edged with hornbeam hedges, decorated with summer-

houses and planted with field maples and wild flowers such as cowslips and ragged robin.

A small walled orchard has old varieties of apple trees; what was once the kitchen garden has now been turfed, and beds of modern roses stand beneath the perimeter walls. To one end stands the orangery, now a tea-room overlooking the lawn, which is partially shaded by unusual trees: a *Cercis siliquastrum* or Judas tree, Christ's thorn and black mulberry. A skilfully constructed ice house is near the stable block, and a shady avenue of holm oaks is punctuated with a statue of Bacchus.

HAMPTON COURT PALACE GARDENS

MAP J

East Molesey
On A308 at junction with A309
Owner: English Heritage
Tel: London (01) 977 8441
Open daily throughout the year
(peak months April to December)

Of all gardens in this country, those at Hampton Court reveal most the changing tastes of centuries. Since Henry VIII, a succession of monarchs and their gardeners have put their stamp upon the flat land surrounding the palace. As long ago as the mid-eighteenth century this fact was respected by Lancelot 'Capability' Brown who, as Surveyor to His Majesty's Gardens and Waters at Hampton Court, uncharacteristically refused to replace the richly-decorated garden with an heroic landscape 'out of respect to himself and his profession'. Lying beside the Thames, the main thoroughfare to the city for many centuries, the palace was a country retreat where the air was fresh and there was ample opportunity to hunt. A royal residence since Cardinal Wolsey presented it to Henry VIII in 1525 until George II's death in 1760 and owned but not occupied by the royal family thereafter, the gardens have never suffered a period of neglect. They were opened to the public by Queen Victoria in 1838, and have given pleasure and the chance to study genuine or reconstructed period features ever since.

Henry VIII's tiltyard to the east of the palace has now been transformed into an ornamental garden of old-fashioned and modern roses, but is still overlooked by one of the five observation towers he had built. Nearby is the wilderness garden where the famous triangular maze, originally formed of hornbeam hedges in 1714, now of yew, stands by the Lion Gate. Far from what its name suggests, as was the fashion of the times, the wilderness was riven with symmetrical paths shortly to be reinstated. Their authentic formality will not detract from the beauty of the lawns decorated with specimen trees and planted with bulbs.

The formal and symmetrical fountain gardens are on the far side of the long broad walk. This runs along the front of the palace and on towards the river; superb and immaculately-kept borders are at one side of this wide gravel path, their rich colouring offset by the deep red of the brick walls behind. The fountain gardens were begun during the reign of Charles II, and various enthusiastic monarchs, such as William and Mary, have added ornamental features. Recently reinstated avenues of limes, first planted by the seventeenth-century garden-makers, London and Wise, are an example. A *patte-d'oie* of paths fans from the central fountain, lined with towering and ancient yews, resembling uneven pyramids set on poles. They were once small topiary pieces and some think their present size detracts from the fine architecture of Sir Christopher Wren's east front. Aligned on the fountain and stretching into the distance is a wide canal flanked by limes. The water which fed this and the fountain was brought, by a watercourse, from the River Colne eight miles distant, during the reign of Charles I.

The most intensely planted areas of the gardens are below the west front of the palace, damaged by fire in 1987. These are walled and hedged individual period gardens, formal and relatively small in scale. The largest is the privy garden with its network of grass paths and beds of shrubs and trees, enclosed by banks. These were constructed from earth which formed a mount topped by a gazebo in Henry VIII's time. There is also a knot, a parterre and a pond

garden, all bright with formal beds of bulbs and bedding-out plants. In the vinery the black Hamburg, planted by 'Capability' Brown in 1768, still produces a rich crop of grapes. Its spreading roots — said to reach the Thames — are fed with a rich dressing of manure, applied to the large empty bed beside the glasshouse.

Those who enjoy letting their imaginations take flight can visualise the lives lived in these gardens and the kings and queens who contributed to their beauty. Others may prefer to seek and admire the magnificent gates and screen by Tijou and the banqueting house on the terrace by the river, or the laburnum arch walk in the wilderness garden. History and horticulture have been well served here.

HARDWICK HALL

MAP C

Doe Lea, near Chesterfield
6½m (10½km) west of Mansfield. 9½m (15km)
south-east of Chesterfield; approach from M1
(junction 29) on A617
Owner: The National Trust
Tel: Chesterfield (0246) 850430
Open regularly from Easter to end October
(peak seasons spring and summer)

This magnificent 'prodigy' house, built by Bess of Hardwick at the end of the sixteenth century, stands proudly on top of a hill more than six hundred feet above sea level. Its symmetry, extravagantly large windows and six towers decorated with her initials, reflect her strong character; the gardens, sensibly, play a sympathetic rather than competitive role.

They are surrounded by eighteenth-century parkland and, like the house, are symmetrical. The perimeter of the walled forecourt with its handsome cedars is decorated with borders, and the lawn is divided into four neat sections. Lady Egerton laid out the south garden in the 1870s, and its restraint and strong architectural character offset the lines of the house. Two hedged alleys, one of yew and one of hornbeam, meet at a central clearing and divide this area into four separate parts. The dark circular hedges of the clearing are a backdrop for lead statues and white garden seats. In the south-west section is an Elizabethan herb garden, with beds of sixteenth-century herbs edged with lavender and divided by hedges of eglantine rose (a flower which appears in the arms of Bess of Hardwick) and sweetbriar hedges. Tripods of golden hop create striking vertical accents, and flowers for cutting; a nuttery and the giant Hardwick lily-of-the-valley also decorate the area. The south-east section has an orchard of old fruiting varieties and a small sixteenth-century gazebo; the north-east contains an ornamental orchard.

Hungarian oaks stand on the lawn of the north-west section, and herb, shrub-rose and herbaceous borders create ribbons of colour. On the lawn east of the house there is a circular pond surrounded by ornamental trees, and an opening in the boundary yew hedge reveals the park beyond the ha-ha. You can see an unusual feature from the east windows of the house: limes, planted around open parkland, form the outlines of a massive, upside-down wine glass.

HAREWOOD

MAP J

Harewood Road, Chalfont St Giles
From A404 Amersham to Rickmansworth road, at mini-roundabout in Little Chalfont Village turn south down Cokes Lane, 200yards (180metres) on left
Owners: Mr and Mrs John Heywood
Tel: Little Chalfont (024 04) 3553
Open several days a year for charity and by appointment
(peak months May and June)
Plants for sale

For those who own gardens abutting on others, this one-acre garden is of particular interest and a model of its kind. The choice and mixture of plant material, and the imaginative use of space have created a private and attractive picture. Within a framework of conifers, yew and box hedges, a wide spectrum of plants has been used to make an informal, well-balanced display with all-year-round interest.

Climbers, including many clematis, hug roses, shrubs and trees, the flowers of another taking over when one dies back. Foliage colour has also been used to extend the season of interest, but the colouring of borders is in no way harsh. The subtle blends have been achieved not by devoting beds to shades of one or two colours, but by excluding one, such as yellow, altogether. Fragrance is provided by daphne, roses and viburnums, and plantsmen will note the good collection of violas, primulas and old roses. Woody plants and climbers are well labelled and a comprehensive plant list is available.

HAREWOOD HOUSE

MAP B

Harewood, near Leeds
8m (13km) north of Leeds at junction of A659 and A61
Owner: The Earl of Harewood (HHA)
Tel: Harewood (0532) 886225
Open daily from April to end of October and Sundays in February, March and November
(peak months late May to October)
Plants for sale

The mid-eighteenth-century house, the home of the Lascelles family for over two hundred years, stands on high ground over the three hundred acres of parkland and pleasure ground. Below lies the vast lake, clumps of trees and belts of woodland laid out by 'Capability' Brown in 1772. The house is on a stage, a grand Italianate terrace designed by the Victorian architect, Sir Charles Barry. It is deep and balustraded and decorated with a parterre of scrolls of box hedging, a long border, urns, fountain and basin. A contemporary bronze statue of Orpheus which stands at the centre of the basin strikes a dramatic note, and ornamental beds of annuals add splashes of bright colour. Steps run down from the terrace to a sloping grass bank planted with specimen trees, which, leads in turn to the woodland garden and lake.

Rhododendrons, spring bulbs and mature trees fill this garden, and the colours of the vast banks of rhododendrons are reflected in the smooth surface of the lake. The walk through the pleasure grounds around the lake is delightful; you will find a cascade spanned by a bridge, the rock and water garden planted intensely with azaleas, primulas, and astilbes, and the striking foliage of *Gunnera manicata*.

Modern and shrub roses are on the terrace, on a bank near the entrance to pleasure grounds and near the walled garden on the far side of the lake. The Victorian terrace, eighteenth-century landscape and pleasure grounds blend well, with fine trees and pockets of intense colour making them an adventure to explore.

HARLOW CAR GARDENS

MAP B

Crag Lane, Harrogate
2m (3km) south-west of Harrogate in Crag Lane
off the B6162
Owner: The Northern Horticultural Society
Tel: Harrogate (0423) 65418
Open daily throughout the year
Plants for sale

All garden-lovers, and particularly those who struggle against the harsh climatic and other conditions in this part of the country, will be encouraged and inspired by these gardens. They were laid out in 1948 by the Northern Horticultural Society, who determined to create a 'Wisley of the North', a garden where a plant's ability to withstand difficult conditions could be tested. The gardens are sixty acres in extent and set on heavy, very acid clay; they lie in a frost pocket and are regularly attacked by rabbits and squirrels. You will appreciate that these gardens do not enjoy especially favourable conditions.

The site is long and narrow and cut lengthwise by a stream which divides the woodland from the intensely planted areas. The stream is sulphurous, and its medical properties prompted Henry Wight to build a bath house here, in 1844, where people could immerse themselves. It can still be seen, though it now houses the Society's study centre and library. The banks of the stream are planted luxuriantly with

moisture-loving and other plants, and the overall picture is not dissimilar to the stream garden at Wisley, which also flows between a rock and a woodland garden.

On the gentle slope running down to the stream are various informal gardens. Areas decorated with specimen trees and island beds, a rockery, individual gardens and trial grounds, are skilfully divided by lawns and hedges. Trial beds of annuals and perennials and Flouroselect free-flowering varieties (Harlow Car is one of only three gardens to have these on show) are hidden and sheltered by beech and other hedges. There are areas planted with slow-growing conifers, ground-covering plants, the National Collection of hypericum, and a herb garden and chronological border showing when plants were introduced to this country.

Delicately scented shrub roses and tree peonies decorate the borders leading to display areas, which contain raised beds and sinks of silver-leafed and other dainty treasures near the alpine house. Beds of foliage plants will interest the flower arranger, while the keen vegetable gardener will head for the fruit and vegetable trial grounds. A section, known as the 'vegetable sanctuary', displays a collection of now unobtainable varieties, as well as part of the National Collection of rhubarb. An area decorated with winter-flowering shrubs and specimen trees contrasts well with the intensely planted and well-constructed limestone rock garden. On the far side of the broad walk, which cuts the slope in two, are a lily pond, heathers, island beds of spring bulbs and the improved rose garden. The woodland garden beyond the stream is enriched with species and hybrid rhododendrons, and an arboretum and conservation garden. You will be astounded at what has been achieved in these difficult conditions.

The range and quality of the plants is matched by the immaculate upkeep of the whole. Set at strategic points are many seats donated by friends of Harlow Car. An invitation to rest and enjoy the beautiful surroundings, they stand witness to the pleasure these gardens give their many visitors.

HARRINGTON HALL

MAP C

near Spilsby
5m (8km) east of Horncastle, A158 Lincoln to
Skegness road, turn left on leaving
Hagworthingham, Harrington 2m (3km)
Owner: Lady Maitland (HHA)
Tel: Spilsby (0790) 52281
Open a few days a week from Easter to end
October
(peak months July and August)
Plants for sale

The sixteenth- and seventeenth-century hall and its surrounding gardens are an intensely English picture of period charm. The unspoilt countryside of Lincolnshire spreads around a scene which has evolved over many centuries. Architectural features like the Elizabethan porch tower of the house, eighteenth-century gate piers in the old brick walls of the garden, the terrace and gazebos, all blend happily into the profusely planted garden. Here Tennyson, who grew up nearby at Somersby Rectory, met and fell in love with Rosa Baring, the inspiration for 'Maud'.

The main part of the garden, covering five acres, is walled and contains a terrace walk. In front of it are the forecourt and drive. Although it has lost the shelter of the old elms, it is protected from north-east winds and a surprising number of tender plants can be seen here. The garden gives the initial impression of a classic country-house garden, but you soon realise that it has been created by a skilled plantswoman, Lady Maitland. Unusual herbaceous and old-fashioned plants and flowering shrubs abound and thrive on the limestone soil. In the walled garden a border below the terrace is planted with cream and yellow flowers; others are devoted to different shades of purple, pink and blue. Low-growing aromatic and silver-foliaged plants spill on to the brick path which runs along the Jacobean terrace, a good vantage point to admire the walled garden and entrance court, decorated with topiary yews.

Climbing roses festoon the walls of the garden

and house — the delicate yellow, *Rosa banksiae lutea* and many others, perfectly complementing the colour of the brick. Old-fashioned roses add fragrance, and ramblers cascade over walls and clamber into trees. A walk between the walled garden and a thick yew hedge has borders densely planted with alstroemerias and day-lilies on one side, and *Crambe cordifolia* on the other. The starry white flowers of the latter are brilliant against the inky hedge. The kitchen garden is divided by borders backed by the claret-coloured foliage of *Prunus* 'Pissardii', and beyond the walled gardens are borders of spring- and summer-flowering shrubs, unusual lilacs, viburnums, hebes and several varieties of potentilla.

HATFIELD HOUSE

Hatfield
Opposite Hatfield station on A1000
Owner: The Marquess of Salisbury
Tel: Hatfield (070 72) 62055
Open regularly from late March to October
(peak season summer)
Plants for sale

Thanks to the present Marchioness of Salisbury's talent as a garden designer and plantswoman, some areas of the gardens at Hatfield are the best examples of reproduction Elizabethan gardens to be seen. The surroundings of the house harmonise so well with its architecture that it is hard to believe they have not always been as they are today.

Robert Cecil, first Earl of Salisbury, built the house early in the seventeenth century and laid out gardens renowned for their waterworks. The planting was the work of John Tradescant the Elder, gardener to the Cecils and later to Charles I. The eighteenth-century vogue, for landscaped parks running up to the walls of the house saw their demise, and it was not until the nineteenth century that the Jacobean-style gardens were reinstated. In recent years great improvements have been made and a scented and authentically planted Elizabethan garden has been laid out.

The east garden, open only one day a week, is

a series of descending formal gardens decorated with a rose parterre, tiered fountain, formal yews, double avenues of standard evergreen oaks and a famous yew-hedged maze. The west garden, open more frequently, is enclosed by yew hedges and contains geometric beds around a central pool. These are generously filled with shrub roses, peonies, herbaceous plants and cushions of delicate violas. A lime walk, a cool tunnel of green, surrounds a lawn and the scented garden, opened in 1979, lies on a lower level. Its paths are patterned with camomile and the beds are filled with well-associated groups of herbs and fragrant flowering shrubs and plants.

A knot garden has been laid out in the court-yard of the Old Palace of Hatfield, but it is vulnerable to erosion from over-visiting and is open only one day a week. Fortunately, being a sunken garden, it can be viewed from above. Patterns of dwarf box-hedging, some of which resemble a miniature maze, lie on either side of paths which strike away from a central pool and fountain. The beds in these knots are planted with subjects which grew during the fifteenth, sixteenth and seventeenth centuries, a number of which were introduced by John Tradescant and his son. Green arbours and standard honey-suckles which resemble large, sweet-smelling bouquet's, roses, acanthus, herbs and much else grow in this delightful period piece.

Quite different from the formal gardens around the house are the thirteen acres of wood-land. Known as the wilderness, this is shaded by fine trees and coloured by rhododendrons, azaleas and bulbs in spring.

Walk of standard evergreen oaks at Hatfield House.

Border in the east garden at Hatfield House.

HEALE HOUSE

MAP I

Middle Woodford, near Salisbury
4m (6½Jm) from Salisbury, on Woodford Valley
Road between A360 and A345
Owners: Major David and Lady Anne Rasch
(HHA)
Tel: Middle Woodford (0722 73) 207
Open regularly from Easter to autumn

The elegant stone house which sheltered the fugitive Charles II after the Battle of Worcester lies in a peaceful valley of the River Avon. Its eight-acre garden, bounded on two sides by the fast-flowing river, blends into the surrounding water meadows, the whole making a delightfully English scene.

Formal gardens stand near the house, which was remodelled by Detmar Blow at the end of the last century. It has retained its Restoration character, but the terrace gardens and flight of steps down to the river have an Italian flavour. They were laid out for the Honorable Louis Greville, the present owner's great-uncle, at the beginning of the century, by the landscape designer Harold Peto. He was well known for his classical, Italian-style gardens and had a talent for marrying the natural with the formal, which was put to good use at Heale, where the river and meadows play such an important role. The terraces rise to a wrought-iron gate, where you can turn and admire the house and the way Harold Peto has transformed an awkward slope into a charming vista. Though the framework

149

may be formal, the planting here and throughout the garden is disarmingly relaxed.

In spring, bulbs cover the banks of the river and crown imperials and small groups of unusual tulips such as 'Apricot Beauty' colour the borders. By June irises, peonies, shrub roses and herbaceous plants are jostling for attention — a wonderfully exuberant display. A border on a low terrace next to the croquet lawn is devoted to pastel shades of musk roses, creamy 'Buff Beauty', pale apricot 'Cornelia' and washed pink 'Felicia'. The old cob-walled vegetable garden, though still fulfilling its original purpose, has been given a pool surrounded by huge balls of box; there is also an apple tunnel (its supports being made out of old piping). Roses, wisteria, clematis and vines tumble over arches, along pergolas and walls.

Painted bridge and magnolias in the Japanese garden at Heale House.

The picture becomes more serene as the frivolity gives way to peaceful lawns running down to the shallow river and the Japanese garden. Made by Mr Greville, this was laid out to a plan of a genuine Japanese garden, and the thatched tea-house and ornamental half-moon bridge were constructed by Japanese craftsmen. Streams weave under and through this area, willows, magnolias, maples and moisture-loving plants creating a scene which is a delightful mix

of the oriental and natural wild garden. Heale is remarkable for the generosity of its planting and the happy blend of garden-making styles. It is not difficult to understand why it was voted 'Garden of the Year' in 1984, a prize awarded annually by the Historic Houses Association and Christies.

HEASELANDS

MAP J

Haywards Heath
1m (2km) south-west of Haywards Heath on A273
to Burgess Hill
Owner: Mrs Ernest Kleinwort
Tel: Haywards Heath (0444) 8084
Open several days a year for charity and by
appointment for parties
(peak month May)

This must be one of the most beautifully-maintained private gardens in England. Part formal, part woodland, it covers thirty-five acres, is richly planted with flowering shrubs and unusual trees and is an excellent example of a twentieth-century garden.

The driveway, through pinewoods underplanted with rhododendrons, gives a clue of what lies in store around the stone, gabled house. When this was built in 1933 by Ernest Kleinwort, incorporating the old farmhouse on the site, there was one handsome blue cedar, which now stands on the terrace. The rest was meadow with oak and pine woodland. Advantage has been taken of the natural beauty of the site and the gardens present a wonderfully-balanced picture of formality and naturalness. Intimate and formal, walled and hedged gardens stand a short distance from the house each richly filled with an appropriate selection of plants, many of which are unusually good specimens of seldom-seen varieties.

Evergreen azaleas and dwarf conifers decorate a sandstone rock garden, and a spectacular *Cornus kousa chinensis* and *Rhododendron yakushimanum* colour the walled garden. A paved yew-hedged garden is bright with herbaceous plants, and the brilliant blue of agapanthus and numerous climbers give a Mediterranean feel to the walled swimming-pool garden. These hidden areas are a series of delightful surprises but it is the terrace behind the house which has the greatest impact. It comes suddenly into view on the far side of an oak door in the forecourt. Suspended above the main garden and backed by the massive spread of the blue cedar, it is decorated with brightly-coloured geometric beds of bulbs and annuals around a central ornamental pond. The South Downs and woodland can be seen in the distance and lawns spread down the slope to the string of ponds in the valley. These divide the more formal garden from the woodland, which is on a gently-rising slope. Its floor is a sea of bluebells in spring. Light filtering through the fresh foliage of young oaks highlights the lively colours of hybrid rhododendrons and azaleas. Primulas grow along the banks of curling streams and there are wild flowers such as spotted orchids. The natural woodland has been enriched so skilfully that its beauty appears artless. The lower branches of trees are lopped to give a feeling of space and to create vistas, and cool mossy or mown grass paths add to the peace of the whole.

A bog and water garden are filled with moisture-loving plants; a young arboretum and glades are radiant with beds of Knap Hill azaleas, the National Collection of which Heaselands tends. Towering Monterey pines, surprisingly only fifty years old, and specimen trees and shrubs produce glowing autumn colours in plenty. For so many reasons — plant content, design, condition and size — this exceptionally lovely garden warrants several visits.

HELMINGHAM HALL

MAP G

Stowmarket
9m (14½km) north of Ipswich on B1077
Owner: Lord Tollemache
Tel: Helmingham (047 339) 363
Open Sundays from May to end September and by appointment for parties
(peak months June to September)
Plants for sale

The Tollemache family have owned Helmingham for nearly five hundred years, but it was not until 1510 that the present redbrick house was built. Though the eighteen generations of the family who have lived here have added to and altered the house and its garden over the centuries, both retain a strong Elizabethan character and a timeless and secure atmosphere. Fortune may in the past have seen the decline and rise of the garden, but today it is a shining example of a period English country-house garden and deserves the Grade 1 status awarded by English Heritage.

Moated, like the house, the main part of the garden is reached by crossing a bridge, but between this and the elegant gates of the original walled kitchen garden is a lawn patterned with a parterre of box-edged beds. These are filled with white, sweet-smelling tobacco plants or hazy blue *Viola cornuta* — a disciplined and attractive introduction to the colourful borders within. These borders divide the garden into its traditional four parts, and are luxuriantly planted with warm colours; stronger subjects support delicate climbers, and froths of white gypsophila decorate each corner. Behind these lie the immaculate and productive beds of fruit and vegetables, which extend to the perimeter walls supporting espaliered fruit trees. Wide grass walks surround this ancient walled garden; they are flanked by the Saxon moat and borders planted lushly with shade-loving and grey-leafed plants. Clipped balls of yew form a military guard along the banks of the moat, on which float waterlilies and, to one side, an avenue of old fruit trees creates a division between the garden and park. Ancient oak trees still stand in the park and provide shade for the herd of deer and highland cattle.

A bridge beyond the walled garden leads to a meadow abundant with wild flowers — cowslips, primroses, ox-eye daisies and orchids. Its unsophisticated charm contrasts with the highly-cultivated and formal areas. Two recent additions stand on the far side of the house: a herb garden and a knot garden. Although not open to the public, they can be admired from above. Both are planted, as is the whole garden, with well-associated subjects, shape, colour and texture all having been taken into account. Shades

Bank of wild flowers beside the moat at Helmingham Hall.

of pink and lavender predominate, and creamy foxgloves rise above shrub roses in the geometric beds edged with dwarf box or lavender.

HERGEST CROFT GARDENS

MAP E

Kington, near Hereford
½m (1km) off A44 on the western outskirts of Kington. Hereford 20m (32km) to the south-east
Owners: Mr R. A. Banks, and Mr W. L. Banks
(HHA)
Tel: Kington (0544) 230160
Open daily May to mid-September; Sundays during October
(peak months May, June and October)
Plants for sale

The proportions and magnificence of the huge trees which surround the Victorian gabled house are so striking, it is hard to believe that the two are of an age, many of the trees having been planted in 1896, when the house was built. Nurtured and added to by the same family for over a hundred years, it was William Banks who first started this outstanding collection of trees and shrubs. As soon as newly introduced seed became available, some collected in China by planthunters such as E. H. Wilson, it was planted. No one knew how fast or large the trees would grow and not enough space was left between them, so, a number have had to be felled to make room for greedier subjects. Despite this and the loss of others due to old age, Hergest Croft is remarkable for its great number of unusual trees, seldom seen at such exceptional size.

Shrubs, particularly rhododendrons from China and Tibet, were also planted at that time and many can be found in Park Wood, across the fields from the gardens. You catch the scent of balsam poplars, *Rhododendron loderi* and common yellow azalea as you explore the fifty-acre garden. *Vitis coignetiae* and Dutchman's pipe cascade out of a gingko near the yew-hedged croquet lawn, and conifers, like skyscrapers, cast shadow over smaller trees and shrubs.

The National Collections of maples and birches can be seen here, together with aralias, variegated sweet chestnuts, magnolias, eucryphias, strawberry and handkerchief trees and unusual hazels, beeches, firs, redwoods and pines. Azaleas, deutzias, berberis and viburnums proliferate, and many other flowering shrubs extend the season of interest. Beyond an orchard is the kitchen garden, with box-hedged beds and herbaceous borders; its cottage-garden charm contrasts with the drama and majesty of the rest of the gardens.

Autumn colour near the yew-hedged croquet garden at Hergest Croft.

153

HERTERTON HOUSE

MAP A

Hartington, near Cambo
Signposted 'Hartington' just off the Hexham to
Alnwick road, B6342; 2m (3km) north of Cambo
Owners: Mr and Mrs F. Lawley
Tel: Scots Gap (067 074) 278
Open several afternoons a week from May to
September and parties by appointment
(peak season summer)
Plants for sale

Thirty miles from the coast and seven hundred feet above sea level, this one-acre plantsman's garden shows that harsh conditions — long, bitterly cold winters and biting winds — do not prevent a garden being filled with fascinating and lovely plants. Well over one thousand varieties find a home here; unusual forms of wild or old-fashioned plants predominate, all having proved themselves hardy. The paths in the various gardens are of river grit and these and not lawns divide the patterns of geometric beds. Because little grows over shoulder height, the impression is of a richly-embroidered carpet, and though there are some strong evergreen shapes the garden has been planted mainly for summer colour.

At the front of the house is a small garden laid out as a parterre. Four different varieties of box hedge beds lined with variegated London pride and golden thyme. At the centre are dicentras, crown imperials and lilies. A herb garden contains a knot and is planted with medicinal and dye herbs — southernwood and camphor, tansy, hyssop and lavender. At the centre is a silver weeping pear underplanted with variegated periwinkle.

The large walled garden also has geometric beds, bursting with well-associated groups of plants. Not an inch of earth can be spied in these, the moisture being retained and weeds suppressed by a dressing of the same river grit used for the paths. The beds have stepping-stones, which allow inspection at close quarters. Old-fashioned 'florist's' flowers jostle for attention — pinks, wild flowers, rare mutations, double and variegated varieties of familiar cottage-garden plants, unusual campanulas, geums, daisies, aquilegia and violas.

The Lawleys have lived here since 1975 and transformed what was a wilderness set around a farmyard and neglected buildings. They have been collecting hardy plants for well over twenty years, propagating them in the adjoining nursery, and are generous with advice on their origins and how to care for them.

HESTERCOMBE HOUSE GARDENS

MAP I

Cheddon Fitzpaine, near Taunton
Off the A361, turn north-west to Cheddon
Fitzpaine, 4m (6½km) from Taunton
Owner: Somerset County Council
Tel: Taunton (0823) 337222
Open weekdays throughout the year and some
Sundays
(peak seasons spring and summer)

Admirers of the work of Gertrude Jekyll and Edwin Lutyens will find this garden — a painstakingly-restored example of their collaborative work — of particular interest. A house has stood on this south-facing site since the twelfth century, but its outward appearance has frequently been changed. Lord Portman bought it towards the end of the nineteenth century and transformed a Queen Anne house into an impressive, but not altogether lovely, mansion. This stands above the garden which his grandson, the Honourable E. W. B. Portman, commissioned the fashionable architect and respected garden designer to lay out in 1903. By 1973 it was in a sorry state; the stone work had subsided and little remained of Jekyll's distinctive plantings. Meticulous research and much hard work over the following five years has resulted in planting almost exactly to her plans; though still causing some problems, the stonework again reflects Lutyens's outstanding skill with this material.

You enter the garden from the top terrace which affords a fine view of the gardens below.

At the centre of the picture is a geometrically-designed plat or parterre surrounded by raised terraced walks. Running the whole length of the far end is a stone-pillared pergola which forms a division between the garden and the natural landscape. The once-famous elms have disappeared and the pergola, covered in climbers, stands somewhat starkly against the rural scene, so you tend to focus attention on the detail within the walled garden. The strong architectural framework married to the natural style of planting is typically Lutyens and Jekyll. Various sorts and shapes of stone have been mixed to form patterns and textures and the rills which run down the terraces either side of the plat; there are stone *claire-voies* and perfectly proportioned, rounded flights of steps. Miss Jekyll's beloved cottage-garden plants are represented by catmint, lavender, lamb's ears and soapwort. Beds of shrub roses, peonies and hellebores are edged with bergenia and, as might be expected, the colouring of the whole is gentle and harmonious. The old millstones, set into stone at significant points, also show her signature.

The circular stone walls of the rotunda on the top terrace alter the direction of attention subtly from south to east. Peaceful and scented, with a central mirror pool, it is a winning architectural device and feature. It leads to the generously-proportioned flight of steps down to Lutyens's symmetrical and classical orangery. The Dutch garden stands on a raised terrace to the east of this elegant building. It has also been planted as Miss Jekyll wished: with roses, her much-loved yuccas, nepeta and lavender.

Edwin Lutyens' and Gertrude Jekyll's formal plat garden at Hestercombe House.

HEVER CASTLE

MAP J

Hever, near Edenbridge
3m (5km) south-east of Edenbridge off B2026
Owner: Broadlands Properties Limited
Tel: Edenbridge (0732) 865224
Open daily from beginning of April to end of
October

The history of this fairytale thirteenth-century castle is touched with romance: Henry VIII courted Anne Boleyn here. The castle resembles a fortress but is a double-moated manor house. The gardens and the Tudor village near Anne's childhood home did not exist in her day; they were laid out at the beginning of this century by the anglicised American millionaire, William Waldorf Astor. He was a great collector of antiquities and acquired many during his ambassadorship in Rome; he decided to make a garden where he could display his fine collection and create surroundings in sympathy with the character of the castle. He sought the advice of his architect, F. J. Pearson, and commissioned the Surrey firm of J. Cheal and Son to lay out the gardens which can be seen today. They cover thirty acres, and were laid out and planted between 1904 and 1908; a further thirty-five acres were used to make a lake. Part formal and part natural, the various architectural and botanical features were placed to complement each other and to suit their situations.

Between the inner and outer moat are period gardens and features in keeping with the age of the castle: the yew-hedged maze and topiary have been clipped to resemble sixteenth-century chess pieces in the enclosed Anne Boleyn garden, and the orchard is strewn with spring bulbs. The vast four-acre Italian garden is quite different; decorated with statuary, busts, sarcophagi, columns and vases, it was designed by Pearson, who also built the Tudor village. The impressive man-made rather than the botanical features have the strongest impact: the immense loggia flanked by colonnades whose steps run down to a piazza and fountain on the lakeside, the half-moon pond, and the classical and renaissance

pieces which decorate the alcoves of the long north wall. A pergola draped with climbers of all sorts runs the length of the south wall; it is screened by yew hedges and is an intimate 'room' where softly-coloured beds surround a pool. The garden has a genuine Italian feeling about it, despite its proximity to an ancient English castle, and its scale, contents and grandeur are quite unlike anything else to be seen in this country.

South of the Italian garden there are rose and rock gardens. The rock garden is planted with blue flowering plants which grow between and over huge slabs of rock from the Chiddingstone Causeway. Rhododendrons and azaleas colour an informal walk and an old quarry, and throughout the garden there are handsome native and specimen trees and unusual shrubs. To imply that plants are a secondary consideration at Hever would be quite wrong — there is much to interest the enthusiast here — but so appropriate is the choice and placing of subjects that it is the overall picture, rather than individual plants, which holds the attention.

HIDCOTE MANOR GARDEN

MAP F

Hidcote Bartrim, near Chipping Campden
4m (6½km) north-east of Chipping Campden, 1m
(2km) east of A46 off B4081
Owner: The National Trust
Tel: Mickleton (0386) 438 333
Open regularly from Easter to end October;
parties by appointment only

This early twentieth-century garden had and continues to have an enormous influence on garden-making in this country. An original when it was created, it is still a source of inspiration. Hidcote covers ten acres and is an extraordinarily successful marriage of contradictory elements: formal bone structure offset by informal planting; the generous nature of a cottage garden juxtaposed with serene simplicity; the 'natural' with the highly cultivated and formal, and cosy intimacy with restrained elegance. No one could fail to relate to the garden and translate, with ease, one of its individual 'rooms' to their own plot.

When Major Lawrence Johnston's mother gave him the two-hundred-and-eighty-acre property in 1907, all that stood on the escarpment was the small Cotswold manor house, the cedar nearby, two clumps of beech trees and farmland. The first priority was shelter and the Major planted hedges of all sorts. These, and others added later, provide the formal framework of a garden which is predominantly formal in layout. These hedged compartments open one into another, or are set on different levels and reveal a gentle string of surprises. Informal areas — the stream garden, the spring slope and shrub and specimen tree garden (Westonbirt) — flow away to the east and west of the wide hedged corridor known as the long walk, a soothingly 'natural' contrast to the formality.

A garden laid out like this is no longer unique, but at the beginning of the century Major Johnston was breaking new ground. An American by birth, his formative years were spent in France and certain features — the unadorned long walk, the stilt garden with its immaculately-clipped pleached hornbeams and architectural hedges and vistas — are reminiscent of the great French and Italian gardens of an earlier age. His education was completed at Cambridge and by 1900 he had become a British citizen. The years before Hidcote obviously engendered in him a love and sensitivity for the English countryside.

A talented plantsman, he took advantage of all the new plants which were being introduced at the time, and accompanied well-known planthunters, like George Forrest and Major Collingwood or 'Cherry' Ingram, on expeditions to China and South Africa. Consequently an amazingly wide collection of unusual plants intermingles with those of a more humble nature. Near the manor house, which stands modestly, almost hiding, at the side of the gardens, are exuberantly-planted 'rooms' of a cottage-garden nature. Herbaceous plants mingle with roses; flowering shrubs and clematis and the dark yew hedges and dumpy box topiary birds in the white garden offset the cream and white-flowering plants and the brilliant red of *Tropaeolum speciosum*, swags of which look like ruby necklaces casually flung on to the hedges.

Plants have been used in a more disciplined manner in the fuchsia garden. Neat box-edged beds of variegated and hybrid fuchsias are enclosed by a 'tapestry' hedge of copper beech, box, holly and yew. A sunbaked Mediterranean atmosphere has been created in a paved area named after the major's mother, Mrs Winthrop, and pots of aloe and cordylines with beds of blue and yellow flowers provide the interest here. The strong shape of the clipped yews in the pillar garden is emphasised by extrovert and blowsy peonies, old-fashioned shrubs and species roses which Major Johnston did much to popularise. They are also generous and fragrant in the old kitchen garden.

There are over a score of different gardens at Hidcote and if all were as luxuriantly planted as these, or as stunningly coloured as the double red borders below the elegant gazebos, the banquet would be indigestible. Like palate-clearing water-ices, eye-cooling features are provided in the shape of the simple and serene bathing pool garden, where the severe lines of dense yew hedges are mirrored in the raised circle of water. Of much larger proportions but equally and courageously restrained in design is the theatre lawn. A handsome beech underplanted with spring bulbs takes the stage at the far end of an 'auditorium' formed of yew hedges and lawn, unadorned, except for a group of hornbeams. The stream gardens and woodland are 'natural' in character but no less thoughtfully laid out and planted. The colours, textures and shapes of a wealth of moisture- and shade-loving plants, bulbs, flowering shrubs and specimen trees make it of interest throughout the season.

Hidcote was the first important garden to be taken over by the National Trust, in 1948 and, with Sissinghurst, it now tops the popularity poll. This poses appalling problems for those tending a garden not specifically designed to accommodate hordes of visitors. The wear and tear on paths and lawns is considerable and to a large extent unavoidable. Certain living features have been lost due to old age or damage by

157

severe weather, and the expert might feel that the planting in certain areas no longer reflects the Major's taste. New plants have become available, others have lost their allure — who is to say how he would have persuaded the gardens to evolve over the years?

THE HIGH BEECHES

MAP J

Handcross, near Crawley
4m (6½km) south of Crawley on A23 at
Handcross
Owners: Mr and Mrs E. Boscawen
Tel: Handcross (0444) 400589
Open a few days a year for charity and by
appointment for parties
(peak months April to June and October)
Plants for sale

Privately owned and less well known than the gardens of Leonardslee and Wakehurst, High Beeches has much in common with those woodland gardens. All three were created by members of the Loder family at the turn of the century, when William Robinson was sounding the death-knell of the artificial Victorian garden and urging garden owners to plan and plant in a naturalistic way. Sussex, like Surrey, offered the perfect terrain to develop such gardens, and the wealth of new hardy plants being introduced from China, India and Japan ideally suited the conditions.

The Loders, — Edmund at Leonardslee, Gerald at Wakehurst and their nephew Giles who inherited The High Beeches — were well-known enthusiasts and had many friends and connections in the horticultural world. They developed and enriched their gardens with plants (often grown from seed) brought back by plant-hunters like E. H. Wilson, Francis Kingdon Ward and George Forrest, and the twenty-eight acres of garden at High Beeches were filled with a glorious collection of unusual trees and shrubs. Many of these have now grown to, an impressive and seldom-seen size and could be said to be in their prime. But the gardens are not a living

museum for unusual specimens: the overall effect has been as carefully considered as the needs of an individual plant.

When Colonel Giles Loder inherited the old house (burnt down in 1942) at the beginning of the century, it was surrounded by a formal garden. He left this untouched, choosing to create a new garden in a wooded valley some distance from the house. The valley lies on the far side of a meadow where wild flowers are now encouraged. The south-facing slope is veined with ghylls or small valleys down which spring-fed streams run. The natural beauty of the woodland has been carefully preserved, and it has a peaceful and open character. The lower branches of the trees have been cut, so there are fine vistas down the ghylls: the mossy and turfed floor is a sea of primroses, wild daffodils and bluebells in spring and of naturalised willow gentian in autumn.

Mown grass paths weave around the woodland, down to the centre pond encircled by gunnera, over bridges draped with the large leaves of a *vitis coignetiae* and around rhododendrons introduced by George Forrest. Ditches and the banks of streams are bright with Asiatic primulas, and a number of unusual and stately conifers are set against the fresh young foliage of woodland trees. Camellias are followed by scores of large-leafed and scented hybrid rhododendrons which have now reached huge proportions. Then there are the brilliant colours of azaleas and the common *Rhododendron luteum* which, having seeded itself freely, fills the air with fragrance. There are a great number of ornamental and specimen trees — magnificent and rarely seen magnolias, Japanese and American maples, a handkerchief tree and *Cornus kousa chinensis* grown from seed collected by Ernest Wilson, handsome cut-leaf beech, and the National Collections of styrax, stuartias and pieris. In autumn the burning foliage of nyssas, parrotias, *Fothergilla monticola* and a host of other trees and shrubs sets fire to the woodland.

HIGHDOWN

MAP J

**Littlehampton Road, Goring-by-Sea, near
Worthing
On A259 3m (5km) west of Worthing
Owner: Worthing Borough Council
Tel: Worthing (0903) 501054
Open regularly throughout the year
(peak months May and June)**

Because Highdown is owned by the Worthing
Borough Council the reader should not think
that this is a park rather than a garden. Nothing
could be further from the truth, for these gardens, in a disused chalk-pit in the side of
Highdown Hill, are unique. If ever there was an
inhospitable site for a garden this was it, but
Sir Frederick Stern, (once secretary to Lloyd
George) was undaunted and began to develop a
garden here in 1909. After much experiment, it
was found that success could be achieved if very
young subjects were planted and allowed to
acclimatise slowly. By the time Sir Frederick,
who was knighted of his services to horticulture,
had died in 1967, the garden was established
and famous.

The lower part of the garden is relatively
formal, but there is a large area of lawn with
informal borders. These are planted with a
glorious array of tree and perennial peonies,
irises, lilies, flowering shrubs and shrub roses.
Lilacs, maples, Judas and other ornamental
trees stand on the lawns and, above, an avenue
of beech divides it from the chalk-pit garden.
Here, a central lawn forms a pool of green, on
and around which shrubs and trees colour the
banks and steep cliff of chalk. Sunken, rock and
water gardens have replaced the pigsties which
once stood here, and an old lime kiln, lined with
local stone, has been made into a cave. Mature
shrubs, like the viburnum on the lawn and
unusual trees — an Indian chestnut and a
handkerchief tree — have grown to impressive
proportions considering that only a thin layer of
soil covers the chalk. Snowdrops were of particular interest to Sir Frederick, and bulbs have
naturalised themselves, together with daffodils,

cyclamen, anemone blanda and crocuses. A
path along the boundary is thickly lined with the
crisp foliage and flowers of hellebores, interspersed with the yellow-flowering peony from
the Caucasus, *P. mlokosewitschii*. There is no
corner of this well-kept garden not worth exploring, and the individuality of its character has
been preserved.

THE HILL

MAP J

**Hampstead, North End Road, London NW11
Entrance to the north side of Inverforth Manor
House Hospital, off North End Road
Owner: The London Residuary Board (until
further notice)
Tel: London (01) 455 5183
Open daily from dawn to dusk**

Set into the hillside overlooking Hampstead
Heath next to Jack Straw's Castle, these are the
gardens of an impressive residence built by Lord
Leverhulme at the beginning of the century. The
advantages of its position were many: there was
a fine view of the heath and the high ground of
Hampstead rose above the smog of the city but
offered easy access to the heart of London for
business and entertainment. Highly architectural, they were designed by Thomas Mawson,
and though part of them is on the verge of decay
they are well worth visiting and should be of
interest to the garden historian.

The soil from the newly-cut Hampstead tube
line was used to build a plateau on the steep
hillside where the house, lawns and pergolas
were built. The scale of these Italianate pergolas
is unusually large. They strike out at various
angles, and bays overhang the Heath like the
prows of old ships. Constructed of Portland
stone and English oak, the vistas down the walks
and the fine detail of craftsmanship are still
evident despite neglect, and what must have
been some of the original climbing plants, such
as wisterias and roses, tumble over stylish pavilions and walks. The ground falls sharply away
below these haunted 'sleeping beauty' tunnels,
and the lower part of the garden lies to one side.

Bluebells in the woodland garden at High Beeches.

This is still well maintained and has a sunken stone terrace and pool. Informal walks and paths flow down the hill past groups of rhododendrons and other shrubs set around the lawn sloping down to the Heath.

HILLIER GARDENS AND ARBORETUM

MAP I

Jermyns Lane, Ampfield, near Romsey
In Jermyns Lane, off the A31, 9m (14½km)
southwest of Winchester
Owner: Hampshire County Council
Tel: Braishfield (0794) 68787
Open regularly throughout the year
(peak months May, June and October)
Plants for sale

For keen gardeners, the name of Hillier is synonymous with excellent hardy trees and shrubs. Since the nursery began in 1864, in Winchester, it has grown to become the largest of its kind in the world, offering an unrivalled wealth of ornamental and specimen hardy woody plants from the five continents. The arboretum, which now covers over a hundred acres, was developed by the late Sir Harold Hillier in 1953 and now contains one of the largest collections of trees and shrubs in the country. In 1977, to ensure its future, Sir Harold gave it to Hampshire County Council and it is now administered by a charitable trust. It is an ideal place for those seeking ideas for planting in their own gardens, to observe and compare varieties and to learn how and where to plant.

Plots of land were planted as they became available, subjects being placed where they would most readily thrive and enhance the natural beauty of the site. Mown grass paths weave between imaginative groupings of shrubs which break up the wide spaces between trees, and large groups of *Magnolia stellata* create lovely groves. No matter what time of year, there is plenty to see, — flowers, foliage and coloured bark and stems of the many different shrubs and trees, as well as carpets of spring bulbs and wild

flowers adding to the well-established picture. Subjects of special interest at a particular time of the year are well marked and listed, and seasonal and special-interest maps are also available, such as those describing where to see Japanese varieties, or those with culinary or medicinal uses.

Around and near to the house are borders planted with herbaceous and late-flowering shrubs, and scree, heather, bog and peat gardens. There are walks to the pond and three-acre paddock where grasses and rowans, oaks and birches that produce good autumn colour have been planted, to the distant acer valley and the whitegate border planted with hibiscus, cotoneasters and the most spectacular of fruiting euonymus, *E. europaeus* 'Red Cascade'. At the far end of the long centenary border are *Acer saccharum*, the sugar maples from which maple syrup is made, and on the western boundary of ten acres is a birch, *Betula lenta*, whose bark is used to produce Wintergreen oil. The arboretum can be enjoyed on many different levels and will give as much pleasure to the amateur as to the professional.

HINTON AMPNER

MAP I

near Alresford
(Bookings and enquiries to Manor Farm,
Bramdean, near Alresford)
Entrance on A272 1m (2km) west of Bramdean
village about 6m (9½km) east of Winchester
Owner: The National Trust
Tel: Bramdean (096 279) 344
Open several days a week from Easter to end
September

In the possession of the Trust only since 1985, this period Hidcote-style garden was the creation of Ralph Dutton, eighth Lord Sherborne. When he inherited the estate in 1934, his knowledge of garden history and of architecture led him to replant and design the park and garden with skill and perception, giving it strong 'bones' and many delightful surprise vistas and features. The framework is formal, the planting relaxed,

Formal walk at Hinton Ampner.

Without knowing their history it would be difficult to date the gardens at Hodnet. The graceful landscape with its lakes and vistas has an eighteenth-century air, but the generosity and character of the planting is of a much later date. The fact that they were laid out after 1922 by the present owner's father, Brigadier A. G. Heber-Percy makes them a unique example of twentieth-century garden-making. It is easy to say now that the site dictated the design, the house commanding a view over a series of lakes to the open countryside beyond, but it must have taken considerable courage and imagination to create those lakes out of swampy ponds and clear the trees to reveal the seventeenth-century dovecote (an eyecatcher) on the far hill.

The soil is lime-free, so the sixty acres of mainly informal gardens are planted generously with rhododendrons, azaleas and camellias, and a rewarding collection of unusual and tender shrubs and trees. The high standard of upkeep achieved by only three full-time gardeners creates a picture of peace and order, with lawns and 'natural' areas acting as a foil to the vitality of the more highly-cultivated parts. They will interest the specialist as well as the garden designer; there are many fine specimens of rare and unusual trees, and a good collection of rhododendrons and azaleas, and the owner has extended the season of interest by introducing a number of summer-flowering subjects.

Balustraded and grassed terraces with a central flight of steps fall away from the south-facing house, which was built in the Elizabethan style around 1870. The top floor and a whole wing of this were demolished to make it more maneagable but the house and the lakes below still play a dominant role. Massed azaleas and other flowering shrubs and trees decorate the lower terrace. Astilbes, hostas, gunnera, primulas and other moisture-loving specimens make huge swathes in the water garden to the west of the main lake. The scene increases in naturalness as you explore: the intensely-planted water garden gives way to woodland which, like so many other areas is carpeted with spring bulbs. The series of lakes, linked one to another, shrink slowly to a stream which meanders into the trees.

with shrubs predominating. The house, now Georgian in style, has been remodelled many times and commands splendid views over the surrounding chalkland.

Set on different levels are a series of gardens linked by features like the straight long walk below the Victorian balustraded terrace, and winding paths, such as the fragrant philadelphus walk to the dell. Stone features — the temple, obelisk and statue of Diana — a rectangular lily pool east of the house, and yew and box hedges give the gardens an air of 'upper-crust' elegance. They are in the process of being restored and can only gain in interest.

HODNET HALL GARDENS

MAP D

Hodnet, near Market Drayton
5½m (9km) south-west of Market Drayton, at
Junction of A53 and A422
Owners: Mr and the Honourable Mrs A.
Heber-Percy (HHA)
Tel: Hodnet (063 084) 202
Open daily from April to end September
(peak months May and June)
Plants for sale

The manmade lake at Hodnet Hall.

On the east a magnolia walk is planted with varieties such as *M. virginiana*, *M. mollicomata*, and *M. sargentiana*, the walk descends between terraces planted with unusual trees, a Chinese maple, contorted hazel, and *Cornus Mas* or cornelian cherry. Together with *Parrotia persica*, *Cercidiphyllum japonicum* and the many different cherries, these add to the brilliant autumn colours of the gardens. An immaculate walled kitchen garden raises fruit and vegetables and plants propagated from the garden, which are for sale. An eye-catching folly in the shape of a classical ruin stands against the sky at the far end of the drive in front of the house. This was saved by Brigadier Heber-Percy from Apsley Castle when it was being demolished and stands as a memorial to the creator of this splendid garden.

HODSTOCK PRIORY

MAP C

Blyth, near Worksop
south-west of Blyth off B6045 Worksop to Blyth
road
Owners: Sir Andrew and Lady Buchanan
Tel: Blyth (090 976) 204
Open a few days a year for charity and by
appointment (peak months May and June)

Over the moat and through the Tudor gatehouse lies a five-acre garden which stands on a site worked since the Bronze Age and recorded in the Domesday Book. The garden is bounded by the moat and ancient earthworks. Features such as the stonework from a twelfth-century chapel, nineteenth-century Italianate terraces around the redbrick house, old yew and ilex hedges and mature trees add touches of romance to what is essentially a twentieth-century garden.

Lawns spread away from terraces enlivened by beds of roses and down to a large pond whose edges are softened by moisture-loving plants. Mixed borders and well-composed groups of shrubs are nearby and areas of acid ground support azaleas and rhododendrons. Bulbs and wild flowers grow on the banks of the moat and there are unusual trees — a contorted willow, swamp cypress, snowdrop tree, maples and superb catalpa. Note the variegated dogwoods near the pond, which have grown to tree-like proportions. A wide range of plants can be grown in the part-acid, part-neutral soil, so there is an interesting mix of contemporary and period features and garden-making styles.

HOLDENBY HOUSE GARDENS

MAP F

Holdenby, near Northampton
7m (11km) north-west of Northampton, off A428
and A50, 7m (11km) from M1 exit 18
Owner: Mr James Lowther (HHA)
Tel: Northampton (0604) 770241 or 770786
Open Sundays and Bank Holiday Mondays from
April to September and Thursdays during July
and August
(peak month June)
Plants for sale

Holdenby was the largest of all Elizabethan 'prodigy' houses and one where the Queen was entertained by her Lord Chancellor and favourite, Sir Christopher Hatton. Not surprisingly the building of the house impoverished Sir Christopher, and after his death it was ceded to the crown in lieu of debts. It then became one of James I's palaces, a prison for Charles I in 1647, the property of the Dukes of Marlborough in the eighteenth century and eventually the home of Colonel John Lowther, the present owner's grandfather. Once a palace in size and concept, Holdenby is now much altered and only one-eighth of its original size. An idea of its former grandeur can be gained from the position of its 1583 entrance arches which stand in an outlying field.

The original twenty-acre Elizabethan garden is buried under grass, but the bones of its terraces can still be detected. The gardens to the east, south and west of the present house cover nine acres, contain period and contemporary features and are a delightful marriage between formal lines and informal planting. They continue to be developed, and new and old features are designed or replanted in a way sympathetic to its great age and character.

In 1980 the garden writer and expert, Mrs Rosemary Verey, designed the Elizabethan garden which contains beds of sixteenth-century plants, particularly herbs, set around a sundial. She also planted the fragrant 'Too Too' borders profuse with lilacs, hybrid musk roses, sweet woodruff and cecily which lead away from the south-facing terraces. Borders along King Charles walk and beside the croquet lawn are filled with shrubs, roses and herbaceous plants, and one beneath the south-facing wall to the east of the house is devoted to grey- and silver-foliaged subjects.

There is an exuberant quality to the planting: the colouring is soft and subjects such as old-fashioned shrub, rambling and climbing roses tumble and clamber over and up walls and hedges. Hidden within a yew-hedged turfed enclosure is an ornamental fish pond and a statue of Hermes surrounded by brightly-coloured beds of perennials, biennials and standard roses. Yew hedges are much in evidence, screening one intensely-planted area from another or emphasising the symmetry and simplicity of a gravelled walk and avenue of young cherries.

Hidden from view behind the hedges of this walk are pens in which Holdenby's rare breeds roam — pigmy goats and Gloucester Old Spot pigs. Ornamental pheasants and a small animals' farm are housed in the walled vegetable garden which is worked in the traditional manner. The outer, older garden, is well worth exploring. A sixteenth-century fish pond can still be seen, as well as a fourteenth-century church. Remodelled by Sir Gilbert Scott in the last century, the church is surrounded with solemn and ancient yews.

HOLEHIRD GARDENS

MAP B

Patterdale Road, Windermere
On Windermere to Ullswater road, 2m (3km)
from centre of Windermere
Owners: Holehird Trust/Lakeland Horticultural
Society
Tel: Lazonby (076 883) 742
Open daily throughout the year
(peak months May and June)

Holehird has one of the most beautiful views of any garden in England, down and over Lake Windermere to the mountains beyond. The aspect is open and a rock garden, terraces and lawns lie on sloping ground above and below the mansion, now a Sue Ryder Home. The garden has been restored and replanted and is tended by members of the Lakeland Horticultural Society. Derelict when they began transforming it in 1971, the garden will absorb the plantsman and give hope to the enthusiast trying to make one on similarly difficult terrain — a glance over the boundary wall at the top of the garden will show the natural rocky ground from which the garden was carved, and climatic conditions include over sixty-eight inches of rainfall a year.

A former owner of the property, Mr H. Leigh Groves, was an enthusiastic nineteenth-century plantsman who commissioned the famous local landscape designer, Thomas Mawson, to build glasshouses for his collection of rare orchids. He also helped finance a plant-collecting expedition to China by Reginald Farrer and William Purdom and enriched his rock and scree garden with a share of their finds. The orchid houses no longer exist but some trees and shrubs from this period survive.

Appropriately, it is the large rock garden which commands most attention today. It is richly and imaginatively filled with alpine, scree- and moisture-loving plants. Dwarf and other conifers and an extensive heather bed give it all-year-round appeal. A recently-planted collection of ferns (increasingly popular) stands in the shade of an oak towards the top of this area, and there are camellias and Himalayan poppies.

A strikingly well-shaped, mature handkerchief tree is a short distance from the entrance to the kitchen garden, which was completely cleared and redesigned in 1981. Climbers and fruit trees decorate the walls, while there are island beds and borders of herbaceous and other plants on and around the lawn. The terraced garden on the far side of the main drive, though not so intensely planted, is attractive with stands of shrubs and specimen trees. The moisture-loving plants along the banks of a stream, pool garden and an old-fashioned fernery add to the interest. The tranquillity, superb position and rich contents of Holehird are matched by the high standards of upkeep.

The Elizabethan garden at Holdenby House.

HOLE PARK

MAP J

Rolvenden, near Cranbrook
on B2086 between Rolvenden and Benenden
Owner: Mr D. G. W. Barham
Tel: Cranbrook (0580) 241251
Open a few days a year for charity and by
appointment for parties
(peak months May, June and October)

Approached along a drive lined with *Metasequoia glyptostroboides*, the sixteen-acre garden at Hole Park will appeal to plantsmen and to all those who appreciate beautiful and well-tended private gardens. They were developed between the wars by the owner's grandfather and contain a fine collection of unusual flowering trees and plants.

Parkland and formal gardens bounded by immaculately-clipped yew hedges spread from the house, and expansive lawns are patterned with the shadows of majestic trees. An admirable balance between restraint and profusion has been achieved — hedges, lawns and trees form a background and foil to intensely-planted areas of the garden. The graceful foliage of a silver weeping pear is accentuated by a backcloth of dark yew, and borders planted with shades of pink and purple or yellow and white decorate formal hedged *allées* and 'rooms'.

Behind the house the policy is planted with eucryphias, a grove of aralias, cornus, cherries, spring bulbs and heathers. Below lie the dell and the woodland garden, where shafts of light filter through the trees and fall on banks of rhododendrons and azaleas, and carpets of bluebells and daffodils. Autumn colour, provided by shrubs and trees such as *Nyssa sylvatica* and maples, make the garden as rewarding to visit in October as it is in May and June. The yellow rose *R. banksiae lutea* climbs the front of the house, which was reduced in 1960 to a quarter of its original size; in a sunny enclosed garden on the foundations of the old house grows *Rosa nitida*, an effective ground-coverer, whose single pink flowers are followed by scarlet prickly fruits and rich autumn foliage.

HOLKER HALL

MAP B

Cark-in-Cartmel, Grange-over-Sands
4m (6½km) west of Grange-over-Sands on
B5277 then a further 4m (6½km) on B5278
Owners: Mr and Mrs Hugh Cavendish
(HHA)
Tel: Flookburgh (044853) 328
Open regularly from Easter to end October
(peak seasons spring, early summer and
autumn)

Only a short distance from the sea, Holker is a soft and lovely contrast to the ruggedness of the Lakeland countryside a short distance to the north. The beautifully-kept gardens, twenty-two acres in all, are part woodland, part formal and essentially Victorian in character, though never heavy or oppressive. Once the home of the Dukes of Devonshire, Holker has seen many changes. An impressive and ornate Victorian wing of the house now overlooks the formal gardens, altered and planted by succeeding generations of Cavendishes. Changes and additions are still being made, like the new shelter belt of trees

recently planted between the park and garden, and the old croquet lawn, which has been turned into an intimate and delightfully-planted garden 'room'.

The formal areas, at their best during the summer, are planted with particularly pretty and well-chosen shrub and rambling roses, peonies and other herbaceous plants. Their gentle colouring is offset by silver weeping pears and well-trimmed hedges. Delicate wrought-iron supports smothered in climbers add to the charm of this area, a light and happy contrast to the somewhat sombre architecture of the house. Herbaceous plants are supported by ingeniously-constructed cages of hazel twigs, typical of the high standards of upkeep.

The woodland garden, on a slope rising to one side of the house, boasts many fine trees — a cut-leaf beech and lime, snowdrop, catalpa, cercidiphyllums and the rarely seen honeysuckle tree as well as a monkey puzzle planted by Joseph Paxton. Rolling grass banks and glades divide groves of mature and recently planted specimen trees and shrubs. Hybrid and other rhododendrons, azaleas and pieris flourish here, as well as enkianthus and cornus. Spring bulbs, wild flowers and bluebells blossom early in the season. A pool and fountain, almost hidden by banks of rhododendrons, appears suddenly, and an elegant flight of steps leads up and past a statue of Neptune to a sunken rose garden designed by Thomas Mawson — a peaceful spot to rest and admire the gardens below.

HOLKHAM HALL

MAP G

Holkham
On the A149 2m (3km) west of Wells-next-the-Sea
Owner: Viscount Coke (HHA)
Tel: Fakenham (0328) 10227
Open a few days a week from late May to late
September

A remarkable number of great landscape architects and garden designers have been involved over the centuries in the development of the landscape at Holkham. Their various contributions make it a fascinating place to visit today. Thomas Coke's 'Grand Tour' in Italy and the growing fashion for picturesque landscape influenced the transformation of the park into a landscape garden in 1718. On his tour Coke had met William Kent, who was to build the supremely-confident Palladian house and develop the park which sweeps up to the walls of the house. Below lies a lake which was once a marsh in a dip, and deer graze and call to each other under majestic clumps of mature trees in the park. You can glimpse Kent's towering obelisk, aligned to the centre of the house, and further energetic exploration will reveal his triumphal arch marking the south approach.

When T. W. Coke, 'Coke of Holkham' later first Earl of Leicester, inherited Holkham in 1776, he wanted to expand the estate and enlarge the lake. This involved moving the old kitchen garden to a new, larger site. William Emes, a student of 'Capability' Brown's, added sluice gates and changed the shape of the lake, and Samuel Wyatt built the vinery and the lodges to the extended park. In the 1780s Humphry Repton created a pleasure garden for Mrs Coke beside the lake, but this romantic feature, incorporating a boathouse, hermitage, pavilion and grottoes, was demolished in the mid-nineteenth century to improve the view of the woodland beyond.

The Victorian era saw the building of the eyecatching monument to the first Earl, a renowned agricultural reformer. Towering against the skyline and aligned through the centre of the house on the obelisk, it was paid for by public subscription and cost an amazing £5,409 19s 3d. Many of the trees and shrubs being introduced to this country were also planted during this period. The second Earl of Leicester commissioned the successful Victorian garden designer, W. A. Nesfield, and the architect William Burn, to lay out the magnificent terraces on the south front. These are decorated with intricate parterres, an elegant basin and a fountain depicting St George struggling with the dragon. Powerful and proud, a large lion and lioness cast by Boehm stand guard at the front of the house, an impressive introduction to the nobility of Holkham.

HOLME PIERREPONT HALL

MAP F

Holme Pierrepont, Nottingham
4m (6½km) east of Nottingham off the A52 at edge of West Bridgford, past National Water Sports Centre
Owners: Mr and Mrs Robin Brackenbury (HHA)
Tel: Radcliffe-on-Trent (060 73) 2371
Open Easter, Spring and Summer holidays, Sunday, Monday and Tuesday, and Sunday, Tuesday, Thursday, Friday June to August. Parties by appointment throughout year, including evenings.
(peak season summer)

Visited in conjunction with the sixteenth-century courtyard house, one of the first brick buildings in the county, the outer and courtyard gardens should be of interest to the garden historian and those involved in restoring period gardens. The formal courtyard was designed to be viewed from the windows above, and contains a French-style box parterre which it is thought was laid out in 1875 by the third Earl Manvers's French wife, the daughter of the Duc de Coigny. Herbaceous borders stand beneath the courtyard walls and rose gardens flank the parterre. To the east of the house, on the site of a seventeenth-century garden, the outer garden is decorated with yew hedges and an avenue of dome-shaped yews. Both house and garden were in a sorry state when the present owners began restoration in 1970, and the work still continues.

HOW CAPLE COURT

MAP E

How Caple, near Ross-on-Wye
5m (8km) north of Ross-on-Wye, 10m (16km) south of Hereford on B4224; turn right at How Caple crossroad, garden 400yds (360m) on left
Owners: Mr and Mrs Peter Lee
Tel: How Caple (098 986) 626
Open daily from April to October
(peak seasons spring and early summer)
Plants for sale

Those struggling to reclaim a period garden will find How Caple, high above a bend of the River Wye, of particular interest. There is an air of drama and romance, engendered by the design of the Edwardian gardens and their partially unreclaimed state. Exploration of the eleven acres is a voyage of discovery, and you may well feel the same excitement as the owners when you alight upon the sunken Florentine garden, yet to be restored. The red sandstone house, part seventeenth-century and part Victorian, hangs over the gardens, the steep slopes on two sides being laid out with terraces which drop to a lawn sunk in a valley.

Herbaceous beds on the west terraces were laid out by Alan Bloom and features like huge copper Japanese vases add interest. Those to the south are divided by hedges and are strongly architectural and intensively decorated with stonework — walls, steps, ponds, statuary, copper dye-vats planted with hydrangeas and seats. They resemble a folly. The Florentine gardens at the edge of the woodland are reminiscent of an illustration from *Sleeping Beauty*: the classical-style stonework, walks and buildings are still partially masked by the wild plants which try to claim it. There are many fine trees in the garden, and spring bulbs, flowering shrubs, roses and unusual herbaceous plants.

HOWICK HALL

MAP A

Howick, near Alnwick
6m (9½km) north-east of Alnwick on B1339
Owner: Howick Trustees Limited (HHA)
Tel: Longhoughton (066 577) 285
Open daily from April to September
(peak months April to June)

Protected from icy winds by a low ridge and woodland, a surprising number of tender trees and shrubs thrive here, and the woodland garden resembles those on the west rather than the colder east coast of the country. The home of the Grey family who played an important role in England's political history, the eighteenth-

Rhododendrons in the woodland garden at Howick Hall.

century hall is surrounded by ten acres of grounds. The mature trees which encircle the estate were planted during the Napoleonic wars, when the Whig Greys, ousted by the Tories, retired to tend their estates.

In 1930 Lord Grey discovered acid soil in an area of old woodland to the east and began to create the woodland garden which is now such a delight to explore. The edges of paths are bright with primulas, and the delicious scent of white rhododendrons and the common yellow azalea fills the air. Magnolias, camellias and cherries add colour to glades, and smaller subjects — scillas, anemones and meconopsis — form carpets of blue. So skilfully has the woodland been planted that the presence of unusual shrubs and trees like pieris, eucryphias and acers does not give it a contrived appearance but enhances its natural beauty.

Lord and Lady Grey's daughter, Lady Howick, has replaced subjects which reached the end of their natural lives and restored neglected areas; she has also planted an arboretum and built up a collection of wild plants. Some of these have been raised from seed collected in North America. Single varieties of all kinds of spring bulbs have naturalised themselves under specimen trees and in the meadow near the well-proportioned stone house. These are replaced by ox-eye daisies in summer and pink and white autumn crocus in late August. An army of red-hot pokers stands against the dark yew hedges enclosing an intimate 'room' overhung by the blue-grey branches of an Atlantic cedar. On the balustraded terraces in front of the house are borders of shrubs, roses and perennials, and agapanthus form vivid ribbons of blue. Northumberland is better known for its castles than its gardens, but Howick, well fortified by its woodland, is a rewarding haven.

HYDE HALL GARDEN

MAP J

Rettendon, near Chelmsford
7m (11 km) south-east of Chelmsford on A130
turn east at Rettendon to East Hanningfield
Owner: Hyde Hall Garden Trust
Tel: Chelmsford (0245) 400256
Open Wednesdays, Sundays and Bank Holidays
throughout the year and by appointment
(peak months April to October)
Plants for sale

Created around a seventeenth-century farmhouse and working farm, the first-rate plantsman's garden at Hyde Hall was begun in 1959 by Dick and Helen Robinson. Their aim was simply to tidy up the neglected areas around the farmhouse but their enthusiasm, knowledge and creative talents grew rapidly and the garden now covers twenty acres, twelve of which are devoted to specimen and ornamental trees.

It is hard to believe that it all began with a sad collection of six trees and a farm pond. These stood on an inhospitable hilltop blasted by winds from every direction and had the lowest rainfall in England, and soil which, though neutral, was a mixture of heavy clay and impermeable gravel. It was hardly the ideal spot for a garden, although there were few frosts and a lot of sunshine. Well sheltered now by judiciously planted trees and hedges and immaculately kept by the Robinsons, the garden comprises a series of different areas varying in character and design, and displays an outstandingly large collection of unusual plants.

South of the house, the pond has been transformed into an ornamental lily pool surrounded by low growing plants and flanked by a long border of modern roses. Adjoining areas are laid out with borders or island beds, divided by grass paths and lawns, such as the woodland garden of camellias, magnolias, cornus, cyclamen and other acid- and shade-loving plants. The gold garden has yellow foliage and flowered or berried plants. A border divided into sections by buttresses of yew creates a series of pictures with different colouring, in which day lilies and peonies play a major role. Bearded irises, the National Collection of viburnums, plants with coloured twigs and bark which provide interest in winter, heathers and dwarf conifers have all been provided with the right growing conditions and suitable positions. Unusual trees abound, such as the National Collection of malus in what is known as the Pig Park, which also contains old roses. Note all the different hedging materials — even field maples have been used to create an effective screen — and the clever way the rampant 'Kiftsgate' rose has been persuaded into a vast mound which perfectly displays its flowers but contains its riotous growth.

If this were not feast enough, there are four greenhouses containing tender and exotic plants. Lapageria, daturas and an intriguing fruit-scented *Michelia figo* grow in the cool house. Alpines and bulbs fill the alpine house, a colourful range of pot plants the conservatory, and lush exotics the warm house. Terraces near the house are decorated with urns and tubs filled with inspired mixtures of bulbs, annuals, foliage and other plants, and the sunbaked walls support unusual clematis, roses and tender climbers.

ICKWORTH

MAP G

The Rotunda, Horringer, near Bury St Edmunds
In Horringer on west side of A143 3m (5km)
south-west of Bury St Edmunds
Owner: The National Trust
Tel: Horringer (028 488) 270
Open regularly from Easter to mid-October

Built between 1794 and 1830, Ickworth was not intended as a home so much as a resting-place for a magnificent collection of furniture, pictures and silver collected on his travels by the fourth Earl of Bristol. An impressive central rotunda rises above the low, curved wings which link it to the neo-classical pavilions at either end. Many architects were consulted before an Italian, Mario Asprucci, was commissioned to design this Italian-style villa on a south-facing site. The gardens were planned to flatter the style of the house and are therefore formal.

There are some highly-cultivated areas but the overall impression is of space punctuated with fine evergreen trees, hedges, lawns divided by wide gravel walks, and woodland. A domed summerhouse has a background of dark cypress trees, and magnolias, one with an exceptionally thick trunk, stand out against the box hedges and evergreens which edge the terrace. The vast sweeping curve of this terrace divides the garden from the countryside and looks like the massive semi-circular prow of a ship. The church tower rises above a distant clump of trees; the village was moved so as not to spoil the view.

A walk decorated with arches of rambling roses and underplanted with hellebores and low-growing subjects leads back to the west pavilion and orangery, where there are fatshederas, scented geraniums and fuschsias. A border lies below the balustraded curve of drive in front of the house, and venerable cedars cast shadows over the lawns. Walks, (one of scented plants) weave through the surrounding woodland. On a fine day it is hard to imagine how vulnerable this garden is to bad weather. Its position is cruelly exposed and its trees have had to battle the elements to survive.

The rotunda at Ickworth framed by cedars.

Flight of steps decorated with antique and classical features at Iford Manor.

IFORD MANOR GARDENS

MAP I

Iford, Bradford-on-Avon
2½m (4km) from Bradford-on-Avon via
Westwood, 7m (11km) from Bath signed
Iford off A36
Owner: Mrs E. Cartwright Hignett (HHA)
Tel: Bradford-on-Avon (022 16) 3146
Open Wednesdays, Sundays and Bank Holidays
May to August and by appointment
Plants for sale occasionally

The warm stone of Iford's elegant façade over-looks an unspoilt valley threaded by the River Frome. Immediately in front of the house this is spanned by an ancient stone bridge with a statue of Britannia. The garden, behind a high boundary wall, is to the back and side of the house on ground which rises steeply to woodland. The woodland provides shelter and a backcloth to the romantic terraces below. There has been a manor at Iford since the days of Edward the Confessor and, though the present house has changed over the centuries, its garden is essentially the creation of Harold Peto, whose home it became in 1899. His love of Italian Renaissance architecture and garden design in which stonework, statuary and water are important is demonstrated in his own garden.

It is decorated generously (perhaps too much so for some tastes) with antique stone and other ornaments he bought or had copied from those seen in Italy. Though strongly architectural in character, it is also a flower garden and beds of shrubs, herbaceous and other plants stand around lawns and colour the rock and water gardens. Low-growing subjects and climbers, including many wisteria, pattern and trail over the sunbaked terraces. Cypress trees create a suitably Italian effect. On one side are the cloisters, which Peto had built in the Italian Romanesque style to house his collection of archaeological objects — a thirteenth-century well-head, Roman sarcophagi, pieces of Renaissance sculpture and much else of historical interest are here and on the terraces. These do not look out of place, despite the intensely English setting.

ISABELLA PLANTATION

MAP J

Richmond Park, Greater London
Between Robin Hood and Kingston Gates in
Richmond Park, entrances off A307, A205, A306
and A3
Owner: Department of the Environment
Tel: (01) 948 3209
Open daily
(peak season spring)

Few, if any, capital cities boast a magnificent deer park like Richmond on their doorstep. It is a pocket of natural beauty which many city dwellers might otherwise never see and, no matter what time of year, it gracefully absorbs the thousands who come to enjoy some of its many delights: fine old trees, peaceful walks, ponds and a lake. Far from all are aware that a beautiful and richly planted garden is set within its woodland.

Covering forty-two acres, the Isabella Plantation was laid out in 1840, but was not properly developed until 1950, when J. W. Fisher began to enrich its contents; its development has continued ever since. Under a canopy of mature trees, beside the stream and ponds and around peaceful glades are massed plantings of classic woodland subjects — rhododendrons, camellias, evergreen and deciduous azaleas and moisture-loving plants. The long view down the stream from the top half of the garden is an unforgettable sight in May, when the azaleas, primulas and hostas make a vibrant and lush serpentine river of interest. Banks of rhododendrons are reflected in the surface of the lake, carpets of spring bulbs and wild flowers cover the woodland floor, and camellias jewel shady walks. In mid-winter the distinctive scent of the witch-hazels is caught well before you reach the entrance to the garden, and they and other specimen trees provide interest through the year. Paths lead down to the heather garden, across bridges and stepping-stones, winding through woodland and around ponds. The pond below the heather garden is surrounded by dogwoods and willows. Though

Path and stream lined with azaleas in the Isabella Plantation.

Moisture-loving plants abound — rheums, rodgersias, hostas and Asiatic primulas decorate a pond bed. Spring bulbs have naturalised themselves under and around trees and shrubs. Inspection will reveal that this is plantsman's garden; many unusual varieties of day lilies, alliums and oriental poppies colour the borders and the damp conditions enable the National Collections of moisture-loving lobelia and trollius to be grown here. Beside the cottage is a small raised bed of alpines, and roses and specimen trees and shrubs grow on higher ground. Anne Stevens is a talented and enthusiastic plantswoman, who has created a fascinating and enchantingly pretty garden: one in perfect sympathy with the character of her home.

at its best in spring, the Plantation is a pleasure to visit throughout the year and is as hospitable to birds as to people.

IVY COTTAGE

MAP I

Ansty, near Dorchester
12m (19km) north of Dorchester. Turn left off A354 from Puddletown to Blandford; after Blue Vinney Inn take first left signposted Dewlish/Cheslebourne; through Cheslebourne, then first right before Fox Inn in Ansty
Owners: Anne and Alan Stevens
Tel: Milton Abbas (0258) 880053
Open several days a year for charity, on Thursdays in April and September, and by appointment for parties
Plants for sale

Ivy Cottage, nestling in the soft Dorset countryside, must be everyone's dream of a thatched country cottage. The garden sloping away from it is planted with traditional generosity and covers one-and-a-half acres. Informal in design, it is divided by a stream, and there are areas of well-drained and damp ground, whose advantages have been exploited to the full.

JENKYN PLACE

MAP I

Bentley, near Farnham
Turn north off A31 at Bentley, 4m (6½km) south-west of Farnham
Owner: Jenkyn Place Garden Trust
Tel: Bentley (0420) 23118
Open Thursday to Sunday and Bank Holidays from mid-April to mid-September parties by appointment
(peak months June and July)
Plants for sale

A six-acre private garden of outstanding beauty and interest, Jenkyn Place is reminiscent of the extended cottage-garden style of famous twentieth-century gardens like Hidcote and Sissinghurst. The high quality and range of its plant content match its part-formal, part-natural design. When Mr and Mrs Gerald Coke began to make the garden after World War II they determined to provide a beautiful setting for the handsome redbrick and tiled seventeenth-century house. They also wanted to create a garden which would reveal itself gradually, have all-year-round interest and grow a wide spectrum of plants.

The site is relatively warm and set on greensand, so a remarkable collection of tender and other plants can be grown here. It was not laid out at one stroke but has evolved over the years and a series of formal 'rooms', enclosed by walls and hedges, now give way gradually to less intensely-planted and more natural areas. The intimate and enclosed gardens are devoted to specific plants and themes. The Dutch garden is filled with scented plants, the sundial garden with pots of various pelargoniums, the rose garden with modern and old-fashioned roses. An unusually rich collection of magnolias decorates an area nearby, and generous borders of lupins, peonies or mixed herbaceous plants are backed by dark yew hedges. Alpines grow along a rock bed set below a hedge in an original and effective way, and herbs surround and fill an old lead tank. Brick and stone paths and steps link the different gardens and form vistas and axes.

The eye is feasted and cooled by undecorated but stylish hedged walks and shrubs which, grown singly in turf, have an opportunity to spread and display themselves. The lower and wilder part of the garden highlights the foliage, shapes and colours of trees and shrubs, particularly those which are at their best in autumn. The return to the house shows how successful the Cokes have been in creating a sympathetic setting for their home. The lawn runs to the terrace and is partly shaded by massive holm oaks and cedars — a flattering frame for the house and an effective vista from it.

The garden contains many garden ornaments. There is a marble statue of Bacchus in the herb garden and a celestial globe adorns another formal 'room'. The stonework — paths, walls, edges to borders, paving and flights of steps — has been skilfully laid and adds to the beauty and composure of the garden. Jenkyn Place offers the professional and the amateur gardener

Herbaceous borders at Jenkyn Place.

a rare opportunity to enjoy and admire an exceptionally high standard of plant content, design and upkeep.

JODRELL BANK VISITOR CENTRE GARDENS

MAP B

near Holmes Chapel
Off the A535 between Holmes Chapel and
Chelford
Owner: University of Manchester
Tel: Lower Withington (0477) 71339
Open daily March to October
(peak seasons spring and autumn)
Plants for sale

The home of the world-famous radio telescope, Jodrell Bank's immediate surroundings have a science fiction rather than a natural look, but a short distance from the Centre itself is a forty-acre arboretum, developed from pastureland since 1972. The majority of the trees are still young but should help those seeking guidance on the choice of suitable specimen and other trees for their gardens.

Mixed groups are planted in areas of rough grass divided by wide sweeps of lawn, the scene becoming increasingly natural as the arboretum is explored. Several thousand different varieties of trees and shrubs can be seen here, including some National Collections, the Heather Society's Calluna Collection and a good number of species and old-fashioned roses. There is a fine selection of suitable hedging plants, and flower beds contain an imaginative mix of trees and shrubs. The merits of a wide variety of, for instance, berberis or maples can be assessed with ease, but no area is devoted to only one genera of plant.

KEN CARO

MAP H

Bicton near Liskeard
Turn north off Liskeard to Callington road at
Butchers Arms in St Ives
Owners: Mr and Mrs K. R. Willcock
Tel: Liskeard (0579) 62446
Open two days a week in May and June and one
only from July to end September
(peak months May and June)
Plants for sale

Flower arrangers as well as plantsmen will find much to interest them here as there are many interesting foliage and unusual plants in this two-acre garden beside a working farm. Begun in 1970 and informal in design, the garden has a cohesive and well-established appearance. This is not only because of the rapid rate of growth of plants in this part of the country but because the garden contains many evergreen trees, shrubs and plants of all-year-round interest.

Variegated subjects and dwarf and other conifers are much in evidence and the perceptive way these have been associated with other evergreens creates a series of striking pictures with strong architectural shapes. As might be expected in a Cornish garden, there are unusual rhododendrons, — the variegated 'President Roosevelt' and Japanese yakushimanum species. A handsome camellia, 'Anticipation', forms a surprisingly dense, columnar shape despite never having been pruned, and evergreens — a variegated yucca, *Senecio reinoldii* whose tough foliage is felted below and glossy above, hollies, euphorbias and hellebores — act as focal points and add texture.

Herbaceous plants have not been neglected, a collection of dicentras being a feature of the gardens, and ground-coverers play a decorative role as well the practical one of suppressing weeds. There are granite troughs of miniatures, and waterfowl and aviaries are imaginatively accommodated around the garden. Ken Caro is easy to relate to, and full of good ideas for the gardener who wants a well-balanced, all-year-round picture.

KENSINGTON ROOF GARDEN

MAP J

99 Kensington High Street, London W8
On the sixth floor, entrance to side of British
Home Stores
Owner: Richard Branson
Tel: (01) 937 7994
Open daily throughout the year

Surprisingly richly planted and supporting stonework and water features, these could be called the 'Hanging Gardens of Kensington'. The climate is that much kinder six floors up and the unexpected presence of water, flamingoes and mature trees — a catalpa, paperbark maple and willow — quickly give the impression of a garden a great distance from the frenetic capital. Only when you glimpse the surrounding rooftops through portholes in the perimeter wall are you reminded of your whereabouts.

When the one-and-a-half-acre garden, designed by the landscape architect, Ralph Hancock, was made on top of a department store in 1938, it was the largest garden of its kind in Europe. It must also have been an engineering feat, for the depth of soil varies from one to two metres and there is a lake, decorative water features and much ornamental stonework. There are three distinct gardens: the Moorish-style Spanish garden with palm trees and terracotta pots; the formal Tudor garden, and the lush and richly-planted English woodland garden. Making such a garden at ground level in a city would be hard enough, but to do so one hundred feet up is amazing. Note the trees: the only ones growing in such a situation which are protected by a preservation order. Roses also thrive here because aphids do not venture more than forty feet above ground.

Mature tree growing on Kensington Roof Garden.

KENWOOD, THE IVEAGH BEQUEST

MAP J

Hampstead Lane, London NW3
Between the A502 from St Pancras to Golders
Green via Spaniards Road and the Al Archway
road via Highgate High Street
Owner: English Heritage
Tel: London (01) 348 1286/7
Open daily throughout the year
(peak season spring)

The mansion commands a superlative view over the landscape and Hampstead Heath, that vital 'lung' north of the city. It was remodelled by Robert Adam for the first Lord Mansfield, in the 1760s, and is renowned for its exceptional collection of paintings. Those who explore its grounds regularly, and enjoy its spacious lawns, fresh air and beauty, would rate Kenwood's surroundings as highly as its contents. In 1793, the landscape gardener, Humphry Repton, was commissioned to advise on the landscape, but it is now difficult to pick out features he might have created, because his 'Red Book' on Kenwood has never been discovered. Much of what can be seen today — the groups of rhododendrons and curving lawns to the front of the house — are characteristic of his work, but the garden has been developed over several centuries by different owners.

The most eyecatching sight is the lakes, backed by woodland, which lie below the house across a wide, gentle slope of lawn carpeted with bulbs in spring. At one end of the lakes, originally fish ponds, there is what appears to be a white ornamental bridge spanning a river. Closer inspection reveals that it is a sham: it is a simple, single-sided construction at the narrow end of the lake; clever and effective *trompe l'oeil*.

The garden around the house is sheltered by woodland and covers twelve acres. On one side, approached through a tunnel of ivy, is the pleasure garden, with its well-kept banks and beds of shrubs — rhododendrons and camellias — and herbaceous plants. A small thatched summerhouse overlooks the scene and an abstract sculpture is at one end of the top lawn, set against a dark backcloth of shrubs. This is not the only sculpture in the gardens: a Henry Moore decorates the more natural landscape below. The old kitchen garden has herbs and other plants chosen to attract butterflies and other nectar feeders.

KIFTSGATE COURT

MAP F

near Chipping Campden
3½m (5½km) north-east of Chipping Campden,
1m (2km) east of A46 and B4018
Owners: Mr and Mrs J. G. Chambers
Open Wednesdays, Thursdays and Sundays
from April to end September
Plants for sale

Inevitably, because they are so close to each other, comparisons are often made between the gardens at Kiftsgate and Hidcote. Major Johnston and the present owner of Kiftsgate's grandmother, Mrs Heather Muir, were good friends and there must have been cross-fertilisation of ideas and knowledge over the years between these two noteworthy garden enthusiasts. They are similar in that they are both composed of collections of separate gardens which vary in character, the framework often formal, the planting generous and imaginative. The most obvious difference between the two is

one of position. The manor at Hidcote hides itself modestly, while at Kiftsgate the mansion dominates the scene.

The house is set high on a dramatic escarpment overlooking the garden and the unspoilt countryside. Built in 1887 of ochre stone, it may not be to everyone's taste, but the garden cannot fail to inspire the plantsman and those who appreciate the sensitive use of colour. Specimen and ornamental trees, many with good autumn colour, and carpets of spring bulbs decorate the lawns beside the drive. Formal gardens stand near the house, on terraces and enclosed by hedges, and paths vein the steep slopes of the escarpment, past informally-planted banks and down to the lower garden, set on a shelf in the hillside. Formal walks lead past mixed borders with colour themes, such as the pink, grey and mauve double borders and the yellow border where delphiniums and bronze foliage have been used with cream- and gold-flowering subjects.

There is a white garden where the tender eucryphias, hoherias, *Carpenteria california* and *Cornus controversa*, roses and alliums, form subtle pictures of colour, shape and texture. This paved garden has a Mediterranean feel, as does the steep bank shaded by pines and the Lower Garden. The latter, with its neo-classical temple and swimming pool in a D-shaped lawn, hangs excitingly over a panorama of fields and grazing sheep. Spiky phormiums, tree peonies, magnolias and the scent of lavender contribute to the Mediterranean atmosphere, and alchemilla and a delicate pink linaria have seeded themselves along the paths made of old staddle stones.

Roses are one of the chief glories of the garden. *Rosa* 'Versicolour', with pink-and-white-striped blooms has been massed in the double rose borders east of the house, and the rewarding *Rosa chinensis mutabilis* climbs a wall, its single blooms changing from cream to pink and purple as they age. One of the most spectacular is, of course, the *Rosa filipes* 'Kiftsgate' which rampages over a tithe barn and up into a copper beech tree, with cascades of white blossom in July. When it was planted in 1938 it was thought to be a musk rose, but thirteen years later Mr Graham Stuart Thomas gave it its present name.

View over Vale of Evesham from the gardens at Kiftsgate Court.

Kiftsgate has not rested on its laurels. It has continued to evolve; new and unusual plants and features are constantly being added and ensure that it is a 'living' rather than a preserved garden. An example is the recently-added effective arch of white hornbeam at the far end of a walk, which frames a unique stone seat carved in the shape of a seated woman.

KILLERTON

MAP H

Broadclyst, near Exeter
6m (9½km) north-east of Exeter off B3185
Owner: The National Trust
Tel: Exeter (0392) 881345
Open daily throughout the year
(peak seasons spring and autumn)
Plants for sale

Killerton is especially interesting for its fine collection of trees and shrubs. It was the home of the Acland family from the time of the Civil War, and the fifteen acres of garden were laid out by John Veitch at the end of the eighteenth century. New subjects were constantly introduced, brought back by planthunters employed by Veitch and Sons, the famous nursery started by John Veitch at Budlake, near Killerton in 1808. They dress the steep, south-facing slope which rises behind the house and overlooks the lawns, terrace and borders.

Little of this can be seen when you approach the handsome house, its walls covered with tender plants and climbers like the dainty, yellow *Rosa banksiae lutea*, fremontodendron and holboellia. A ha-ha runs close to the side of the house, and the fields stretch away over flat land cut by the Clyst and Exe rivers. Only when you round the corner of the house is the main part of the garden revealed — the borders planted with feathery maples, daphnes and perennials at the back of the house, the wooded slope, and the low-walled terrace garden striking out along the

179

level ground. The terrace garden was designed by William Robinson at the beginning of the century and did not meet with general approval at the time. He was an energetic advocate of 'natural' gardens, and it is an unusually formal example of his work.

The energetic should cross the lawn to explore the richly planted hillside and seek out the great and rare trees, especially some of the conifers which were original introductions. Many other specimens planted by succeeding generations of the Acland family produce flowers in spring, or have good autumn foliage and bear berries. There are tulip trees, unusual maples and sorbus, a weeping silver lime and a rare *Zelkova serrata*. In spring the magnolias, rhododendrons and azaleas are at their best, and the massed blooms of naturalised bulbs colour the lawns and slopes of Dolbury Hill.

In front of a thatched summerhouse, the Bear's Hut, hypericums and graceful wand flowers have been planted, and behind there is a rock garden made in a defunct quarry. Somewhat dark and heavy in character, it contains no alpines but quantities of naturalised cyclamen and shrubs, such as the sweet-smelling osmanthus. An avenue of beeches pre-dating the arboretum stands majestically high on the hill, providing shelter for this well-kept and notable garden.

KNEBWORTH HOUSE

MAP G

Knebworth, near Stevenage
28m (45km) north of London. Own direct access off A1 (M) at Stevenage, junction 7
Owner: The Hon David Lytton Cobbold
Tel: Stevenage (0438) 812661
Open regularly from Easter to end of September
(peak months June and July)

The Lytton family has owned the garden at Knebworth since 1490. The most dramatic change to it was during the Victorian era when the romantic novelist and statesman, Edward Bulwer-Lytton, laid out an intricate and formal garden in the walled area behind the house.

This was designed to complement the high Gothic architecture of the mansion he had re-modelled, but very little of it now exists, apart from a fraction of a maze and an informal wilderness garden.

The most important features today are those created by Edwin Lutyens in 1909. Having married into the family not long before, introduced to his wife by Gertrude Jekyll, he was on hand to give advice on the simplification of the formal layout. He created the pleached lime enclosure around the pool on the main lawn and a garden beyond the formal yew hedges which has recently been restored and planted in the Jekyll style. Her rediscovered planting plan was followed when the herb garden was created — an unusual quincunx pattern of circular beds which attractively contains and displays the diverse shapes and textures of the plants. The three mounts survive from the garden's earliest days; their original role was as viewpoints to survey the garden below and the parkland beyond.

KNIGHTSHAYES COURT

MAP H

Bolham, near Tiverton
2m (3km) north of Tiverton, turn right off A396
Owner: The National Trust
Tel: Tiverton (0884) 254665
Open regularly from Easter to end October
(peak season spring)
Plants for sale

During the late nineteenth century the impressive architecture of the Victorian Gothic house was matched by an extravagant and intricate garden. It was laid out by Paxton's pupil, Edward Kemp, and had work-intensive bedding-out areas, greenhouses of exotics, a water garden, a bowling green and handsome terraces. When Sir John and Lady Heathcote-Amory inherited the house in 1937, the style and upkeep of such a garden was no longer practical, but it was not until after World War II that they embarked on the sensitive transformation and creation of what is now one of the National

Knebworth House.

Trust's most beautiful and richly-stocked gardens.

Part formal, part woodland, the gardens are on the terraces below and to one side of the house and on the wooded hillside. The creation of the hillside terrace was prompted by the removal of trees damaged by a plane which crashed there during the war. Fighter pilots billeted at Knightshayes would 'buzz' the house; towards the end of the war, one miscalculated his height and ploughed across and into the woodland.

A wide gravel walk runs along the top terrace in front of the house, whose walls are festooned with climbing roses. These terraces have been simplified, emphasising the view over the park and countryside. Beds below the retaining wall are exuberant with large, softly-coloured tree peonies and shrub roses. Flowering shrubs and tender plants edge the walk which leads to the two formal gardens, hidden behind old yew hedges resembling battlements. A sloping scree border of alpines and dwarf shrubs introduces these delightful 'rooms', the first of which is paved and planted with low silver, white and pink plants. These harmonise with the lead tank, the focal point, flanked by standard wisterias. The bowling green is now a pool garden — wonderfully restful. The graceful habit of a silver weeping pear next to the pool is set against the dark yew hedge, which hides the trunk but not

the salmon-pink spring foliage of an *Acer pseudoplatanus* 'Brilliantissimum' behind it. On the far side of the wide path is another hedged room. The simple carpet of lawn focuses the eye on the urn, stone seats and the topiary hunt, fashioned in the 1920s, which races across the top of the hedge.

Justly famous, the thirty-acre woodland garden spreads up and away from the terrace. Many mature trees had to be felled so that the light could penetrate the dense canopy of foliage, and year by year more patches were cleared and painstakingly planted. Paths thread around beds banked with peat blocks and open on to peaceful glades. As might be expected, superb rhododendrons, azaleas, camellias and maples flourish here, but it is the amazing variety of other shade-tolerant bulbs and woodland plants of all kinds that provide a delightful surprise: roses clambering into trees; unusual hostas, hellebores and euphorbias; stately white and yellow foxgloves, trilliums, erythroniums, cyclamens and primulas — all contribute to the richness of this garden, which cannot fail to absorb the most demanding of plantsmen. Some distance from the back of the house the Heathcote-Amorys developed a willow garden: as decorative in winter, when the naked branches burn orange in the sunshine, as in spring and summer, the willows and Ghent and other azaleas surround a pond.

LADHAM HOUSE

MAP J

Goudhurst
North-east of village, off A262
Owner: Betty, Lady Jessel
Tel: Goudhurst (0580) 211203
Open several days a year for charity and by
appointment
(peak months May and July)

Divided by the charming nineteenth-century neo-Georgian house are two quite different gardens. At the front of the house, there is formality in the shape of a fountain garden decorated with beds of low-growing shrubs, and double mixed borders backed by camellias and magnolias, one of which is appropriately called *M. campbellii* 'Betty Jessel'. To the far side of the house, spacious lawns flow between informal groupings of shrubs and mature trees; there is a heather garden and a bog garden provides a lush and colourful surprise at the far end. Ten acres in all, the gardens attest to the horticultural talents of the late Sir George Jessel and his wife. Plantsmen will delight in the many unusual varieties and the way they have been associated; its immaculate condition emphasises the spacious feel and peaceful atmosphere of this obviously much-loved garden.

cypresses at the far end has been made to seem much farther away than it actually is, by being placed beyond a long rectangular pond. A steep, dry, bank has been planted with heathers and rhododendrons; herbaceous plants and shrubs fill informal borders, and large areas of scree are bright with alpines and other low-growing subjects. Though planted for effect more than as a collection, the garden displays an unexpected wealth of unusual plant material. It will appeal to plantsmen and to those like the owner, who can spend only one day a week on maintenance but demand high standards of upkeep.

LAND FARM

MAP B

Colden, near Hebden Bridge
From Hebden Bridge follow road to Burnley for
3m (5km), bypass Heptonstall, turn right in Edge
Hey Green at wooden garages
Owner: Mr J. Williams
Tel: Hebden Bridge (0422) 82260
Open daily from April to September
(peak months June and July)
Plants for sale

To create a garden one thousand feet up on a north-facing slope requires skill and imagination which the owner of Land Farm obviously possesses. Young but far from shapeless, this garden spreads away from the ancient stone farmhouse which looks across the valley to hills. Its one acre is divided into sections, linked but with distinctive and individual characters.

The condition and lie of the land have dictated the design and plant content of these different areas. Walls, steps and paths, made from the old stone to hand on site, form boundaries or link informal, scree and hedged gardens. Evergreen and deciduous foliage plants play an important role, and conifers give it year-round shape and colour. Predominantly informal in design, the upper and lower halves are divided from each other by a long hedged 'room', providing a formal contrast. There is an interesting exercise in perspective: the modernistic figure set between

LANE END

MAP I

Sheep Lane, Midhurst
In North Street turn left at Knockhundred Row,
left into Sheep Lane, left to garden
Owner: Mrs C. J. Epril
Tel: Midhurst (073 081) 3151
Open for charity by appointment

Planted to give year-round interest, this garden is set on the eastern edge of the charming old town on a high platform above a romantic view of the ruins of Cowdray Castle and park. It was once part of the grounds of an eighteenth-century house, so it contains some mature trees and features, such as the retaining wall on the northern boundary. These and other features have been cleverly incorporated into or form a frame to a series of pictures.

Around the house, areas of lawn, divided by paths and low walls, are surrounded by raised beds of shrubs, dwarf conifers, ground-coverers and other suitable plants. The soil is acid, so rhododendrons and azaleas flourish, and alpine and other dwarf plants colour the rock and scree garden. Espaliered fruit and specimen trees decorate the old kitchen garden, which continues to raise soft fruit and vegetables. Hostas and other shade-tolerant plants are framed between the buttresses of a boundary wall. Roses, and free-standing and well-associated groups of shrubs, stand nearby and the dell garden lies below, reached by a flight of steps against the ancient boundary wall. A path weaves through a lake of bluebells and other wild flowers, and there are tree peonies shaded by handsome old chestnuts, limes and quince trees.

LANHYDROCK HOUSE

MAP H

Bodmin
2½m (4km) south-east of Bodmin. Turn off A38
Bodmin to Liskeard or B3268 Bodmin to
Lostwithiel roads and follow signs
Owner: The National Trust
Tel: Bodmin (0208) 3320
Open daily throughout the year
(peak seasons spring and summer)
Plants for sale

This important Cornish house, sheltered by a glorious backdrop of trees and overlooking the valley of the River Fowey, has an air of permanence and security. Delve into the history of the house and garden though and you find that all is not quite as it seems. Some features are genuinely ancient, others are recent additions.

The garden is unusual for Cornwall in that it is composed of three distinct parts — strictly formal, informal and woodland. Entered through the charming seventeenth-century gatehouse, formal terrace gardens decorate what was once the quadrangle of the original house. This was built in 1670 by the Robartes family who lived at Lanhydrock until it was given to the National Trust in 1953. A little over a century later the east wing of the house was demolished, leaving the two-storied stone gatehouse stranded in the park.

The period when a landscape rather than a garden was fashionable was followed by the Victorian return to formality. In 1857 the architect Gilbert Scott was commissioned to modernise and enlarge the house and link the gatehouse to the whole once again. He built the wall, punctuated with obelisk-shaped finials matching those decorating the gatehouse, which now links the house, gateway and church. He enriched the reinstated enclosed area with a pattern of formal, box-edged flower beds and

dark sentinel yews. Today these give the impression of having stood here for several centuries rather than a little over one hundred years. They cast finger-like shadows across the lawns and the now simplified geometric beds, each of which is devoted to a brilliantly-coloured and thickly-planted subject such as roses or bedding-out plants. This feature matches the Victorian interior decoration of the house but does not clash with its misleading exterior: the major part of the mansion was gutted by fire in 1881 and rebuilt of local stone. It is typically Cornish rather than neo-Gothic; Sir Gilbert Scott's assistant, Richard Coad, was responsible for its reconstruction.

Camellias and magnolias are particularly splendid in the informal part of the garden, which is laid out with lawns and planted with mature trees and groups of shrubs. A circle of yew hedge encloses a pattern of wedge-shaped beds filled with herbaceous plants; the banks of a small stream are bright with primulas, and hostas grow on the side of the hill. High above the house a path leads to the woodland garden, where a constantly-growing collection of large-leafed and other rhododendrons and deciduous azaleas thrive under a canopy of oaks.

LEA GARDENS

MAP B

Lea, near Matlock
Off A6 at Cromford or Whatstandwell to Lea,
garden signposted
Owners: Mr and Mrs Tye
Tel: Dethick (0629) 534380
Open daily from end of March to end of July
(peak month May)
Plants for sale

Set on the side of a steep hill, this four-acre garden contains a fine collection of rhododendrons, azaleas and rock plants. So richly have these been planted over the slope that the overall picture is of a vibrant and multi-textured wall-hanging. John Marsden-Smedley first began to create the garden on the site of an old quarry in 1935. He devoted the next twenty-four years to developing it and increasing his collection of unusual rhododendrons, some of which have reached an impressive size. In 1952 the gardens became the property of the Tye family, who have continued the work and enriched the collection further with newly-introduced and rare specimens.

There are two distinct parts: the expansive rockery spreads away around the modern house and beyond is the older, woodland garden. A superb range of plants embroiders the rocky bank below the house — *Rhododendron yakushimanum*, heathers, conifers, meconopis and kalmias to name a mere handful. Beside the house a tufa bed supports unusual alpine and dwarf subjects — star-like lewisias and dwarf varieties of rhododendron. Beyond lies the highly-cultivated woodland, veined with a network of hard paths, laid to ease maintenance and movement around the stone-edged beds. These are voluptuously filled with rhododendrons of all kinds: sweetly-scented *R. loderi*, early-flowering *R. fargesii* and *R. thomsonii*; large-leafed *R. sinogrande* species and others with intriguing metallic or peeling bark, or foliage with chocolate-coloured felted undersides. A bowl-shaped area has been luxuriantly planted with occidental, and Ghent azaleas, and specimen trees such as magnolias and summer-flowering eucryphias. The garden is sheltered from the wind and frost rolls off the slope before it can do any damage, so a surprising number of tender subjects thrive at Lea.

LEONARDSLEE GARDENS

MAP J

Lower Beeding, near Horsham
4m (6½km) south-east of Horsham on A281.
3m (5km) from Handcross at bottom of M23
Owner: Loder Family (HHA)
Tel: Lower Beeding (040 376) 212
Open daily from mid-April to mid-June; also
weekends only in summer and autumn
(peak month May)
Plants for sale

This eighty-acre site is naturally beautiful. A chain of lakes formed from old 'Hammer' ponds runs through a valley, whose steeply-sloping sides are dressed with a glorious collection of rhododendrons, azaleas, camellias and specimen trees. In spring and autumn, the first sight of Leonardslee is unforgettable: the colours of the countless flowering shrubs and the bronzed foliage of trees are mirrored in the water far below; the scent of the common yellow azaleas and *Rhododendron loderi* is caught on the breeze. Exploration of this important garden is a delight, because the planting has preserved its natural woodland character and at the same time evokes a Himalayan hillside. The Loder family have developed it for nearly a century, and it is of great interest to the rhododendron buff, the plantsman and the dendrologist.

The name Loder is much respected in gardening circles, members of the family having created the outstanding gardens at Wakehurst and High Beeches. In 1889 Sir Edmund Loder bought the land and nineteenth-century Georgian-style house from his parents-in-law and was the first of the family to plant the rhododendrons for which the garden is famed. Leonardslee is the home of the scented *Rhododendron loderi* hybrids, whose treelike proportions were produced by crossing *R. fortunei* and *R. griffithianum*. Sir Edmund also planted magnolias, acers, unusual and rare conifers, birches, oaks and camellias, many of which were new introductions to this country. The collection was added to by his son, Sir Giles Loder, whose own son is now in charge of the gardens.

Shrubberies and mature trees shelter the drive and rock garden near the house, with lawns sloping from the back. This is a good spot to admire the scene below. Paths snake through groves and dells full of camellias and rhododendrons, and reach the bridge which crosses one of the lakes. Surprising specimens here are the wallabies, brought to Leonardslee by Sir Edmund and allowed to roam a large fenced area.

The far side of the valley is more thickly wooded and wilder. Splendid with the warm colours of deciduous azaleas in May, it is also fragrant with the scent of common yellow azaleas which have propagated themselves freely. The lake at the far end of the valley is spanned by a Chinese-style bridge, and it is from here that the most spectacular view of the garden can be enjoyed; the sheet of water reflects and intensifies the beauty of the richly-clad hillsides. The slopes on the far side of the Chinese bridge are veined with paths weaving through more plantations of hybrid rhododendrons and specimen trees, maples, magnolias, eucryphias, and towering conifers.

Whether in spring or autumn, you must be prepared to expend time and energy exploring, to discover all the garden has to offer.

LEVENS HALL

MAP B

near Kendal
5m (8km) south of Kendal, near Kendal Bridge on
A6
Owner: Mr O. R. Bagot (HHA)
Tel: Sedgwick (05395) 60321
Open Sundays to Thursdays from Easter Sunday
to end September
(peak months June and July)
Plants for sale

Levens is quite unlike any other garden. To enter it is to step into an *Alice in Wonderland* fantasy. Its topiary is as extraordinary as the Mad Hatter, as rounded as Tweedledum and Tweedledee, as spiky as the Red Queen, and altogether unforgettable. When Monsieur Beaumont, a pupil of the great Le Nôtre, was commissioned by Colonel James Grahme to design a parterre in 1690, it is doubtful whether he visualised his neat yew and box shapes reaching such massive proportions. Few other parterres were left undisturbed, nurtured and encouraged to grow to such a size. Obviously some of the yew and box have had to be replaced, but the picture is still one of a living chessboard of giant figures. They stand in geometric beds filled with a particular annual or variety of rose, their matt, dark or golden shapes offset by a carpet of vibrant colour, and bright red necklaces of the delicate climber *Tropaeolum speciosum* decorate the inky green of hedges and topiary.

Beyond this unique and busy part of the garden, Beaumont laid out restrained features, *allées* and walks, flanked by the fresh green of beech or sombre with yew. Herbaceous borders lead to a rondel of beech hedge which encloses a peaceful pool of turf; vistas to the far end of the garden and to a cedar on the topiary lawn are channelled down hedged walks, and others are flanked by yews clipped to resemble battlements. The writhing trunks of ancient specimens, like dinosaurs' twisted ribcages, form tunnels and arches, and an arbour nestles beneath a vast mound of yew. Although the period topiary, lively bedding-out and disciplined hedges immediately capture the attention, closer inspection reveals the interesting plant material used in the borders and against the walls, and unusual trees such as a gingko and a *Metasequoia glyptostroboides*.

Now sadly cut off from the Elizabethan house by the main road, a fine park, laid out at the same time as the garden, extends down the valley of the River Kent. Though it pre-dates the picturesque landscapes of the eighteenth century, it is not dissimilar in character and is a home for a herd of black fallow deer and 'Bagot' goats.

Topiary at Levens Hall.

185

LIMEBURNERS

MAP F

Lincoln Hill, Ironbridge, Telford
Turn off B4380 at west end of Ironbridge, top of
Lincoln Hill on left
Owners: Mr and Mrs J. E. Derry
Tel: Ironbridge (095 245) 3715
Open by appointment April to September for
charity

Few would have the guts and imagination to transform a council refuse tip into a well-designed and attractive nine-and-a-half-acre garden planted specifically to attract wildlife — butterflies and moths in particular. This is what the Derrys set out to do in 1977, and it is now so well established, it is hard to imagine the garden's former use and state.

On a south-facing slope a spacious lawn fans out from the house over a vista of woodland. A wide range of shrubs and trees of year-round interest are banked either side, and the ground-cover material massed below is delightful. The farther the garden stretches from this central point, the wilder it becomes. Oaks, alders and willows have been planted to attract moths, and the wild flowers, encouraged to naturalise in the rough grass under the trees, are magnets for butterflies. The vogue for wild gardens has reached epidemic proportions today and enthusiasts, naturalists and plantsmen will be fascinated by the success of the garden at Limeburners. A tip worth noting is the way the Derrys protect their cuttings grown in the open: jam jars placed over them prevent them from drying out and act as mini-greenhouses.

LING BEECHES

MAP C

Ling Lane, Scarcroft, near Leeds
At Scarcroft, 7m (11km) nort-east of Leeds on
A58, turn west Ling Lane, garden 600yds (550m)
on right
Owner: Mrs Arnold Rakusen
Tel: Leeds (0532) 892 450
Open several days a year for charity and by
appointment
(peak month May)

Carved out of and embraced by woodland, this two-acre informal and woodland garden has been planted to give perennial interest. It contains many foliage, unusual and surprisingly tender plants, which have all been used to create an harmonious picture. The house, with its green pantiled roof, nestles into its surroundings; the woodland on the far side of the lawn, though depriving the garden of day-long sunlight, gives it a sheltered and secure feeling.

Low-growing and scented subjects like thyme form neat cushions on the paving of the terrace around the house, and the outer edges of the lawn are decorated with island beds of shrubs, shrub roses, herbaceous plants, ground-coverers and bulbs. The golden foliage of a large number of shrubs — *Lonicera nitida* 'Baggesen's Gold', *Philadelphus coronarius* 'Aureus', golden maple and privet — stands out against the dark background of trees, and dispels any feeling of gloom. The paths which wind away into the woodland have been dressed with gravel, an unusual but surprisingly attractive material in a garden of this nature. The deeper you penetrate into the wood, the more natural the scene becomes: rhododendrons, azaleas and other shade-tolerant and woodland plants form layers of interest; maples, parrotias, conifers, hostas, ferns, lily-of-the-valley, white foxgloves and spring bulbs abound.

Ground-coverers have been particularly well used: to soften the edges of the paths, form colourful or textured carpets and — with generous helpings of home-made compost — cut down the work. Despite being five hundred feet above sea level and vulnerable to cold winds, eucryphias survive here and a *Cistus battandieri* thrives against a sheltered wall.

LINGHOLM GARDENS

MAP A

near Keswick
West shore of Derwentwater off A66 at
Portinscale, 1m (2km) on left
Owner: Viscount Rochdale
Tel: Keswick (07687) 72003
Open daily from April to October
(peak months April to June and September and
October)
Plants for sale

The woodland gardens of the Lake District have a noteworthy and welcome quality: the ground is never over-cultivated or the woodland robbed of its natural beauty. Lingholm is a good example of this sympathetic treatment, and it is generously endowed with late-flowering varieties of rhododendrons.

Beatrix Potter wrote *Squirrel Nutkin* here when her family rented the house, but the garden looked very different then. It was not until the beginning of this century that Colonel George Kemp, later Lord Rochdale, began to develop it and enhance the woodland with hybrid and species rhododendrons in the 1920s and 1930s. Spacious lawns, shaded by handsome conifers, surround the house, which was built in 1880; behind it lie seven acres of formal garden. There is the sunken, secluded memorial garden and a sunbaked terrace with a border of herbaceous plants and azaleas. This is divided into sections by buttresses of yew, and a long bed on the terrace is massed with roses.

A gateway at the far end of the terrace leads away from the formal garden to a large area of rough grass planted thickly with spring bulbs. An avenue of cherries strikes towards the woodland, beyond which is a fine view of Catbells Fell.

The woodland garden covers twenty-eight acres, with a winding path forming a giant loop. Though retaining its wild nature, this part of the garden is far from neglected, and a happy marriage has been achieved between the natural and cultivated plants. Mosses, wild bugle, oxalis and bilberries cover the ground; the sunlight, filtered through oak and beech trees, highlights fine

rhododendrons and azaleas. The huge blooms of *Rhododendron loderi* and the common yellow azaleas scent the air; the fascinating foliage, bark and new growth of large-leafed and other specimens prolong the season of interest, as do early- and later-flowering hybrids such as *Rhododendron* 'Polar Bear'.

A vast sweep of blue Himalayan poppies, *Meconopsis betonicifolia*, is a splendid sight, as are the candelabra primulas which thrive in an area of boggy ground. Willow gentians and the burning foliage of deciduous trees and shrubs colour the garden in autumn. Do not miss the opportunity of going 'behind the scenes', to inspect the impressively well-kept and stocked propagating house, greenhouses and potting-sheds.

LITTLE MORETON HALL

MAP B

near Congleton
On A34 4m (6½km) south-west of Congleton
Owner: The National Trust
Tel: Congleton (02602) 2722018
Open regularly from Easter to end September

The architecture of Little Moreton Hall is so distinctive that to compete with it would be folly. Consequently, in 1975, the National Trust laid out a garden which would harmonise with the style of the half-timbered and gabled sixteenth-century house. Surrounded by a square moat, the house stands to one side of the one-acre garden and now overlooks a beautifully-reproduced knot garden. The design for this was found in a book called *The English Garden* by Leonard Meager, published in 1688. It is an elegant but restrained pattern of beds made up of smooth mown grass, edged with dwarf box and divided by gravel. Viewed, as intended, from the top of the mound or from the windows of the house, it resembles a charming and well-executed tapestry.

Borders of old-fashioned herbs and flowers, interspersed with small standard lavenders, strengthen the period picture and a hedge of honeysuckle, thorn and hornbeam forms a boundary. Apple, pear and quince trees stand on the lawn above the knot which, like all the plants in the garden, might have been grown in the sixteenth century.

LLYSDINAM

Newbridge-on-Wye, near Llandrindod Wells
Turn west off A479 at Newbridge-on-Wye, right
immediately after crossing River Wye, entrance
up the hill
Owner: Lady Delia Venables Llewelyn and the
Llysdinam Charitable Trust
Tel: Newbridge-on-Wye (059 789) 200
Open for charity and by appointment for parties
only
(peak months May and June)

The handsome house, set into a hillside and with a superb view over the upper Wye valley, is splendid in spring, when the mass of naturalised bulbs in the surrounding gardens are at their best. A huge Turkey oak and copper beech stand on the lawn near the house, adding to the beauty of the scene but not interrupting the view. The flower gardens at Llysdinam are mostly hidden from view; only a colourful border of irises, peonies, astilbes, dahlias and geraniums, backed by a yew hedge, is immediately visible. At the far end of the long lawn, shrubs and a collection of Ghent azaleas herald the entrance to the wood.

This beech and pine woodland is a backdrop to the azaleas which stand to one side of the path along the hillside. To the other lies a bog garden, the surrounds of its small ponds planted with moisture-loving plants and maples. A rock garden nearby has low-growing and spreading plants such as heathers, bergenias and perennial geraniums, as well as more azaleas. These all provide colour at different times of the year. Through a gate in the long yew hedge beside the house is the kitchen garden, its central paths flanked by herbaceous plants and herbs. Greenhouses against the sunbaked boundary walls raise plants for the house, and figs, grapes, peaches and nectarines. This garden is as productive as it is beautifully situated.

LONG CLOSE

Main Street, Woodhouse Eaves, near
Loughborough
From A6, turn west in Quorn on to B591
Owner: Mrs George Johnson
Tel: Loughborough (0509) 890 376
Open for charity and by appointment
(peak months April to June)

The forecourt of Long Close, planted with *Schisandra rubriflora*, crinodendron, campsis and magnolia, should alert the enthusiast to what is in store on the far side of the high wall. Though it is in the middle of the village, the long narrow garden, set on an east-facing slope, is secluded and sheltered by trees.

The upper part is laid out with formal terraces, their lawns decorated with massed groups of dwarf azaleas, rhododendrons and other shrubs, conifers, a pond and a fountain. Below these, though there are formal features like the pond surrounded by high yew hedges, the garden takes on a woodland character. Bulbs and wild flowers colour the rough grass, and there are specimen trees and unusual shrubs of impressive size, handsome shape and obvious beauty. The magnolias — *M. kobus, obovata, stellata* and *salicifolia* — are fine specimens and, together, with other ornamental trees — *Cornus kousa*, snowdrop and Judas trees, a paulownia and a vast *Prunus padus* or bird cherry — contribute greatly to the beauty of these gardens.

The soil is very acid, so rhododendrons, azaleas and camellias thrive, and autumn foliage subjects such as parrotia persica, spring-flowering *Viburnum tomentosum*, shrub roses and moisture-loving plants such as gunnera and skunk cabbage extend the season of interest.

LONGLEAT

MAP I

near Warminster
On A362, 4m (6½km) south of Frome
Owner: The Marquess of Bath (HHA)
Tel: Maiden Bradley (098 53) 551
Open regularly throughout the year
(peak seasons spring and autumn)
Plants for sale

The most spectacular view of Longleat is from a beech-covered escarpment south-east of the house. This spot is aptly called Heaven's Gate, and from it you can see the panorama spread below, the park and the mansion flanked by a long narrow lake or 'leat' from which it gained its name.

In late May and early June the drive to this viewpoint, designed by Russell Page, is lined with banks of azaleas and rhododendrons. These are set against mature beeches, and occasional specimen trees, such as monkey puzzles and Wellingtonias, form strong dark vertical shapes. The drive is about a mile in length and leads down to the splendid prodigy house and through open parkland, where the original formal Elizabethan garden once stood. Trees planted by 'Capability' Brown in the eighteenth century are grouped with characteristic skill and two fountains break the severe lines of the symmetrical courtyard in front of the house. Formal gardens and tightly trimmed yews on the north side echo the classical lines of the warm stone. Redesigned by Russell Page, these include such sixteenth-century features as a knot garden and a pleached lime avenue, and marry the house to the orangery built by Wyattville in 1802. The orangery houses tender plants and leads through to the secret garden behind. This is guarded by peacocks and planted with fragrant roses and shrubs. There are also the pet's cemetery and a yew-hedged maze planted in 1978. With almost two miles of paths, it is thought to be the largest of its kind in the country, if not in the world. A recently rediscovered arboretum is being restocked and incorporated into a pleasure walk abundant with spring bulbs and wild flowers.

Though not of particular interest to the plantsman, Longleat is a fine example of English landscape gardening, which provides a superb setting for the proud and splendid house.

LONGSTOCK PARK GARDENS

MAP I

near Stockbridge
2m (3km) north of Stockbridge from A30 turn
north on to A3057, signposted on open days
Owner: John Lewis Partnership
Tel: Andover (0264) 810894
Open a few days a year for charity from April to
September on the third Sunday in each month
(peak seasons early spring and summer)

Longstock is one of the loveliest water gardens in the country, possibly in Europe. The gardens were developed between 1946 and 1953 on ten acres of chalk and flint downland. The River Test was used to feed a rural Venice of lagoons and channels, islands and bridges. The garden is a considerable distance from the house and looks wonderfully natural: well kept but not over-disciplined, an entity in itself. Lawns, old oak woodland where a number of acid-loving shrubs and trees thrive (surprising, considering the underlying chalk), and fine views over the surrounding countryside make a picture of peace and beauty. Wild flowers have been encouraged to play as important a role as moisture-loving plants and spring bulbs. Along the banks and around the islands varieties of iris, primula, hosta and skunk cabbage mingle with native waterside plants, and in summer waterlilies cover the surface of lagoons. There are many unusual bog and water-loving plants and specimen trees, but the triumph of the garden is its deceptively 'natural' beauty.

Longleat House.

LOWER HOUSE FARM

MAP E

Nantyderry, near Abergavenny
7m (11km) south east of Abergavenny, turn off
B4598 Usk to Abergavenny road at Chain Bridge
Owners: Mr and Mrs Glynne Clay
Tel: Nantyderry (0873) 880257
Open for charity and by appointment from April
to October

Chestnut trees line the drive to the house, and a bed of well-associated shrubs provides a welcoming introduction and a clue to the good things to be seen here. Set around a farmhouse, the garden is the joint creation of Mr and Mrs Clay and, as with many gardens created by a husband and wife team, he is responsible for the layout and she for the planting. The original way in which the best and frequently unusual varieties of plants have been associated is particularly noteworthy.

A walled courtyard garden, although still young, is profuse with roses, and low-growing plants colour the York stone paving. At its centre, built around an old water pump, is a raised scree bed planted with alpines. There is a small formal garden beyond the courtyard, divided from the main part by a pergola. A long bed of iceberg roses runs below the wall of the house, against which an apple tree has been beautifully trained. Beds surrounding the neat lawn are filled with auriculas planted in generous groups, or are devoted to white and green flowering plants and variegated foliage.

The layout of most of the garden is informal; island beds, generously filled with mixed plants, create different colour schemes and foliage effects. The use of red and orange foliage and flowers — never easy colours in a garden — is particularly successful, as is the marriage of yellow and gold. There are effective small flower beds beneath trees; brilliant blue grape hyacinths have been massed beneath a gleditsia, and white shasta daisies surround a *Malus robusta*. Along the banks of what was once an old ditch, moisture-loving plants make lush growth and at the far end of the garden is a bed lively with Mr Clay's one indulgence: an exuberant bed of annuals. A short walk across a field, planted with trees which produce good autumn colour, is a small wooded island where alders and hazels shade ferns and wild flowers like bluebells, wood anemones and Solomon's seal.

LUTON HOO

MAP G

Luton
2m (3km) south-east of Luton, turn west off A6129
Owner: Mr Nicholas Phillips (HHA)
Tel: Luton (0582) 22955
Open several days a week from late April to
mid-October
(peak season summer)

The impressive mansion is balanced by the spaciousness and grandeur of its park and gardens. The park was laid out by 'Capability' Brown between 1764 and 1770 and is a good example of his genius for putting clumps of trees exactly where they will produce picturesque effects. At Luton Hoo, as in so many other parks, he used an existing source of water — the River Lea in this case — and swelled its banks dramatically to form a serpentine lake. A high proportion of the stately trees were planted in the nineteenth century and are a striking feature, the cedars being particularly noteworthy.

Falling away from the south-east front of the house are the formal terraced gardens, designed by the architect William Henry Romaine-

Walker. There is much handsome stonework on these, balustrading, twin-domed pavilions, ornamental ponds and fountains and wide flights of steps. Architecturally splendid, the lower terrace has a delightful rose garden. Edwardian in design, its box-edged beds are filled with over three thousand modern hybrid tea and standard roses, their liveliness offset by tight-clipped topiary and dark yew hedges.

A short distance away, set in a dell, is the recently-restored rock garden, built at the beginning of this century when such 'natural' features (but in reality highly contrived) were all the rage. Its peat-walled scree beds, planted with ericaceous subjects, can be admired from the bridge over its central pool. Much restoration work is going on: the collection of ornamental trees and shrubs and woodland plants is being added to and the herbaceous borders are being completely replanted.

LYME PARK

MAP B

Disley, near Stockport
6½m (10½km) south-east of Stockport, on A6
on western outskirts of Disley
Owner: The National Trust
Tel: Disley (06632) 2023
Open daily throughout the year

Over a thousand acres of hunting rather than landscaped park and moorland surrounds the part-Tudor but predominantly eighteenth-century Palladian house. On exceptionally high ground at the edges of the Peak District, the elegance and colour of the fifteen acres of formal gardens come as a surprise. They are reached through the stylish Italianate central courtyard of the house, decorated with standard box trees and a wellhead erupting with bright flowers. The magnificent west front, designed by Giacomo Leoni in 1725, overlooks the formal gardens, lawns and lake.

An orangery containing a fountain, glossy camellias, fig trees and tender plants stands to the east, above a parterre whose beds are packed with bulbs in spring and annuals in summer. A yew-enclosed rose garden lies beyond, and borders and stands of evergreen holly and yew give this area strong, year-round shape. A statue of Neptune is at the apex of the west façade, surveying the lake below, whose far banks have recently been planted with rhododendrons. This lake is fed by a moorland stream which runs through a ravine known as 'killtime', because the gardeners laboured there when all other work had been completed. It now displays a pleasing collection of shade- and moisture-loving plants such as hostas, astilbes, ferns and primulas.

The formal gardens at Lyme were made by Lord Newton in the late nineteenth century and one of the most interesting is the Dutch garden. It lies hidden below a high terrace wall west of the lawn, and its pattern of beds, surrounding an ornamental pool, resemble a richly-coloured carpet. Individual beds are neatly edged and planted with low-growing subjects — each bed devoted to a single variety. A sloping walled area displays a collection of unusual trees and shrubs, giv n to Lyme by Vicary Gibbs, the well-known gardener at Aldenham. They provide an informal but botanically fascinating contrast and finale to these beautifully-maintained gardens.

grass paths, and they create vistas to features such as a pool with a central statue, a vase encircled by variegated weigela, a stone seat at the far end of an *allée*, and the house itself. The thick lower trunks and roots of the yew hedges are like lions' claw feet digging into the soil, and a long hedge opposite a border is divided into sections by buttresses. Between each of these is a pillar supporting a stone vase planted with spider plants, whose graceful pale fronds are highlighted against the dark yew.

The long border provides a colourful contrast and is profusely planted with shrubs, roses, herbaceous plants and climbers. At its far end, separated by hedges from the wide ribbon of colour, is a small garden filled with white flowering plants. Marvellously uniform lines of clipped yew topiary march either side of the central path of the forecourt. Textures, shadows, varying shades of green and the sympathetic colour of the stone paths, house and features, contribute to the restful character of this disciplined and pleasing garden.

MAENLLWYD ISAF

MAP D

Abermule, near Newtown
5m (8km) north-east of Newtown, 10m (16km)
south of Welshpool, 1½m (2½km) from
Abermule on B4368
Owner: Mrs Denise Hatchard
Tel: Abermule (068 686) 204
Open by appointment throughout the year
for charity

The River Mule acts as a boundary to this three-acre plantswoman's garden, set around a beautifully restored yeoman's sixteenth-century farmhouse and outbuildings. The successful design embraces formal, informal, woodland and orchard areas; as an architect, Mrs Hatchard has a good eye for shape and form and a great love for plants and skill with them.

An old bowling green near the house has been transformed into small, formal garden 'rooms', neat with dwarf box hedges. The redundant pigsties have become a miniature neo-classical orangery where ferns, orange and lemon trees

LYTES CARY MANOR

MAP I

Charlton Mackrell, Somerton near Ilchester
1m (2km) north of Ilchester bypass A303,
signposted from roundabout at junction of A303
Owner: The National Trust
Tel: Somerton (0458) 223297
Open two days a week from April to end of
October

Essentially formal, the three-acre garden of the part-fourteenth and part-fifteenth-century stone house is stylish and restrained in design. So well does it suit the character of the house that it is hard to believe that it was laid out only at the beginning of this century.

Yew hedges form the symmetrical framework to a series of garden 'rooms' linked by walks. They surround an orchard of medlars, quinces, apples and pears cut diagonally with mown and a loquat are housed. Spring bulbs bedeck the orchard of damsons and other fruit trees; at the far side of the drive a rockery — made of stone rescued from a nunnery which was being demolished — is planted generously with alpines such as gentians and lewisias. Typical of the ingenious way inhospitable sites and available materials have been put to good use is a giant sink for alpines, formed from tufa stone, and an old ash pit turned into a primula bed.

The flower beds are planted in an informal manner and contain well-associated collections of unusual plants, only the most suitable and attractive varieties being given precious space. Dwarf conifers and foliage plants are well represented and there are many species rhododendrons in the woodland area, also hostas, ferns and wood anemones. A steep bank, shaded by beeches and oaks, runs down to the fast-flowing river and is planted with Solomon's seal and more rhododendrons.

borders, planted to provided perennial interest; each warrants close inspection, because the creation of a long-lasting picture in a small space takes great skill.

At the far end, hidden by groups of shrubs and trees, and entered through an arch, is a shady circular garden. An urn set in a small circular flower bed is a lively focal point, and around the lawn borders are planted with strong foliage shapes and white-flowering plants. In contrast, what was once the old vegetable garden has been transformed into a sunbaked rectangular 'room', at one end of which is a raised pool, Moorish in design. Mediterranean in character, this 'room' is decorated with aromatic and tender subjects — herbs, alliums, oleanders and roses. Moisture-loving plants like rodgersias and hostas occupy a bed beneath an old lead pump in the wall by the house; against another between the garden and the street, pleached hornbeams give extra height and privacy.

MAGNOLIA HOUSE

MAP G

Yoxford, near Saxmundham
On A1120 in Yoxford
Owners: Mr Mark Rumary and Mr Derek Melville
Tel: Yoxford (072 877) 321
Open a few times a year and by written
appointment
(peak months May to August)

This delightful and cleverly-designed walled garden covers only one-third of an acre. It is irregular in shape and every bit of space has been put to good use. Divided into a series of areas which vary in character and treatment, it is richly planted with thoughtfully chosen and well-associated plants to interest the most fastidious of plantsmen.

Private and peaceful, no part of the garden is muddled or indigestible; long views have been made and each garden 'room' is an entity. There are contrasts between shade and light, space and intimacy, and the sound of water and cooing doves emphasises the soothing atmosphere. Around the lawns near the house are narrow

THE MAGNOLIAS

MAP J

18 St John's Avenue, Brentwood
From A1023 turn south on to A128; after 300yds
(270m) right at traffic lights, over railway bridge,
St John's Avenue third on right
Owners: Mr and Mrs R. A. Hammond
Tel: Brentwood (0277) 220019
Open several days a year for charity and by
appointment for parties from March to October
(peak months May and June)
Plants for sale

Arriving outside this modest suburban house, only the shrewdest of plantsmen will spot the clues to what lies in store in the back garden. Those who think they have come to the wrong place will miss a remarkable living museum of rare and unusual plants which will stay in their memories for many years. The Magnolias is only half an acre in size, but it contains enough plants, trees and shrubs to fill a garden twenty times its size. Not an inch of the sloping site has been wasted; when you explore the curling paths you have to move slowly and inspect the garden at all levels so as not to miss anything.

Immediately behind the house, the narrowest part is filled by an unexpected sight: four raised pools of koi carp. Apparently, some visitors are so taken aback by these that they fail to notice the superb magnolia behind them. The garden runs away from the pools down the slope, a many-layered forest of diverse and unusual plants which the neutral soil supports. Ornamental and specimen trees abound — magnolias, stuartias, maples and conifers jostle for attention, and large specimens are hosts to climbers and ramblers.

Rhododendrons, camellias and azaleas thrive and evergreen foliage and over one hundred varieties of hosta, the National Collection of arisaema and a fine collection of ferns crowd into the shade of trees and shrubs. Foliage plants are also favourites here and specimen bulbs and herbs. All are well labelled; the date when a subject was planted is listed with its name. There is a small area of lawn where a child's swing is entwined with several, seldom-seen climbers. The only other shaded but relatively open spaces of ground are the two water gardens. One of these, decorated with a wisteria-clad bridge and pagoda framed in luxuriant foliage and flowers, has an authentic Japanese air. Apricots and nectarines grow in the greenhouse and, as might be expected in a plantsman's garden such as this, a further greenhouse is devoted to raising plants.

THE MALT HOUSE

MAP I

Chithurst, Rogate near Midhurst
From A272, 3½m (5½km) west of Midhurst turn north signposted Chithurst then 1½m (2½km); from A3 2m (3km) south of Liphook, turn south-east to Milland, then follow signs to Chithurst for 1½m (2½km)
Owners: Mr and Mrs Graham Ferguson
Tel: Rogate (073 080) 433
Open for charity several days in spring and by appointment for parties only
(peak month May)
Plants for sale

Dating from 1560, the interesting and beautiful house lies on a west-facing hill with views to the South Downs. Terraces surround the wisteria-clad building, then the garden becomes increasingly natural and eventually melts into woodland. In spring the flowering shrubs and ornamental trees capture the attention; in summer the spectacular and triffid-like rambling rose, 'Kiftsgate'; and a clematis montana clamber up a cliff, leaving below the more delicate, pale yellow *Rosa banksiae lutea*. There are fine rhododendrons, Exbury hybrids producing colour over a long period, and many different varieties of hydrangea.

Specimen trees such as *Cornus nuttallii*, eucryphias and standard wisterias are attractive, and the brilliant blue-flowered *Lithospermum diffusum* 'Grace Ward', which dislikes limy soil, thrives on this peaty sand. You can also explore the fifty-acre woodland with its massive western hemlocks and redwoods and the incense cedar native to California and Oregon.

MANNINGTON HALL GARDENS

MAP G

Saxthorpe, near Holt
18m (29km) north of Norwich, between Aylsham and Holt, turn north-east at Saxthorpe for Mannington
Owners: Honourable Robin and Mrs Walpole
(HHA)
Tel: Saxthorpe (026 387) 284
Open one day a week from April to December and several days a week in June, July and August
(peak months June and July)
Plants for sale

The gardens which surround the friendly fifteenth-century, moated manor house have a homely and welcoming air. They belie the fierceness of an inscription near the front door: 'A tiger is worse than a snake, a demon than a tiger, a woman than a demon, and nothing worse than a woman.'

Between the flint-faced manor and the moat

are intimate gardens devoted to herbs and scented plants, roses or sympathetically-composed beds of herbaceous plants and shrubs in a mixture of yellows and oranges. The gardens on the far side of the moat are more relaxed. Informal beds of trees and shrubs and old-fashioned roses are set around lawns and reflected in the smooth surface of the moat and a man-made lake; a temple sheltering a statue representing Architecture is glimpsed between groups of trees and shrubs. The chapel garden across the lane has a natural wildness; paths weave through rough grass and woodland, and you will light upon the ruins of a Saxon church and Victorian follies.

In complete contrast, but also of historical interest, is the Heritage rose garden laid out in the old kitchen garden. Roses through the ages, from the very old to the modern hybrid, are planted in individual gardens designed in a period style. There is a wattle-enclosed medieval garden, a Tudor knot, a turn-of-the-century trellis garden and others, fragrant and colourful with over a thousand roses.

THE MANOR HOUSE

MAP F

Bledlow, near Princes Risborough
½m (1km) off B4009 in middle of Bledlow
village
Owners: Lord and Lady Carrington
Open one day a year for charity and by
written appointment on weekdays only
(peak months second half of April, May to July)

The simplicity of the driveway to the Manor House — a cool spread of well-kept lawns and mature trees, is a serene contrast to more intensely-planted and formal gardens hidden behind hedges. These were created to add interest, break up the space and allow different elements of design and content to live in harmony. Spread around three sides of the house, with a working farm to the west, the garden is on level chalk ground. South of the house, a path lined with standard *Viburnum carlesii* (the scent in spring can be imagined) leads to the sunken

garden, with beds of shrub roses, polyanthus and a lily pool. A path edged with catmint leads to a white-painted gazebo. An avenue of pleached hornbeams leads to a small informal garden planted with spring-flowering subjects — lilac, brooms and the unusual 'incense' rose.

On the far side of the drive, beyond the lawn and hedges, are the yew-hedged 'rooms'; the astrolabe garden of cubed, clipped box and yew; St Peter's garden where box-edged beds fan out from the statue, filled with santolina, rue, variegated dwarf hostas or golden marjoram; finally, there is a garden planted with yellow and white roses, lavender and irises. Relaxed open areas decorated with shrubs, trees and borders lie beyond, and there is a kitchen garden.

A particular strength of this delightful and well-balanced country-house garden is the discerning use of colour, texture and shape. There are many interesting and unusual plants, but it is the way they have been used and mixed which immediately captures the attention.

Lord and Lady Carrington have also made an informal garden in the village, a short distance from the house. The steep slopes of a valley falling down to a stream are planted with shrubs and moisture-loving plants, and wooden walkways and bridges have been built over the water, giving the garden an uncontrived and subtle Japanese air.

Mellow brick walls, herbs and shrub roses in the garden at Goodnestone Park.

THE MANOR HOUSE

MAP E

Walton-in-Gordano, near Clevedon
On the B3124 1½m (2½km) from Clevedon
Owners: Mr and Mrs Simon Wills
Tel: Clevedon (0272) 872067
Open several days a week April to
mid-September and by appointment
(peak months May and June)
Plants for sale

The four acres of garden which surround the early eighteenth-century manor house will be of special interest to the plantsman. Though still young and constantly being added to, the exceptionally wide range of plant material, which includes the National Collections of cercis and dodecatheon, is matched by the high standards of upkeep. Everything is well labelled and mulches of shredded bark and gravel are used liberally to condition the light sandy soil and suppress weeds. Mature trees, such as a London plane over two hundred years old, and a monkey puzzle add stature to the well-sheltered garden which has been intensively developed since 1977.

At the front of the house are beds of silver and white plants, and an orchard and spring garden to the side of the drive contain unusual bulbs, hellebores and specimen trees. The main part, to the north, is informal, with mown grass paths weaving between collections of acid-loving, winter-flowering, foliage or other unusual and sometimes rare trees, shrubs and plants. A rockery displays tender specimens from the Mediterranean and New Zealand and a border nearby has plants grown from seed collected by the owners on their travels in Greece.

Island beds — one containing subjects with red flowers, berries, bark or foliage — can be seen near the house and an old tennis court has been transformed into an attractive formal pool garden. When the yew hedges around this mature, it will make a delightful resting place — the sight and scent of lavender and pinks trapped in the hedged 'room' and the overall picture to be admired from one of the thoughtfully-placed seats. An increasingly popular feature is the meadow garden of native wild flowers such as cowslips and orchids.

MARWOOD HILL

MAP H

Marwood, near Barnstaple
4m (6½km) north of Barnstaple on B3230 turn
west for Marwood at Muddiford
Owner: Dr J. A. Smart
Tel: Barnstaple (0271) 42528
Open daily throughout the year
(peak seasons spring and summer)
Plants for sale

Plantsmen will thrill to the contents of this twenty-acre garden which, since 1962, has spread out from the original walled garden to embrace a wide expanse of pastureland. Since 1949 it has been developed by Dr J. A. Smart, an expert plantsman and dendrologist who has collected and grown from seed a range of unusual subjects from all over the world.

Many can be seen on the hillside which runs down to the bog garden and three small lakes formed by damming the stream running through the valley. The edges of the lakes accommodate an exceptionally rich and generously planted collection of moisture-loving plants, their dramatic shapes and colours matched by the size and quantity of the carp in one of the lakes. Day lilies, candelabra primulas, ligularias, irises, gunnera and skunk cabbage present a lush picture. An old quarry has been transformed into a rock garden on the hillside, and huge greenhouses filled with Australasian plants and camellias lie within the walls of the original garden. These walls are clad with tender and other climbers; the varieties of clematis are particularly eye-catching. Heathers, roses and hostas abound, and tree and herbaceous peonies and cyclamen are shaded by shrubs.

Rhododendrons and a wealth of specimen and ornamental trees — eucalpytus, magnolias and cornus — and many other subjects decorate the hillside below the modern house. New plants are added constantly, and specimens of unusual trees have been planted recently on the hill to the far side of the lakes. Marwood will be an inspiration to those seeking new and interesting plants for their own garden, because it offers an opportunity to observe the growing habits of several different varieties of any one genus and introduces the enthusiast to new treasures. A large number of these, propagated from stock in the garden, are available from the excellent nursery run by Dr Smart.

MELBOURNE HALL GARDENS

MAP F

Melbourne, near Derby
8m (13km) south of Derby on A514
Tel: Melbourne (033 16) 2502 (HHA)
Open a few days a week from April to end
September
(peak months June, July and September)

The garden at Melbourne is one of the very few formal seventeenth-century gardens to be seen in this country. Saved by past neglect, it is laid out in the French style originated by Le Nôtre at Versailles. By the time that Queen Anne's Vice-Chamberlain, Sir Thomas Coke, had inherited Melbourne in 1969, he had studied architecture and garden design in France and had obviously been much influenced by the grandeur and formality of all he had seen. He wanted to translate this style for his own garden, drew up a design and employed nurserymen London and Wise to lay the gardens out. Since the completion of the work, little of note has been added. Due to the political activities of subsequent generations of the family and the fact that they owned another property nearer London, the original design was left unchanged. The garden is much smaller than its seventeenth-century French counterpart and does not display the intricate parterres so popular in such gardens. But it has other vital elements such as hedged *allées*, symmetrical walks, vistas, water and elegant features like stone vases and lead figures. It is autocratic in character and highly disciplined in design.

East of the house, aligned on the façade and flanked by yew hedges, are large rectangular lawns set on terraces and divided by gravel paths. Cherubs and mythological figures by van Nost decorate the symmetrical scene, which overlooks the grand basin, a large formal pool. Behind this is a magnificent and unique wrought-iron feature — an arbour or birdcage. Partly gilded, domed and unashamedly ornate, it was made by Robert Bakewell at the beginning of the eighteenth century and cost Sir Thomas £125. South of the basin, groves of trees are divided by avenues of limes and yews which radiate from axes such as the famous Urn of Four Seasons. As one focal point at the end of an *allée* is reached, a further beckons from the far end of another avenue. The sixteen acres of garden give an illusion of stretching to infinity. The sight and sound of fountains add to the atmosphere — part sylvan, part grandiose. The smooth rounded shapes of a long yew tunnel of enormous proportions resemble reclining abstract figures by Henry Moore; the rib-cage of twisted and tangling trunks reveal its great age.

MIDDLE HILL

MAP H

Washfield, near Tiverton
4½m (7km) north-west of Tiverton. Through
village of Washfield, leaving church on right,
1¼m (2km) on the left
Owners: Mr and Mrs E. Boundy
Tel: Oakford (039 85) 380
Open several days a year for charity and by
appointment from middle of April to
beginning of September
(peak month May)
Plants for sale

When the Boundys came to Middle Hill in 1964 their first priority was to plant a shelter belt, because the garden is exposed on a high and windy site. The soil of the third of an acre was not ideal either, being heavy clay. They made a series of raised scree and other beds whose specially created soil conditions allow many different sorts of plants to thrive.

Melbourne Hall from the entrance of the wrought iron birdcage.

Divided into different sections by hedges and groups of shrubs, the garden has a cottage air. The owner is an insatiable propagator, so much on show has been grown from seed collected from all over the world. No one family of plants dominates the scene, the only obvious common factor being the unusualness of so many of the plants. Foliage is as important as flowers and pleasing plant associations are here in plenty. Suitable conditions have been created for growing specimen bulbs, alpines, grasses, moisture-loving and herbaceous plants. Shade-tolerant hostas, hellebores and pulmonarias grow beneath shrubs and trees, fragrant plants beside sunny garden seats and wild flowers on grassy banks.

MINTERNE

MAP I

Minterne Magna, near Sherbourne
On A352 2m (3km) north of Cerne Abbas, 9m
(14½km) south of Sherbourne
Owner: Lord Digby (HHA)
Tel: Cerne Abbas (03003) 370
Open daily from April to end October
(peak months April to July and October)

Once the home of the Churchill family, Minterne became the property of the Digbys in 1768. Five generations of this family are responsible for the beauty and interest found throughout the garden today. Though composed of two quite different elements, an eighteenth-century landscape and a nineteenth-century woodland garden, the lie of the land lets the two meld into and complement each other. The landscape, possibly influenced by 'Capability' Brown, surrounds the Edwardian Hamdon stone house and flows down towards the valley. Maximum use was made of the river flowing through it, and an elegant stone bridge spans it. Fourteen dams and cascades form different levels, and the surroundings become increasingly natural the deeper it cuts into the valley. A shelter belt of beech and pines was planted, making a woodland garden possible in the valley a century later.

Wandering the paths, punctuated by bridges and stepping-stones across the water, and weaving through the woodland is an adventure. The atmosphere is that of a lush Himalayan forest; the skilful planting successfully masks the hand of man. Paths circle around and through a superb collection of rhododendrons, a number having been grown from seed brought back by the planthunter George Forrest at the beginning of this century. Many of the most exciting varieties of azaleas, maples and magnolias decorate the route, and enkianthus and azaleadendrons, handkerchief trees, bamboos and swamp cypress, as well as moisture-loving plants, make a lush and colourful picture. Scent is easily trapped in the valley, as is the soothing sound of tumbling water. This garden can be savoured on several different levels — historical, botanical, or simply visual — all three are equally satisfying.

MISARDEN PARK

MAP F

Miserden, near Stroud
In the village of Miserden, 7m (11km) north-east
of Stroud
Owners: Major and Mrs M. T. N. H. Wills (HHA)
Tel: Miserden (028 582) 309
Open a few days a week from late April to end of
September and on other days by appointment for
charity
Plants for sale

High above Golden Valley and surveying wooded hills and countryside is an Elizabethan manor house with a twelve-acre garden. The handsome stone house and its immaculately-kept surroundings present a classical picture of stability and old-fashioned charm. Topiary, a scented garden and herbaceous borders, containing the seldom seen white willow herb, stand on the terraces near the house. Below lie lawns punctuated by a flight of grass steps which are embroidered with lobelia and were laid out at the suggestion of Sir Edwin Lutyens. These lead down to the pleasure grounds — an open and informal area planted with shrubs, spring bulbs and some ornamental and specimen trees. Below this lies a woodland walk to a lake, but the less energetic can explore the more highly-cultivated areas on the terraces west of the house.

There is a yew-enclosed rose garden planted with floribundas, and the splendid double herbaceous borders, unusually deep and luxuriantly planted, are at their best in June and September. Hidden behind hedges is a well-ordered kitchen garden. Miserden has many noteworthy features: the martagon lilies which have seeded themselves so freely; the new grey-and-silver border beneath an ancient sycamore which has grown through a wall; the fiery autumn tints of a *Vitis coignetiae* which clambers over an old yew, and the clipped, lollipop hornbeams at one side of the house. The uniformly good condition of every part of the garden gives no hint that it is prey to severe weather conditions and damage by deer, forty-six once having been seen grazing on the top lawn.

MONTACUTE HOUSE

MAP I

Montacute, near Yeovil
4m (6½km) west of Yeovil on south side of A3088;
3m (5km) east of A303 near Ilchester
Owner: The National Trust
Tel: Martock (0935) 823289
Open daily throughout the year

This superb Elizabethan mansion, confident and richly embellished, was built by Sir Edward Phelips at the end of the sixteenth century on the site of an ancient fort, Mons Acutus. The Phelips family lived here for three hundred years and though only the framework of the original Elizabethan garden now exists — alterations and planting having been done in the nineteenth century — the soft yellow Ham Hill stone features and sympathetic plant material create a seductive period atmosphere.

More architectural than floriferous, the garden is divided by walls into several definite sections. Chestnuts and cedars, a garden house decorated with arches, and a small circular pool garden can be found on the enclosed cedar lawn. North of this, against a dark yew hedge, are two elegant white seats reproduced from a design by

Sir Edwin Lutyens. The east court garden with its central lawn was the original forecourt and entrance before it was turned back to front in 1785. The warm stone of the charming pavilions and balustraded walls topped with obelisks is offset by borders which make a ribbon of colour around its perimeter.

Once the original garden to the house, the north court is surrounded by a raised terraced walk from which the countryside as well as the layout of this garden can be admired. This was simplified in the mid-nineteenth century by William and Ellen Phelips and their gardener Mr Pridham — lawns and flowerbeds were laid out and an ornamental pond built. This stands at the centre of the picture and replaces the ancient mount which was originally there. Radiating out from it are wide gravel paths which cut the lawn into four sections. Their outer edges are lined with sentinel yews whose columnar shapes contrast with the rounded American thorns along the terrace walk. A yew hedge, of whale-like size, runs in undulating, velvety humps down the west side of this court; borders of old-fashioned roses and hostas were planted beneath the terrace on the advice of Vita Sackville-West. Jasmine, standard fuchsias

The early eighteenth-century wrought iron birdcage by Robert Bakewell at Melbourne Hall.

and ferns decorate the eighteen-century orangery, and from the west side of the house the long drive dips and rises between an avenue of sentinel yews backed by beeches, limes and Lebanon cedars. A fine specimen of the fragrant winter-flowering *Chimonanthus praecox*, variegated holly, towering *Cupressus macrocarpa* and Californian redwoods can be seen at the top of the drive near the house.

MOSELEY OLD HALL

MAP F

Moseley Old Hall Lane, Wolverhampton
4m (6½km) north of Wolverhampton: south of
M54 between A449 and A460; 2½m (4km) south
of Shareshill Island; traffic from south on M6 and
M54 take Junction 1 to Wolverhampton
Owner: The National Trust
Tel: Wolverhampton (0902) 782808
Open from mid-March to late December a
varying number of days a week, depending on the
season
(peak season summer)

Though reproduced and not original, these seventeenth-century-style gardens will appeal to the historian and to those interested in old-fashioned plants. When the Elizabethan house — now almost completely masked by a nineteenth-century brick shell — became the property of the National Trust in 1962, the walled garden was derelict. After much hard work and research the present gardens had been laid out by 1963 and were gradually enriched with a fascinating range of plants and trees which might have been grown before 1700.

At the front of the house, which sheltered Charles II after the Battle of Worcester, are lawns decorated with topiary box in spirals and cones. Beds edged with germander are planted with hypericum and perimeter borders with old gallica and sweet briar roses, madonna lilies and plants like soapwort whose sap was used to clean fabrics. Beyond a wrought-iron gate in the wall is the wonderfully-disciplined knot garden. Its geometric pattern reproduces a design of 1640 by the Reverend Walter Stonehouse illus-

trated in a manuscript at Magdalen College, Oxford. The pattern is made up of dwarf box and coloured gravels, standard balls of box adding vertical interest. Further period features are a hornbeam walk, a nut alley edged with fritillarias and autumn crocus, a sixteenth-century arbour, an orchard filled with old varieties of fruit trees, and a box-hedged herb garden.

Seventeenth-century gardens were not planted purely for effect. They had to supply the household with fruit, nuts and culinary herbs, as well as material for medications and strewing plants to scent the house. There is a delicacy and charm about these fragrant centuries-old plants, which makes some of those introduced later seem coarse and gaudy in comparison.

MOTTISFONT ABBEY

MAP I

Mottisfont, near Romsey
4½m (7km) north-west of Romsey; ¾m (1½km)
west of the A3057
Owner: The National Trust
Tel: Lockerley (0794) 40757
Open several days a week from Easter to end
September
(peak months June and July)

Monasteries were usually established near a good source of water, and the Augustinian priory which forms the inner core of Mottisfont Abbey was no exception. A short distance from the once Tudor (now mid-eighteenth-century) house, a spring or 'font' rises, and a sparkling tributary of the River Test runs beyond the rolling lawns. The overall impression is one of light and space, punctuated by pools of shade thrown by dignified and impressive planes, oaks and sweet chestnut trees.

Pockets of formality lie within this handsome landscape: a pleached lime walk designed by Geoffrey Jellicoe, underplanted with *Chionodoxa luciliae*; a box and lavender parterre near the house, laid out by Norah Lindsay in 1938, and a stylish yew-hedged octagon decorated with lead vases. A *Schizophragma hydrangeoides* growing against the north-east wall of the house is a seldom-seen beauty from Japan akin to the hydrangea petiolaris.

The jewel in the crown at Mottisfont is the unforgettably lovely and fascinating collection of old-fashioned roses in the walled garden. Created in 1972 by the renowned rose expert and the National Trust's Garden Adviser, Graham Stuart Thomas, it gives a rare chance to enjoy and study the diverse beauty and origins of all the roses raised before 1900. Thanks to the National Rose Society and Mr Thomas's perseverance in collecting roses from all over the world over many years, it is now a hard-to-rival panorama of this much-loved genus. The scent and colour of the myriad damask, musk, gallica, centifolia and other roses which ramble and climb over walls and poles and mingle in borders is concentrated and trapped by the surrounding walls. The layout is formal: dwarf box edges the beds and Irish yews encircle a fountain, but the planting is exuberant and relaxed. Herbaceous borders and spring-flowering edging plants extend the season of interest.

MOUNT EDGECUMBE COUNTRY PARK

MAP H

Cremyll
By road via A374 and B3247 from Torpoint or by the Cremyll ferry from Admiral's Hard, off Durnford Street, Stonehouse, Plymouth
Owners: Plymouth City Council and Cornwall County Council
Tel: Plymouth (0752) 822236
(Peak seasons spring and summer)

On a headland with panoramic views over the Sound to Plymouth and the moors beyond, Mount Edgecumbe has one of the most superb positions of any public park in the country. The natural beauty of the site has been enhanced by landscape and formal gardens, and decorated with architectural features. It can be enjoyed on several different levels by the historian, the botanist, the naturalist and the country-lover; it was recently given a Grade 1 listing by the

Historic Buildings and Monuments Commission. The park shows the Edgecumbe family's enthusiasm and talent for garden-making over the centuries, and their ability to keep smartly in step with fashion. Artistic and cultured, they did not need to employ the fashionable garden designers of the day being well able to interpret current styles themselves.

An eighteenth-century landscape with serpentine walks, punctuated with classical and other features, winds around the park. It was laid out by Sir Richard Edgecumbe on his retirement from politics in 1742, and the natural drama of the terrain has been accentuated and romanticised by his clever placing of buildings like the temple and the folly. From afar, the folly looks like a massive ruin set against the sky on the hilltop. Closer inspection discloses a surprisingly modest and cleverly sited flight of steps supporting a platform from which there is a magnificent view of the Sound.

The intimate formal gardens, hidden behind high hedges, were laid out bang on cue at the end of the eighteenth century, on the site of an old wilderness garden. The fine flight of steps decorated with statues in the Italian garden looks down on an imposing orangery, all of them offset by an impressive hedge of bay. The sheltered English garden is the home of a neo-classical garden house which surveys a lawn dotted with specimen trees, twisting cork oaks and magnolias. Amid the neat, bright parterre beds of the French garden a fountain of four huge shells stands in front of an elegant conservatory.

There are many other period botanical and architectural features: a fern garden; an ancient towering ilex hedge next to the old tennis court; the National Collection of camellias: a grotto, a Doric pavilion and an amphitheatre. Plymouth County Council took over the park in 1971 and began restoration and replacement planting of trees and shrubs, work which continues today. The concrete paths which thread through some areas of the park are a reminder of the American troops who were here in 1944 in preparation for D-Day.

MUNCASTER CASTLE

MAP B

Ravenglass
West of Ravenglass off A595
Owner: Mrs Patrick Gordon-Duff-Pennington
(HHA)
Tel: Ravenglass (06577) 203
Open regularly from Easter to September
(peak months April to June and September and
October)
Plants for sale

The castle's position on a hilltop overlooking the Esk valley is magnificent, and the view over the valley to Scafell and the Lakeland hills is stunning. The scale and position of Muncaster, as well as its extensive woodland enriched with rhododendrons, azaleas, camellias and specimen trees, make it an exciting place to visit. Built of red sandstone, the oldest part of the castle dates from the thirteenth century; the collection of plants (once the largest of species rhododendrons in Europe) from after World War I.

The present owner's grandfather, Sir John Ramsden, began the collection and developed the woodland garden between 1920 and 1958. He subscribed to planthunting expeditions, raised his own hybrids such as 'Muncaster Bells' and 'Muncaster Mist', and transplanted seedlings brought from his garden at Bulstrode in Buckinghamshire. Unfortunately, some of the late eighteenth-century and other woodland trees are reaching the end of their lives and the garden is in danger of losing its shelter. The new rhododendrons, a number of which were grown from seed collected by the planthunter Francis Kingdon Ward, were planted in the shade of these trees. No one at that time had any idea how large or fast they would grow; due to the garden's proximity to the warm Gulf Stream, the high rainfall and the loss of light through the rapid growth of some specimens, a number of the unusual rhododendrons have grown leggy and distorted. Muncaster is far from being the only woodland garden of its age to be faced with these problems, and great efforts are being made to replace trees and plant young shrubs.

A small valley and stream lie immediately below the castle walls, their steep banks glossy with voluptuous crimson rhododendrons, unusual maples and magnolias. A long grass terrace walk stretches away from the far side of the valley; set into the side of the hill, this eighteenth-century feature was obviously devised for enjoyment of the glorious view. A yew hedge, clipped to resemble battlements, stands on the outer edge, and a belt of shrubs and interesting trees — maples, cercidiphyllum and cornus — line the inner edge. Lawns and a formal garden are on the far side of the castle, and in spring the woodland garden creates a brilliant frame.

Along the drive are a number of handsome nothofagus, eucryphias and conifers, and the large and glossy leaves of skunk cabbage catch the eye beside a stream. The steeply-sided banks of the woodland are ideal to display the azaleas and rhododendrons: large-leafed and scented varieties of the latter thrive here, and in summer the hydrangeas come into their own.

MYDDLETON HOUSE

MAP J

Bulls Cross, Enfield
3½m (5½km) north of Enfield on the A105 or
Junction 25 of M25
Owner: Lee Valley Regional Park Authority
Tel: Lee Valley (0992) 717711
Open on several Sundays between March and
October and every weekday except public
holidays, throughout the year
(peak seasons spring and early summer)

Those who have enjoyed the gardening books of E. A. Bowles will find this Edwardian plantsman's garden particularly fascinating. It was neglected for several decades, but is now being restored and the visitor will recognise features and plants he wrote about so vividly: the 'Lunatic Asylum' bed which still contains the twisted hazel and other freakish plants; the meadow and rock garden rich in unusual snowdrops and other naturalised bulbs; 'Tom Tiddler's Ground', which has once again been filled with unusual variegated plants, and the iris beds which now contain the National Collection of this genus.

A plantsman's garden suffers more than any other when left to its own devices, and it will take a few years before newly-planted varieties mature and the battle against perennial weeds has been won. Some trees will have to be replaced, though a fine Dawyk beech stands near the pond, palm trees have survived recent severe winters, and the short avenue of eucalyptus trees in the pergola garden has recently been replanted.

Informal, and on a human rather than a grand scale, the garden has a distinct period air. Attached to the handsome early-nineteenth-century house is Mr Bowles's conservatory, which now contains his eighty-year-old pepper tree, together with succulents, tender subjects and a vigorous and always seductive *Rosa banksiae lutea*.

NEWBURGH PRIORY

MAP C

Coxwold
3½m (5½km) south-east of Thirsk on A19 turn
east to Coxwold and Newburgh Priory
Owner: Sir George Wombwell
Tel: Coxwold (034 76) 435
Open one day a week from mid-May to end
August
(peak months May and June)

The gardens of Newburgh, cultivated from the twelfth century onwards, are once again enjoying a period of renovation thanks to the energy and enthusiasm of their present owner. In unspoilt countryside beneath the Hambledon Hills, the priory has been in the same family since the Dissolution of the monasteries in 1538; subsequent centuries have laid a patina of period features on the house and over the (now) fifty acres of well-kept grounds.

The approach to the house is through handsome wrought-iron gates and down a drive flanked by lawns. On the lawns stand yews that have been intriguingly clipped into the shape of

coronets. On one side are beds of shrub roses, peonies and hostas, and there is a border of perennials beneath a long wall. Behind this is the kitchen garden, now turned into an ornamental flower garden. On the far side of the house lawns cut by gravel paths lined with yew topiary — nesting birds, dogs and other shapes — flow down to an eighteenth-century lake and spread to the edge of the woodland and surrounding countryside.

A large number of trees planted by royalty and a half-mile walk of ornamental cherries and crab-apple trees, draw the eye from the house and towards the water garden, a delightful and highly-cultivated surprise on the hillside. First developed in 1938 by the owner's uncle, Captain V. M. Wombwell, this twentieth-century 'wild garden' is fed by springs and is lush and colourful with the foliage and flowers of many acid- and moisture-loving plants. The garden is set on limestone, so quantities of peat had to be brought in, and mature and newly planted azaleas, rhododendrons and handsome acers now thrive, together with bamboos, flowering shrubs and trees. Paths weave around streams and groups of plants on the hillside, and dwarf conifers and alpines grow in stone troughs and raised beds, the stone walls of which are jewelled with the star-like flowers of *Ramonda myconi*. An ancient roofless building beside the house has been turfed and turned into an intimate garden: narrow borders contain lily-of-the-valley and nerines, and fig trees and roses decorate its walls. *Magnolia grandiflora*, *Actinidia chinensis*, *Clematis alpina*, roses and Virginia creeper grow against the house.

NEWBY HALL AND GARDENS

MAP C

near Ripon
2m (3km) south-east of Ripon; 1m (2km) west of
A1 on the B6265. Turn south at Bridge Hewick
Owner: Mr R. E. J. Compton (HHA)
Tel: Boroughbridge (0423) 322583
Open regularly from spring to autumn
Plants for sale

The gardens of Newby Hall earned the prestigious Christies/Historic Houses Association 'Garden of the Year' award for 1986; the present owner has served as President of the Northern Horticultural Society and on the National Trust's Gardens Panel. These facts should alert the garden-lover to the treat in store.

Laid out with great style and imagination, the gardens cover twenty-five acres, are a well-balanced mixture of informality and formality, and contain a fascinating and wide-ranging collection of plants. They are one of the loveliest and most rewarding gardens in the north of England and very much more than a frame for the fine eighteenth-century house. Visitors, especially plantsmen, should be prepared to spend considerable time exploring them.

When the present owner's father, Major Edward Compton, inherited the property in 1921, there was little of what can be seen today — only the statue walk, the curving pergola now restored and draped with *Laburnum vossii*, and the rock garden designed by the Edwardian plantswoman Ellen Willmott. The major determined to give it a strong 'bone structure', and created the various compartments either side of the main axis running from the balustraded south terrace down to the River Ure. This splendid central vista from the high terrace, decorated simply with an ornamental lily pool reflecting the façade of the house, through the lower terrace (restrained, with clipped yew), flows on down through the luxuriant double borders set against yew hedges. Like the Russian dolls, the various gardens to east and west of this long view, gradually reveal themselves.

A number of features have been added since Mr Robin Compton inherited Newby in 1977: new gardens have been made and others replanted with sympathetic and eyecatching arrays of unusual plants. A sunken and paved 'room' named after Mr Compton's mother, Sylvia, is planted with grey, purple and blue foliage and flowers — artemesia, purple sage and irises. Other 'rooms', such as the rose and the autumn gardens, are equally intimate, their disciplined design offset delightfully by the exuberance and generosity of their planting. Straight paths and tightly-clipped hedges give way to curving walks

and glades planted with ornamental and specimen trees and shrubs. One contains a grove of Himalayan birches, their luminous white trunks rising out of a pool of pale pink primulas and tiarella. The way shrubs and low-growing subjects have been massed rather than dotted under trees is particularly effective, and highlights the appealing qualities of the plants used.

A handkerchief tree and an *Acer griseum* are in an area known as 'Wilson's Corner', named after the planthunter who introduced them to this country, and a long wall next to the orchard garden is swathed with surprisingly tender plants. Nearby is a white garden set on either side of a gravel walk. Shrub roses are at one side and beds of white-flowering and interesting foliage plants flank a stylish garden seat on the other.

The diversity and richness of the plant material, the way it has been associated — colour, shape and texture all taken into account — is absorbing enough. But the design of the different areas and the skilful way features like urns, wellheads, seats and gateways have been used as focal points, ensures that the overall picture seduces rather than the detail. The gardens also

Vista of the gardens at Newby Hall.

The double borders at Newby Hall.

accommodate an adventure garden for children and a miniature railway, but neither has been allowed to intrude on the private and peaceful atmosphere. Owners of gardens open to the public, as well as enthusiasts, will find much at Newby to inspire them to greater efforts. The excellent guide-book — a separate one for each season — is typical of its uniformily high standards.

NEWSTEAD ABBEY

MAP C

Lindy, near Mansfield
4m (6½km) south of Mansfield on A60 turn west
at Ravenshead
Owner: Nottingham City Council
Tel: Mansfield (0623) 793557
Open daily throughout the year
(peak seasons spring, summer and autumn)

The large scale, constantly changing mood and surprise elements of the gardens at Newstead could be likened to the character of its most famous owner — Lord Byron. Originally a twelfth-century Augustine priory, it became the property of the Byron family in 1540, but was sold in 1817 to meet the debts of the man who was 'mad, bad and dangerous to know'. The stump of an old oak which he planted and the tomb of his beloved Newfoundland dog, Boat-swain, are reminders of his time here.

The remains of the ancient priory now blend with buildings of a later date, successive owners having added various features to the abbey and its grounds. The nineteenth-century Tudor-Gothic front surveys spacious rolling lawns and a large lake, fed by the River Leen. Mock eighteenth-century forts stand on its banks; their size typifies the bold proportions to be seen in the twenty-five acres of garden and three-hundred-acre park.

Beside the abbey, ancient stew ponds adjoin a sombre walk of yews which leads, through a tunnel, to the eagle pond. Formal and restrained terraces, wide gravel paths and lawns surround the pond which gained its name from the (still undiscovered) brass eagle lectern thrown into it by the monks at the time of the Dissolution of the monasteries. Two statues with cloven feet gaze down from a spot once known as devil's wood, and in front of the east wing a Spanish wellhead is surrounded by flower-filled, boxed-edged beds. A short distance to the south, wisteria-clad gate piers lead into the first of two walled gardens; it contains geometric beds of irises set around a sundial, and borders and arches of trained fruit trees. The second has a central fountain and is fragrant with old-fashioned roses such as 'The Holy Rose' or *R. sancta*, discovered in an Egyptian tomb of 6000 BC.

A walk between mountainous and undulating yew hedges widens into an informal area planted with flowering shrubs, conifers and heathers. The sound of tumbling water hastens your steps onwards, past a rockery, to the early-twentieth-century Japanese garden, a craftily hidden surprise. Water was channelled from the garden lake nearby, over cascades and through tunnels into streams and lily pools spanned by stepping-stones and humpbacked bridges. The garden was laid out by a Japanese landscape architect and has an authentic oriental character; it contains the traditional ornaments of a tea-house and lanterns and appropriate trees, shrubs and moisture-loving plants. The path winding away from this richly-planted area makes a sudden turn and you have a panoramic view of the lake. More cascades can be seen on the far side of the lake — one constructed of huge rocks resembles a vast abstract sculpture. A long pergola walk of roses runs beside the water's edge, and the path gradually gives way to the lawns shaded by venerable trees by the Abbey.

7 NEW STREET

MAP D

Talybont, near Aberystwyth
On A487 in Talybont, 6m (9½km) north of
Aberystwyth
Owner: Miss M. J. Henry
Tel: Talybont (097 086) 529
Open throughout the year by appointment
for charity
(peak season spring)
Plants for sale

Measuring five by twenty-five yards, the garden behind this small terrace house is the creation of a trained horticulturist and offers good ideas to those faced with a similarly tiny plot. More a large rockery covered with miniature shrubs, rock plants and alpines, than a landscaped garden, every inch of space has been used to advantage. Paths made of bricks and pebbles from the beach weave around the beds set on different levels, past sinks studded with dwarf plants and trees, such as a witch-hazel and a golden elm, which have been espaliered along a boundary. Tall conifers and a columnar 'Amanogawa' cherry make full use of the vertical space available and room has even been found for a small sunbaked 'room' at the far end. The stone steps from the house down into the garden support scores of pots of miniature and dwarf plants; a glasshouse, used to propagate old favourites and new finds, stands nearby.

NORTHBOURNE COURT GARDENS

MAP J

Northbourne, Deal
West of Deal turn off A258 to Northbourne
Owner: Lord Northbourne
Tel: Deal (0304) 360813
Open for charity several days a year and one day a
week June, July, August, and by appointment
(peak months June and July)
Plants for sale on occasion

A short distance from the sea and sheltered from the harsh east wind by mature trees, the walled gardens at Northbourne have a sunbaked air. A series of 'rooms' varying in size and set on different levels, the gardens are much older than they appear. Though a part-eighteenth- and part-nineteenth-century house stands above them, they once belonged to an Elizabethan house destroyed by fire. The site has Saxon origins and the priory of St Augustine's, Canterbury once stood on this spot.

In the largest of the brick-walled enclosures are three tiers of terraces overlooking a rectangular lily pond. They once fulfilled the same purpose as a mount, affording views over the surrounding countryside, but are now decorated with borders. The planting of the seven-acre garden dates from 1925 and is largely the work of Walter, Lord Northbourne. A talented artist and enthusiastic botanist, he filled it with romantic, softly-coloured old-fashioned roses, peonies and silver- and grey-foliaged plants which thrive on the thin chalky soil. Around the house terraces, some intimate and sheltered, are lively with geraniums, fuchsias and silver-foliaged plants. Pinks and other low-growing subjects spill on to the stone and brick paths and jasmine and roses climb the house walls. The sweet and peppery scents entrapped here are reminiscent of a Mediterranean garden, and the presence of many tender plants and filled tubs enriches the romantic and relaxed feel of the whole.

NYMANS GARDENS

MAP J

Handcross, near Haywards Heath
4½m (7km) south of Crawley on the B2114 at
Handcross
Owner: The National Trust
Tel: Handcross (0444) 400 321
Open regularly from Easter to end October
Plants for sale

One of the great gardens of the Sussex Weald, Nymans is famed for its superb collection of trees and shrubs, a good number of which bear its name. Five hundred feet up on light acid loam and relatively frost-free, it has formal and enclosed gardens, a pinetum, woodland and a park. Separate areas display different design styles and varied plant collections; certain subjects, like the vast mounds of rhododendrons, have grown to an awesome size. Those who regularly attend the Royal Horticultural Society's shows must have noticed how often flowering trees and shrubs from Nymans win prizes. This fact alone would single it out for the plantsman's interest, but it is as visually satisfying as it is botanically fascinating and can be enjoyed on many different levels.

Nymans is the creation of successive generations of the Messel family who gave the gardens to the National Trust in 1954 but continue to oversee development. Ludwig Messel arrived here in 1890 and the mass of rhododendrons and azaleas, which play such an important role, were his creation. He also began the pinetum, and laid out the heather garden and the raised pergola walk above the croquet lawn. In 1916 his son, Lieutenant-Colonel Leonard Messel, inherited the property and became as enthusiastic and energetic in developing the garden as his father before him. He planted many of the now outstanding collection of magnolias and eucryphias, invested in plant-collecting expeditions and laid out the gardens as we see them today. His wife, Maud, made the rose garden — a pattern of beds filled with old-fashioned varieties, some of which originally came from Italy and France and were part of a collection made by the author of *The Genus Rosa*, Ellen Willmott.

The Victorian house, which the Colonel had transformed into a neo-Jacobean mansion, was almost completely burned down in 1947. Only one end is now inhabited; the rest, a roofless ruin draped with climbers, has a romantic *Sleeping Beauty* character. Topiary birds stand by the terrace and a yew hedge, decorated with clipped obelisk shapes, forms an architectural enclosure at one end. There is more topiary around the fountain, the focal point of the walled garden, which is divided by intersecting paths. This area has a distinctly Edwardian flavour: the planting of its spring and summer borders was inspired by William Robinson, the advocate of 'natural' gardens. Behind them is a valuable collection of tender, mature specimen trees and flowering shrubs. The camellias were grown from cuttings brought back from Portugal in 1973 by Ludwig Messel's grand-daughter and her husband (Lord and Lady Rosse) who continue to live at Nymans and care for the garden.

There is generosity in the way the more highly-cultivated parts have been planted: camellias completely surround the sunken garden of formal bedding; climbers intertwine with each other up walls and over arches, and tree-like and mountainous rhododendrons almost eclipse the beauty of the many rare and handsome magnolias. The heather and dwarf shrub garden, laced with narrow paths and set around a mound patterned with boulders of local stone, is decorated with Chinese ornaments and topped by an oriental-style platform, from which you can admire the varied texture and colour of all that lies below. The park, the pinetum and the woodland across the road, though more natural in character, are no less beautiful and well endowed with unusual shrubs and trees. In spring quantities of naturalised daffodils and narcissi carpet a meadow, and Tasmanian and Chilean rhododendrons colour the rhododendron and wild garden. It may be impossible to please everyone all of the time, but there is so much on offer at Nymans that the garden-lover cannot fail to be entranced by some of its different aspects.

THE OLD MANOR

MAP F

Twyning, near Tewkesbury
3m (5km) north of Tewkesbury via A38; follow signs to Twyning, garden at crossroads at top end of the village
Owner: Mrs Joan Wilder
Tel: Tewkesbury (0684) 293516/299878
Open one day a week throughout the year and by appointment
Plants for sale

Gardens whose *raison d'etre* is the display of a collection of unusual plants are an increasingly popular feature of our times. The garden of the Old Manor is a rewarding case, and even the most rabid plantsmen will find a good number here which he will not have seen previously. Many of the plants have been raised from seed collected by or exchanged with likeminded enthusiasts all over the world.

The Queen Anne cottage is surrounded by a one-acre garden enclosed within old walls; more walls divide it into different sections which vary in character. Once the old kitchen garden to the nearby manor house, its soil is neutral and so an extraordinarily wide range of plants can be grown, though the rainfall is only twenty-four inches a year and the ground is free-draining. When the owners began to develop it thirty years ago, the site was bare but for an old sycamore tree and an ancient mulberry; the present size of, for instance, the tulip tree and the Oriental plane should be an inspiration to those who think they will not see a fine tree mature in their lifetimes.

On the terrace next to the house, paved with old tombstones, are stone sinks of small subjects which enjoy alpine conditions, and beds of small shrubs. An informal area nearby is planted with specimen and ornamental trees, an unusual feature being an *Acer griseum* grown from seed by the owners. Collections of peonies, clematis and ferns have been planted, and beyond lies a water garden. A lawn in the main walled garden is surrounded with borders, scree and peat beds which provide ideal conditions for subjects collected from the wild — found on a Greek beach or high in the Andes and the Himalayas. Those expecting to see run-of-the-mill plants will be disappointed; only the choicest and most unusual varieties, a large proportion of them alpines, find a home here. The overall picture evolves all the time as new discoveries are made, and fellow collectors will be delighted to see a large number of these 'specials' for sale in the small nursery.

The twentieth-century plantsman's garden is now not complete without an arboretum, however small. At the Old Manor it stands on what was once a pig field where Korean limes and poplars, a paulownia, a catalpa from Zagreb and other specimen trees now thrive. The owners'

The garden by the ruins of the neo-Jacobean house at Nymans.

good 'eye' for sympathetic plant associations has made the garden more than simply a living museum of rare plants — it is as aesthetically pleasing as it is botanically intriguing.

THE OLD RECTORY

MAP I

Burghfield, near Reading
5m (8km) south-west of Reading. Turn west off
A33 and went to Burghfield
Owners: Mr and Mrs R. Merton
Tel: Burghfield Common (073 529) 2206
Open on several days a year for charity and by
written appointment
Plants for sale

Though belonging to an eighteenth-century house, the six-acre garden at Burghfield has been created by Mr and Mrs Merton over the last thirty-five years. Like many beautiful gardens made by a husband and wife team, the layout was planned by Ralph Merton and the planting was added by his wife, an enthusiastic and green-fingered plantswoman, a relatively late but avid convert to gardening. The wide range and imaginative and generous use of unusual or rare plants is impressive. Many have been brought back from trips abroad, and Mrs Merton's enthusiasm and botanical knowledge contribute to the enjoyment of a visit. To call this a plantswoman's garden would be correct but perhaps misleading, because the success of its design matches the diversity of its contents.

Divided by walls and yew hedges, each area is planted with candidates which suit a particular atmosphere or situation. In an intimate paved area at the back of the house is a collection of stone sinks planted with small plants which could be lost in thickly-planted flower beds. Beyond the door in the wall is a series of gardens, a secret swimming pool and a spring garden around a pond which mirrors a Roman statue of Antinous. These lead ultimately to what Mrs Merton calls her 'Camberley area' which as might be expected, is planted with unusual rhododendrons and azaleas. Running down the centre of the garden, to one side of the long lawn shaded by a venerable cedar, are long, deep double borders fronting yew hedges. Massed with lively herbaceous and other plants, they create a colourful vista from the south terrace, where there are pots luxuriantly planted with an imaginative mixture of annuals and other (often surprising) subjects. Spring bulbs and wild cyclamen colour the natural areas of the garden, and hellebores thrive in the shade of shrubs and trees. Ferns abound, but the most seductive of all the collections of plants are the fragrant Asiatic roses which rampage into trees, cascade over walls and frame doorways. Their exuberance typifies the generosity of this charming garden.

THE OLD RECTORY

MAP I

Farnborough, near Wantage
4m (6½km) south-east of Wantage off B4494
Owners: Mr and Mrs Michael Todhunter
Tel: Chaddleworth (048 82) 298
Open a few days a year for charity and by
appointment
(peak months May, June and July)
Plants for sale

Once the home of Sir John Betjeman, the eighteenth-century rectory stands eight hundred feet up on the Berkshire Downs. The flourishing appearance of the garden, only partially sheltered by mature limes and beeches, belies its vulnerability to weather conditions.

Lawns framed by trees run from the front of the house to a ha-ha which skilfully obscures the road running along the boundary; enclosed and other gardens stand at the back. Borders display a sensitive use of colour, a particular strength of this garden. A number are planted in shades of pink, but the one in the enclosed swimming-pool garden is a warming mix of cream, yellow and apricot. Roses — 'Golden Wings', 'Sombreuil' and 'Paul's Lemon Pillar' — adorn the walls and scent the air, and in front of the Gothic summerhouse pots of lilies and daturas add to the exotic and sunbaked feeling.

A rose garden has shrub roses underplanted with foliage plants, and the orchard has been enriched with ornamental trees and shrubs. Shrubs also feature in the vegetable garden hidden behind a beech hedge. Many of the best and unusual varieties of plants have been used throughout the garden, an unpretentious example being white rather than purple foxglove, the seldom seen variegated tulip tree and the charming rose Fimbriata or 'Phoebe's Frilled Pink', with delicate soft pink blooms like carnations. Species peonies abound, as do violas, daphnes and euphorbias, and a number of small-flowered clematis grow against the house with the wisteria and roses.

OLD RECTORY COTTAGE

MAP I

Tidmarsh, near Reading
½m (1km) south of Pangbourne, midway
between Pangbourne and Tidmarsh turn east
down narrow lane; left at T-junction
Owners: Mr and Mrs A. Baker
Tel: Pangbourne (073 57) 3241
Open frequently throughout the year and by
appointment
(peak months June and July)
Plants for sale

At first glance, the garden surrounding the red brick cottage, almost obscured by an outer skin of climbers, appears to be of an unassuming cottage nature. At closer quarters it is a plantsman's treasure chest. Fellow plantsmen are warned to allow several hours to appreciate it fully, and the wild garden Mr and Mrs Baker have made nearby has much to offer. Insatiable plant-collectors, they have never missed an opportunity on their frequent trips abroad to acquire seed or specimens of new and unusual plants, particularly wild varieties. A tour of the garden is a geographical and botanical education.

The highly-cultivated area around the house has been planted with shrubs, trees and plants with good year-round structure and interest. The borders and informal beds are not devoted to either perennials or shrubs but are a mixture of a wide range of subjects. Bulbs, irises, violets, lilies and wild perennial geraniums and peony species are in evidence, and different varieties of pulmonaria and less-invasive, decorative lamiums are used as ground-coverers. Old Rectory Cottage is a particularly good place to seek new varieties of such useful plants. A rock garden is a home for small and precious bulbs and dwarf plants, and stone sinks with tufa rock are filled with alpines. Hardy agapanthus and day lilies are planted between blue, columnar Lawson cypresses which line a walk to a white-painted garden seat, the one formal feature of the garden. Small-flowered clematis, many of which have been bred by the Bakers, clamber up stouter subjects against the house, and unusual ferns find a home in a shady corner.

A curved beech hedge leads to the wild garden, bounded by the River Pang, the source of water for the lake in what was once an old orchard. Varieties of willow and specimen trees, such as the handkerchief tree and weeping silver pear, provide shade here. Honeysuckles and roses romp into trees, giving the wild garden a wonderfully carefree air. In generously mulched beds edged with logs are wild flowers from all over the world, lilies bred by the Bakers, and the show-stopping blue meconopsis poppy and *Lilium giganteum*. A wide range of bulbs, carpets of cyclamen, fritillaria and martagon lilies thrive, and perennial geraniums and other ground-coverers have been used to great effect. Moisture-loving plants like primulas grow in areas of boggy ground and at the water's edge the local wild flower, the Loddon lily or *Leucojum aestivum*, flourishes.

OSTERLEY PARK

MAP J

Isleworth, London
Entrance in Jersey Road, north side of Great West
Road (A4)
Owners: The National Trust/Victoria and
Albert Museum
Tel: London (01) 560 3918
Open daily throughout the year

This landscaped park is now only a fraction of its original size, having been cut by a motorway, and is set on flat rather than undulating ground. However, its fine architectural features, handsome trees, serpentine lakes and all-important vistas to and from the porticoed mansion mark it as dating from the eighteenth century. Formality and floral displays do not find a home here.

The original house was built in 1577 by the fabulously wealthy merchant adventurer, Sir Thomas Gresham. Apart from the corner turrets which acted as belvederes to survey the original park, the entire house was encased in a Palladian-style shell by Robert Adam in the second half of the eighteenth century. Commissioned by the rich Child banking family who then owned the property, he and the fashionable landscape architect, Sir William Chambers, transformed the surrounding park. The Childs, like Sir Thomas Gresham, were not chary of displaying their wealth; it is said that one of their reasons for purchasing Osterley was the capaciousness of the vaults beneath its courtyard.

Chambers was responsible for the layout. He created the serpentine lakes, winding paths and vistas through clumps of trees. Cedars form a striking feature next to the lake and nearer the house stands his Doric temple, its interior decorated with stuccoed medallions representing the seasons, and two British worthies: the architect Colen Campbell, who was instrumental in introducing the neo-classical vogue, and the scientist, Sir Isaac Newton. This temple and Adam's semi-circular greenhouse were far from being simple decorative garden features. They were garden rooms in which to entertain and to dine. The park's proximity to urban development emphasises its maturity and space. Work goes on all the time to replace dead or dying trees, and to preserve these and important architectural features, but its surrounds are constantly under threat.

OVERBECKS GARDEN

MAP H

Sharpitor, Salcombe
1½m (2½km) south-west of Salcombe off road
to South Sands
Owner: The National Trust
Tel: Salcombe (054 884) 2893
Open daily throughout the year
(peak seasons spring and summer)

The superb position of this plantsman's six-acre garden, high above the mouth of the Salcombe estuary, could lead the visitor to believe that he or she had been transported to an unspoilt Mediterranean resort. Yachts sail down the sparkling estuary and out to the sea, and Chusan palms, with the sweet and peppery scents and bright colours of many interesting and tender plants strengthen the impression. The steep banks which were terraced at the beginning of this century are now covered with mature trees and shrubs. These were planted by Mr and Mrs G. M. Vereker between 1913 and 1928, when the property was bought by Mr Otto Overbecks. He amassed the fascinating collection of tender plants and left Overbecks to the National Trust.

From the lawn in front of the house, paths thread along banks shaded by mature trees and open up to intimate and sheltered areas like the fairly formal statue garden with its herbaceous borders. In spring the magnolias are a wonderful sight, particularly the splendid *Magnolia campbelli* planted in 1901. Hellebores flourish with cyclamen and primroses. In the summer exotic daturas, the electric blue flowers of a *Puya alpestris*, a Chatman Island forget-me-not and other rare specimens revel in the warmth. Trees, shrubs and plants grow to an unusual size here and varieties like the ebullient and long-flowering *Chrysanthemum frutescens* 'Jamaica

Primrose' survive through the winter. The shiny, strap-like leaves of New Zealand flax offset towering echiums, and the blue of agapanthus reflects the azure of the sky.

Beehives and rustic seats in the cottage garden at Eastgrove.

OXBURGH HALL

MAP G

**Oxburgh, near King's Lynn
7m (11km) south-west of Swaffham turn
north off A134 to Stoke Ferry
Owner: The National Trust
Tel: Gooderstone (036 621) 258
Open weekends only in April and October and
daily except for Thursdays and Fridays from May
to September
(peak season summer)**

This late-fifteenth-century moated manor has fairytale charm, an open aspect over the flat Norfolk countryside and a garden which displays some minor and one outstanding period feature. On the level lawns beside the house with its tall Tudor gatehouse is an immaculately-kept parterre.

This was created by Sir Henry Paston Bedingfeld and his wife Margaret in about 1845 and was copied from an early-eighteenth-century example they had seen in a garden in Paris. This in turn was taken from a design by the French gardener Dezallier d'Argenville, illustrated in his book *La Théorie et al Pratique du Gardinage*. In such a way do fashionable garden features cross the Channel and become Anglicised. Rectangular in shape and set on gravel are swirling and intricate shapes of box and santolina filled with brilliant blue ageratum, yellow tagetes and the blue and grey foliage of rue and stachys. Cones and balls of yew add vertical interest to this richly-patterned carpet.

A long yew hedge on the bank above hides from view an herbaceous border which might otherwise rob the parterre of its impact. It is bounded by a blue ribbon of catmint and displays a repetitive and effective colour scheme, plants like brilliant blue aconitum and dwarf golden rod giving long-lasting interest. A fine Judas tree stands in the spring shrub border, and white crinum lilies against a warm wall. You go through an ancient stone gateway to the kitchen garden, which is surrounded by walls punctuated with towers. This has now been turfed and planted with plum, quince and medlar trees, while cistus, potentilla, lavender and ceanothus flourish against a sunbaked wall near the potting shed. There are informal walks, carpeted with spring bulbs, through what was once a Victorian wilderness garden; these and expansive and beautifully-kept lawns running between the moat and the ha-ha, add to the tranquillity.

OXFORD UNIVERSITY BOTANIC GARDENS

MAP F

**Rose Lane, Oxford
In High Street, entrance opposite Magdalen
College
Owner: University of Oxford
Tel: Oxford (0865) 242737
Open regularly throughout the year
(peak season summer)**

These Botanic Gardens are the oldest in Britain. In 1621, Henry Danvers, Earl of Danby, leased from the University five acres of land belonging to Magdalen College. It was beyond the city walls and formerly used as a burial ground for Jews. Danvers embarked on transforming it into a physic garden to benefit medicine. Developed over the centuries and added to by various keepers, they have been enriched by a flow of plant material from all over the world, as the boundaries of botanical knowledge were extended. It was the first garden of its kind to circulate a seed list towards the end of the seventeenth century and by 1840, with the realisation that the study of plants could benefit wider fields than medicine, they had become botanic rather than simply physic gardens. The great planthunter, Sir Joseph Banks, who had sailed with Cook on the *Endeavour*, studied here and thanks to him and likeminded botanists the gardens now display a wide-ranging and fascinating collection of plants.

Though their *raison d'etre* is educational, they are far from being simply of scientific interest and of dry, academic appearance. Sheltered and peaceful, a pocket of calm near the heart of the busy city, they are aesthetically pleasing and botanically absorbing. The main part of the garden, entered through a gateway designed by Inigo Jones's master mason, Nicholas Stone, is formal in design. Graced by mature and unusual trees, it is divided into sections by intersecting paths which meet at a fountain in the centre of the original walled garden. Many of the three hundred different sorts of climbers, some tender, grow against these walls. Beds of shrubs, planted in family groups, and classic rectangular order beds of herbaceous plants (laid out to Benthall and Hooker's classifications) stand on lawns in the different sections. Roses, planted to display their development over the centuries, decorate an area beyond the main walled garden; overlooking the Cherwell are glasshouses with exotic tropical plants, alpines, tender climbers, ferns, waterlilies, orchids, palms and carnivorous and succulent plants. The conservatory, near a side entrance to the walled garden, is filled with fuchsias, geraniums and tender plants from warmer climates which are vulnerable to frost.

Part of the Botanic Gardens, but situated next to the University Parks, is the Genetic Garden.

This one-acre experimental area shows the processes flowering plants go through as they develop. Roses, gourds, alliums and variegated plants are grown in beds especially designed to aid this study. The University Arboretum off the A423 at Nuneham Courtenay, is the third part of the Botanic Gardens. Originally an eight-acre pinetum planted by Edward Harcourt in the mid-1800s, it was acquired by the University in 1968 and now covers fifty acres. Towering North American conifers rise above groups of camellias, rhododendrons, pieris and azaleas and mown grass paths meander around carpets of heather and groves of ornamental and specimen trees such as cornus, maples and ginkgos. Original specimens which have reached the end of their lives are being replanted, and the woodland is constantly enriched with new and unusual subjects.

PACKWOOD HOUSE

MAP F

Lapworth, near Solihull
Off the A34 2m (3km) east of Hockley Heath. 11m
(18km) south-east of central Birmingham
Owner: The National Trust
Tel: Lapworth (056 43) 2024
Open several days a week from Easter to end
September

One of the walled enclosures in the garden of this Tudor House contains an historically puzzling feature which some say dates from the seventeenth century and others from only the last. The topiary garden is intriguing in design and in history and the visitor will have to decide: are the extraordinary conical yews of all different sizes an overgrown nineteenth-century topiary garden or were they really planted to evoke a scene of Christ preaching to the multitude?

Viewed from the handsome wrought-iron entrance gate, they form a definite avenue. This leads to a mount patterned by a spiralling box-edged path which winds up to a single tall yew, the 'Pinnacle of the Temple' or 'The Master'. It is easy to accept that this was once a formal garden and that the yews, standing on open

215

Yew topiary leading to the house and Carolean garden at Packwood.

ground either side of the avenue, were originally planted to replace fruit trees in what had once been an orchard. From different angles, the dark clipped shapes have the haphazard look of a crowd gathered below a preacher. The shadows thrown by the various shapes and the way smaller trees stand close to towering specimens — like children nestling up to a parent — intensifies the impression of a crowd jostling to hear the 'Sermon on the Mount'. The answer lies in the imagination and eye of the beholder. It is known that some of the yews are over two hundred and fifty years old, that others are about one hundred and fifty, and that they vary in texture, grow at different rates and are now clipped with the help of hydraulic lifts.

Through the gate in the wall, which is impressed with thirty alcoves once used to house bee skeps, the lawn stretches to the gabled Tudor house; Packwood was the home of the Fetherston family until the middle of the nine-

teenth century. On the right is the formal Carolean garden, its corners decorated with gazebos which acted as viewpoints to the surrounding countryside. They were built at different periods; the one to the north-east dates from the reign of Charles II and contains a fireplace and chimney, which was used to warm the inhabitants and also heat the wall and speed the ripening of peaches growing against it. The sunken garden nearby was remodelled during this century by Mr Graham Baron Ash, the last private owner of Packwood. It has a rectangular pool with raised beds of flowers surrounded by a low hedge. There are imaginatively-planted borders beneath the long wall next to the house. The flowers in these display a repeated colour scheme and are planted singly or in small groups rather than in large clumps.

Another historically interesting feature stands in a yew-hedged enclosure north-west of the house: a seventeenth-century plunge pool.

Entered down a flight of stone steps, it was originally fed by a tap set in the plinth at one end. Beyond the walled gardens a lake is surrounded by handsome old trees, reminders that Packwood is in the Forest of Arden, an ancient and unspoilt pocket of countryside only a few miles from the centre of Birmingham.

PAINSHILL PARK TRUST

MAP J

near Cobham
Only entrance off A245 by River Mole, Cobham
(no entry at Painshill House on roundabout)
Owners: Elmbridge Borough Council and leased
to Painshill Park Trust
Tel: Cobham (0932) 68113 or write to
Painshill Park Trust, Portsmouth Road,
Cobham, Surrey KT11 1JE
Open Saturday afternoons
and by arrangement for parties only

Undiscovered for two hundred years, Painshill offers those interested in eighteenth-century landscapes an opportunity to observe the restoration of one of the finest examples of the genre. Like Stourhead, it was the work of an enthusiastic amateur, the Honourable Charles Hamilton (1704–86), who was an artist and an inveterate traveller. He had a particular sensitivity in recreating scenes and atmospheres; a series of set pieces decorated with architectural features, which were the all-important components of the 'sublime' landscape.

Follies and other man-made features around the fourteen-acre lake have been, or are in the process of being, restored. Work on the Gothic temple with its fan-vaulted ceiling has been completed, and the floor of the Roman mausoleum has been discovered, buried nine inches deep. Other features which stood around the park and pleasure grounds include a folly built to hide the Painshill tileworks, which imitated the ruined walls of an abbey; another resembled a Turkish tent. There were also a cascade, Chinese bridges, a waterwheel and an amphitheatre.

Perhaps the most impressive construction under excavation is an unusually large grotto: forty feet wide, it had several openings on to the lake and reflections off the water played on its walls and mineral-encrusted ceiling. It was built by Joseph Lane of Tisbury and Charles Hamilton described its intention to '... fill the mind with that sort of delightful horror which is the best genuine effect and truest test of the sublime ...' The park covers two hundred and sixty acres and still displays some of the North American conifers planted by Hamilton who the Victorian garden writer John Claudius Loudon claims was the first to introduce rhododendrons and azaleas to this country. It is hoped in time to replant the vineyard, which once produced a sparkling white wine. Thanks to the generosity and advice of the National Heritage Memorial Fund, the Garden History Society and the Elmbridge Borough Council, work is continually going on to reconstruct, restore and replant this fascinating period garden.

PAINSWICK ROCOCO GARDEN

MAP F

The Stables, Painswick House, Painswick
On B4073 ½m (1km) from Painswick
Owners: Lord and Lady Dickinson (HHA)
Tel: Painswick (0452) 813204
Open regularly from May to September

This recently-reclaimed rococo garden will be of especial interest to garden historians. It was laid out between 1738 and 1748 by the then owner of Painswick, Benjamin Hyett, and its style falls between the intensely formal Renaissance period and the eighteenth-century vogue for landscapes. The gardens are set in a valley below the converted stables and to the east of the Palladian mansion; they cover six acres. On a sloping bowl of open ground lie an orchard, and kitchen and formal gardens encircled and sheltered by woodland. On its edge are the many and varied architectural features.

Lord and Lady Dickinson have been guided in their restoration work by a 1748 painting of the original gardens by Thomas Robins. Renovation was begun in 1984 — the removal of trees, thick scrub and silt, and the painstaking repair of the decorative architectural features like the Doric seat, red and eagle houses, and Gothick alcove. Water from a spring now runs freely into a plunge pool at the far end of the garden and *allées*; avenues of yew and beech and the orchard have been replanted. All the plant material, from centifolia roses to medlars, would have been available when the gardens were originally planted. Vistas to the charming rococo buildings have been engineered with skill in the relatively small space available, and the overall picture is delicate and lighthearted. Its charm is accentuated by the thick carpets of snowdrops in March, the wild daffodils in April and the bluebells which are being encouraged to spread through the woodland.

PARCEVALL HALL GARDENS

MAP B

Skyreholme, near Skipton
12m (19½km) north of Skipton, east of
Grassington on B6265 to Pateley Bridge; turn off
south to Burnsall and Appletreewick
Owner: Walsingham College (Yorkshire
Properties) Ltd
Tel: Burnsall (0756) 72 311 or 214
Open daily from Easter to end October
Plants for sale

A fertile haven lying in a dip of the fells, the character of the garden borders on the exotic and is in direct contrast to its wild and dramatic setting. The hall nestles into a south-facing hillside overlooking the spectacular Wharfedale Valley. The journey to Parcevall is rewarding; an exploration of its terraced and woodland gardens is even more so. These are the creation of Sir William Milner who bought the estate in 1927 and restored and enlarged the sixteenth-century farmhouse. This involved blasting out rock and destroying ancient cellars and an old

barn; the stone was put to good use in the terraces below the house. Thirty men were employed for three years, during which the woodland was planted to provide protection, and a stream was diverted to run through the 'natural' garden. Until his death in 1960, Sir William continued to enrich the twenty acres with fine trees, shrubs and plants, many of them surprisingly tender. The gardens are on limestone and millstone grit, so the range of plants that flourish is wide.

View of the moors from Parcevall Hall gardens.

There is a series of interlinking formal, woodland and open areas, all planted with subjects to suit their situation. Paths wind up through the shady woodland filled with a fine collection of rhododendrons and azaleas. The orchard and grassy banks are carpeted with naturalised daffodils and narcissi, shaded in places by stately conifers. Nearer the house, startling blue meconopsis and a paperback maple decorate the intimate and tranquil chapel garden and exotic and tender plants comes into view as you approach the terrace gardens. The hoheria, crinodendron and eucryphias and magnolias are particularly splendid, together with climbing roses, vines, herbs and unusual shrubs.

The design of the terraces is vaguely reminiscent of Lutyens: architectural features like lily pools, viewpoints, elegant flights of steps and buttressed walls form a handsome frame to the well-grouped plants. The stonework is softened by graceful cherry trees and swags of wisteria. A long bed of thickly-planted agapanthus is a ribbon of azure blue, and formal beds contain annuals and other flowering plants. Further exploration reveals the collection of camellias, conifers and many other rewarding shrubs and trees. Your eye will inevitably be drawn to the stunning view down the valley, but perhaps only when it has feasted on the immediate beauty of this disarming garden.

PARHAM HOUSE

MAP J

near Pulborough
3m (5km) south of Pulborough on A283
Owner: Mrs P. A. Tritton (HHA)
Tel: Storrington (090 66) 2021
Open several days a week from Easter to end
September
(peak months June to August)
Plants for sale

The great age of the house, the earliest part of which dates from the Dissolution, and the spaciousness of its surroundings strike a romantic note. It stands secure and confident in the deer park, only venerable cedars and the small church being allowed to compete with its impressive exterior.

Initially, there is no hint of the gardens which are some distance from the house and reached through a doorway in the wall on the far side of the forecourt or fountain court. A sloping path runs down to the gates of a four-acre kitchen garden which has retained its period character though it is now an ornamental flower garden. Traditional, wide intersecting paths divide the garden into four sections, and are now lined with borders. The four sections are turfed and decorated simply with fruit and May trees and wild flowers, or contain features such as a yew-hedged ornamental herb garden and a greenhouse lively with fuchsias, pelargoniums,

orchids, plumbago and passion flower. Backed by espaliered fruit trees or stylish wooden trellis-work interwoven with climbers, the mixed and herbaceous borders have colour themes, some devoted to shades of purple and golds and others to lime and yellow. The foliage of shrubs such as *Cotinus coggygria* 'Atropurpureus', purple berberis and golden spiraea, hops and the ground-covering golden marjoram, ensure that these have long-lasting colour. Seven acres of pleasure gardens, divided from the house and park by a tall yew hedge and ha-ha, flow away from the kitchen garden down to a lake. Japanese cherries, magnolias and mature trees including a handsome specimen of a cut-leaf beech, add colour and interest to the informal, peaceful scene.

In the Green Room of the house there are some fascinating memorabilia of the eighteenth-century plant-collector, Sir Joseph Banks, who could be called the father of the botanic gardens at Kew. Among the various pictures of him is a portrait by Sir Joshua Reynolds and another which depicts the return of *Endeavour*, on which he sailed around the world with Captain Cook.

Borders in the old walled vegetable garden at Parham House.

219

PARNHAM HOUSE

MAP I

Beaminster
¾m (5/6km) south of Beaminster on A3066; 5m
(8km) north of Bridport
Owners: Mr and Mrs John Makepeace
(HHA)
Tel: Beaminster (0308) 862204
Open Sundays, Wednesdays and Bank
Holidays from April to end October

The terraces are the most striking feature of the fourteen acres of gardens surrounding this Hamdon stone neo-Gothic house. Strongly architectural in design, there are no floral displays or shrubberies here; the stylish effects have been achieved with the simple ingredients of stone, water, yew and turf. Built, surprisingly, at the beginning of this century, they have a delicacy and symmetry which reflects the garden-making style of a much earlier period. At the corners of the balustraded top or Ladies Terrace are elegant stone gazebos. Only rectangles of turf surrounded by wide gravel paths and cherry trees modify the restrained layout. Two further turfed terraces lie below; the central vista through them channelled between stone-lined rills and an avenue of fifty cone-shaped topiary yews. Divided from the park by a ha-ha on one side and bounded on the other by a river, the terraces flow down to an expansive lawn and melt softly into the surrounding countryside. Mighty planes and dark, spreading cedars stand to either side of the serene composition, framing the picture but not impinging on its disciplined formality.

Stonework also plays the major role in the forecourt of the house, remodelled by John Nash in 1810. The balustrading is decorated with obelisk-shaped finials; roses are the only decoration, climbing up stone pillars and against the gate posts. An intimate courtyard nearby contains the Dutch garden, planted with white-flowering subjects, and a short walk from the house is the Italian garden, its herringbone brick path and herbaceous borders set against the rosy brick wall of the old kitchen garden.

Informality now takes over. A woodland walk, part of which follows the line of the river, leads past handsome trees and shrubs, beside a small water garden. Larger-than-life statues of Morecombe and Wise by Nick Munro are almost hidden by rhododendrons. Much restoration work has been carried out by Mr and Mrs Makepeace since their arrival in 1976, ensuring that these unusual twentieth-century gardens will not be lost through neglect. Well known as a school for craftsmen in wood, Parnham deserves to be better known for its garden.

PECKOVER HOUSE

MAP G

North Brink, Wisbech
On north bank of River Nene in Wisbech
Owner: The National Trust
Tel: Wisbech (0945) 583463
Open several days a week from Easter to
mid-October
(peak season summer)

Its warm and homely atmosphere and sheer prettiness make the garden at Peckover House one of the National Trust's most winning; it would take a hard heart not to fall under its spell. Behind the Georgian house which was once the home of a Quaker banking family, Peckover, it is laid out in a series of intimate, walled 'rooms'. Although essentially Victorian in character, it is not dry and dusty or pompous and gloomy.

There are a number of trees that were fashionable features of gardens of this period — redwoods, monkey puzzle, ginkgo, Chusan palms and laurels, — but also a frivolity of rambling roses, honeysuckle arches, brilliantly-coloured borders, and generously-filled old-fashioned greenhouses. At first glance it appears unremarkable, despite the fine specimen trees and unusual shrubs which surround the lawn, but on exploration it gradually reveals its various parts.

A charming white-and-green-painted summerhouse looks over a small pond, through a break in a hedge topped by topiary peacocks and down between double borders punctuated by pillars of clematis. At the far end the unpretentious orangery really does house fruit-bearing orange trees thought to be over two hundred years old, as well as a colourful display of pot plants. There is a shrub and rose garden; the gravel path near the orangery is spanned by arches of honeysuckle and ramblers, and lawns are patterned with beds planted in the Victorian 'gardenesque' manner. Neat collars of annuals edge evergreens or foliage plants, and scalloped ribbons of low-growing subjects, such as thrift and London pride, surround semi-circles of herbaceous plants and bulbs.

The kitchen garden, now grassed over, has specimen fruit trees, mixed borders and an old-fashioned nursery bed, filled with flowers for picking, such as sweet peas grown the traditional way — a single stalk strictly trained to produce impressive blooms. An appropriate addition to a garden of this period is the fern house; like the propagating glasshouse and the whole garden, it is kept in immaculate order. Peckover's friendly atmosphere — possibly a legacy from the prosperous and philanthropic family who once lived here — makes the visitor feel instantly at home. Strangers strike up conversations, chat to the friendly garden staff or make full use of the many seats to relax and soak up the surrounding beauty.

PENPOL HOUSE

MAP H

Penpol Avenue, Hayle
From Foundry Square, Hayle, take road to left of
White Hart, Penpol Road, second left into Penpol
Avenue at top of which stands Penpol House
Owners: Major and Mrs T. F. Ellis
Tel: Hayle (0736) 753146
Open a few days in summer for charity and by
appointment
(peak months June and July)

A charming old-fashioned garden surrounds the fifteenth-century house on a hill above the town. Covering three acres, it is quite different in character to the majority of those in Cornwall open to the public, which are woodland, filled with rhododendrons and azaleas and at their best in spring. The soil at Penpol is alkaline, which rules out ericaceous plants. Their place is taken by a bobbish array of trees, shrubs and herbaceous plants which can withstand the salt-laden winds from the sea nearby. The garden was formerly sheltered by a belt of elms which of course, succumbed to Dutch elm disease and had to be felled. Its contents and layout are reminiscent of those described in turn-of-the-century novels, where a child is sent to stay by the sea with a much-loved old aunt.

A glorious border of delphiniums, pots of agapanthus, neat box hedges, a hundred-year-old vine and almost equally mature, vibrant red climbing geranium in the greenhouse, a walnut and a medlar tree, all join to create the period atmosphere. Old stone walls, and dwarf box, fuchsia and yew hedges divide the various areas: the kitchen garden with its espaliered apple trees and box-edged beds; an area planted with silver and grey foliage plants; a hybrid tea and shrub rose garden, beds filled with flag irises and borders of herbaceous plants. Climbing and rambling roses dress walls and clamber over rustic trellises, and imaginatively-placed granite grinding stones, troughs and staddle stones are reminders of the days when Penpol was a working farm. Projecting from the outside wall of what is now a convenient potting shed, but was once the old cider house, is a white-painted ship's figure-head, straining for a better view of the beautifully-kept garden.

PENRHYN CASTLE

MAP D

Bangor
1m (2km) east of Bangor, at Llandegai on A5122
Owner: The National Trust
Tel: Bangor (0248) 353084
Open daily from Easter to late October
(peak seasons spring and summer)

The high and beautiful position, vast proportions and splendid period interior and contents of this nineteenth-century neo-Norman castle reward the visitor well. It is also well worth strolling through its grounds. On the lawns and rough turf shaded by handsome old trees are carpets of spring bulbs, cyclamen and wild flowers, and a short walk brings you to the Victorian walled garden. Though not large, this has a rich collection of unexpectedly tender subjects. The rainfall is high (forty-five inches a year) and the climate surprisingly mild, which allows eucryphias and Chilean plants, like the fire bush and holly, to flourish.

The garden is set on a slope and is terraced. The top terrace, with loggia and lily ponds, is decorated with a dwarf box parterre, and tender and hardy climbers cling to the walls. Specimen trees thrive in this sheltered and peaceful garden — a stuartia, a handkerchief tree, metasequoia, styrax and *Cornus kousa chinensis*. Below them a pergola entwined with honeysuckles scents the air, and beyond is a water garden where the giant foliage of *Gunnera manicata* has a backcloth of red Japanese maples. The walk back to the castle is decorated with rhododendrons, camellias and azaleas.

The nineteenth-century neo-Norman Penrhyn Castle.

PENSHURST PLACE

MAP J

Penshurst, near Tunbridge Wells
In Penshurst village on B2176, west of Tonbridge
and Tunbridge Wells
Owner: Viscount De L'Isle
Tel: Penshurst (0892) 870307
Open every afternoon from 1 April to 4 October
(peak months June and July)

Apart from being 'the Orchard of England', Kent is renowned for its glorious gardens and historic houses; Penshurst Place has all three. Over six hundred years old, the ancient stone house is overlooked by a fourteenth-century tower which stands guard between its south-facing forecourt and grounds. There have been gardens at Penshurst for many centuries, but it was the present owner's grandfather who laid out those seen today, to a seventeenth-century design.

Encased in ancient walls is an uneven checkerboard of enclosures varying in size and character; nearly a mile of yew hedging acts as a formal bone structure. Surprises are engineered and vistas created to distant features by a network of symmetrical paths and *allées*. The immaculate condition, variety and treatment of these individual gardens makes them an adventure to explore and ensures interest, in one or several areas, from early spring to autumn.

The Italian garden has geometric patterns of box and beds of polyantha roses around an oval ornamental pool; it strikes a note of high formality and covers the largest area. To the east, paths lead to the spring and rose gardens, passing between glorious double, mixed and herbaceous borders, and gradually revealing a host of boldly-planted and stylish features. The way plants and trees have been massed and trees trained gives a French flavour. Parallel to a seemingly-endless bed of peonies is a long line of the delicate hybrid lilac 'Bellicent', their soft pink echoing that of the delightfully blowsy peonies. The velvety grey foliage of *Stachys lanata* forms a carpet beneath standard roses, and a line of golden topiary balls lines a yew *allée* like guardsmen. Two well-known twentieth-century garden designers have advised on the development: the late Lanning Roper designed a border and John Codrington laid out the magnolia and grey gardens.

The Italian garden at Penshurst Place.

Spring bulbs colour the turf of the ordered apple orchard, and the trees in the nut garden have been persuaded to arch like umbrellas. A yew-hedged 'room', decorated simply with a lily pool known as Diana's bath, is a restrained contrast to more intensely-planted areas — one surrounded by pleached limes and planted to represent the Union Jack. Behind this runs a venerable avenue of limes dating from the time of William III, a reminder that though the gardens continue to evolve this ground has been worked for a very long span of time.

PEOVER HALL

MAP B

Over Peover, near Knutsford
3m (5km) south of Knutsford off A50
Owners: Mr and Mrs Randle Brooks
Tel: Lower Peover (056 581) 2135
Open two days a week from May to end of October
(peak months mid-May to end July)
Plants for sale

The gardens at Peover Hall are an unusual but well-balanced mix of garden-making styles. There are many stately homes in England with vast gardens which have evolved over the centuries, but the human scale and sympathetic atmosphere of Peover, with its period features, make it especially easy to enjoy.

A series of immaculately-kept garden 'rooms', part walled and part enclosed by yew hedges, stand at the back of the rosy, redbrick Elizabethan house. These individual enclosures are decorated with topiary, beds of white or pink plants, box-edged beds of herbs, a box knot garden, or geometric beds of sweetly-scented shrub roses. The cleanly-clipped hedges, with topiary balls, pierced by spy holes and shaped into an arbour give a charming Tudor air in keeping with the architecture and age of the house. Topiary also decorates the lawn in front of the house, and a wide grass walk, bounded by pleached limes, leads to the theatre garden with its pavilion. This looks on to an unadorned circle of yew, the restrained and disciplined design of the walk and the garden having a formal, seventeenth-

century character.

Nearby is the woodland garden with its huge chestnut trees and a view down the beech avenue, which introduces a nineteenth-century wilderness garden and dell. These have a 'natural' character: The bowl-shaped dell, at its best in spring, is coloured by rhododendrons, azaleas and the foliage and flowers of specimen trees like maples and magnolias. Cedars and redwoods and a huge rockery add to the Victorian feel of this shady and informal garden, carpeted in spring with naturalised bulbs and bluebells. A pleached hornbeam walk leads to the church (whose tower often catches your eye as you explore the gardens) and back to the formal gardens behind the house. The tour has taken you through several centuries, the surrounding park with its lake and woods providing the missing link — it was laid out in the mid-eighteenth century.

PLAS NEWYDD

MAP D

Llanfairpwll, Anglesey
1m (2km) south-west of Llanfairpwll and A5 on
A4080 to Brynsiencyn; turn off A5 at west end of
Britannia Bridge
Owner: The National Trust
Tel: Llanfairpwll (0248) 714795
Open regularly from Easter to end October
(peak season spring)

On sloping ground overlooking the Menai Straight, the long, eighteenth-century house designed by James Wyatt is a fine sight. It is almost completely surrounded by lawns which run down to the water's edge and enjoys superb views of Snowdonia and the dramatic terrain on the far side of the water. The high rainfall, sunny situation and proximity to the sea which, thanks to the Gulf Stream, staves off destructive frosts, means that a remarkable number of tender plants and trees can be grown. Humphry Repton advised on the landscape at Plas Newydd and his 'Red Book' has recently been discovered, though, not surprisingly, many changes and additions have been made since that time.

Stretching away from the south end of the house is a wide expanse of lawn framed by mature trees and informal beds of shrubs. Handsome red oaks and dignified conifers provide a background to flowering specimen trees such as magnolias, eucryphias and styrax. In spring the azaleas, camellias and vast mounds of the white-flowering *Viburnum tomentosum* make an eyecatching display. Abelias and hydrangeas take over later in the season, and the glowing foliage of deciduous flowering shrubs, Japanese maples, cercidiphyllums and red oaks stage a superb finale in autumn.

On the south side of the house is a small, Italianate terraced garden, built partially on the foundations of an Edwardian conservatory. The formality of this area is emphasised by the neat clipped yew hedges and the classical statue set against a background of foliage. Mediterranean cypresses reinforce the Italian character of the two terraces. Borders are planted with roses, heathers and rhododendrons like the compact *R. yakushimanum* variety.

For the energetic, a three-quarter mile walk through the woodland north of the house leads to a rhododendron garden planted with an exciting collection of Himalayan, rare and tender hybrids and species. The initial planting was done by the sixth Marquess of Anglesey in the 1930s, but a period of neglect intervened before the present marquess began to maintain the woodland and add to the collection. Many of the new additions were a wedding gift from Lord Aberconway of Bodnant, whose collection is renowned. The area has retained its 'wild' nature and the large-leafed varieties, lush scented blooms and vast proportions of other, seldom-seen subjects give it an exotic air.

POLESDEN LACEY

MAP J

near Dorking
3m (5km) west of Dorking, 1½m (2½km) south of Great Bookham, off A246 Leatherhead to Guildford road
Owner: The National Trust
Tel: Bookham (0372) 58203/52048
Open daily throughout the year
(peak seasons spring and summer)

No matter the time of year, Polesden Lacey has much to offer the visitor. A former house on the site was once the home of the eighteenth-century playwright Richard Brinsley Sheridan, but its heyday was probably the period when it was the gracious country home of the Edwardian hostess, the Honourable Mrs Ronald Greville and her husband. Much of what can be seen to day dates from that time and reflects a lavish, turn-of-the-century, garden-making style.

On a ridge of the North Downs with fine views over wood and farmland, the site is ideal from the point of view of an architect but a tricky one for gardeners. The ridge lies on chalk, with only a thin layer of moisture-retaining soil. Thanks to the hard work of a skilled team of gardeners — thirty-eight before World War II and only five today — there is little evidence that plants and trees suffer. The garden is a mixture of formality and naturalness: the informal walks past groups of rhododendrons, through the pinetum and along the lip of the ridge to the terrace are offset by the intimate and formal gardens enclosed by walls and hedges.

Large expanses of lawn spread out from the early-nineteenth-century house remodelled by the Grevilles, to fine mature trees; a number to the west of the main lawn were planted by their royal guests. To the east lies the last surviving feature of Sheridan's time — the long walk. A quarter of a mile in length and bounded by a ha-ha, it leads to the six Doric columns which formed the portico of the original house. A series of formal and enclosed gardens are west of the house. They were made by the Grevilles in the old walled garden; with an ample Edwardian nature, they are profusely planted with flowers of soft rather than strident or hot colours. Any available scent is trapped within the hedges and walls surrounding these individual 'rooms'.

The rose garden has box- and lavender-edged paths, and the pergola walk tumbles with ramblers and beds containing over two thousand shrub and other roses. Borders are planted with peonies, lilies and bearded irises, and another enclosure displays varieties of lavender. The winter garden is living proof that this season is far from barren of flowers and interest. It is fragrant with sweet box, mahonia and daphne, and coloured by hellebores, early bulbs and the delicate blossom of the romantically-named Japanese apricot 'Flight of Red Plovers'. A herbaceous border one hundred and fifty yards long stands against the far side of the sunny wall sheltering these gardens, and below are croquet lawn and sunken garden. The lawns and banks of the sunken garden are planted with young cedars and shrubs, and hydrangeas, lilacs and silver weeping pears add further interest and colour. Stone ornaments and figures — the Venetian wellhead in the rose garden, the Roman sarcophagus in the loggia on the west front, the various urns and classical and other figures depicting Diana the Huntress, a discus thrower or one of the four seasons — add greatly to the atmosphere and beauty of these satisfying gardens.

PORT LYMPNE GARDENS

MAP J

Lympne, Hythe
3m (5km) west of Hythe; 6m (9½km) west of
Folkestone; 7m (11km) south-east of Ashford off
A20
Owner: Mr John Aspinall
Tel: Hythe (0303) 64646
Open regularly throughout the year
(peak seasons spring and summer)
Plants for sale

When the name Port Lympne is mentioned, the threatened fauna of the world, not a display of flora, immediately leaps to mind, but there is a garden as well as a zoo on the three-hundred-acre estate. Of interest to the designer and historian, it is an individual and stylish example of early-twentieth-century garden-making. It lies below the gabled, Dutch-colonial-style house, and was laid out just before World War I, having been designed by Philip Tilden for Sir Philip Sassoon, MP for Hythe.

The strong architectural framework of the layout, terraces, hedges and stonework, which so closely link the house to the garden, has an Italianate quality, but is also reminiscent of the garden design of Edwin Lutyens (note the semi-circular stone alcove on the terrace immediately below the house, a distinctive Lutyens feature). Interestingly, Sir Philip's architect, who no doubt advised on the construction of the garden, was Sir Herbert Baker. He was later to collaborate with Lutyens on the building of New Delhi.

The most important part of the fifteen-acre garden is the terraces, which stand below the house on a steep south-facing slope. These overlook the woodland and a panorama of open countryside and marshland which seemingly stretch to infinity. A dramatic Cumberland stone stairway, flanked by evergreen hedges, leads down to the terrace gardens. Formal, with clipped hedges and stonework playing the major role, these are divided into a series of 'rooms' where water, turf and geometric beds of annuals create an ordered picture enriched with vistas and surprise elements. The wonderful sound of falling water is provided by fountains and water spouts in the lily ponds and the old bathing pool; statues stand in alcoves cut into a crescent yew hedge, and parterres make colourful patterned carpets. There is a yew-enclosed chessboard garden, its immaculately-kept squares either turfed or massed with low-growing red or white flowers. In the striped garden, annuals are bright rivulets of colour.

A spectacular eighteen-foot-wide border, planted with shrubs and herbs, runs below the western terrace and beneath the formal gardens. A terraced vineyard of white grapes is at one side of a long flight of steps, fig trees are on the other. The garden then melts into the natural woodland, where wild flowers are encouraged.

Sir Philip Sassoon welcomed a stream of illustrious guests to Port Lympne, from the Prince of Wales to Charlie Chaplin, but by the start of World War II the house had been abandoned and the gardens left to decline. It was not until 1973 that Mr Aspinall saw the property and determined to rescue the gardens from extinction, with the advice of the late Russell Page. We live in an age when many period gardens are being restored; the work already done and continuing on this exciting and original creation is an example of the way our heritage is being preserved.

POWIS CASTLE

MAP D

Welshpool
1m (2km) south of Welshpool, on A483
Owner: The National Trust
Tel: Welshpool (0938) 4336
Open regularly from Easter to September
(peak months June, July and October)

Everything about Powis makes it a thrilling place to visit — its setting high on an escarpment overlooking the rolling Welsh countryside, its unique Italian baroque terraces of grandiose proportions, its richly planted borders, the natural contours of its landscape garden and, of course, the castle itself. There is something for everyone: the garden historian, landscape designer, plantsman and lover of beautiful places, and none could fail to fall under its spell and be awestruck by its drama.

The castle, parts of which date from the thirteenth century, is constructed of sandstone, the terraces below of rosy brick. Built in the late seventeenth century by the first Marquess of Powis and completed during his exile by a Dutch compatriot of William III, the Earl of Rochford, the terraces survived through neglect. The eighteenth-century landscape movement mercifully passed them by and, when notice was once again taken of them, their period design was appreciated rather than deemed 'old-fashioned'.

Old yews which once formed neat rows of topiary have grown to mammoth architectural proportions, and spill over the top terrace to form buttresses. Those at the far end end of the top terrace now form a mountainous backcloth of dark green to a statue of Hercules. Lead statues of shepherds and shepherdesses by van Nost, painted white in the eighteenth-century manner, stand along the balustrade on the aviary terrace, and the seven arches of the loggia, which now shelters Himalayan rhododendrons and other tender subjects, acts as a focal point when the terraces are seen from afar. At the centre of the third terrace is an orangery, hollowed into the retaining wall, which is draped with climbers and from which flow double borders edged with box.

The lower apple slope is decorated with shrubs, ornamental and specimen trees, and the great lawn lies in the bowl of ground between the terraces and the wooded ridge. The majority of these features have decorated the terraces for a considerable time, but its rich dressing of plants was added early in this century when Lady Powis began to develop their potential. They stand on limestone rock, so the soil is alkaline in this part of the garden. Magnolias and maples grow well and obviously tolerate the alkaline conditions, and the herbaceous borders are planted with a superb collection of unusual and often tender, lime-tolerant plants. A skilful blend of shape, texture and colour, these borders are one of the garden's most glorious features, their colouring in autumn being as satisfying as in summer.

At the far side of the great lawn is a ridge where a wilderness garden was laid out in the nineteenth century. It is a superb platform to view the castle and terraces, and is shaded by mature trees underplanted with rhododendrons which flourish on its acid soil. The old kitchen gardens to the north-east have been transformed into a series of large hedged enclosures. On their lawns are topiary pieces, old-fashioned varieties of fruit trees and, around the perimeters, borders of roses and herbs. The treatment of the fruit trees is delightful. Trained into an unusual pyramid shape, they stand in individual beds planted with lamium, *stachys lanata* or golden marjoram. Your eye is constantly drawn to the dramatic terraces and castle no matter where you are in the garden. The impressive picture may prompt the observer to wonder how gardens

The terrace gardens of Powis Castle.

in this country might have looked if they had not been so radically altered by the eighteenth-century vogue for landscapes.

PREEN MANOR

MAP D

Church Preen, near Much Wenlock
3m (5km) south-west of Much Wenlock on B4371 turn right to Church Preen and Hughley; after 1½m (2½km) turn left for Church Preen, over crossroads, ½m (1km) drive on right
Owners: Mr and Mrs P. Trevor-Jones
Tel: Longville (069 43) 207
Open a few days a year for charity and by appointment for parties
(peak months May to July)
Plants for sale on occasion

The remains of a twelfth-century Cluniac priory and of a Norman Shaw mansion, which once stood on this site, have been put to good use in this rewarding private garden and continue to influence its development. The six-acre garden has three distinct parts, each of which makes maximum use of the changing character of the slope with its view to Wenlock Edge.

Sheltered and intimate 'rooms' have been created on the foundations of the demolished nineteenth-century Shaw house, which stood a short distance from the present manor. The long buttressed walls of the former kitchen garden are now a boundary between these 'rooms' and the restrained formality of the grassed terraces below. On the sloping ground between this and the surrounding countryside lies the park and the water garden with its handsome cedars and mature rhododendrons. The range and beauty of the plants are of equal interest to the plants-man and those in the throes of developing their own gardens, and match its imaginative design.

Generously fed and watered, young but thick, shoulder-high yew hedges divide areas devoted to subjects such as roses and tender climbers, and stonework from the old house has been skilfully used to make a rock garden. Rare varieties of ivy dress an ancient wall and form an unusual and tight edging to a circular rose bed; the highly polished bark of a *Prunus serrula* glistens among a collection of unusual shrubs, and a cottage-style garden at the front of the house displays thoughtfully arranged foliage and other plants. Each part of this garden reflects the talent and hard work of its owners and is a source of good ideas.

Borders and exuberant rambling rose at The Priory.

THE PRIORY

MAP F

Kemerton, near Tewkesbury
5m (8km) north-east of Tewkesbury off B4079
Owners: Mr and the Hon Mrs Peter Healing
Tel: Overbury (038 689) 258
Open for charity on Thursdays from May to
September, and on certain days in June, August
and September
(peak months June to September)
Plants for sale

This exceptionally lovely private garden is an example of how it is possible in four acres to forge a happy marriage between well-balanced design and a well-chosen and well-used collection of plants. The success of the owners' efforts, since their arrival in 1940, is immediately apparent.

A welcome is provided by peaceful lawns shaded by mature trees, their simple design emphasising the elegance of the eighteenth-century house. A series of discoveries are slowly made: borders, secret enclosed gardens, a small arboretum, a stream, a shady sunken garden and other surprises. The character and effect of any one garden does not interfere with another, and eye-cooling features like dark yew hedges and smooth lawns punctuated with specimen trees are a foil to the lively and inspiring arrangements of plants.

The discerning use of colour is an outstanding quality of these gardens which, allied to the considerable horticultural talents of the Healings, has produced a collection of memorable pictures. The three borders are particularly noteworthy, their subtle colour combinations and mix of shapes and textures is skilfully engineered; the way groups of unusual annuals have been mixed with shrubs and herbaceous plants is highly imaginative. In one, grey, silver and white build up to warm yellow, and ultimately to red, which gradually gives way to cooler shades. A 'red' border, so tricky to compose successfully, is a stunning orchestration of bronze, purple, and red foliage and flowers. The garden is a fascinating collection of plants of all kinds, from dainty violas and exotic orchids to the Giant Lily, *Cardiocrinum giganteum*, and its beauty is matched by the warmth of its atmosphere.

THE PRIORY

MAP G

Water Street, Lavenham
10m (16km) south of Bury St Edmunds
Owners: Mr and Mrs Alan Casey (HHA)
Tel: Lavenham (0787) 247417
Open regularly from end March to end October
(peak season summer)

Lavenham is justly famous for being one of England's best preserved medieval towns. Just to wander through the old streets is pleasure enough, but some of the ancient buildings are open to the public and The Priory, once the home of Benedictine monks and now a private house, is one of these. The Caseys came here in 1979, restored the derelict house and laid out a small formal herb garden. Its design depicts the de Vere Star, the emblem of the Lords of the Manor and the shaped beds, divided by stone

Clipped yew providing a background to red flowering and foliaged plants at the Priory.

paths, are filled with over one hundred and twenty different herbs. There are collections of culinary, aromatic and medicinal herbs, as well as plants used for dyeing. The sweet and peppery scents of these and the layout of the small sheltered garden can be enjoyed at ground level or from the upstairs windows.

PROBUS DEMONSTRATIONS GARDEN

MAP H

Probus, near Truro
On A390 between Truro and St Austell
Owner: Cornwall Education Committee
Tel: Truro (0872) 74282 ext 3401
Open regularly throughout the year

Near the entrance to the gardens is a notice stating: 'Most plants grown in gardens originated as wild plants in other parts of the world'. A suitably down-to-earth statement, in keeping with the admirably practical and informative nature of all to be seen here. The seven and a half acres at Probus could be described as a living guide to better gardens and gardening.

Resembling a giant jigsaw, no two pieces alike, the garden is divided into scores of different areas. These vary in size and display well over fifty aspects of horticulture and garden-making — from propagation to mulches, dry-stone walling to labelling methods. There are individual gardens laid out to suit a variety of situations and needs — patio, rock, scree, front and labour-saving — and others are designed with the elderly or disabled in mind. One section displays historical plants such as the leek, the peony and the mulberry tree, which were brought here by the Romans, and others which were introduced by planthunters through the centuries. There are beds of culinary and medicinal herbs, and religious plants such as the Glastonbury thorn. Design ideas, building materials, greenhouses and frames, a spray calendar and samples of seeds are on display, and groups of plants suitable for exposed, shady, acid or alkaline conditions can also be assessed. As well as col-

lections of ivies, lilies, narcissi, hebes, heathers and hydrangeas, different hedging materials are on show and a good number of specimen and ornamental trees.

The gardens are set on the local shaly soil, and were first developed in the early 1970s, their purpose being educational. For those seeking guidance on the why, how and wherefore as well as what to plant, Probus has a tremendous amount to offer; few, will leave without learning or seeing something new.

PUSEY HOUSE

MAP F

near Faringdon
5m (18km) east of Faringdon; 12m (19½km) west of Oxford, ½m (1km) south of A420
Owner: Pusey Garden Trust (HHA)
Tel: Buckland (036 787) 222
Open regularly from April to late October (peak months June, July and August)
Plants for sale

These popular gardens were created after World War II in what was once an eighteenth-century landscape. When Mr and Mrs Michael Hornby came to Pusey in 1935 they were faced with a silted-up man-made lake and areas gasping for breath beneath Victorian shrubberies. A quantity of wall space and water seemed the two elements worth keeping, and today you can see what good advantage these have been put to.

Geoffrey Jellicoe, then just embarking on his career as a landscape designer, was commissioned to create a terrace south of the house. Generously proportioned and with a wide flight of steps, this provides a superb platform to admire the vista over the lawns and lake and through the stands of trees and shrubs to the countryside beyond. The lake, now free of silt and debris, plays an important dual role, both as a division and as a link between the two parts of the garden. The near side provides interest of a more formal nature. Highly-cultivated and colourful features are to the west and east of the house, divided from the more natural areas by the lawns and lake, which give the gardens a spacious and open feeling.

The borders at Pusey are one of its most rewarding features, their colouring is noteworthy, as is the clever use of unusual plants. Double rainbow-coloured borders divide the walled kitchen garden and introduce the main part, which lies beyond the wrought-iron gates in the wall. Stretching away east and west beneath the sunbaked outer side of this wall are herbaceous borders backed by climbers. Lady Emily's Garden, to the east, is a walled enclosure divided into four parts by stone paths. It is a fragrant bower, generously planted with roses, clematis, peonies, irises and other plants like the eyecatching *Hydrangea sargentiana* with its outsize, flat heads of lavender-pink florets. There are beds of shrub roses on the west of the terrace and a border planted with shrubs and roses.

The western end of the long, serpentine lake is spanned by a stylish, white-painted Chinese bridge, which leads to the water gardens. On either side of the central vista from the house, the far banks of the lake are softened by groups of shrubs, trees and shade- and moisture-loving plants. A bed is devoted to variegated subjects and farther afield paths wander around shrubberies, an area named Westonbirt planted with specimen trees, a glade and a pleasure garden. The soil is alkaline, so only lime-tolerant material has been used at Pusey, but so exceptional is the range that each part of the garden demands close inspection.

The long, low, Elizabethan manor house gives the impression of having taken root in the ground. Painted and thatched, it is a classic Devonian picture of security and contentment. The walled, sheltered garden is only half a mile from the sea, and is divided into two parts. Unlike a great number of west-country, Gulf-Stream gardens, it is on alkaline soil and level rather than undulating ground.

The main part is at the back of the house, whose walls are clothed with an immaculately-clipped 'waistcoat' of myrtle. An expansive croquet lawn is centre stage, and the intensely-planted areas are at either side. A stream weaves its way down one side, its banks lush with moisture-loving plants like primulas, hostas, astilbes and willow gentians. An ancient mulberry tree sprawls and the giant leaves of a paulownia or foxglove tree cast their shade over this 'natural' area. By contrast the far side of the lawn is a profusion of colour with old-fashioned roses, herbaceous and other plants in borders and on the long rockery set into a bank. Part of the old walled kitchen garden in front of the house has been converted into an ornamental flower garden. A grass path, flanked by mixed borders and backed by fruit and specimen trees, leads up to a tunnel of trained apple trees. On either side of this are neat beds of soft fruit, vegetables and flowers grown for picking. A small herb garden, espaliered fruit trees against sunbaked walls, and further climbing and shrub roses add to the fruitful and joyous character of this garden.

PUTSBOROUGH MANOR

MAP H

Georgeham, near Barnstaple
North-west of Barnstaple; A361 Barnstaple to
Braunton road; B3231 to Croyde, ½m (1km)
north of village
Owners: Mr and Mrs T. W. Bigge
Tel: Croyde (0271) 890484
Open a few days a year for charity and by
appointment in summer
(peak month late June)

QUEEN ELEANOR'S GARDEN

MAP I

The Great Hall, Castle Avenue, Winchester
Set behind the Medieval Great Hall in Winchester
Owner: Hampshire County Council
Tel: Winchester (0962) 841841
Open regularly throughout the year

Designed by Dr Sylvia Landsberg, a triangle of
land bounded by buildings has been transformed

The woodland garden at Ramster.

into a facsimile of a thirteenth-century garden. It was created at the behest of the Hampshire Gardens Trust, an organisation doing much to save and restore period gardens in the country. It displays plants known to have been grown in the thirteenth century and reproductions of features — an arbour formed of bent poles supporting climbers, a 'pentice' or covered walk, a Purbeck stone fountain, and oak, turf and stone seats. It is named after Queen Eleanor of Castile who, on her marriage to Edward I, introduced plants like the much-loved hollyhock to this country.

The garden is not a genuine but a painstaking reproduction of a medieval garden: plants grown for practical reasons, such as herbs used to flavour food (or for their healing properties), and those which had a symbolic meaning (such as ivy for eternity), and the hawthorn which stood as a reminder of Christ's crown of thorns. A surprising addition is the usually unwelcome weed, marestail grass, which was used to clean pewter and armour. There are collections of wild and ancient flowers — sweet violets, rocket and woodruff, single white and pink roses, vines, lavender and lilies. As was traditional in those times, the turf is decorated with daisies, celandine and other subjects, and set in a corner enclosed by trellis is a chamomile lawn with turf seats.

QUEEN MARY'S ROSE GARDEN

MAP J

Regent's Park, London NW1
Within the Inner Circle in Regent's Park,
approach from Outer Circle via Chester Road or
York Gate
Owner: The Crown; administered by the Royal
Parks Division of the Department of the
Environment
Tel: (01) 486 7905
Open daily throughout the year
(peak months June to September)

When the Prince Regent commissioned John Nash to design Regent's Park in 1811, the site was farmland. It was a highly ambitious and expensive project — a huge outer circle was encompassed by elegant Palladian-style terrace houses; within lay the six hundred and seventy one acres of park. Queen Mary's Rose Garden, which was laid out in 1932, lies like a jewel within the Inner Circle, and is one of the major collections of roses in this country. The original collection was donated by the British Rose Growers' Association and over sixty thousand roses of all sorts now find a home here, new varieties being added as they become available.

Apart from beds planted with modern and old-fashioned shrub roses, climbers adorn pillars and ramblers make high swags of colour along roped trellises. The sight, scent and colour in summer is a magnet to a multitude of city workers and inhabitants, but the garden is not solely devoted to roses. On one side a pattern of beds is tightly packed with brilliant begonias, and a long border is imaginatively planted with herbaceous plants. An avenue of cherry trees leads up to a pool and fountain and a mound planted with evergreen and acid-loving shrubs, such as azaleas, overlooks the lake. There is a delightful waterfall, set unexpectedly high, and an island reached over a bridge, which is covered with rock plants and others. A short distance north of the Rose Garden is St John's Lodge, where an elegant circle of pleached limes surrounds beds of roses. A further feature, beautifully maintained and generously planted (as is the whole garden) is the long border of scented flowering shrubs.

RAMSTER

MAP J

Chiddingfold
1½m (2½km) south of Chiddingfold on A283
Owners: Mr and Mrs Paul Gunn
Tel: Haslemere (0428) 4422
Open every afternoon late April to mid-June
(peak month May)

Unspoilt by being over visited or too highly cultivated, the twenty acres of woodland and flowering shrub garden at Ramster are unusually soothing. Cool, mown grass paths weave through the oak and larch woodland, around groups of flowering shrubs and areas of rough grass carpeted with bluebells and wild flowers. Vistas to distant features and the scent of the numerous *Rhododendron loderi*, beckon you down through the woodland to the bog garden, splendid with the giant, architectural foliage of *Gunnera manicata*.

On Wealden clay and sandy soil and laid out by Gauntlett Nurseries in 1904, the garden has a fine collection of camellias, Exbury and Mollis azaleas, species and hybrid rhododendrons, and rare trees, one of which is a mature specimen of the Japanese *Kaloponax pictus*. The brilliant colour of the massed deciduous azaleas, the camellia garden and an impressive avenue of *Acer palmatum* 'Dissectum' are a lively introduction to the woodland, whose peace is undisturbed by harsh colour; the pale shades of pink and white rhododendrons and the specimen trees — styrax, magnolias, cedars and redwoods — enhance its natural beauty in a subtle and effective way.

The owners have worked very hard over recent years, and there is now little evidence of the garden having suffered a period of neglect. The flowering shrubs are not leggy or misshapen, and the clearing of scrub, opening up of glades and admirable upkeep of the grass paths, give a well-groomed but not over-disciplined appearance.

RIEVAULX TERRACE

MAP C

Rievaulx, near Helmsley
2½m (4km) north-west of Helmsley on B1257
Owner: The National Trust
Tel: Bilsdale (043 96) 340
Open daily from April to end of October
(peak month May)

If you took someone to see Rievaulx Terrace for the first time, it would be tempting to tell them nothing about it beforehand. The surprise element and its natural drama and romance make it an exciting place to visit.

It is not difficult to understand why Thomas Duncombe decided to create such a feature around 1758. The view of the abbey ruins in a wooded valley below the escarpment must have seemed a heaven-sent gift to an eighteenth-century gentleman wanting to make a 'sublime' landscape garden. It boasted the most vital ingredient: the paintings of an idealised version of the Italian countryside by Claude, Poussin and Salvator Rosa, which inspired the vogue for eighteenth-century landscapes, almost without exception depicted a ruin set in dramatic terrain. The ruin at Rievaulx was that of a twelfth-century Cistercian abbey rather than a classical temple, and the setting was English rather than Italian, but the opportunity was not to be missed.

The terrace resembles that built by Thomas Duncombe's grandfather, earlier in the eighteenth century, at nearby Duncombe Park. Both are long turfed walks with classical-style buildings at either end, but Rievaulx is more natural in character. The half-mile-long wide walk is serpentine rather than crescent-shaped, with a series of viewpoints along its outer edge becoming visible only gradually. These have been cut in the line of trees along the outer edge and present softly-framed pictures of the ruins, the river, ridge, moors and hills. Cowslips and other wild flowers paint the grassy banks on the edge of the escarpment, and on a still day voices of people exploring the ruins float up from the valley. An undulating line of trees — variegated sycamores and beeches — forms an inner boundary to the walk, which provides shelter and focuses attention on the temples as they come into view.

The Tuscan temple, circular with a Doric colonnade and domed roof, is at the southern end of the terrace, while an Ionic, porticoed temple, stands to the north. Used as a banqueting house, the Ionic temple has rich interior decoration which must have impressed the Duncombe family's guests and convinced them of their good taste and standing.

You are recommended to take the woodland path which leads to the southern end of the terrace, to enjoy the full impact of the first sight.

RIPLEY CASTLE

MAP B

Ripley, near Harrogate
On A61 3½m (5½km) from Harrogate
Owner: Sir Thomas Ingilby
Tel: Harrogate (0423) 770152
Open daily from April to mid-October
(peak season summer)
Plants for sale

The Ingilby family have lived at Ripley Castle since the fourteenth century — an achievement when one thinks of the dramatic events which saw the demise of so many families. The main part of the house consists of a tower dating from 1555, which was added to in the 1780s. Successive generations have been keen gardeners but it was Sir William Amcotts Ingilby who was responsible for the castle's superb setting, believed to have been developed by 'Capability' Brown in the first half of the eighteenth century.

A terrace overlooks a landscape which certainly reflects Brown's radical and heroic style. The park, with its fine old trees that provide shade for grazing deer and cattle, boasts two serpentine lakes with islands, fed and drained by cascades. In contrast, a short distance from the castle, there are walled gardens dating from the 1820s. The first contains herbaceous borders, formal beds of roses, handsome stone summerhouses and an orangery. A wrought-iron gate leads to the reserve garden, with its circular rose pergola, ornamental beds and espaliered fruit trees. A third walled garden, narrow in shape to contain the heat and encourage early growth, is planted with vegetables and fruit.

ROATH PARK

MAP E

Cyncoed, Cardiff
Approach city via A48 (M) down Eastern Avenue;
at Gabalfa interchange take first left, signs to
Roath
Owner: City of Cardiff
Tel: Cardiff (0222) 751235/7
Open daily throughout the year
(peak seasons spring and summer)

In the middle of a city remarkable for its many beautifully-kept parks and open spaces, Roath is noteworthy for its fine range of unusual plants, shrubs and trees, and its attractive and unmunicipal appearance. The design, the presence of water and the fact that the buildings beyond its confines are on the whole low and hidden behind trees and shrubs create a wonderfully peaceful impression.

The park is cut in two by a main road; though the larger half has more to offer the garden-lover, the smaller contains a rewarding number of mature specimen trees. There are also beds of bulbs, annuals and roses in this area and Chinese-style bridges span the stream which runs through it. This stream also flows through the main part of the park: its source is a vast lake at the far end. It is set on higher ground and initially hidden from view, so the first sight of it is a wonderful surprise. The great expanse of water has a backdrop of mature trees and distant hills which totally belie its position close to the centre of the city.

Laid out in the 1880s, Roath originally contained an extensive botanical garden. Only three of the original order beds, once stocked by the Royal Botanic Gardens at Kew, still exist, the rest having been replaced by an extensive rose garden where over fifty different varieties are displayed. Six beds contain roses currently being assessed by the National Rose Society. Richly planted herbaceous and mixed borders, a grove of maples and numerous other ornamental and specimen trees lie to one side of the stream. The far side has a more woodland and informal character and contains unusual and mighty conifers. An absorbing feature in the park is the conservatory, built in 1975; it is imaginatively designed and its contents cannot fail to please. It boasts an exciting collection of tropical and temperate plants and exotic fruits, and a rocky bank, a pool, a cascade and a fountain. Terrapins and eleven different types of fish as well as birds seem to be at home here, as do the orchids, loquats, lemon and orange trees, bananas, ornamental vines, bougainvillea, ficus, hibiscus and cacti.

ROCKINGHAM CASTLE

MAP G

near Corby
2m (3km) north of Corby, 8m (13km) from Kettering on A6003
Owner: Commander Michael Saunders-Watson
Tel: Corby (0536) 770240
Open a few days a week from Easter to end of September
(peak months June to August)

The picture of permanence and strength, this castle built by William the Conqueror commands a spectacular view over five countries. It is built of honey-coloured limestone and set on the Welland Valley escarpment; the ground falls away sharply on three sides. Rockingham was a royal residence until the sixteenth century, when it became the home of the Watson family who live there today. Over the centuries, they have developed the gardens which lie on the terraces around the castle and beyond.

The proportions, position and design of features on the terrace gardens flatter those of the castle — examples are the elephantine and undulating shape of the clipped yew hedges and the circular yew-hedged rose garden on the site of the old Norman keep. Modern standard and bush roses line a walk beside the castle and fill the geometric beds of the yew-hedged rose garden. Mixed borders beneath the walls have been planted with a colour theme: shades of blue and pink flowers lie to one side, and warm oranges and yellows to the other.

The wild or grove garden in the ravine below

was developed at the end of the nineteenth century; it reflects the tastes of the time, and is filled with contemporary subjects. There are a rewarding number of mature specimen trees — unusual conifers, maples, *Pterocarya rehderana* (wing nut) and handsome handkerchief trees. Cherries, old yews and balsam poplars scent the air in spring, and naturalised bulbs add to the charm of this area.

RODMARTON MANOR

MAP F

Rodmarton, near Tetbury
Off A433 6m (9½km) south-west of Cirencester, 4m (6½km) north-east of Tetbury
Owner: Mrs Anthony Biddulph
Tel: Rodmarton (028 584) 219
Open for charity several days a year, once a week from March to August and by appointment
(peak months May and June)
Plants for sale

The gardens surrounding the Cotswold stone house display a particularly high standard of craftsmanship, both horticultural and architectural. They are blessed with a warm and unpretentious atmosphere, and are tended with obvious love and care by their owner. Some are yew-hedged 'rooms', others are set on the terraces behind the house or in natural areas near the boundary; they will interest the plantsman and charm the lover of English country-house gardens.

At the beginning of this century, Ernest Barnsley was given the brief to build a house constructed of stone and timber taken from the Biddulph's estate, which would involve the talents of local craftsmen. Every detail was designed and made with care, from the plasterwork to the furniture. The owner's mother-in-law was a trained horticulturist, so this ensured that the gardens would be well planted and carefully designed. Stonework and yew hedges play a major role; the hedges shelter the winter, rose and topiary gardens from the cruel winds which sweep across the this part of the country. Double borders flank a colourful vista to a summerhouse with a steep roof, hung with stone tiles, and on the terrace is a colony of stone sinks, collected from all over the farm and planted with alpines.

Formality gives way to a cherry orchard planted with species roses; fruit trees and bushes, vegetables and greenhouses lie within the kitchen garden, whose walls are festooned with climbers. Note the circular stepping-stones in the topiary garden, which were cut from pillars found on the farm; the huge wooden tubs made from elms which died; the fine array of plants with variegated foliage; the 'Gothic aisle' of hornbeams, and the unrivalled collection of snowdrops.

ROSEMOOR GARDEN TRUST

MAP H

Torrington
On B3220 1m (2km) south-east of Great
Torrington
Owner: The Royal Horticultural Society
Tel: Torrington (0805) 22256
Open regularly from April to end October
(peak season spring)
Plants for sale

This important west-country garden, developed by Lady Anne Palmer from 1959, was donated to the Royal Horticultural Society in 1987. It is now administered by the Society and is their first major outpost — a focal point for keen gardeners and horticultural societies. It is set on heavy clay and lies in a wooded valley of the River Torridge; at present it covers eight acres. It is hoped that the thirty-six acres of surrounding farmland will also be developed in time, and that trial grounds and demonstration gardens will be laid out, similar to those at Wisley.

The gardens around the house are of exceptional interest to the plantsman; they contain a wealth of unusual plants associated and positioned with great discernment. Lady Anne was a late convert to gardening and all she had to begin with were the mature trees. As her knowledge and enthusiasm grew, the gardens spread and were enriched with interesting plants. The surroundings of the homely, white-painted house are now intensely cultivated. The gardens are only fifteen miles from the sea and are sheltered from destructive east winds by the wooded hill behind the house and the shrubbery and belt of trees which mask from view the Exeter to Bideford road.

Essentially informal in character, different areas display diverse collections, though no one part of the garden is slavishly devoted to a particular genus. A rewarding feature is the extensive collection of rhododendrons, the yellow-flowered Exbury hybrid 'Crest' being noteworthy near the house. Magnolias flourish, as well as herbaceous plants and many specimen trees. A pool at the far end of the lawn is surrounded with moisture-loving subjects: rogersias, astilbes and swamp cypress, and the stylish foliage of hostas flatters more delicate subjects.

The drive divides the lawn, punctuated with island beds, from the more intensely-planted areas beside the house. The foundations of the old conservatory have been planted with tender subjects and a pattern of informal beds contain alpines, a splendid range of flowering shrubs

The Royal Horticultural Society's west country garden, Rosemoor.

and unusual ornamental and flowering trees, such as Japanese maples and tulip trees. Dwarf conifers and roses have been planted on what was once a tennis court, silver weeping pears adding graceful vertical points of interest. A paddock has been transformed into a young but flourishing arboretum (Lady Anne also became a keen and knowledgeable dendrologist). There are peat and scree gardens, and the woodland garden is filled with azaleas, rhododendrons and appropriate ground-coverers, such as *Gaultheria shallon*. Mahonias, hollies, cistus and roses are well represented, some roses romping into trees and tumbling over walls.

It was the well-known plantsman Collingwood ('Cherry') Ingram who inspired Lady Anne to collect plants and create this garden; apart from a great number of wild species, there are some of his own hybrid cherries, a *Prunus kursar* being an example. A *Prunus serrula* in the gravel path behind the house is an eyecatching feature and Japanese cherries, such as the double pink-flowering 'Taoyoma Sakura' and the double white 'Shimidsu Sakura', add charm in May. The nursery sells a gratifyingly wide range of unusual plants propagated from those in the garden. Roses are grown on their own roots and plants on display can be propagated to order.

ROUSHAM PARK

MAP F

Rousham, near Steeple Aston
14m (22½km) north of Oxford on A423 turn east
Owner: Mr Charles Cottrell-Dormer
Tel: Steeple Aston (0869) 47110
Open daily (No children under fifteen admitted)

Horace Walpole once said that Rousham 'was the most engaging of Kent's works. It is Kentissimo'. Time has dealt kindly with this important early eighteenth-century landscape and, though it is now somewhat overgrown and smaller than others, it is the least-changed example of his landscape design. Here, as at Claremont and Stowe, he followed Charles Bridgeman who, though making the first moves away from rigid formality, still used geometric

shapes. William Kent's aim at Rousham was to create an idyllic landscape, decorated with surprises and romantic man-made features which enhanced the 'natural' design of the whole. These features were to be seen in a particular sequence, to ensure that the impact and individual character of each was admired to the full and that the correct sequence of emotions was experienced.

The landscape lies on gently sloping ground some distance from the house; it runs down to the River Cherwell, which acts as a natural boundary. From the level expanse of lawn behind the house, which was Bridgeman's bowling green, the visitor plunges into Kent's artificial reconstruction of the Elysian Fields. Paths meander through woodland and glades, and architectural features are glimpsed in the distance: the Dying Gladiator rests on top of the Praeneste terrace, a sombre introduction to what lies below; the Vale of Venus where statues by van Nost decorate Kent's primeval-looking cascades; the eel-like stone rill which runs through the woodland to a plunge pool set in front of a grotto; a statue of Apollo, and a temple which contains the 'tomb' of the gladiator seen in his death throes on the Praeneste terrace.

On a hill beyond the river is a construction of three arches, a folly which serves no practical purpose but is simply an eyecatcher. The Praeneste terrace, now viewed from below, turns out to be a stone loggia, whose design was possibly inspired by the aqueducts built by the Romans — engineering feats Kent would doubtless have seen during his period studying painting in Italy. This is a good point to rest and admire the river and surrounding countryside and drink in the atmosphere, before making the climb back up through the woodland to the bowling green and the 'real' world. Despite the size to which the yews have grown in the woodland, and the distant views beyond the garden which have been altered since Kent's day, his landscape is still an ingenious mix of the highly-artificial and the natural. It has retained its Arcadian, god-inhabited character and evokes an era of classical antiquity when primitive man tended sheep and was seduced by nymphs and fauns.

A satyr surveys William Kent's garden at Rousham.

Older and quite different in character are the walled gardens next to the house. In the first of these, a wide gravel path runs between borders on one side of the old kitchen garden. Backed by espaliered apples on one side and a rosy brick wall on the other, these ribbons of colour lead to a further walled enclosure containing the pigeon house. It was built in 1685, is topped by a cupola and contains its original revolving ladder. Nearby there is a parterre of box-edged beds planted with roses, a lighthearted and colourful contrast to the contemplative character of the landscape.

ROYAL BOTANIC GARDENS, KEW

MAP J

Richmond
On A307 (Kew Road) south of Kew Bridge
Tel: London (01) 940 1171
Open daily throughout the year, except on
Christmas and New Year's Day

Famous throughout the world as a major repository of botanical knowledge and life, these great gardens are a magnet to the expert and the amateur gardener. Their purpose might be scientific: the conservation of and investigation into the habits of rare, vulnerable and productive plants is part of their work, but it is the beauty and diversity of character of Kew Gardens which is of immediate appeal. They inspire affection as well as admiration; generations of visitors return time and again to visit a part of the three hundred acres which they consider particularly their own. Seemingly infinite in extent, they might shrink with familiarity but no visitor, however well acquainted with even its most hidden corners, leaves without having discovered or learnt something new. It is impossible to see all Kew has to offer in one visit and a mistake even to try. Individual taste and the season should guide your footsteps. Some prefer to explore the peaceful, wild or woodland areas, others to admire the formal beds and period gardens, shelter from a passing shower in one of the many glasshouses or be transported to a different world — steamy tropics or arid desert. The 'menu' is long and rich and guarantees satisfaction for even the most fastidious of tastes.

Kew cherishes a fine heritage of botanical and garden-making history, a large number of our renowned landscape designers, planthunters and botanists having been involved in their development. Originally two royal estates — the first in Richmond acquired by George II and the second in Kew by his son Frederick, Prince of Wales — they were amalgamated on the death of Frederick's wife, Augusta, when the two estates were inherited by George III. Augusta had overseen the birth of the botanical gardens at Kew, assisted by William Aiton and Lord Bute. The handsome orangery which now houses an exhibition and a shop, the 163-foot-high Chinese pagoda, classical-style temples of Aeolus, Bellona and Arethusa and the Roman arch, designed by the landscape architect Sir William Chambers, all date from this time. Sir William's rival, 'Capability' Brown, was also involved and, without conscience, swept away a Georgian garden to form a natural landscape. This is now the rhododendron dell which is colourful with Himalayan and hybrid rhododendrons in spring.

Due to the work of Sir Joseph Banks the planthunter, member of the Royal Society, botanist and entrepreneur, George III's reign saw the emergence of Kew as a major botanical garden. The success of his planthunting expeditions to Newfoundland and around the world prompted him to encourage other talented and courageous botanists. They discovered and returned with new plants from all over the world, which signalled the beginning of one of Kew's most important roles — as a 'bank' of newly-introduced botanical material.

The gardens became the property of the nation in 1841 and were given one of its most-loved features, the palm house, shortly afterwards. Designed by Decimus Burton, it was the technical masterpiece of its time, and the vast scale of the structure as well as its tropical contents, create a sense of wonderment in all who enter it. Burton was also responsible for the giant temperate house, once the largest greenhouse in the world, which now displays plants from countries such as South Africa, New Zealand and Chile. Architecturally and botanically thrilling to explore, both houses have recently undergone restoration. The palm house is the focal point of three vistas created by the Victorian landscape designer, William Nesfield, who also laid out the formal rose garden of floribundas and hybrid teas and the now-simplified parterre beds in front of the palm house. These beds, and those which run down either side of the broad walk, are filled at every season with imaginative and sometimes highly-original bedding-out schemes, sources of inspiration for both the amateur and the amenity gardener.

Succeeding years have seen many changes as new botanical specimens, period gardens and architectural features have been added. In 1969 the charming seventeenth-century-style formal garden behind Kew Palace was named after, and opened by, Her Majesty the Queen. It is overlooked by a rotunda set on a mound, and laid out with a disciplined pattern of period features: parterre beds, clipped hedges and a pleached hornbeam alley. All its plants are known to have been grown before 1700. There are sweet-smelling subjects used for strewing or nosegays, culinary and medicinal herbs, old varieties of trees and shrubs and a tunnel dripping with laburnum.

The two most recent and spectacular additions are the Sir Joseph Banks Building — which houses the library, reference collection and a 'Plants for the People' exhibition — and the Princess of Wales conservatory, which replaces the old T-shaped collection of greenhouses. The Banks Building, surrounded by lakes, has an exciting science-fiction appearance. Energy conservation and ideal atmospheric conditions for the storage of the collection of plants were prime considerations in its construction. The conservatory, a technical masterpiece which encompasses ten different environments, is like a tented village of low-pitched, overlapping glasshouses rising out of the ground. Imaginatively landscaped, the changing levels, rocks and water are a background to the thrilling collections of plants. These come from widely-differing climates: tropical rain and cloud forests, mangrove swamps and deserts. Each environment has been made to look as natural as possible — pillars are masked by cork bark; mosses, peat and rock provide a home for plants such as orchids and bromeliads, and ferns and even algae have a well-established look. A collection of succulents is set against a diorama of the Mojave desert; cacti thrive in the arid zone, and the staggering six-foot-wide *Victoria amazonica* waterlily has been catered for as well as stately tree ferns. It is an impressive technical and horticultural achievement. The multifarious needs of the plants, attractive appearance of the conservatory, running costs, and the requirements of the visiting public have all been taken into account.

Farther afield you will come upon other smaller greenhouses: the new alpine house, the Australian house, which shelters ninety percent of that countries endemic species, and the fern and tropical waterlily houses. Seek out the collection of specimen bulbs and irises in the intimate walled Cambridge cottage garden; the alpines in the rock garden, its path sunk like the course of a river between mounds of sandstone, so that you can admire the tiny specimens without constantly bending down; the waterside plants by the lakes, and the wild flowers, heaths, azaleas, bamboos and many other collections within these gardens.

Exceedingly old, rare and magnificent trees are, of course, Kew's crowning glory. The habits and beauty of countless specimens could absorb the enthusiast's time completely and has inspired countless amateurs to resist the temptation to plant run-of-the-mill subjects ever again.

ST HELEN'S CROFT

MAP C

Halam, near Southwell
½m (1km) west of Halam, 2m (3km) west of
Southwell
Owner: Mrs E. Ninnis
Tel: Southwell (0636) 813219
Open a few days a year for charity and by
appointment
Plants for sale

When Mrs Ninnis embarked on transforming an area of farmland into a garden in the early 1950s, she decided that it should blend into the unspoilt countryside. The design is informal; island beds and paths form subtle divisions between one area and another which all have a distinct character. Planted by a talented plantswoman, the contents will absorb the enthusiast for many hours — not an inch has been wasted.

Colouring has been carefully considered, some borders being devoted to soft blues, pinks and white, others to shades of orange, yellow and gold. The distinctive shape, texture and colour of interesting foliage plays a major part — subjects like the golden elder 'Nigra Aurea', spiraea 'Gold Flame', artemisias and willows are used to good effect, though variegated plants are not the owner's favourites. The garden is set on neutral soil, so the range of plants grown is wide: old-fashioned shrub and rambling roses like 'Souvenir de la Malmaison' and 'Rambling Rector' (which romps into an old apple tree) pinks, alpines, seldom-seen herbaceous plants, and rhododendrons and heathers. Many specimen trees have been cleverly positioned to enhance the rewarding plant associations: the foliage or flowers of a golden catalpa, false acacia, magnolia and eucryphia, and an unusual elm

'Jaqueline Hillier', with a dense habit and fan-like foliage, all contribute to the series of 'pictures'.

Traditional farm features — staddle stones, stone troughs, millstones and even old stable bricks have been put to good use. The summer-house with a pantile roof set on brick piers is draped with roses and a *Vitis coignetiae*, whose large heart-shaped leaves turn a brilliant crimson in autumn.

ST PAUL'S WALDEN BURY

MAP G

Whitwell, near Hitchin
On the B651 5m (8km) south of Hitchin; ½m
(1km) north of Whitwell
Owners: Simon Bowes-Lyon and family
Tel: Whitwell (043 887) 229
Open a few days a year for charity and by
appointment
(peak month May)
Plants supplied by Herts and Middlesex
Trust for sale on open days

One of the very few formal seventeenth-century gardens to survive the onslaught of the landscape movement, the main part of the forty acres is reminiscent of the great gardens of France. There are no intricate parterres or waterworks around the house and the ground is rolling rather than level, but the autocratic way in which the native woodland has been treated is evocative of certain parts of the garden at Versailles.

Allées fan out through the woodland from the rectangular lawn to the north-east of the house. Lined with hedges, these wide mown paths enclose blocks of boskage, native hornbeam and oak woodland, and swoop down and up the far side of a shallow valley, creating vistas to romantic features. A neo-classical temple designed by Sir William Chambers stands on the far bank of the lake, mirrored in the surface of the water; another was designed by Wyatt, and an octagonal pavilion, on high ground, is the focal point of a long ride lined with limes. There is no firm

boundary between the countryside and the garden. Like the later eighteenth-century landscape gardens it blends imperceptibly into the surroundings, and views to features, such as a distant church tower, make the garden seem much larger than it actually is.

It was the childhood home of Queen Elizabeth the Queen Mother. The Bowes-Lyon family have lived here for over two hundred and fifty years and it was her brother, Sir David Bowes-Lyon, who did much to restore the seventeenth-century garden. A past President of the Royal Horticultural Society, he also created flower gardens where they would not detract from the clean lines of the formal period garden. A further feature is the twentieth-century woodland garden to the west of the house, which has been enriched with azaleas, primulas, and lilies since 1960. Together with bluebells and rhododendrons, some of which were raised from seed collected in the Himalayas by Simon Bowes-Lyon, these create pools of colour beneath the canopy of trees.

SALING HALL

MAP G

Great Saling, near Braintree
3m (5km) west of Braintree on A120 turn north to
Great Saling
Owners: Mr and Mrs Hugh Johnson
Open several afternoons a week mid-May to
mid-October and by appointment for parties

The twelve-acre garden belonging to the charming, Dutch-style, redbrick house has been blessed in the last two decades with owners who were and are creative and talented gardeners. The present owner, Mr Hugh Johnson, is known not only for his writing on wine but increasingly for his gardening books and articles. He and his wife have developed the gardens and introduced variety in a series of compartments differing in mood and design. There are sheltered 'rooms', formal and restrained walks, a lush water garden, peaceful glades and an arboretum, and sometimes sharp contrasts between formal and informal areas. Sheltered from the bitter east winds by belts of trees, the garden is secluded and the visitor is unaware of the flat farmland beyond.

Shortly after World War II, Lady Carlyle planned the old walled garden with its mushroom-shaped apple trees and tall clipped cypresses. The Johnsons preserved the formal layout of this enclosure, but enriched it with plants and added a pergola. It has a light-hearted air; its long box-edged beds punctuated with Lawson cypress are generously filled with grey-leafed Mediterranean plants, spring bulbs, herbs, shrubs and herbaceous plants with blue, pink or white flowers. It is overlooked by a conservatory which contains Australasian plants and other tender and sun-loving specimens. The kitchen garden nearby displays some unusual varieties of vegetables, all well labelled. Thereafter the garden is a slow revelation of stylishly-designed and attractively-planted areas increasingly informal in character.

From intimate yew-hedged 'rooms' containing features like a border of white-flowering plants, the picture opens up to grass walks, and vistas to features such as an elegant urn. There is a rose glade planted with pink-flowering shrub roses, a Japanese and a pond garden enhanced by stone lanterns and a grove of *Betula jacquemontii*. Trees are one of the garden's great strengths; the loss of mature elms prompted the owners to plant an arboretum. Many unusual, even rare, specimen and ornamental trees can be seen here, as befits the garden belonging to the author of the *International Book of Trees*. None of these was planted in this open and spacious area before 1975 but, though it is still in its infancy, the arboretum offers the enthusiast an opportunity to observe the different characteristics of rare birches, sorbus, cherries, willows, junipers and others which flourish on the boulder clay.

There is a cool and shady water garden luxuriant with moisture-loving plants near the house that overlooks what was once the village green. Lawns run down to a duck pond overhung with willows and a striking avenue of Lombardy poplars, like the aisle of a Gothic cathedral, link the village and the church beside the Hall.

SALTRAM HOUSE

MAP H

Plympton, near Plymouth
2m (3km) west of Plympton. 3½m (5½km) east of Plymouth city centre, between Plymouth to Exeter road (A38) and Plymouth to Kingsbridge road (A379); take Plympton turn at Marsh Mills roundabout
Owner: The National Trust
Tel: Plymouth (0752) 336546
Open daily throughout the year
(peak seasons early spring and summer)

The eight-acre garden, long and thin and set above the River Plym, is to the east of the large, white-painted George II mansion. It was first developed in 1770 and contains some interesting and elegant architectural features dating from that time, but was much altered in the nineteenth century. Its outlook over the river and estuary, masked by a belt of trees, is now somewhat urban and industrial. The layout is informal, and paths wind around lawns shaded by fine trees which lead to the woodland garden. The only straight line is created by a superb avenue of limes, underplanted with old varieties of narcissi and autumn-flowering cyclamen.

Near the house is an enclosed garden called the orange grove, in which stand the stylishly-designed tubs of orange and lemon trees that are overwintered in the nearby orangery. This also shelters a Norfolk Island pine and tubs bursting with agapanthus. Paths weave through glades and the woodland, which has shade-loving, ericaceous, flowering shrubs and specimen trees such as magnolias, Japanese maples and rhododendrons. At the far end of the garden is the castle, an octagonal belvedere which was a viewpoint as well as a place to dine. Walks through the park are laid out in a Brownian style, one leading to the amphitheatre whose classical façade and grass terraces overlook the Plym.

SANDLING PARK

Hythe
North-west of Hythe, entrance off A20
Owners: The Hardy family
Tel: Hythe (0303) 66516
Open for charity several Sundays in spring
(peak months May and June)

The original Georgian mansion, destroyed by a bomb during World War II, has been replaced by a smaller modern house, but the thirty-acre gardens were mercifully unharmed. The large walled garden and terraces are of the same period as the original house, but the woodland garden dates from the beginning of this century. It was developed by Major Hardy's grandfather, who took advantage of a pocket of greensand overlayed with leafmould, and the availability of the exciting plants which were being introduced at the time.

The first rhododendrons were planted in 1900, and today the garden boasts a fine collection of these and later additions. Together with Ghent azaleas, camellias, pieris, magnolias, Japanese maples and unpretentious bluebells, wild orchids and lilies-of-the-valley, these provide the interest in the woodland and give it a vigorous and luxuriant appearance. Despite being richly planted — even the banks of streams and ditches are embroidered with moisture-loving primulas and arum lilies — the woodland has retained its natural beauty and never appears contrived.

A mighty alder, the tallest in Europe, towers above the garden, and there are fine specimens of cut-leaf and weeping beeches, abies and nothofagus. A yew-hedged rose garden is beside the walled kitchen garden, which is run in the traditional manner. Worth noting is the way gooseberries have been grown as climbers against the walls. The advantages will be obvious to those familiar with tending this often vicious plant.

SANDRINGHAM

near King's Lynn
8m (13km) north-east of King's Lynn on B1440
2m (3km) north of its junction with A148
Owner: Her Majesty The Queen
Tel: King's Lynn (0553) 772675
Open regularly from Easter Sunday to September
when the Royal Family is not in residence
(peak seasons spring and summer)
Plants for sale

Despite the large scale of the grounds and house, Sandringham has been a home rather than a palace for the Royal Family since Edward VII, then Prince of Wales, bought it in 1862. There are formal features in the immaculately-kept gardens but the design is predominantly 'natural'. The woodland, expansive lawns and lakes are planted with mature trees and informal groups of shrubs and plants, rather than straight borders and avenues. The redbrick and local carstone house, was rebuilt in Jacobean style in 1870, and the grounds were opened to the public at the Queen's express wish in 1977.

Those familiar with other gardens with royal connections, such as the Savill and Valley Gardens in Windsor Great Park, will note some similarities. The sandy loam of the area offers ideal conditions for rhododendrons, camellias and azaleas as well as other woodland and acid-loving plants such as heathers. T. H. Findlay, who worked with Sir Eric Savill at Windsor and helped to develop these gardens, must also be a link.

Woodland walks and shrubberies open on to glades and lawns, whose fine trees are surrounded by carpets of spring bulbs. Cercidiphyllum and sorbus trees, lilies and flowering shrubs such as hydrangeas, moisture-loving plants around the two lakes and dwarf conifers and heathers on the rock garden, extend the season of interest. To the north there is a formal garden of pleached limes, box hedges, lawns and beds of herbs, roses and annuals. Designed by Geoffrey Jellicoe for King George VI, this was positioned for enjoyment from the windows of the king's rooms on that side of the house. A statue of Father Time stands at the far end of its central walk, one of the features added over the years — like a gold-plated bronze Chinese statue known as 'Chinese Joss'; the summerhouse built for Queen Alexandra, the gravestones of royal dogs and the cave-like carstone boat house by the lake. Trees and plants are well labelled, with both the name and the planting date.

SAVILL AND VALLEY GARDENS

MAP J

The Great Park, Windsor
Clearly signposted in the district, particularly
from Egham and from Windsor
Owner: The Crown Estate Commissioners
Tel: Windsor (0753) 860222
Savill Gardens open daily except for three days
over Christmas, Valley Gardens open daily
(peak months April to October)
Plants for sale

The name Sir Eric Savill is well known to lovers of temperate woodland gardens, with good reason. His transformation of a large area of Windsor Great Park into one of the finest twentieth-century gardens of this type was a supreme achievement, acknowledged in 1951 when King George VI commanded that it should take his name.

Work began in the 1930s when, as Deputy Surveyor, he decided to turn a damp area of the park near Englefield Green into a bog garden. The Savill Gardens, now covering thirty acres, grew from this. The fast-flowing stream was formed into two ponds and various vistas, meadows and glades were opened up and planted. A relatively formal area containing herbaceous borders, rose gardens, raised alpine beds and a dry garden was made next to a wall. Now decorated with climbers, this was built to

create the illusion of a garden belonging to a house. Of year-round interest, these gardens will absorb the plantsman (particularly the rhododendron buff) for many hours.

The Savill garden is small and intensely planted, whereas the Valley garden has concentrated pockets of interest. The magnificent trees in the Great Park, its open spaces, undulating ground and vast sheet of water contrast with the liveliness of the Valley garden; the Savill garden is more inward looking and protected.

An informal network of paths weaves around the collections of peat, moisture-loving and woodland plants, shrubs and ornamental and specimen trees in the Savill Garden. The three 'layers' of interest — the trees which give shelter and produce flower and autumn colour, the flowering and other shrubs, and the ground-coverers and low-growing subjects — form a rich composition. Trilliums, species bulbs, Asiatic primulas and meconopsis have been planted generously; hardly an inch of bare earth can be spied and all is in immaculate order. The magnolias such as *M. campbellii* 'Alba' and 'Charles Raffill' and *M. liliflora* 'Nigra', together with cherries, rhododendrons and azaleas, are a memorable sight in spring.

The Savill tends the National Collection of magnolias and has also raised several hundred hybrid rhododendrons, some of which have won the Royal Horticultural Society's Award of Merit. Other National Collections here are of hollies, dwarf and slow-growing conifers and species rhododendrons, tender varieties of which, along with scented hybrids and camellias, are on display in the temperate house. Although of year-round interest, the garden is at its best in spring and autumn, when the foliage colour of styrax, maples, sorbus, liquidambars and fruiting subjects is triggered by the fall in temperature. Note the mossy floor of the beech wood near the entrance, a sea of pale bubbling velvet with an appealing silky texture.

In 1949 Eric Savill began to develop the Valley garden. Situated on the north bank of Virginia Water and covering some three hundred acres, it has three parts: a mixed woodland interplanted with camellias and rhododendrons (including the natural amphitheatre of vivid azaleas in the punch bowl); the hardy varieties of species rhododendrons which are part of a collection made by J. B. Stevenson and were moved from his home in Ascot to the gardens in the 1950s; and the ten-acre heather garden on what was once a gravel pit. Part of the National Collections mentioned can be seen here; the hardy species rhododendrons introduced by planthunters such as George Forrest, Francis Kingdon Ward and Ernest Wilson, are the largest collection in any one garden. The hollies are concentrated in the south-west and the dwarf conifers add to the subtle textures of the heather garden, whose large informal beds form serpentine islands of colour in a green sea. Hydrangeas add colour in summer and the lofty redwoods and other conifers are an impressive sight in the pinetum at any time of the year.

Both gardens are constantly being added to as new and better varieties are raised or become available; they have not been allowed to ossify. The present Keeper has been awarded (as was

Moisture-loving plants beside one of the ponds in the Savill Gardens.

Sir Eric Savill) the Royal Horticultural Society's highest honour, the Victoria Medal — an assurance of the gardens' safe future.

SCOTNEY CASTLE

MAP J

Lamberhurst, near Tunbridge Wells
1½m (2½km) south of Lamberhurst on A21
Owner: The National Trust
Tel: Lamberhurst (0892) 890651
Open several days a week from April to October
Plants for sale

The farther one advances into the gardens of Scotney, the faster reality recedes, for this is one of the best 'picturesque' landscapes in the country. Romantic and in parts dramatic, it was created at a time when the eighteenth-century landscape was taking its bow and a new style of formality was about to take the stage. It differs from 'Capability' Brown's purist style in that it has much more variety, is better endowed with unusual trees and plants and boasts romantic and dramatic features. The garden was laid out by William Sawrey Gilpin, whose book *Observations relating to Picturesque Beauty* had inspired Uvedale Price and others to break new ground and form a bridge between the landscape and the formal garden.

There has been a dwelling at Scotney since the twelfth century, and this evolved into a moated castle, which was then joined by an Elizabethan manor house. The Hussey family acquired the property towards the end of the eighteenth century but by 1835 had decided that its situation was damp and unhealthy. Anthony Salvin was commissioned to build a neo-Gothic mansion on the higher ground overlooking the castle. This involved blasting stone from the hillside, the effects of which formed one of the garden's 'picturesque' features. Gilpin transformed the quarry into a giant rock garden, and accentuated the castle's romantic air by pulling down part of the old Tudor manor house and creating a ruin.

The moss floor beneath the beech trees in the Savill Gardens.

This is now the focal point of the gardens; the trees and shrubs he planted on the sloping ground above create vistas to the fairy-tale picture of the moated ruins and fortified building draped in climbers. The trees planted at that time — many of them fine specimens of North American conifers — and those planted in this century by Christopher Hussey were specially chosen and placed to accentuate the romance of the scene. Paths lined with trees and shrubs lead down from the commanding formal terrace of the nineteenth-century mansion, through the quarry planted with rhododendrons, *Magnolia stellatas*, Japanese maples and azaleas, to the open ground below. The castle is reached over a bridge which spans the moat; on being drained for repairs recently, this was found to contain an interesting legacy: eight-inch-long, fresh-water mussel shells. A small garden of herbs and old-fashioned plants decorate the courtyard of the castle, whose walls and those of the ruin support roses and a magnificent white wisteria. Royal ferns are planted by the moat and on a lawn nearby there is a group of impressively large *Kalmia latifolia*, their flowers resembling tiny parachutes.

An intriguing feature on the northern end of the slope below the mansion is an ice well, covered by a tent-shaped hat of thatched heather. Lanning Roper helped to design an extension to the garden, which contains a memorial walk winding beside the river and up to a spring. It is planted with American subjects, and its informal and peaceful nature adds to the enchantment of Scotney.

SEWERBY HALL

MAP C

Bridlington
2m (3km) north-east of Bridlington on B1255 turn south at Marton
Owner: East Yorkshire Borough Council
Tel: Bridlington (0262) 673769
Open daily from 9 a.m. to dusk
(peak months May and late August to early September)

A justly popular port of call for residents and visitors to Bridlington, the grounds of the hall contain not only a zoo and a wide range of recreational activities but beautifully kept gardens. These have a surprisingly sheltered atmosphere, considering that the North Sea laps the beach only yards from the garden.

The most interesting part of the grounds, from a gardener's point of view, is on the far side of the putting green to the back of the house. There is the formal garden with its avenue of towering monkey puzzle trees, which march up either side of a central path to a temple summerhouse. Some of these have been lost to old age, but young ones have been planted to ensure that future generations will enjoy this unusual sight. Ornamental beds are filled with bulbs in spring and fuchsias, geraniums and annuals in summer; the pendulous foliage of the handsome weeping beeches on the lawns is offset by the straight trunks of the monkey puzzles.

A short distance away, on the far side of Moor Road, are the old walled kitchen gardens which have been transformed into formal, old-fashioned flower gardens. In the first of these are beds of seasonal flowers whose brilliant colouring is a lively contrast to the immaculately-clipped topiary yew and dwarf-box hedging. Greenhouses on one side display tender climbers like bougainvillea and plumbago, as well as pelargoniums, fuchsias and calceolarias. An ornamental goldfish pond is centre stage, and a charming summerhouse against a wall is a focal point at the far end of this walled enclosure. The second walled garden, with scented plants labelled in braille, should give especial pleasure to the blind. Box-edged beds of roses stand on an area of gravel, and climbers, shrubs and shrub roses line the perimeter walls. The walk back to the house is down a 'corridor' of tender and hardy plants — witch-hazels, pittosporum, cistus, roses and hydrangeas.

SEZINCOTE

MAP F

Moreton-in-Marsh
On A44 to Evesham, 1½m (2½km) from
Moreton-in-Marsh
Owners: Mr and Mrs D. Peake (HHA)
Open on Thursday and Friday and Bank Holiday
Mondays throughout the year, except December

There is nothing quite like Sezincote anywhere in Western Europe, except, perhaps, the Brighton Pavilion, which it inspired. Completed in 1805 by Samuel Pepys Cockerell, for his brother, Sir Charles Cockerell, this superb 'Mogul Palace' overlooks an intensely English landscape. The two make a surprisingly happy marriage between east and west. Built of local stone, the mansion's onion dome, peacock-tail arched windows and small minarets reflect the Islamic and Hindu architecture Sir Charles must have seen while working for the East India Company. This style was not carried through to the interior decoration of the house, which is classical, but appropriately influenced the design and decoration of the gardens.

The artist Thomas Daniell, who had spent eight years in India, advised on both house and garden and designed the bridge topped with Brahmin bulls and the temple to the sun god Surya. Humphry Repton was also consulted on the layout, the shape of the serpentine lake and the planting of woodland in the park. His subsequent designs for the Brighton Pavilion reveal that he was much inspired by all he saw here. He would have loved to have secured the commission to build the Pavilion but, despite the fact that it was he who originally suggested its distinctive style of architecture, shrewd Nash won the day.

Water plays a strong role in the area north of the house known as the Thornery. The temple to Surya overlooks the first of a string of pools, which lie one below another, linked by streams and cascades. The design of the Indian bridge and a realistic snake, slithering up a trunk of dead yew, give the gardens a mystic and eastern feel. This is strengthened by the choice of the

wide range of plant material, and by the manner in which it has been used. Edges of lawns are planted with mature and unusual shrubs and trees, and the ponds and streams with moisture-loving plants whose interesting foliage has been blended with skill. The architectural shapes, varied texture and colour of these have been used to offset more delicate flowering plants and create a lush, almost exotic picture. Trees with distinctive shapes and textures — dark spreading cedars, tangled honey locusts and feathery Japanese maples — balance the overall picture. Much of the planting here was devised by Graham Stuart Thomas and Lady Kleinwort in 1944.

They also collaborated on the creation of the 'paradise garden' which lies below the sweeping curve of the delicate Indian orangery beside the house. The lawn, punctuated with slim, fastigiate yews, is riven by canals which meet at a central pond, each element of the design having a traditional and symbolic Mogul meaning. Here again the skilful use of foliage is much in evidence — variegated ivy, bergenia and the large-leafed vine, *Vitis coignetiae* decorate flights of steps which lead to the grotto and the charming tennis pavilion. A majestic arc of trees shelters this part of the garden, the rich, port-wine colour of the copper beeches being flattered by an underplanting of dogwoods.

SHAKESPEARE GARDENS

MAP F

in and around Stratford-upon-Avon
New Place, entrance Chapel Lane; Elizabethan
Knot Garden, entrance via Nash's House, Chapel
Street; Anne Hathaway's Cottage, Shottery, 1m
(2km) from Stratford
Open regularly throughout the year
(peak months May to August)

Though the design of these gardens reflects the spirit of the Elizabethans, they do not date from Shakespeare's time and contain a much wider range of plants than were available during that period. Rather, they provide colourful frames for the timbered houses which were significant in the poet's lifetime. An Elizabethan knot garden has been laid out on the old foundations of New Place and its formal box-edged beds, divided by paths and surrounded by an arboured walk of trained apple trees and laburnum, are a bright patchwork of herbs and flowers. The four beds represent the suits of a pack of cards: diamonds, spades, hearts and clubs. Nearby, the great garden which once supplied the hall with vegetables is planted with yew and box topiary hedges whose buttresses frame variously planted beds. Thatched and timbered, Anne Hathaway's old home has a classic cottage garden and orchard, the old-fashioned charm of which seldom fails to delight. Hall's Croft in the old town and Shakespeare's birthplace in Henley Street also have gardens.

Conifers rising above a bank of azaleas at Sheffield Park.

SHEFFIELD BOTANIC GARDEN

MAP C

Clarkehouse Road, Sheffield 10
Off the A57 near the Royal Hallamshire Hospital
Owner: Sheffield Town Trust, administered by
the Sheffield Metropolitan District Council
Tel: Sheffield (0742) 671115
Open daily

The noise of traffic penetrates only faintly the peace of this twenty-acre garden a short distance from the city centre. On a south-west-facing slope four hundred and fifty feet above sea level, a fine collection of mature and unusual trees and shrubs forms a buffer between the hurly-burly of the city and the peace of the gardens. They were developed by the Sheffield Botanical and Horticultural Society in 1833 and laid out in the gardenesque style by their first curator, Robert Marnock. A far cry from the municipal parks created at this time, Marnock designed a garden of weaving paths, whose exploration would prevent visitors from retracing their steps and give an impression of gardens of great size. They also provided opportunities to display a diverse collection of plants, which would have to be

sought out rather than observed from a distance. Victorian features — the pavilions built in the style of, and named for, the curator's contemporary, Sir Joseph Paxton; the ornamental bedding-out (albeit with modern varieties) in the Victorian gardens, and the impressive size of certain specimen and ornamental trees — are reminders of the gardens' early beginnings.

Like all botanical gardens, it has an educational purpose and certain areas are devoted to plant trials, conservation and endangered varieties, or demonstrate what can be grown in various conditions. Over five thousand plant species find a home here, a surprising number of which are tender, and it is interesting to note that the policy is to work with the soil conditions rather than try to transform the quick-drying clay. A rockery, formal rose garden, trial beds of dahlia cultivars, island beds devoted to themes such as dwarf conifers, floral art and plants with silver or gold foliage, the National Collection of diervilla and weigela, a garden for the disabled and borders displaying some of the plants holding the Royal Horticultural Society's Award of Garden Merit are a small sample of all that can be seen here. An old bear pit which resembles a deep well and the fossilised stump and roots of giant club moss or *Lycopod* are two unusual features at the centre of the gardens. The higher reaches support the majority of ornamental floral features, the lower have an informal woodland nature.

SHEFFIELD PARK GARDEN

MAP J

near Uckfield
Midway between East Grinstead and Lewes, 5m (8km) north-west of Uckfield, on east side of A275
Owner: The National Trust
Tel: Danehill (0825) 790655
Open regularly from Easter to beginning of November
(peak seasons spring and autumn)

This richly embellished landscape garden is famed above all others for its glorious autumn colours, but at all times of the year the hundred acres set around four man-made lakes present a memorable picture. The heroic design and grand scale of the landscape is well matched by its superb trees and flowering shrubs; the smooth sheets of water provide a mirror to everything around them, and a T-shaped backbone to the whole.

There has been a dwelling on this site since the thirteenth century, but the most important periods in the garden's development were in the late seventeenth and early twentieth centuries. The Gothic house designed by James Wyatt for the Earl of Sheffield in 1775 stands on high ground and enjoys fine views over the landscape. The house is still privately owned and is somewhat detached from the garden, but efforts are being made to create an effective link between the two. While the house was being built, 'Capability' Brown was fashioning the landscape, creating two of the four lakes and building a cascade. The first of the two lakes that come into view and the waterfalls were made in the late nineteenth century by James Pulham, of Pulham and Son, renowned for their skill in constructing dramatic rock and water features. It was after 1909, when Arthur Soames bought the property, that the gardens were given their exciting collec-

tion of rare and unusual trees and shrubs, maximum advantage being taken of the existing landscape. A large number of these were planted between 1909 and Soames's death in 1948, and are now in their prime. The conifers do not have that scraggy look which marks so many of those planted in the Victorian era. The rhododendrons are of haystack proportions and when not in flower provide a dense and dark background to livelier subjects.

Walks ring the lakes and strike out into the surrounding woodland, which is enriched by a humbling array of unusual shrubs and trees; they weave through glades carpeted with wild flowers and spring bulbs and open up to vistas of the lake or striking botanical features. In spring, the hundreds of different rhododendrons, azaleas, kalmias, cherries and other flowering shrubs and trees create bold banks and mounds of colour beneath the fresh green canopy of oaks and beeches. In summer, there are the late-flowering varieties of rhododendron, waterlilies on the lakes, and gunnera, astilbes, hostas and other moisture-loving plants along the banks. The drop in temperature brings about the grand climax in autumn. Dark and stately cypress, cedars, pines, hemlocks and junipers and the evergreen foliage of rhododendrons are the perfect backcloth to a veritable bonfire of colour produced by deciduous subjects like maples, *Nyssa sylvatica* on tupelo trees, red oaks, Spanish chestnuts, amelanchiers, spindles, parrotias, fothergillas, and cornus. The brilliant colours are reflected in the water, light up the glades and woodland and almost eclipse the beauty of autumn crocuses and the gentians which form rivers of brilliant blue either side of a path. The views from the bridges suspended over the cascades and waterfalls are superb. The vast expanses of water accentuate the dramatic scale of the trees and the mounds of rhododendrons which appear to float on its surface. There is nothing mean or petty about any aspect of these gardens, thrilling to all, though of especial interest to the plantsman and dendrologist.

Rhododendrons and towering conifers beside the lake at Sheffield Park.

SHELDON MANOR

MAP I

Chippenham
1½m (2½km) from Chippenham turn south off
A420 at Allington
Owner: Major M. A. Gibbs
Tel: Chippenham (0249) 653120
Open a few days a week from April to October
(peak months June and July)

The gardens around this medieval manor house will appeal particularly to the lover of old-fashioned shrub roses and unusual trees and shrubs. There are no spectacular displays of bedding-out or herbaceous plants here and, though there are formal yew-hedged areas and a water garden, the predominant quality is one of agreeable rural charm. The damask, gallica, musk, moss and other roses which flourish on the heavy Oxford clay have been planted singly in turf, which emphasises their individual beauty and characteristics. In various parts of the garden, from orchards whose trees are tangled with clematis and rambling roses, to converted rickyards, are seldom-seen varieties of sorbus, thorns, magnolias, a mature specimen of a white Judas tree and an *Acer pseudoplatanus* 'Brilliantissimum'. An old apple store set on staddle stones, the Dutch copper vats now containing plants but once used to make cheese, Muscovy ducks, bantams and rare breeds of sheep add to the homely charm of the garden.

253

SHERBOURNE PARK

MAP F

near Warwick
3m (5km) south of Warwick off A429, ½m (1km)
north of Barford
Owner: Honourable Mrs Smith-Ryland
Tel: Warwick (0926) 624255
Open a few days a year for charity and by
appointment
Plants for sale

The high standards of this large private garden and the fact that it has been developed from scratch in just over twenty-five years mark it out as exceptional. The early Georgian house was originally surrounded by parkland and relatively flat, open countryside. The symmetrical façade still faces this scene, for the garden is at the back of the house, initially hidden from view by a redbrick wing.

A series of gardens set within one, hedges, walls, pergolas and groups of shrubs create divisions between the areas and form walks, intimate enclosures and vistas. The eye is directed down an avenue of limes in the park beyond the ha-ha, and to architectural features such as a temple by the lake and the spire of the Gilbert Scott church on the far side of a wall. Formality is present in the shape of the Dutch garden, which contains a pattern of box-edged beds, and the yew-hedged enclosure planted with white-flowering plants.

These give way to areas treated in a more relaxed and 'natural' manner — the young arboretum around the lake at the far end of the garden, and the banks of the stream nearby. One of the garden's strengths is its wide collection of unusual plants and the way they have been used. Tender subjects such as campsis, solanum and bignonia grow against the walls of the south-facing terrace and the swimming-pool garden; standard wisterias and honeysuckles decorate the Dutch garden, and roses the pond garden. Shrubs and specimen trees play an important part in the borders, giving them height and strong shapes. Imaginative plant associations abound, and the way cream- and buff-coloured flowers have been used make subtle blends between stronger shades is noteworthy.

SHERINGHAM PARK

MAP G

Upper Sheringham
1½m (2½km) south-west of Sheringham on
B1157
Owner: The National Trust
Tel: Aylsham (0263) 733084
Open daily throughout the year
(peak seasons spring to early summer and autumn)

The deft hand of Humphry Repton fashioned this beautiful park for the Upcher family at the beginning of the nineteenth century. It was completed towards the end of his career as a landscape gardener, and he considered the house and landscape his masterpiece 'my most favourite monument' and one 'more durable than brass'. He was correct because today it is considered the finest surviving example of his work. His eldest son, the architect John Adey Repton, helped to design the neo-classical house, whose elegant simplicity is set against a south-facing wooded hill. Planted in the 1950s with rhododendrons, camellias and azaleas, this hill protects the house from the harsh winds blowing off the North Sea and though the house is deprived of sea views, it looks instead on to beautiful undulating land and wooded hills.

Open spaces which allow views to the sea are as important in the landscape as the woodland and impressive mounds of cultivated and ponticum rhododendrons. Repton was loath to 'make one dull, vapid, smooth and tranquil scene, wrapt all o'er in everlasting green' and he cleverly left the cornfields between the hills and the house to form a contrast to the intense planting elsewhere. To give an idea of the balance, there are three hundred acres of woodland in the park, ninety acres of grass and fifty acres of 'wild garden'. His design ensured that the eye would be drawn to features beyond the park as well — to the windmill along the cliffs at Weybourne, the (newly-replaced) temple set on a hill, and the undulating line of mature trees on high ground. The more highly-cultivated, domestic garden is open to the public occasionally.

SHUGBOROUGH

MAP F

Milford, near Stafford
5½m (9km) south-east of Stafford on A513;
entrance at Milford
Owner: The National Trust
Tel: Little Hayward (0889) 881388
Open several days a week from mid-March to
late October

The approach to the late-seventeenth-century house, with its handsome pillared portico added by Samuel Wyatt, is through a large park embellished with impressive neo-Grecian monuments — the Lanthorn of Demosthenes, Triumphal Arch and Tower of the Winds. These were built by Admiral Lord Anson who circumnavigated the world and in 1744 brought back an immense fortune and a variety of everlasting pea which has come to be known as 'Lord Anson's Blue Pea'. He and his brother, Thomas, lavished the fortune on Shugborough.

Very much smaller in scale than the heroic monuments, a feature of the gardens added at this time was the Chinese tea-house designed by one of the admiral's officers. Surrounded by plants from China, this beautifully-restored building is reached over a wrought-iron bridge painted lacquer red. The oriental building strikes an intimate note in a garden which has a pleasing feeling of space. Lawns run down to the River Sow and great trees have room to display their proud size; an ancient yew whose low branches cover a staggering area of ground is particularly eyecatching.

A dainty, Victorian-style rose garden, designed by Graham Stuart Thomas, is near the terraces on the west front, which William Nesfield created in the mid-nineteenth century. Delicate arches and pillars support froths of rambling roses and hoops of clematis which, together with standard roses, provide vertical interest above the formal pattern of beds. The shady wild garden south of the house is a peaceful walk which opens up to banks of rhododendrons and azaleas near the river, and in spring there is the always welcome sight of daffodils and bluebells.

SISSINGHURST CASTLE GARDEN

MAP J

Sissinghurst, near Cranbrook
1m (2km) east of Sissinghurst village on A262;
2½m (4km) north-east of Cranbrook and 13m
(21km) south of Maidstone
Owner: The National Trust
Tel: Cranbrook (0580) 712850
Open regularly Easter to mid-October

The shrine to which all true garden-lovers make a pilgrimage at some time in their lives, Sissinghurst is in danger of being loved too well and worn down by the thousands of pilgrims. Only the consummate skill of its custodians protects its special qualities. So often when a garden ceases to be nurtured by the hand which created it, it loses its unique personality and becomes simply a preserved masterpiece with a strangely 'dead eye'. This is not so at Sissinghurst where the spirit rather than the letter of the law dictates. The disciplined bone structure of the design is unchanging, but the planting, like nature itself, has been allowed to evolve.

When Vita Sackville-West and her husband Sir Harold Nicolson came here in 1930 they were faced with a disconnected collection of ancient buildings: stables, cottages, Tudor gatehouse, Elizabethan tower, old walls and a garden which had become a farmyard dumping-ground. Few would have had the vision to know what could be made of this sad scene, which resembled a neglected folly and not the fairy-tale castle of the Nicolsons' dreams. It is mistakenly thought that Vita Sackville-West was its sole creator, perhaps because of her still immensely readable articles about her garden-making experiences here. In fact it was the ideal marriage of their talents which brought about its birth and growth to maturity. Harold Nicolson laid out its strong basic design and worked out how existing irregular features could be incorporated into a plan of square or rectangular compartments where vistas and surprises play an important role. Vita Sackville-West's sense of history, her romantic nature, considerable horticultural talents and love of beauty filled the 'rooms' with informal and inspired arrangements of plants. These were chosen to create a particular atmosphere, a colour theme or a seasonal display. Sir Harold was the architect, Vita Sackville-West the interior decorator.

Similar to Hidcote in many respects, and inspired by it, the design is formal and the planting generous and relaxed; cottage-garden and wild flowers intermingle happily with a wealth of more sophisticated and unusual plants. Each compartment has an individual character, but contributes a necessary element to the well-balanced whole. What begins as a feast of scent and colour in formal, highly-cultivated enclosures gives way to restrained formality in the shape of the unadorned rondel and walks of tight-clipped yew. These cool the eye before it is once again seduced, this time by the unsophisticated charm of the orchard and moat. In such a way has the garden been made to blend with the period buildings and the surrounding countryside. To appreciate fully the cohesive layout of the six acres, climb to the top of the tower and enjoy an unforgettable bird's-eye view of the whole.

The imaginative use of colour is a major feature — the purple border in the tower courtyard; the flower beds around the large copper in the garden of South Cottage, filled with warm oranges, golds and yellows (shades many gardeners find tricky to place and consequently reject); the soothing white garden, surveyed by a lead statue of the Virgin beneath a silver weeping pear, with its glorious central 'wedding cake' eruption of a *Rosa longicuspis*, and box-edged beds of white- and lime-flowering foliage plants. Roses abound, flattering the old walls, rioting through the trees in the orchard and massed in the rose garden. Note how well the old-fashioned shrub varieties are staked and trained here: striped gallicas, tissue-paper-white to wine-dark blooms being shown to their best advantage and underplanted with sympathetic violas and

irises. This fragrant 'room' is at its best in June, whereas the flagged, pleached lime walk, flanked by beds of anemones, fritillarias and spring bulbs of all kinds, and the Azalea Walk down to the moat, catch the attention in spring.

The nuttery, a feature which predates the Nicolsons, is now underplanted with euphorbias, perennial geranium, sweet woodruff, ornamental grasses and trillium, and two thyme lawns introduce the yew-hedged herb garden at the far end. The moat, its banks treated in a natural way, is a boundary to the far end of the garden. This can be reached by a formal grass walk, scented by yellow azaleas. The sensitivity with which features have been chosen and placed — the statue against a crescent of yew hedge, urns and terracotta pots — adds greatly to the atmosphere and beauty of these gardens.

Every layer of the plant content warrants close inspection, from the roses and unusual climbers which shoot up and over walls, to the rich variety of ground-hugging subjects and tiny specimen bulbs. The overall effect of any one compartment is of prime importance, but the way each has been planted, more often than not with unusual and particularly lovely varieties of plants, makes the gardens unique. Botanically fascinating and aesthetically pleasing, Sissinghurst feasts the eye and feeds the spirit.

SIZERGH CASTLE

MAP B

Sedgwick, near Kendal
3½m (5½km) south of Kendal on A591
Owner: The National Trust
Tel: Sedgwick (05395) 60070
Open from Easter to end October
(peak seasons spring and autumn)

The most absorbing feature at Sizergh is the rock garden, laid out in 1926 by the well-known Ambleside nursery of T. R. Hayes and Son. It is in a natural dell on one side of the castle, which was built around a fourteenth-century pele tower. The rock garden covers quarter of an acre, and is constructed of weathered lakeland limestone. Small ponds, linked by a stream fed

Maples on the rockery at Sizergh.

nests on the island.

The far banks of the lake are an ideal spot to admire the castle, and to note the false perspective of the steps running down to the cleverly-designed terrace and parapet. The retaining walls of the deep grass terraces support tender climbers, and vivid blue gentians stand at the foot of the tower draped with Boston ivy. On the now modified grass terraces of the Dutch garden are balls of variegated box and in the rose garden nearby is an avenue of young *Sorbus aucuparia* 'Beissneri' and island beds of shrub roses underplanted with perennial geraniums, violas and lamium 'Beacon Silver'. Magnolias, spindles, hydrangeas and a eucryphia also decorate this area. Sizergh is far from the forbidding castle with rugged surrounds which might be imagined in this part of the country. It is surprisingly easy to relate to and a pleasure to explore.

from the lake above, provide ideal conditions for bog and water plants and, though many alpines can be found here, it is the National Collection of hardy ferns (approximately 120 species), dwarf conifers and Japanese maples which are the most eyecatching subjects. The varying textures, shapes and shades look marvellous against what appears to be a natural, rocky slope. Rare forms of the royal fern, lady, Japanese painted and hart's tongue ferns fan out of crannies and offset the brilliant colours of primulas, astilbes and willow gentians. The maples, such as the bold *Acer palmatum* 'Atropurpureum' at the centre of the garden, have now reached a considerable size, and the compact shapes of 'bun' Norway spruces, unusual golden yews, and powdery mounds of Japanese white pines prompt a new appreciation of the diversity of conifers.

Above the rock garden, hidden behind a bank of conifers, is an herbaceous border with soft-coloured flowers gradually building up to warm reds and oranges towards the centre. A grassy bank, running down to the lake below the castle, is peppered with spring bulbs, orchids, ox-eye daisies and other wild flowers which thrive on the limestone. The lake is surrounded with shrubs, willows and dogwoods, and a Camperdown weeping elm shades the swans'

SLEDMERE HOUSE

MAP C

Sledmere, near Driffield
3m (5km) north-west of Great Driffield on A166
turn north-west on to B1252
Owner: Sir Tatton Sykes
Tel: Driffield (0377) 86637
Open Easter weekend, Sundays in April and daily
from May to late September
(peak month July)
Plants for sale

'Capability' Brown's original plans for the park at Sledmere can be seen in the beautiful library of this Georgian house. Commissioned to lay out the park in the late 1770s, Brown's design involved the removal of the village to its present position, out of sight of the house so that it would not detract from the nobility of the newly-fashioned landscape. Unlike so much of his work, because of underlying chalk there is no lake at Sledmere, only a circular stone pond on the grass terraces behind the house. Beyond lies the open countryside and vistas, channelled through woodland, to a neo-classical deer shed on a hill to the west and to Sledmere Castle to the east. Handsome chestnuts and copper beeches shade the lawns around the house and a church can be spied above a neatly-clipped hedge.

The gardens, village and the famous stud farm have never suffered a period of neglect, and have a wonderfully ordered and cared-for appearance. In many gardens of stately homes period features are being developed or reinstated. Those at Sledmere are the recently-laid-out knot garden and the reconstructed neo-classical orangery, saved from ruin by the National Trust. The knot, set around a Venetian fountain, is west of the house. Laid out on gravel, its pattern of dwarf box hedging, interplanted with vari-egated ivy, appropriately incorporates the letter S. The orangery, which originally came from Fairford in Gloucestershire, overlooks the Italian garden with its statues and stonework.

A short woodland walk leads to the kitchen garden, now simplified, which contains fruit trees such as crab-apples and cherries and also goose-berry and currant bushes. Against the walls are immaculately-trained fruit trees and roses and clematis and, in a secluded smaller walled sec-tion, there are beds of mixed modern roses, peri-meter borders of spring- and summer-flowering plants and old-fashioned shrub roses.

SLEIGHTHOLME DALE LODGE

MAP C

Fadmoor, near Kirkbymoorside
3m (5km) north of Kirkbymoorside, 1m (2km) from Fadmoor
Owners: Dr and Mrs O. James
Tel: Kirkbymoorside (0751) 31492
Open a few days a year and by appointment for charity
(peak months May to July and September)

Well off the beaten track, this peaceful three-acre garden clings to the side of a steep south-west-facing valley. It is divided into two parts: the older, more formal garden, laid out in 1910, hangs above an informal spring garden devel-oped by the present owner's mother during World War II.

Sheltered by walls, the top flower garden is

patterned with borders and geometric patterns of beds divided by stone paths, pergolas, es-paliered fruit trees and oak trellis-work. These are hosts to an abundance of clematis, fragrant honeysuckles and rambling roses. The borders have a voluptuous array of herbaceous plants, subjects with purple foliage (such as sage and berberis) cleverly used to flatter the soft colour-ing of peonies, shrub roses and flowering herbs.

Japanese cherries and huge hummocks of species roses decorate the paddock below, which is carpeted with daffodils and bluebells. The way a warm, glowing group of occidental azaleas has been made to erupt out of a mound of variegated cornus is particularly effective. Below the house, dry-stone terraces run down to a pond and ha-ha. Shrubs, dwarf conifers and small specimen trees tumble over retaining walls: finely-textured maples; a philadelphus aptly named 'Avalanche'; *Lonicera syringantha* which has scented, soft-lilac flowers, wild red tulips and an abundance of other lovely and unusual plants create a waterfall of interest.

SNOWSHILL MANOR

MAP F

Snowshill, near Broadway
3m (5km) south-west of Broadway, 4m (6½km) west of junction of A424 and A44
Owner: The National Trust
Tel: Broadway (0386) 852410
Open a few days a week from Easter to end October

Set in a charming Cotswold village, the hillside gardens at Snowshill were once a semi-derelict farmyard described as being 'a wilderness of chaos'. Their transformation into a series of 'rooms', specifically designed as an extension of the fifteenth-century manor house, was the work of the architect, artist-craftman, poet and col-lector, Charles Wade, who came to Snowshill in 1919. Given the talents of this unusual man, parts of the garden are understandably archi-tectural in character; like the house itself, they shelter an intriguing and often eccentric collection of features.

The restrained entrance to Snowshill Manor.

Charles Wade knew the importance of creating a balance between peaceful, restrained and highly-decorated, formal areas. The introduction to the gardens is deliberately simple. A gravel path flanked by lawns leads up to the classical eighteenth-century front of the house, grass terraces falling away to an orchard on one side. A walk lined with borders marks the start of the series of intimate gardens below the house, divided by walls and paths, which have a sun-baked nature. A Venetian wellhead, a dovecote, columnar sundial, zodiac clock, painted statue of St George and the Dragon, pools and sinks fed by a spring, all decorate or are the focal point of a 'room'.

Doors and garden seats are painted an unusual dark blue turquoise, known as 'Wade Blue'; Wade, with justification, deemed that this colour was an ideal foil for grass and foliage. Though the borders in the various 'rooms' are no longer predominantly filled with the blue and mauve flowers he thought flattering to the honey-coloured Cotswold stone, they and the walls boast a generous and colourful display of plants. The doorway beneath a statue of the Madonna leads to an informal garden shaded by shrubs and trees, a secluded and subtle contrast to the liveliness of all that came before. Stylish and idiosyncratic, these gardens are unusually welcoming and easy to relate to; though the attention is focused on the immediate surroundings, there are delightful views of the surrounding countryside and peacefully grazing sheep.

SOMERLEYTON HALL

MAP G

near Lowestoft
On B1074 5m (8km) north-west of Lowestoft
Owners: Lord and Lady Somerleyton (HHA)
Tel: Lowestoft (0502) 730224
Open regularly from end March to end September
(peak month June)

The original Jacobean house is masked by the confident and ornate Victorian additions made, in the mid-nineteenth century, by the railway magnate Sir Morton Peto. No expense was spared on them or on the making of the gardens, which once boasted a crystal palace with a mosque dome and a flamboyant parterre. The work ultimately bankrupted Sir Morton, and the property was then sold to the present owner's grandfather, Sir Francis Crossley. Of historical and botanical interest, the gardens still reflect the unembarrassedly grand and sumptuous style of Victorian garden-making. Visitors have been welcome to them for over a hundred years and though they continue to impress their friendly atmosphere prevents them from being intimidating.

As might be expected in a garden of this period, there are many fine trees: cedars, beeches, tulip trees and the Victorian favourite, monkey puzzles, form vast pools of shade on the expansive lawns. Spread around them are groups of evergreen shrubs and conifers; the rhododendrons provide mounds of brilliant colour in spring and shelter hidden pockets of interest. Borders decorate the otherwise grassed-over walled kitchen garden, where one of the greenhouses displays rare exotics, and a three-hundred-foot-long pergola nearby is draped with roses, vines and wisterias.

Two of the best-known designers of the time were involved in the development of Peto's gardens. Paxton contributed the glass wall cases against the outer wall of the kitchen garden — like thin, lean-to greenhouses, they were built to protect subjects like peach trees. William Nesfield designed the now radically-modified parterre, and the yew-hedged maze. Its entrance is through a huge wedge of yew which, if you take the correct paths, is only four hundred yards from the central point, a pagoda set on a mound.

The parterre, on a terrace overlooking the park beside the house, was grassed over during World War II, and rose beds, Irish yews, standard rhododendrons and stone ornaments now provide the interest. Striking away from the house, a colonnade is a boundary to the winter garden, patterned with paths, lawns, a central pond and perimeter beds of seasonal flowers. This area was once covered by the vast crystal dome, which was once described as being 'unsurpassed by anything of its kind in Europe'. The gardens are obviously much loved and admirably tended and offer a rare opportunity to admire the garden-making skills of the Victorians.

SPETCHLEY PARK

MAP F

Spetchley, near Worcester
3m (5km) east of Worcester on A422
Owner: Mr R. J. Berkeley (HHA)
Tel: Spetchley (090 565) 213/224
Open regularly from April to September
(peak months April to June)

The gardens belonging to the Bath stone Palladian mansion built in 1811, though developed over several centuries, have an ample Edwardian character. Much of what can be seen today was the creation of Rose Berkeley whose sister, Ellen Willmott, was a much-respected plantswoman of the Edwardian era. The four yew-hedged enclosures known as the fountain gardens originally contained beds devoted to individual plant families, and were thought to have been Miss Willmott's idea. They no longer contain a living 'museum' of plants, but the gardens as a whole display a wide-ranging col-

lection of unusual plants. These can be seen in walled and hedged enclosures and in the informal and woodland gardens.

Tender subjects — a bignonia, double pomegranate *Punica granatum* 'Flore-Pleno', paulownia or foxglove tree, fragrant osmanthus, and *Fremontodendron californicum* — inhabit the sheltered walled gardens. Mixed borders of old-fashioned shrub roses, herbaceous plants and flowering shrubs surround the rosy brick walls, their contents overflowing on to the paths. In the yew-hedged 'rooms' of the fountain gardens, the thirty-six order beds still exist, but are now planted with several varieties of magnolia and a number of plants which bear Miss Willmott's name.

The picture now opens up: the spacious lawns flattering the handsome cedars and other fine trees, the white bridge spanning the moat, the park, lake and house can be spied. A rose garden with individual beds of modern varieties stands near the conservatory and beyond lies the Garden Pool, its banks smothered in daffodils. What is known as New Lawn has been planted with shrubs and trees which produce good autumn fruits and colour; the flowering trees and shrubs such as maples, cornus, rhododrons and azaleas are at their best in the woodland garden in spring. Spring bulbs proliferate, and fritillarias and self-seeded Turk's cap lilies create a haze of pink in an area of rough grass near the house. Features such as the thatch-roofed root house, the Bath stone loggia or alcove, and the fountain supported by dolphins and lead figures representing the four seasons further the period feel of the whole. The intensely-planted, more formal areas may not be maintained to the high standards demanded during their heyday, but they still have charm.

SPINNERS

MAP I

School Lane, Boldre, near Lymington
From A337 Brockenhurst-Lymington road, turn
east for Boldre; RAC signposted through village
Owners: Mr and Mrs P. G. G. Chappell
Tel: Lymington (0590) 73347
Open every day from mid-April to end
August (nursery all year)
(peak months May and June)
Plants for sale

Roy Lancaster has called Spinners a 'Mecca for plantsmen'; it is not difficult to see why. Developed from scratch in the 1950s, the upper reaches are set on gravel, the lower on clay, and the water which drains freely through the gravel forms moist areas below the sloping oak woodland. Informal in character and with year-round interest, it is the lavish planting and extraordinarily wide variety and quality of the plants which first catches the eye. Acid-lovers abound as do shade-loving perennials and ground-coverers.

Paths wind up through the woodland past imaginatively-grouped plants, from delicate trilliums to bold and unusual rhododendrons and handsome magnolias. An impressive variety of hostas, primulas, meconopsis, rogersias and ferns are lush and colourful in the bog garden and, below the house, the paths open on to the lawn surrounded by large beds of perennials and flowering shrubs and trees. Seek out and admire maples such as *Acer pennsylvanicum* 'Erythrocladum', whose young foliage is shrimp pink, *Cornus kousa chinensis*, the grove of eucalyptus trees and the rarely seen *Nyssa sinensis* which provides superb autumn colour and produces young shoots of bright red throughout the growing season.

The garden is filled with unusual plants, particularly those better-than-average varieties which the Chappell's consider pay their way: unusual magnolias; free-and long-flowering *williamsii* camellias like 'Francis Hanger' and 'Anticipation'; the *Dicentra* 'Langtrees' which has beautiful foliage and white flowers; the wide collection of perennial geraniums which are ideal ground-cover; fragrant daphnes and delicate spring- and autumn-flowering cyclamen. Apart from the rarity of so much to be seen here, there are lessons to be learnt on how to cut down labour and improve growing conditions while creating satisfying plant associations of long-lasting interest. The owners run an exceptionally good nursery and are generous with their knowledge and enthusiasm.

SPRINGFIELDS GARDENS

MAP G

Camelgate, Spalding
1m (2km) north-east of Spalding on A151 turn
north
Owner: Springfields Horticultural Society
Tel: Spalding (0775) 4843
Open daily from end March to end September
(peak months April to mid-May, July and
September)
Plants for sale

Since 1966 Lincolnshire has had a showcase, in the shape of Springfields Gardens, for its best-known product: spring bulbs. They cover twenty-five acres and display several thousand varieties of bulbs and corms in spring, with roses, dahlias and annuals prolonging the season well into September.

Once through the turnstile gate in the high perimeter fence, beds on the lawns and terraces create a brilliant patchwork of colour. Waterlilies cover the surface of a lake; a pergola walk is draped with scores of different clematis; glasshouses shelter hundreds of varieties of tulips, and there are annuals grown from seed: geraniums, impatiens and profusely-filled hanging baskets. A woodland garden is planted with suitable subjects, such as the blue Himalayan poppy, *Meconopsis betonicifolia*.

Much of what is on show has been supplied by the horticultural industry, experimental stations and various plant societies. Springfields is an ideal place for amateur gardeners to make comparisons and select varieties for their own

Massed flowering bulbs at Springfield Gardens.

gardens; it is also a rewarding day out for those who revel in generous and lively displays of plants.

STAGSHAW GARDENS

MAP B

Ambleside
½m (1km) south of Ambleside on A591
Owner: The National Trust
Tel: Ambleside (05394) 32109
Open daily from Easter to end of June, and by appointment from July to September
(peak season spring)

Having been brought up at Killerton in Devon — a garden filled with rare and unusual trees and shrubs — it is not surprising that Cuthbert Acland wanted to transform the lower part of a rugged and wooded fell into a woodland garden. Covering eight acres and planted between 1959 and 1979, it is an example of how the natural beauty of a site can be preserved and enriched with cultivated and unusual plants. The wild character, native trees and flowers play as important a role as the more sophisticated newcomers.

The charm of the woodland is enhanced by the glades which were opened up and planted with azaleas, rhododendrons and camellias. The sensitive use of colour is an outstanding feature. Planted for overall effect rather than simply as a collection of flowering shrubs, the subtle blends of pale or brilliant shades prevent the woodland from ever appearing contrived or hard. There are some fine magnolias, maples, cherries, embothriums and cornus, and a stream veins the hillside, tumbling over cascades and rocks. Native wild plants, such as bilberies, ferns and grasses, act as ground-coverers and an outcrop of rock supports a moss garden, its grey-green velvety cushions seemingly dusted with frost. Large-leafed rhododendrons make striking features, and spring bulbs, roses, hydrangeas and eucryphias, with the autumn foliage of maples, nyssas and parrotias ensure that there is a long season of interest. You can savour the views and tranquillity of Stagshaw from well-placed seats.

STODY LODGE

MAP G

Melton Constable, near Briston
Off the B1110 to Holt
Owners: Mr and Mrs Ian MacNicol
Tel: Melton Constable (0263) 860572
Open for charity on Sundays from mid-May to early June, including Spring Bank Holiday Monday, and open by appointment for parties on weekdays
(peak months May and June)

There are two separate gardens at Stody. One fans out from the house built by Lord Rothermere in the 1930s and another, a water garden, lies in woodland on the far side of the road. Both contain good collections of acid-loving plants such as azaleas and rhododendrons. From the expansive lawns at the back of the house, wide grass avenues divide large areas boldly planted with mature conifers, ornamental trees, heathers, rhododendrons and azaleas: their colour and scent is spectacular. This part of the garden was designed by the architect Walter Sarel, but the water gardens, in a depression of a one-hundred-and-fifty-acre wood, were created by Ernest Horsfall at the turn of the century. Paths weave around ponds and islands are ringed by channels, the whole area being planted with over two thousand rhododendrons and azaleas. The season of interest may be short at Stody, but the generosity of planting and the skilful way evergreens have been used to create strong shapes near the house create a memorable picture.

STONE COTTAGE

MAP G

Hambleton, near Oakham
4m (6½km) east of Oakham, turn south off A606 for Hambleton
Owner: Colonel John Codrington
Tel: Oakham (0572) 2156
Open a few days a year and by appointment from April to October for charity
(peak months May and June)

Belonging to the plantsman and garden designer John Codrington, this two-acre garden is in a class of its own. It lies on a finger of land which juts out into the massive man-made lake, Rutland Water, whose surrounds were landscaped by Dame Sylvia Crowe and are well worth making a detour to see. When Colonel Codrington and his sister first began to develop the limestone garden in the 1950s, it lacked protection from the harsh easterly winds which tear across the flat countryside of these parts. Creating a shelter belt was a top priority, and today the garden is embraced by a woodland-like mix of willows, conifers and poplars. Informal in design, it has both a wild and a cottage-garden character, though there are also stylish touches, vistas, points of drama and surprises.

The Colonel's love of, and fascination with, plants is obvious as an absorbing collection of wild and cultivated varieties have been allowed glorious freedom to display their beauty and seed themselves freely. There are many rare plants, a large number of which he collected on his travels abroad to advise on and design gardens — a jacaranda from Guavi; pines grown from seed collected in Tokyo; a false fennel from Carthage; and many beauties from Italy, New Zealand, North America and the Himalayas. These thrive side by side with a host of native wild plants, grasses, herbs, liquorice which actually came from Pontefract, and other more common but no less loved plants.

The garden is composed of a series of separate gardens, some devoted to a colour theme such as hot reds and oranges, silvers and whites or blues and yellows, or to foliage and moisture-loving plants, culinary or medicinal herbs. Allspice, sago, chili peppers, papyrus and plumbago can be seen in a small tropical house, and an old cowshed, converted into a neo-Georgian orangery, has plants tumbling out of a manger. Fellow plantsmen must leave plenty of time to explore this exciting and unconventional creation.

STONE HOUSE COTTAGE GARDENS

MAP F

Stone, near Kidderminster
2m (3km) south-east of Kidderminster, off A448
Owners: Major and the Honourable Mrs James Arbuthnott
Tel: Kidderminster (0562) 69902
Open on certain days for charity, and Wednesday to Saturday from March to November (peak season summer)
Plants for sale

Sheltered and confined by walls, this one-acre plantsman's garden will be of special interest to those who despair of growing tender plants. The Midlands have far from mild weather conditions but, thanks to the walls, the owners' horticultural skills and, most important, courage, they have managed to grow to maturity much that the majority of gardeners would confine to a greenhouse.

When the Arbuthnotts came here in 1975, the old kitchen garden to Stone House, with a gardener's cottage in one corner, had been neglected for a long period. The triangular plot, set on well-drained sandy loam, is now filled with interesting shrubs, climbers and herbaceous plants. Paths flanked by yew hedges, already surprisingly thick considering their youth, fan out from the gateway in the south-east corner. Four large borders are at the centre of the gardens; they sport old-fashioned roses, hardy fuchsias, herbaceous plants, tree mallows and romneyas. A hedge of the claret-coloured *Prunus Pissardii* divides a small arboretum from the formal borders. Not a foot of the rosy brick walls has been wasted; the tender climbers are one of the garden's specialities: lobster's claw or *clianthus puniceus*, the Tasmanian bell-flowered *Billardiera longiflora*, bignonias and many others. These join with scores of clematis, climbing roses, honeysuckles and a good collection of unusual climbers to create a beautiful display.

Other tender plants, helped to withstand the harsh winters by a dressing of potash in autumn, are the white-flowering hoheria, fremontodendron, drimys, and plumbago *Ceratostigma griffithii*. Obviously there are casualties, but the Arbuthnotts are skilled propagators, constantly raising plants for the excellent nursery, so gaps are seldom left unfilled for long; untried tender specimens are experimented with or old favourites reinstated.

STONESTACK

MAP B

283 Chapeltown Road, Turton, near Bolton
4½m (7km) north of Bolton, via A666 leading to
B6391
Owners: Mr and Mrs Frank Smith
Tel: Turton (0204) 852460
Open several days a year for charity and by
appointment
(peak months May and August)

Created from scratch around a house built in 1959, the two-acre garden contains not only a wide range of plant material but a series of imaginatively-constructed compartments. Mr Frank Smith is a surveyor, as is evident in the care and ingenuity with which stone and other building materials have been used to create divisions, paths and flower beds. The framework of the garden is a lesson in how various materials, which the average person might consider useless, can be put to good use. Old tiles have been laid under some beds to improve the drainage of the wet, acid soil, and the strawberry beds, on a steep narrow slope, have been terraced with abandoned concrete paving and edging. Easy to maintain, the terracing has put to good use a sunny but otherwise awkward site.

Informal beds on lawns near the house are planted with shrubs, herbaceous plants or annuals which provide bright splashes of colour, and a pond is surrounded by a scree bed. Initially out of sight, on a lower level or screened by hedges or walls, are bog, rock and rose gardens, a small orchard, and a raised alpine bed. Plants for the garden are raised in a solar dome which shelters tender subjects such as fuchsias and oleanders, and in greenhouses, one of which contains a camellia. The 'business' area is as

well organised and kept as the rest. Wooden boxes filled with sand, grit or compost are set on castors beneath the benches, the needs of the gardener being as well considered as those of the plants.

STOURHEAD

MAP I

Stourton, near Warminster
At Stourton off B3092, 3m (5km) north-west of
Mere on A303
Owner: The National Trust
Tel: Bourton (0747) 840348
Open daily

Stourhead must rank with Stowe and Blenheim as one of the most beautiful classical landscapes, not just in Britain but in the world. It is a superb example of the eighteenth-century English ideal of the classical villa, in a setting of water, trees, grass and temples. The garden has also become an arboretum, with a fine selection of conifers and rhododendrons.

Henry Hoare ('The Magnificent'), director of Hoare's bank, inherited Stourhead in 1741. It consisted of the house his father had built on his acquisition of Stourton manor in 1717 (a Palladian cube which forms the nucleus of the modern house) and the pasture surrounding it. Prior to developing the gardens he had returned from an Italian tour, where he must have seen the landscapes of Claude and Poussin and the Italian countryside, which so inspired the landscape movement. His banking work also kept him in touch with the ambitious landscapes being realised by his clients at Stowe, Castle Howard and Studley Royal. On the death of his wife in 1743, Hoare began the improvements at Stourhead, and the paddocks in the valley below the house were transformed into a lake and landscape. Hoare's Arcadia was complete by the 1770s, and received great public attention, so much that a new inn had to be built in the village to house the tourists.

He was succeeded by his grandson, Richard Colt Hoare, who stocked the garden with the unusual trees and shrubs being introduced at

Early autumn at Stourhead.

that time but, realising the greatness of his grandfather's masterpiece, he did not alter the bones of the landscape. Colt's example was followed by his descendants with occasional lapses in the assiduous care the garden demands, until Henry Hoare gave the estate to the National Trust just before World War II. Stourhead is the Trust's most important landscape, and is beautifully maintained. Excellent guides to the garden are available, including a tree guide and several histories of the grounds.

When Hoare created his landscape, he was in a sense celebrating the settling of the Hoare family in a permanent home. He saw Stourhead as being the well-spring of his family; the gardens are in the valley where the Stour rises, which is probably why his father changed the name of the house from Stourton to Stourhead. Henry Hoare was steeped in classical literature, and saw an analogy between his founding of Stourhead and Aeneas' founding of Rome: the landscape is full of references to Virgil's *Aeneid* and the journey around it is an allegory of Aeneas' travels from Troy to Rome.

Stourhead does not need a knowledge of the classics to be appreciated, however. The diversity of its ornament, and its almost religious calm cannot fail to excite a reaction; but those who want to concentrate on the eighteenth-century landscape are recommended to go in winter when the rhododendrons do not distract and the classical lines of Hoare's landscape are revealed. As with all landscapes, the vistas of Stourhead were designed to be seen in a particular order: working anti-clockwise around the lake, starting from the house. The modern entrance is in the village and its view, which takes in nearly all of the garden, was intended to be the grand finale to the tour. So, if you use this entrance, much of the garden's drama and surprise is lost. Between Easter and October, the approach from the house is open, but in winter you must take' all paths to the right, up the hill to see the lake from above — a view of breath-taking grandeur.

Continuing around the lake anti-clockwise, you descend to the level of the water and begin to see the temples through the trees. The grotto, concealed in a yew thicket, is not to be missed because it is a temple where the Stour gushes out of the hillside below two statues. It is Hoare's well-spring, and in a sense the inner sanctum and *raison d'etre* of Stourhead. The focus of the garden, and Aeneas' destination, is the Pantheon, whose excessive grandeur seems out of place in this quiet 'sanctuary'; but the journey carries on, the path going over and under the road by a rustic bridge and a tunnel. The round Temple of the Sun gives more sublime prospects of the water from above before you descend at last to the village, which — after cosmetic surgery — was incorporated into the classical vision.

The history of Stourhead can be seen as the corruption of the original landscape through subsequent planting, or its enrichment for the same reason. Either way, the garden has outstanding appeal: as an eighteenth-century masterpiece, a fine arboretum, or simply as a beautiful work of art.

STOURTON HOUSE GARDEN

MAP I

Stourton, near Warminster
2m (3km) north-west of Mere off A303, on road to Stourhead
Owners: Colonel and Mrs. A. S. Bullivant
Tel: Bourton (0747) 840417
Open a few days a week from April to end November and by appointment for parties

The popularity of dried flowers today is well known but the majority are imported from Holland, so the opportunity to see them growing is rare. At Stourton, much of the four acres of gardens is given over to a wide range of plants which are dried and sold. The majority are confined to the vegetable garden which is in four sections, the lines of annuals and perennials being divided by fruit and vegetables. There are seventy varieties of hydrangea and many of these and the seedheads and blooms of shrubs and plants all over the garden are also dried.

This is far from being the only aspect of interest because there are enclosed and other areas containing much that is unusual. The owners have a talent for making the tour as entertaining as it is instructive by pointing out the intriguing habits or particular beauty of certain plants. Superb tree peonies and herbaceous plants decorate the four corners of an area enclosed by an attractively-swagged cupressus hedge, and carnivorous pitcher plants and lilies thrive in the central pond adorned with an urn. Unusual bulbs, (quantities of narcissi being outstanding) are found next to the rock and water garden. On the far side of the lawn is a woodland garden where magnolias, acers, and tender and unusual shrubs and trees, enjoy the shelter of mature hornbeams. A secret 'room' of acid-loving plants is hidden within mounds of rhododendrons.

STOWE

MAP F

Buckingham
2m (3km) north-west of Buckingham on A422,
turn north to Dadford
Owners: Stowe School, Allied Schools Ltd
Tel: Buckingham (0280) 813650
Open Easter weekend, August Bank Holiday
Monday, and a few days a week during the school
summer holidays

The influence of the eighteenth-century landscape at Stowe on the garden-making style of the time could be likened to that of the Acropolis on architecture. It is a classic. Its transformation from a formal seventeenth-century garden of terraces, parterres and ponds to today's Arcadian scene, took seventy-five years and involved many of the major designers of the period. Consequently, the history of Stowe's development is the story of the revolution which swept over English garden-making in the eighteenth century.

The first plans were drawn up by Charles Bridgeman for its owner, Viscount Cobham, in about 1715. Bridgeman's design was superficially similar to the popular French Baroque style in its use of geometric shapes, but its disregard for symmetry and the inclusion of surprise elements were the first tentative steps towards a new attitude to the relationship between nature and the garden. Most significant was Bridgeman's use of a ha-ha which gave the illusion of a garden without clearly defined boundaries, which extended into the countryside.

Cobham then rather perversely called on the real hero of the story — William Kent — to help Bridgeman. Kent enriched the gardens with more architectural monuments, and then swept away the tidy geometry of his predecessor's work, softening the shape of the octagon lake and banishing straight walks. Kent took the idea of the ha-ha a step further: if this allowed the garden to extend into nature, why not join the two together imperceptibly? However, as Kent reconstructed it, nature was not the English

countryside but an English imitation of the paintings of Claude and Poussin. These were idealised representations of the Italian landscape where lakes, cypress trees and rocky crags decorated with classical remains were the major elements. The development of the gardens was later overseen by the young 'Capability' Brown; due to Kent's frequent absence because of his success as a landscape designer, Brown was involved in making important decisions and doubtless added features of his own. He learnt much from working with Kent, particularly on the architectural side, but the landscape at Stowe does not reflect his fully-fledged heroic and purist style. It is Kentian and not Brownian in character.

Lord Cobham was a staunch Whig, as a look at the many monuments proves. An example is the strange Gothick Temple by James Gibbs, part medieval and part Gothic in style, built to glorify the virtues of the British people: liberty and equality. He also made a wry comment on the morals of his day in building two temples close to each other: one, the Temple of Ancient Virtue, was conscientiously looked after; the other, the Temple of Modern Virtue, was allowed to become derelict.

The mansion is on high ground overlooking the lakes, which are linked by a cascade. In the far distance, on the crest of a distant hill, is the mighty Corinthian arch which lies at the end of the grand avenue to Stowe. On the undulating ground spreading away from the house, in partially wooded areas such as the Elysian Fields and around the lakes, are various monuments and architectural features — the Temple of British Worthies and the Temple of Venus by Kent; the rotondo and lake pavilions by Vanbrugh (who preceded Kent as Lord Cobham's architect); the Boycott pavilions and Cobham monument by Gibbs, and the Palladian bridge, which is a replica of that designed by Lord Pembroke at Wilton. There are many more and you should allow plenty of time to seek them out.

STUDLEY ROYAL

Fountains, near Ripon
2m (3km) west of Ripon off B6265 to Pateley
Bridge
Owner: The National Trust
Tel: Sawley (076 586) 333
Open daily throughout the year, except Christmas
Eve and Christmas Day

As with many of our most beautiful gardens, the unique landscape at Studley Royal was designed by an amateur. John Aislabie was Chancellor of the Exchequer in 1716, the year of the South Sea Bubble (the Wall Street Crash of the eighteenth century). Forced to resign for his part in that fiasco, he retired in disgrace to Yorkshire and spent his time, until his death in 1742, building the house (since burnt down) and garden which form the nucleus of Studley Royal today. His son William continued his work, and bought the neighbouring estate of Fountains Hall, including the ruins of a Cistercian abbey. William also created a new garden at nearby Hackfall, now, sadly, in ruins.

Studley Royal was an extremely revolutionary garden in its day. It stood between the formal style in imitation of Versailles and the informal landscapes of William Kent and of the later eighteenth century. It is out of sight of the house, standing as a landscape in its own right not as an extension of the house, as most formal gardens are. It uses the lie of the land, and does not impose itself on it. Temples are sited dramatically on the steep sides of the Skell valley; the curves of the river are modified into the crescents of the moon pools; and the straight part of the valley was tidied up (but not regularised) to provide better views of the impressive remains of Fountains Abbey.

The grounds of Studley Royal can be approached either from the Fountains end or from the park surrounding the site of the old house. The ruins of the abbey itself are striking enough and through them one enters a long valley. At its end, indicated by a Gothic arcade, just discernible in the trees from this point, are the crescents

themselves. There are no parterres or fountains or statues, simply two refreshing, austere spaces where grass and water take sinuous shapes. It is not difficult to imagine how supremely beautiful they must look by moonlight. The River Skell runs through the gardens and ends up as a forlorn-looking straight canal, which pours between two pretty pavilions into a larger and more conventional lake. The whole garden seems to be squeezed between the steep sides of the valley, which is covered with trees. A few temples (assumed to be by Colen Campbell) decorate the space, and lend it a rather ceremonial or sacred feeling, but do not be deceived — the garden was built as a stage for many beautiful nocturnal *fêtes-champêtres*.

SUTTON PARK

MAP C

Sutton-on-the-Forest, near York
8m (13km) north of York on B1363
Owner: Mrs N. M. D. Sheffield (HHA)
Tel: Easingwold (0347) 810249
Open daily from Easter until October
(peak months April to July)

Facing south, the Georgian house surveys its stylish garden and the park planted with clumps of eighteenth-century and older woodland trees. The most intensely-planted areas of the garden are the terraces, linked by a long and a short flight of steps, which flow away from the house. They are gracious in design and have been planted with a well-chosen collection of flowering plants, whose colouring is soft and cleverly blended. Running east to west on the top terrace are borders, rectangles of lawn and a long path paved with old York stone, jewelled with self-seeded plants. The weathered paving stones came from the kitchens of old houses being demolished in Otley; like the numerous other garden ornaments — urns and gazebos tumbling with climbers — they add to the elegance and charm of the garden.

An ancient font from Lincolnshire decorates the centre of the second terrace. There are beds of shrub roses edged with catmint and mixed borders coloured with shades of purple, blue, yellow, grey and white. Silver weeping pears strike a graceful note, their vertical accents and the strong columnar shapes of the conifers along the bottom terrace creating an effective contrast. Known as the water garden, the restrained lower terrace supports a rectangular ornamental lily pool. One side of it is punctuated by a semi-circle of water which echoes the curve of the marble seat in a niche of the beech hedge. Topiary balls of holly are along the top of this hedge, which is the boundary between the garden and the park, and cedars nearby have cascades of Kiftsgate and 'Wedding Day' roses.

Either side of the terraces are informal lawns, island beds, ornamental trees and a laburnum walk. There is a semi-wild walk, at its best in spring when the cherry blossom and narcissi are out, and a nature trail through the park and woodland. In the garden at the front of the house are venerable cedars, a walk of 'Amanogawa' cherries and a well-preserved ice house.

SWANNINGTON MANOR

MAP G

Swannington, near Norwich
10m (16km) north-west of Norwich, off A1067 to
Attlebridge
Owners: Mr and Mrs Richard Winch (HHA)
Tel: Norwich (0603) 860700
Open Wednesdays and Bank Holiday Mondays
from end of Easter to September
(peak months June and July)
Plants for sale

The delightful garden belonging to this seventeenth-century redbrick house with Dutch gables has a three-hundred-year-old framework of topiary box and yew hedges. They are the background to the herbaceous borders planted generously with fragrant and unusual plants, imaginatively associated and well labelled. There is also a knot and herb garden, and the banks of a stream flowing through the three acres are lush with moisture-loving subjects.

The woodland, peaceful and shaded by limes, a mature copper beech and young specimen trees, is carpeted with bulbs in spring.

This garden is constantly being enriched with new and better varieties of plants and is full of good ideas for those seeking sympathetic plant associations. Note the silver weeping pear underplanted with the crisp blue-grey foliage of *Hosta sieboldiana*, which is further enhanced in early summer by white foxgloves emerging through the curtain of grey foliage.

There are many beautifully-kept greenhouses, one of which contains a collection of orchids.

SWISS GARDEN

MAP G

Old Warden
Approximately 2m (3km) west of Al, off
Biggleswade to Old Warden road, adjoining the
Shuttleworth Aircraft Museum
Owner: Leased to Bedfordshire County Council
Tel: Bedford (0234) 56181
Open several days a week from April to end
October
(peak season spring)

Bedfordshire County Council, with a grant from the Historic Buildings Council, have made a marvellous job of restoring this individual and lovely nineteen-acre woodland garden, and well deserved their 1984 Civic Trust award for it.

Originally created in the early nineteenth century by the third Lord Ongley, this unique example of a 'picturesque' garden had fallen into sad disrepair by 1975; the serpentine paths were hidden and the now delightful buildings were begging to be restored: the Swiss cottage, on a mound carpeted with spring bulbs and shaded by a cedar; the tiny garden cottage which resembles a chapel; a kiosk; humpbacked ornamental bridges; and a grotto constructed of tufa rock and fernery, a forerunner of the greenhouse. Fortunately, it still boasted a fine collection of mature trees and these, with banks of rhododendrons, handsome pieris and many other shrubs, plants and spring bulbs, give it welcome colour and form. The paths lead beside ponds, over bridges to islands and open on to well-dressed glades and vistas; they make exploration of the eight acres an exciting experience.

Note the detailed construction of the interior and exterior of the thatched Swiss cottage, the fretwork, pine-cone decoration and twisted twig work. Approached from one angle it seems to be a single-storey building, and from another reveals itself to have two. Nearby, screened by trees, is a two-seater privy; farther along the route, a thatched tree-shelter and seat encircle an old oak. The early-nineteenth-century vogue for all things Swiss was extended by Lord Ongley to the estate village of Old Warden, which has equally 'picturesque' features. He even persuaded the women living there to wear tall hats and red cloaks!

SYON PARK GARDEN

MAP J

Brentford
2m (3km) west of Kew Bridge off Twickenham Road
Owner: The Duke of Northumberland (HHA)
Tel: London (01) 560 0881
Open regularly throughout the year
(peak seasons spring and autumn)
Plants for sale

Syon offers a well-presented collection of attractive and interesting features, which cater to all ages and tastes. The castellated Tudor palace with its corner towers looks over the River Thames to Kew, a peaceful picture which belies the estate's proximity to bustling urban life. The Thames was the most convenient and busy thoroughfare for many centuries, and its banks were considered an ideal spot to build a fine mansion. The wealth and power of the owners was on display to all who passed — a mixed blessing in troubled times: several of Syon's inhabitants made the journey, not up-river to Hampton Court, but down, to the Tower. Fortunately, before suffering this fate, some of Syon's owners contributed to the beauty of the garden and estate. The Lord Protector, Edward Seymour, Duke of Somerset, who built the

handsome house, had laid out the now-extinct botanic garden which was the first in this country, and around 1550 he planted the mulberry trees which still stand in the private garden.

By the middle of the eighteenth century, the fashion was for picturesque landscape, and the Duke of Northumberland employed 'Capability' Brown to transform the formal gardens. He created the two lakes, one draining into the other, and distinctive clumps of trees, some of which are still to be seen. In the 1820s Charles Fowler built the innovative and impressive domed conservatory with curved wings, for the third Duke of Northumberland. It was an inspiration to Joseph Paxton, and was the father of the great glasshouses at Chatsworth and, subsequently, the Crystal Palace. Today it houses a fascinating collection of temperate plants and cacti, its original heating system no longer being used to protect tender orchids. A formal garden of geometric beds and topiary, around a pool and statue of Mercury, spreads away from the conservatory. The six-acre rose garden is magnificent, its colours offset by dark cedars and mature oaks. The gardens are rich in unusual and mature trees and the imaginative way shrubs and plants are grouped (such as on Flora's lawn) provides a series of memorable pictures.

Syon House.

An unusual feature at Syon is the garden for the disabled. It is a great pity that this is not a more common feature in gardens open to the public, as it is full of good ideas and an inspiration to those seeking a new hobby or believing they may have to give up a much-loved one. Regular demonstrations are given, using specially designed or adapted tools, techniques and suitable plants.

The old riding school designed by Charles Fowler now contains a comprehensive garden centre, and there is also an aquarium and a butterfly house with an exciting collection of butterflies, spiders and scorpions.

TAPELEY PARK

MAP H

Instow, near Bideford
On A39 between Barnstable and Bideford
Owner: Mrs Rosamond Christie
Tel: Instow (0271) 860528
Open regularly from end March to October

Visitors are encouraged to make themselves at home in the thirty acres of garden at Tapeley; games are set out on the lawn and deck-chairs on the verandah; a parrot chatters to those taking tea outside the Queen Anne dairy. Italianate terraces fall away from the William-and-Mary-style house. Fine stone statues stand against dark fastigiate yews, palm trees reach for the sky, a flight of steps is hidden within an unusual arbour of holm oaks, and borders beneath the retaining walls are colourful with herbaceous plants and flowering shrubs.

Period features with old-fashioned charm have obviously been tended with loving care over the years: shell and ice houses and a circular sundial garden. The walled vegetable garden is kept in the traditional manner, with cordoned apples, fig trees and an impressive vine house which runs the length of one wall. Peacocks strut across the lawns and busy chickens range near the yard, geese and rabbits being confined to runs. From the top lawn there is a superb view over the Taw and Torridge estuaries, and a woodland walk leads to the lily pond on the estate.

TATTON PARK

MAP B

Knutsford
3½m (5½km) north of Knutsford, 4m (6½km)
south of Altrincham,
3½m (5½km) from M6 at Manchester
interchange No. 19, or leave M56 at Junction 7,
travel south on A556 and look for signposts;
entrance on Ashley Road, 1½m (2½km) north-
east of junction A5034 with A50
Owner: The National Trust
Tel: Knutsford (0565) 54822/3
Open regularly throughout the year
(peak season spring)
Plants for sale

The sixty acres of garden and one thousand acres of park which surround the neo-classical Regency house boast a beautifully-kept collection of period features. The Egerton family lived here from the sixteenth century until 1958, and succeeding generations had developed the property to reflect the tastes of their times.

Towards the end of the eighteenth century, Humphry Repton drew up one of his famous 'Red Books' recommending various changes at Tatton, some of which were implemented. The meres to the south were expanded but his suggested break-up of the majestic avenue of beeches and pines was rejected. Half a century later, the pendulum had swung from the informal landscape back to formality. Fashion dictated that the surrounds of the house should be softened by intensely-planted and formal architectural features. The first Lord Egerton commissioned Joseph Paxton to lay out the Italianate terraces, with their flights of steps, urns, central fountain and parterres. Though now simplified, the parterres have once again been planted with the pastel pink and blue flowers he recommended, and they have a disciplined and rich appearance. An impressive introduction, these terraces are also a viewing point to admire the gardens and park spreading below.

A typically Victorian feature is the fernery near the house, thought to have been designed by Paxton, and one of the best examples of its kind. Tree ferns from New Zealand diffuse the light and though Lord Egerton's frogs and snakes no longer inhabit the humid jungle their presence can easily be imagined. Wyatt, who built Tatton, was responsible for the orangery nearby which still houses orange and lemon trees and exotics.

Farther to the west are borders, their different and subtle colour themes prevented from clashing by buttresses of yew. A topiary yew hedge at the far end hides a sunken rose garden of pompom and polyantha roses, and the summerhouse overlooking these pretty beds provides a peaceful resting place. The contrastingly shady, but similarly intimate, tower garden is planted with specimen trees and shade-tolerant plants; the tower is no longer inhabited by a salaried hermit, but the atmosphere is still rustic and romantic. Mature and interesting trees play a strong role throughout; a glade of *Metasequoia glyptostroboides* is particularly noteworthy, as are the conifers in the pinetum.

In 1910 the third Lord Egerton created one of Tatton's most popular features. He imported Japanese workmen to build the Japanese garden with its Shinto temple set on an island and an ornamental bridge. Here, as elsewhere, water enhances the sympathetic and traditional planting of maples and azaleas. A small beech maze and an African hut are concealed in the woodland — the hut was built by the third Lord Egerton during World War I when he was prevented from hunting big game in Africa. During the 1940s the collection of rhododendrons and azaleas was widened, and over six hundred species and hybrids offer a superb display in spring. Lord Egerton welcomed the young and underprivileged of Manchester to share the delights of Tatton, and the warmth of that welcome can still be felt today.

THORPE PERROW ARBORETUM

MAP B

Park House, Bedale
2m (3km) south of Bedale, turn east off B6268 to Thorpe Perrow
Owner: Sir John Ropner (HHA)
Tel: Bedale (0677) 22480
Open daily from March to mid-November
(peak seasons spring and autumn)

Peaceful and unspoilt, the arboretum is the only one of its kind in this part of the country. It offers to the keen enthusiast, or to those simply seeking a walk with a difference, an opportunity to enjoy a collection as interesting as it is beautiful. It was begun in 1927 by Sir Leonard Ropner, when his father gave him sixty-five acres of farmland set in the park. Until his death fifty years later, Sir Leonard enriched this land with rare and unusual specimens, many of which he collected himself all over the world. Not all of them enjoyed the rigours of the northern climate, and some quick-to-mature subjects are now past their best, but replacement planting and the hundreds of majestic trees now in their prime make it an exciting place to explore.

There are avenues of red oaks and cherries and winding rides, cut through the woodland, open on to glades and create views to the lake and the more formal garden in front of the house. Thorpe Perrow is far from being simply a living museum of trees and shrubs; the thoughtful planting makes delightfully varied pictures. Autumn and variegated foliage, blossom, and the intriguing shapes and textures of evergreen and deciduous trees flatter one another or form massive dramatic effects. Some areas are devoted to sorbus, pears and whitebeams, others to autumn colour or crab-apple and cherry blossom. There are rare willow, Hungarian and Algerian oaks, spruces and hazels and a host of other seldom-seen trees are divided by rides and paths.

Part of the impressive collection of azaleas and rhododendrons at Tatton Park.

TINTINHULL
HOUSE GARDEN

MAP 1

Tintinhull, near Yeovil
5m (8km) north-west of Yeovil, 12m (19½km)
south of A303 on east outskirts of Tintinhull
Owner: The National Trust
Tel: Martock (0935) 822509
Open several days a week from Easter to end
September

Though covering barely an acre, this important garden is one of the National Trust's most valued possessions. A series of formal gardens surrounded and divided by walls and hedges, it has an inward-looking nature, its elegance and secure atmosphere unaffected by views to distant features and the surrounding countryside. It is a plantsman's garden but one where carefully-chosen and often unusual plants create a well-balanced overall picture. The 'bones' are formal, but the planting is generous and relaxed.

The oldest part of the Ham Hill stone house dates from 1700; its elegant Queen Anne front overlooks the formal eagle court and gardens. They are thought to be have been laid out by Dr S. J. M. Price, who was a tenant of Tintinhull at the beginning of this century. In 1933 Captain and Mrs F. E. Reiss bought the property and began to develop the rest of the gardens, Phyllis Reiss giving the compartments their famous compositions of plants. Great care has been taken to preserve the character of her garden; tended by Penelope Hobhouse, it has not been allowed to atrophy and, evolving, it has retained its personality — a quality easily killed by slavish preservation.

A path edged with balls of box runs down the centre of eagle court from a terrace decorated with handsome stone pots, its low walls draped with clematis. This path runs to the far west end of the garden, creating a delightful vista through a series of compartment gardens. The azalea garden has perimeter borders filled with fragrant, yellow blooms offset by the variegated foliage of Japanese honeysuckles and glowing *Philadelphus coronarius* 'Aureus'. Hellebores, perennial geraniums and cyclamen are planted in the shade of an old holm oak and beyond is a small 'room' hedged with yews. These are an effective dark background to the pale spreading foliage of a *Cornus controversa* 'Variegata', luminous white flowers of honesty and the washed lilac of hostas.

At the far end of the walk is the fountain garden, where yew hedges are once again an ideal foil to the white-flowering and silver plants in beds around a pool. Standard silver-leafed salix provide a vertical accent — an attactive change from the more common silver weeping pear. The kitchen garden to the north is cut by intersecting paths edged with catmint, and beds of a rose much used by Gertrude Jekyll, 'Nathalie Nypels', provide colour between the ribbons of purple and espaliered fruit trees.

Vistas to, from and through the various 'rooms' add to the garden's charm; the one over the rectangular pool to the pillared loggia, bright with pots of tender and other plants, is particularly lovely. The mixed borders either side of this pool garden are one of Tintinhull's finest features. Set against yew hedges, their colouring is soft pinks, blues and greys on one side and warm shades on the other. From this sunbaked compartment you enter the cool shade of cedar court, dominated by a Lebanon cedar standing on one side of the lawn. This is surrounded by borders, one beneath a purpled leafed prunus being a striking mix of plum- and gold-foliaged flowers and shrubs such as berberis and dogwoods.

THE TRADESCANT GARDEN

MAP J

St Mary-at-Lambeth, Lambeth Palace Road, London SE1
Next door to Lambeth Palace in Lambeth Palace Road
Owner: The Tradescant Trust
Tel: London (01) 261 1891
Open regularly throughout the year and by appointment

Garden historians will find the churchyard and the interior of St Mary-at-Lambeth of great interest. The churchyard contains a facsimile of a seventeenth-century knot garden filled with plants which England's first true planthunters, the two John Tradescants, father and son, would have found familiar, and the latter has a permanent exhibition about the Tradescants and other garden history material. Their own sixty-acre garden, in what was then rural Lambeth, was half a mile from the church and there John Tradescant the Elder propagated the many plants gathered on his travels and housed his famous and eccentric collection of 'rareties'. Acquired in dubious circumstances by Elias Ashmole after the deaths of father and son, the remains of this extraordinary collection can be seen in the Ashmolean Museum in Oxford; Ashmole's tomb is in the churchyard at Lambeth.

The knot is composed of box, santolina and ilex hedges, and almost completely fills the small churchyard bounded by the crenellated wall of Lambeth Palace. The beds between the low hedges are filled with plants introduced by or well known to the Tradescants: violas, crown imperials, pinks, alliums, salvias, dianthus, aquilegias, daphnes and a surprising number of other shrubs, bulbs, perennials and herbs. Roses such as *R. gallica versicolor* and *officinalis*, *R. de Meaux* and *R. burgundica* have been planted around an arbour and seats set in the perimeter borders. In a corner is the Tradescants' tomb, decorated with a weird fantasy of animals, plants, shells, obelisks, pyramids and an epitaph describing their life and work. A further tomb, of Captain

Bligh of the *Bounty*, is an apt feature in a garden devoted to botanical history. If the *Bounty* had not been held up for five months in Tahiti so that its cargo of breadfruit grown from seed could reach maturity before making the voyage to the West Indies, the mutiny might have been avoided and the reputation of one of England's great sea-captains left unstained.

TREBAH

MAP H

Mawnan Smith, near Falmouth
3m (5km) south-west of Penryn turn south off
B3291 to Mawnan Smith
Owners: Major and Mrs J. A. Hibbert
Tel: Falmouth (0326) 250448
Open every day from late March to September
and by appointment
(peak months April, May and June)
Plants for sale

Several different factors make this a particularly exciting garden to visit: its dramatic and beautiful position in a deep ravine which drops two hundred feet to the Helford River; the fact that it was developed by Charles Fox, a member of the renowned Quaker garden-making family, whose shipping interests helped them to collect outstanding new plants which thrived in the Cornish climate; and the enthusiasm and work of the present owner, which have saved the mid-nineteenth-century garden from extinction.

Trebah covers twenty-six acres, flowing away from the eighteenth-century house poised above the ravine. A stream punctuated with pools runs through its centre, its banks rising ever more steeply and providing superb 'stages' for the display of a formidable collection of trees and shrubs. Tree ferns, echiums and meconopsis are here in plenty as are bog and water plants — astilbes, irises and ligularia; a two-acre swathe of hydrangeas colours the stream's lower reaches. Unusual rhododendrons and magnolias have grown to vast proportions and they, with Chusan palms and other sub-tropical exotics, can be admired from a network of paths running along the steep sides and floor of the valley down to a

private cove. Much clearing and replanting has been carried out, and near the terrace below the house is a recently-built waterfall, constructed of vast boulders, which splashes into a pool of Koi carp.

TREGREHAN

MAP H

Par
On A390 opposite the Britannia Inn
Owners: The Carlyon family
Tel: Par (072 681) 2438
Open by appointment for parties only
(peak months mid-March to May)

Tregrehan has been the home of the Carlyon family since the reign of Elizabeth I. Its thirty-acre garden houses an outstanding collection of camellias and a pinetum of rare and outsize conifers. Though it is predominantly informal in design and of especial interest to the camellia enthusiast and the dendrologist, the bones of an earlier garden can be seen — the Italian terrace garden south of the house, the quarter-mile yew walk and the walled kitchen garden. There are over nine thousand camellia bushes including a one-hundred-and-fifty-year-old *C. japonica*; award-winning hybrids raised by the late Miss Gillian Carlyon and former members of the family and new varieties from America, New Zealand and Australia. All were collected or raised over the years and now make an almost indigestible feast beneath the canopy of trees.

The conifers in the pinetum, over twenty of them the largest specimens of their kind in the country, were planted towards the end of the nineteenth century, when many new introductions were being made. There is a Japanese fir, *Abies firma*, a *Picea omorika* and *jezoensis*, *Pinus parviflora* and *patula*, *Chamaecyparis obtusa* 'Lycopodioides' and 'Tetragona Aurea', *Podocarpus totara*, *salignus* and *macrophyllus* and a *Tsuga dumosa*.

In spring, there is a blaze of colour from magnolias, vast tree rhododendrons, a huge sprawling *Kalmia latifolia*, other woodland and acid-loving flowering plants, spring bulbs and the humble bluebell. Glasshouses in the old walled kitchen garden are filled with tender subjects — waxy-flowered lapagerias, new Carlyon and other hybrids and vireya rhododendrons from New Zealand.

TRELISSICK GARDEN

MAP H

Feock, near Truro
4m (6½km) south of Truro, on both sides of
B3289 above King Harry Ferry
Owner: The National Trust
Tel: Truro (0872) 862090
Open regularly from March to end October
(peak seasons spring to late summer)
Plants for sale

Cornwall is famous for its woodland gardens which, blessed by the Gulf Stream and a mild climate, are adorned with exotic and tender flowering shrubs and trees. Many also enjoy fine views over an estuary or the sea. Trelissick overlooks the Fal, views of the sparkling water in the creek being framed by trees or thrown open across parkland running down to the water's edge. The pleasing proportions of the white porticoed house are echoed by the spacious and flowing design of the gardens. There is nothing mean here: the gently-twisting gravel paths are wide, the overhanging trees handsome and mature, and the planting, particularly of hydrangeas and rhododendrons, is bold and generous.

Trelissick has had many owners since 1750 when the original house was built by an eccentric and convivial captain in the Cornwall militia. It has been owned by a tin-mining magnate whose investments earned him the name of 'Guinea-a-minute-Daniell'; by a neighbouring landowner, the Earl of Falmouth; the Gilbert family who planted the many fine pines, cedars and holm oaks; Lord Cunliffe who was a Governor of the Bank of England; and finally, in 1937, Mr and Mrs Ronald Copeland, who ran the family business making Spode china, W. T. Copeland and Sons.

The majority of the magnificent flowering shrubs were planted by the Copelands and they transformed the somewhat colourless but well-treed scene into a lively and sensitive series of pictures. A list of the rich collection of species and hybrid rhododendrons would take a great deal of space — from *Rhododendron thomsonii* and *R. cinnabarium* with their bell-shaped and tubular flowers to 'Trelissick Port Wine' and 'Trelissick Salmon' — but the scent, varied foliage, colour and habits of this classic woodland plant contribute greatly to the overall beauty. These, and many rare varieties of hydrangea, are not planted *en bloc* but imaginatively mixed with other shrubs and plants; they form luminous pools of colour beneath dark canopies of trees and exuberantly fill informal borders. There is an exotic dell, planted with the varied textures of tree ferns, hardy Japanese banana, colourful shrubs and moisture-loving plants.

On the far side of the bridge spanning the road, an old orchard has been cleared and more hydrangeas break up the space between specimen trees. Near the house are borders with unusual and tender climbers and shrubs and in summer one running beneath the old kitchen garden wall is a purple haze of sweet-smelling heliotrope. Immaculately tended, Trelissick can absorb a great number of visitors without appearing crowded; the peace of its woodland walks and resting places is unassailably tranquil.

TREMEER

MAP H

St Tudy
8m (13km) north of Bodmin, west of B3266
Owners: The Haslam-Hopwood family
Tel: Bodmin (0208) 850313
Open daily March to September
(peak months April to June)

The first blood transfusion was carried out by King Charles I's doctor in the basement of this fourteenth-century granite house. When Major-General E. G. W. Harrison bought the property in 1939, he might not have made a major breakthrough, but he did save the then derelict garden from ruin. Its development did not begin until after World War II when the general, though an amateur, raised many of his own hybrid camellias and rhododendrons and built up a rewarding and wide collection of plants over the years.

The seven acres of the more formal garden are near the terrace at the front of the house. A wide expanse of level lawn divides it from the natural, water and woodland gardens beyond. An unusually large *Euonymus fortunei* 'Variegata' softens the austerity of the house, and beneath the terrace Japanese azaleas form a long bank of colour. The edges of the lawn are planted with specimen trees and interesting shrubs, such as a *Parrotia persica* of handsome, tree-like proportions. Beyond, paths weave through groves of rhododendrons, camellias and other flowering shrubs and ornamental trees, their colouring reflected on the surface of a lake. Many of the general's own hybrids can be seen here and in the gardens behind the house. Although he left Tremeer in 1978, much new planting has prevented the garden becoming frozen in time.

TRENGWAINTON

MAP H

near Penzance
2m (3km) north-west of Penzance, ½m (1km) west
of Heamoor on Penzance-Morvah road B3312,
½m (1km) off St Just road A3071
Owner: The National Trust
Tel: Penzance (0736) 63021
Open several days a week from March to end
October
(peak season spring)

No plantsman or garden-lover could go to Cornwall and not visit Trengwainton, a garden filled with exotic, tender, woodland and moisture-loving plants. Four hundred feet above sea level on lime-free soil overlooking Mount's Bay, it is sheltered by a belt of beech trees which, due to old age and storm damage, are gradually being replaced. This is an important point; due to recent exceptionally hard winters, the garden's more tender subjects, which have thrived for several decades, will be under threat without shelter.

It was not until after 1925, when Lieutenant-Colonel E. H. W. Bolitho inherited the property from his uncle, that the gardens were really developed, the propagating talents of its head gardener, the generosity of Cornish neighbours and seed collected by Kingdon Ward in Burma and Assam all contributing to the evolution of Trengwainton's collection of rare plants. Even a small list of its contents would prove dry reading; suffice it to say that the eyes of the most jaded of plantsmen will light up on seeing the magnificent rhododendrons, Asiatic magnolias and tender-flowering shrubs and unusual trees. Those which need extra protection are grown within the walled gardens on one side of the drive up to the house — the creamy blooms of *Magnolia cylindrica* flowering on naked stems; brilliant pink flowers of *M. sprengeri diva* and other seldom-seen subjects such as *Chilean Lomatia ferruginea* with its velvety stems and fern-like foliage; the white-flowering tree from China, *Rehderodendron macrocarpum*, eucryphia and styrax and climbers like the striking lobster's claw feasting the eye.

Around glades and in woodland or either side of the long drive are specimen trees and flowering shrubs like pieris, azaleas and rhododendrons. A stream tumbles over rocks on one side of the walk, its banks lush with native and exotic palm-leafed ferns such as *Dicksonia antartica*, bamboos, spectacular swathes of crimson, magenta and golden-yellow candelabra primulas and other moisture-loving plants. Lawns spread from the house, with large groups of shrubs and trees opening to reveal a fine view over open countryside and the sea beyond. Mixed borders lap the edges of the lawn, on which stands a hundred-year-old *Myrtus luma* with its distinctive cinnamon-coloured, powdery bark. The garden gradually melts into the woodland, carpeted with bluebells and spring bulbs. South of the house is a magnolia garden where, in April, the mountain of flowers produced by a *Magnolia sargentiana robusta* almost eclipses a number of unusual rhododendrons. These abound and give the enthusiast a superb opportunity to admire the myriad combinations of flower and foliage size, texture and shape; the colouring of the velvety undersides of many leaves are as fascinating as the blooms themselves.

New Zealand tree ferns in the gardens of Tresco Abbey.

TRERICE

MAP H

St Newlyn East, near Newquay
3m (5km) south-east of Newquay via A392 and
A3058 (turn right at Kestle Mill)
Owner: The National Trust
Tel: Newquay (0637) 875404
Open daily from Easter to end October
(peak season summer)

Belonging to an Elizabethan manor house built of Crowan stone, this small summer garden has a charming appearance and friendly atmosphere, with no period pretensions. On different levels there are enclosed courts, lawns and a bowling green, but no original or reconstructed Elizabethan garden features. There is an orchard of Cornish fruit trees, and an interesting collection of perennials, climbers and shrubs. The front court is attractively decorated with purple- and gold-flowering plants and a hayloft contains a collection of old lawn mowers, some over one hundred years old.

TRESCO ABBEY GARDEN

MAP H

Tresco, Scilly Isles
South-west corner of island, take ferry from St
Mary's or helicopter from Penzance. (Booking
office Tel: Penzance (0736) 63871)
Owner: Mr R. A. Dorrien Smith (HHA)
Tel: (0720) 22849
Open regularly throughout the year
(peak months March to June)
Plants for sale

Nowhere else in the British Isles does such an exotic and exciting collection of plants grow in the open. Many people must have shaken their heads sceptically when the philanthropist, Augustus Smith, embarked on its creation in 1834. The two-and-a-half-mile-long island was racked by salt-laden winds and was the resting-place of countless wrecked ships. Apart from a

collection of tiny allotments, the land had never been cultivated and boasted only the odd gorse bush. But he must have done his homework before taking on the lease of the Scilly Isles and deciding that, as their Lord Protector, he would make his home on Tresco. The island's position in the eye of the warm Gulf Stream must have been a deciding factor, and the ruins of the Benedictine abbey of St Nicholas was a strong indication of a good source of water. The climate was exceptionally mild, all that was lacking was shelter, and he provided this by planting belts of Monterey pine and cypress which had proved their 'seaworthiness' on the coast of California.

He built his home of locally-quarried granite and set about constructing the terraces on a south-facing slope incorporating the ruins of the abbey. The fifteen acres are divided by two long walks; the lighthouse way with its superb views and long flights of steps, and the long walk which cuts across the whole. Within these divisions are many others, a veritable box of surprises. The style is quite unlike an English country garden; a sailor suffering shock after being wrecked might well think he had been washed up on the far side of the world. The plants grow to dazzling proportions, tumble down rock faces, form massive eruptions of colour and luxuriance and fill the air with scents which evoke pictures of faraway places.

Five generations of the family have enriched the garden with tender plants collected from all over the world. Species from the southern hemisphere and the Mediterranean play the strongest role, different areas being devoted to those from South Africa, Australia and Mexico. Seed is constantly exchanged with botanic gardens all over the world, and the hardiness tested of a constant flow of new plants. Augustus Smith propagated or planted about fifty percent of the garden's present content.

After World War I and up to his death in 1955, Major Arthur Dorrein-Smith built up the collection of New Zealand plants, his son, Commander Thomas M. Dorrien-Smith turning his attention to tender specimens from South Africa. The unprecedented sub-zero temperatures of January 1987 caused considerable damage, but only those familiar with the gardens will notice the changes. Fortunately, the rate of growth is rapid and seed of rare and unusual specimens no longer so hard to come by. The all-important shelter belts have been reinforced over the last ten years and the widespread re-planting of many tender subjects will ensure the garden's future.

Palms shoot skywards, stately echiums resemble burning rockets, agapanthus makes sheets of azure blue and agaves, aloes, proteas, cacti, bromeliads and countless plants normally grown under glass flourish within the secure embrace of the massive holm-oak hedge which helps to protect the garden. Many flowers, like mesembryanthemum, seed themselves freely, and have crept beyond the bounds and begun to wander the island.

The lively colour of sunbacked, aromatic walks and intimate 'rooms' is contrasted with the cool lushness of a grove of tree ferns, and features like the old Gothic arch, once part of the original abbey, add touches of romance. High on the top terrace, a head of Neptune gazes down light-house walk and out to sea. Before Augustus Smith came to Tresco, the inhabitants of the island lived off the loot from wrecks, and a Valhalla of old ships' figureheads is on display. From its early days Tresco has welcomed visitors, though their numbers, like the range and size of its contents, have swelled considerably. The garden now warrants visiting at different times of the year to be fully appreciated.

TREWITHEN

MAP H

Grampound Road, near Truro
On A390 east of Probus
Owners: Mr and Mrs A. M. J. Galsworthy (HHA)
Tel: St Austell (0726) 882585/882764
Open daily except on Sundays from March to end
September
(peak seasons March to June and August to
September)
Plants for sale

When George Johnstone inherited Trewithen in 1904, the garden and eighteenth-century park were well endowed with mature trees, particularly holm oaks and beeches, but little else. He embarked on a clearance programme, created glades and planted a shelter belt of laurels to protect what is now a superb collection of plants. Introduced from Asia, America and Australasia by planthunters such as E. H. Wilson, George Forrest and Francis Kingdon Ward, these flourished and grew to a great size in the soft Cornish climate. Johnstone especially loved magnolias, and they are one of the most seductive features of the gardens. An awesomely large specimen of *M. campbellii mollicomata*, a mountain of washed pink, waterlily-shaped blooms, is a spectacular sight next to the south lawn, which flows away from the handsome stone house. Boldly-planted banks of flowering trees and shrubs flank the lawn; the bell-shaped white flowers followed by the brilliant red fruits of a *Rehderodendron macrocarpum* are noteworthy.

Paths strike off through woodland decorated with specimen shrubs and trees, magnolias and camellias playing a strong role. Many of the latter were raised by Johnstone himself — e.g. 'Trewithen Pink', 'Trewithen Salmon' and one named after his daughter 'Elizabeth Johnstone'. Williamsii camellias are generously represented; they are a cross between *C. japonica* and *C. saluenensis*, raised by Johnstone's friend and neighbour at Caerhays, J. C. Williams. One of the most popular members of this family is 'Donation', which is not only a visual delight but interesting for being propagated from the original plant raised by Colonel Stephenson Clarke at Borde Hill in Sussex. This died before others could be propagated and the 'Donation' at Trewithen became the parent plant. The pale-yellow-flowered, large-leafed *rhododendron macabeanum*, is an eyecatching sight in a glade near the house, as are the tree ferns in the cockpit.

Specimen trees such as eucryphias, stewartias, myrtles and acers abound, with shrubs from Chile, China and Australasia, embothriums, pieris and evergreen lomatia. George Johnstone died in 1960 but his garden is still owned by the family and has continued to evolve. New and interesting subjects are planted and old ones replaced; there is an arboretum in the park and a water garden at the western end of the gardens.

One area of formality is now an introduction and a finale to this plantsman's garden: the walled enclosure which was once the old drying ground. Beds of roses stand on the lawn and borders of perennials line walls dressed with tender climbers. A pergola heavy with wisteria runs along the terrace to one end, and nearby, if the winter has not been too harsh, the deep-blue flowering *Ceanothus aboreus* 'Trewithen Blue' makes itself felt in spring.

An early flowering rhododendron at Trewithen.

TURN END

Townside, Haddenham, near Aylesbury
3m (5km) north-east of Thame, from Thame
Road turn at Rising Sun into Townside. Backbone
of group of three houses 300yds (280m) on left
Owners: Margaret and Peter Aldington
Tel: Haddenham (0844) 291383
Open several days a year for charity and by
appointment
(peak months May to July)
Plants for sale

Begun in 1965, the one-acre walled garden belongs to a house which is part of an award-winning complex built by the owners. It illustrates well their ingenuity with unusual building materials and their skill with plants. Full use has been made of the space available, mature trees have been taken advantage of, and various compartments made which give an illusion of a garden much larger than one acre. Salvaged materials, such as railway sleepers, have been used to make paths and steps and to edge flower beds, an olive jar and a cast-iron dough mixing bowl, planted with cordyline, are focal points.

Once an orchard, the site now contains a series of small hidden gardens which fan out from a long glade shaded by apple, walnut and chestnut trees and planted with roses and shade-tolerant plants. These small 'rooms' are diverse in character: the box court has box-edged beds planted with 'daisy'-type plants; a pool and pergola garden with raised beds of acid-loving plants; raised alpine beds; a sheltered, sunbaked area planted with silver-leafed and sun-loving plants, which has a Mediterranean feel; and a peaceful courtyard shaded by a robinia and lush with moisture-loving plants around a pond. All are filled with carefully-chosen and associated foliage and flowers. A garden of surprises: discovering its small rooms is like dismantling a Russian doll, no one room impinges upon another or confuses its individuality.

TYNANT

Moelfre, near Oswestry
From B4580 in Llansilin, 8m (13km) west of
Oswestry, follow signs to Moelfre
Owners: Mr and Mrs D. J. Williams
Tel: Llansilin (069 170) 381
Open throughout the year by appointment for
charity
(peak months early May, July and October)

Well off the beaten track, in an idyllic valley threaded by a stream running from Moelfre lake, this five-acre garden is split into individual areas widely different in character. The low stone house, once a smithy and mill, overlooks the stream; the ground either side of this has been laid out with scree beds covered with a layer of a pea-like local gravel. A low bed of succulents, treated in this way, is an unusual and effective addition and the spreading branches of a 'Tai Haku' cherry hang over beds planted with small herbaceous plants and shrubs.

Beyond the house lies the dingle garden, where the banks of another stream are lush with moisture-loving plants. There is a good collection of specimen trees, many planted in this area, which is bounded by a steep bank planted with shrubs. The natural beauty of a woodland walk beside the main stream has been enriched by azaleas, loderi and large-leafed rhododendrons, planted to catch your eye as you round bends in the walk. The path veers away from the stream and leads to an informal area planted with spring bulbs and interesting trees and shrubs. There is something for everyone in this well-stocked and well-tended garden set on neutral soil, from tiny alpines and moisture-loving primulas to unusual maples and eucalyptus.

UNIVERSITY OF BRISTOL BOTANIC GARDEN

MAP E

Bracken Hill House, North Road, Leigh Woods, Bristol
Far side of Suspension Bridge from Clifton, take first right; garden ½m (1km) on left
Owner: University of Bristol
Tel: Bristol (0272) 733682
Open on weekdays throughout the year; at weekends for parties by appointment
(peak season late spring)

Put together for educational and research purposes, the Botanic Garden at Bracken Hill displays over four thousand plants belonging to two hundred plant families. Though there are only a few order beds — the traditional rectangular beds where plants of one family would be displayed — trees, shrubs and plants of all kinds have been planted in specific groups. These are set around the large, walled garden once the property of the Wills family, who built the gabled house in 1886. Another interesting feature is the rock and water garden, constructed by the well-known firm of Pulham and Son of Chelsea. This period piece is formed of sizeable chunks of an artificial rock called Pulhamite, the invention of the garden designer, James Pulham. It provides ideal conditions for moisture-loving primulas, gunnera, irises and hostas. The striking, pink and green foliage of an Actinidia kolomikta, a tender loquat, and the huge, glossy leaves of a *Magnolia delavayi* soften the walls of the house.

Predominantly informal in design, areas are devoted to widely-differing collections of plants: tender shrubs, conifers, insectivorous plants, endangered species, wild flowers and ferns. Another rock garden a short distance from the house displays subjects from Australasia and rare limestone plants from the Bristol area. Borders contain herbaceous plants grown to produce seed; beds in the formal garden are filled with rare and variegated wild flowers; an area of woodland has been planted with native trees and shrubs and one of the order beds displays economic plants.

Four greenhouses of varying sizes and temperatures protect a rich collection of crop-producing, water- and shade-loving plants. Succulents, orchids, bromeliads and other exotic and temperate subjects make these houses rewarding to explore. Do not expect to see beds of brightly-coloured annuals at Bracken Hill or be surprised at what might appear to be the unkempt condition of certain areas. These, like the lawn purposely left unweeded, are ecological and other research areas under observation or development.

UNIVERSITY OF DURHAM BOTANIC GARDEN

MAP A

Hollinside Lane, Durham
1m (2km) south-west from the centre of Durham, between Grey and Collingwood Colleges in Hollinside Lane
Owner: University of Durham
Tel: Durham (091) 3742671
Open daily throughout the year
(peak seasons spring and summer)

The general public are welcome to explore this garden but should bear in mind that its primary purpose is research and education. That is not to say that its sixteen acres have not been attractively laid out — quite the contrary — but it is the keen plantsman and botanist who will find its contents particularly absorbing. Trial plots are devoted to experiments being carried out by students, such as testing for the hardiness and suitability of certain plants or crops which might boost the economy of a Third World country or be of medicinal use. The main part displays collections from different parts of the world. Among these is a small replica of a Scandinavian forest, trees and shrubs from China and Japan, a sample of temperate Himalayan vegetation, and beds of bog and alpine plants. Greenhouses shelter tropical and desert plants. The garden is young, having been laid out in 1970, but the trees and shrubs are now well on their way to making an effective display. The garden staff are enthusiastic and helpful and few visitors leave without having seen or learnt something new.

UNIVERSITY OF EXETER

Exeter
On the north west-side of Exeter within the area bounded by Pennsylvania Road and New North Road
Owner: University of Exeter
Tel: Exeter (0392) 263263
Open daily throughout the year, parties by appointment
(peak months April to June)

Covering four hundred acres, the University of Exeter estate is recognised as one of the most beautiful and interesting of any British university, complementing and providing a superb setting for the modern campus buildings. The University received its charter in 1955 but, as the University College of the South West, it came to the house and grounds of Streatham Hall (now Reed Hall) in 1922. These grounds, which included the Victorian arboretum planted by Veitch and Sons of Exeter, now form the nucleus of the estate. Here are fine specimens of unusual trees, many of which must have been the first of their kind grown in this country. The terraced gardens around the hall have retained their Victorian character — conifers, bold groups of rhododendrons, the site of an old conservatory now transformed into a garden of floral bedding, and sunken garden of scented plants all combining to form a contrast to the spaciousness of the twentieth-century landscape.

One of the finest post-World War II examples of soft landscaping, the main part of the estate is set on hills overlooking the city. The mild climate and soil conditions enable a wide range of plants, from cacti to ferns and alpines to palm trees to flourish here. Micro-climates created by hills, streams and buildings have been used, growing the widest possible range of plants,

shrubs and trees. The original arboretum has been expanded throughout the campus, but with concentrated plantings on the hillsides and in the valley to create a woodland garden. There are comprehensive collections of acacia and eucalyptus, and the National Collection of azara. These, with deciduous trees and shrubs, camellias and conifers such as the *Pinus gregii* from South America, enhance the landscape. The estate is constantly being developed: several thousand rhododendrons and azaleas have been planted on the slopes above the ponds in the Higher Hoopern Valley. Plants of special interest are a double-flowered *Myrtus communis* 'Flore Pleno'; the Lucombe oak, a cross between the cork and Turkey oak, discovered as a seedling growing in an Exeter nursery by a Mr Lucombe in 1763; the yellow-flowered climbing rose 'Maréchal Niel' growing against the wall of Reed Mews. It has a girth of over two feet and might well have been the first of its kind in Britain.

A colour booklet describing a tour of the grounds is available at the supermarket at the University, or from the Director of Domestic Services at Devonshire House on the campus. With its aid, a number of hidden areas with fine collections of plants can be found. Bird-lovers may be interested to know that, apart from the water-fowl which make their homes around the ponds, some fifty-three different types of birds from buzzards to wrens have been seen in the grounds.

UNIVERSITY OF LEICESTER BOTANIC GARDEN

Beaumont Hall, Stoughton Drive
South, Oadby, Leicester
On south-east outskirts of Leicester, opposite Oadby racecourse
Owner: Council of the University of Leicester
Tel: Leicester (0533) 717725
Open weekdays throughout the year
(peak months May to October)
Plants for sale

The sixteen-acre Botanic Garden spreads over what was formerly four private gardens. These belonged to large, turn-of-the-century houses which were converted to student residences in 1947. Although devoted to the scientific study of plants and their uses, the gardens, which flow one into the other, have retained their private character. Original and newly introduced features have been skilfully blended and the formal and natural areas enriched with a wide-ranging collection of plants.

The garden is a long rectangle running from north to south; its informal southern end contains many handsome and unusual conifers and other specimen trees, all well labelled. Wild flowers grow in a meadow, witch-hazels on what was once a lawn tennis court, and moisture-loving plants on the edges of a pond on the lawn of Knoll House. The terrace of Hastings House is decorated with wisteria and 'Nevada' roses, and that of Southmead Hall with a herb garden. At the centre of the gardens is the National Collection of skimmias, a limestone scree and rock garden, and a display of roses showing their development through the ages. At the northern end is the water garden, with its long ornamental pool of waterlilies flanked by rose-entwined pillars. This was one of the original features of the gardens of Beaumont House, once considered among the finest private gardens in the county. A pergola draped with vines and clematis divides the pool and the brick-paved sunken parterre patterned with box-edged beds.

Other points of interest are the maples on the sandstone rock garden, the yew-hedged conservation area of raised beds filled with bedding violas and violettas, and the nine glasshouses. These house collections of succulents, alpines or ferns, or are devoted to research or propagation. Note the way certain borders have been planted with a well-associated mix of shrubs, small and large specimen trees and ground-coverers: the bronze foliage of an *Acer palmatum* 'Heptalobum Elegans Purpureum' underplanted with golden and variegated spireas, and the spreading skirts of a *Cotoneaster dammeri* on the sandstone garden being an effective composition of textures and colour.

A blue and yellow herbaceous border.

UNIVERSITY OF LIVERPOOL BOTANIC GARDENS (NESS)

MAP B

Ness, Neston, South Wirral
10m (16km) north-west of Chester, 5m (8km) from western end of M56 on Neston road between Ness and Burton, 2m (3km) from A540 Chester to Hoylake Road
Owner: University of Liverpool
Tel: Liverpool (051) 336 2135
Open regularly throughout the year
(peak months, May to August)
Plants for sale

When the cotton broker Arthur K. Bulley (1861–1942) began to develop the sixty-acre garden on the Wirral Peninsula in 1898, his aim was to grow an exceptional range of hardy plants from all over the world. This brought about a dramatic leap forward in the planthunting world and gave the gardens of this country a new dimension. His initial efforts to raise plants from seed collected on journeys was a failure — his wife described the results as an 'international collection of dandelions' — so Bulley sought professional advice. He became the first major twentieth-century patron of plant-collectors, financed the first expeditions by George Forrest and F. Kingdon Ward and contributed to many others. Ness was the first garden to grow the new introductions. Philanthropist as well as keen naturalist, Bulley welcomed visitors from the gardens' early days and by 1909 his nursery and seed firm, Bees Ltd, was offering the new introductions to its customers. His daughter, Miss A. L. Bulley, gave the gardens to the University in 1948, with the stipulation that they should remain open to visitors.

The undulating site on the southern tip of the peninsula overlooks the River Dee to the Clywd Hills and is protected from the harsh winds blowing off the Irish sea by shelter belts of poplars, Scots pines and holm oaks planted by Bulley. The soil is part sandstone, part boulder clay, with areas of sand and silt, and the rainfall is surprisingly low. The gardens suffered neglect during World War II but have been restored since, replanted and developed, and an area shaded by pines has been transformed into a woodland garden. The atmosphere and design is still that of a much-loved private garden; the changing levels and belts of trees form vistas to, or serve to frame, the various areas.

There is a long view down a serpentine border of unusual rhododendrons such as the *R. roxieanum*, from China which was grown from seed sent by George Forrest; lilies and hydrangeas extend the interest. A collection of china, noisette, bourbon, hybrid perpetual, floribunda, tea and other roses has been planted to show the development of the modern rose. A wide grass walk divides a long border glowing with deciduous azaleas underplanted with bulbs and an herbaceous border tightly planted with a collection of perennials which provide colour from early June to late autumn. Specimen trees and shrubs like the dazzling original *Pieris formosa* 'Forrestii', and the finest collection of sorbus in existence, have been planted in the arboretum, in informal groups or borders.

A spectacular feature is the heather garden planted with *Calluna vulgaris*, Connemara, Cornish and other heaths; it seeps down a south-facing slope like rainbow-coloured lava from a volcano. Beside one of the ponds in the valley are endangered and other native plants — alliums from the Avon Gorge, veronica from Llandudno and an erica from Galway. A meadow is carpeted with bulbs and tender shrubs and climbers can be seen on the terraces of the house. In a valley below these lies a rock garden, constructed of lime, sandstone and tufa rock, which is almost hidden beneath soft mounds and cushions of dwarf and alpine plants, specimen bulbs and conifers. There is much else to seek out in this fascinating year-round garden — the Ledsham herb garden, for instance, with its laburnum arch and fragrant plants especially planted for the blind — the unifying factor being that interesting plants abound throughout.

UNIVERSITY OF YORK GARDENS

MAP C

Heslington, York
In Heslington on the south-east outskirts of York;
University signposted off A64 avoiding city centre
Owner: University of York
Open daily
(peak months May to July and September to October)

The twentieth century will not go down as a time when large private properties were landscaped, but it has seen a dramatic improvement and change of attitude to public spaces. The general public's heightened awareness of their surroundings and the vulnerability of areas of great natural beauty means that the designer's job no longer stops at the walls of a factory, housing estate, dam or school but includes the immediate environment. The quads and gardens of ancient colleges at Oxford and Cambridge have been cultivated for centuries, but the building of a new university at York, shortly after World War II, offered an exciting opportunity to lay out a twentieth-century landscape. This would link the faculty, residential and other buildings and create a sympathetic environment for those who lived and worked there. H. F. Clark of Edinburgh University architectural school decided to use water in the landscape to emphasise the contrast between a ridge and a valley, parts of which were marshy and posed a drainage problem. The detail and development were done by a committee and the architects Robert Matthew, Johnson-Marshall and Partners. The architects were responsible for planting the groups of ornamental and large forest trees linking the various buildings, which relate the landscape to the surrounding countryside and form shelter belts.

What meets the eye today is a successful marriage between a man-made 'natural' landscape and a series of intimate gardens on a smaller scale. Groups of trees frame or form vistas to buildings and the vast sheet of water, and break up the wide expanses of undulating turf. Like a cathedral set beside a Venetian lagoon, its steps descending into the water, the hexagonal central hall juts out into the lake, with a water spout as focal point beyond. In the shelter of the buildings are small gardens, covered walkways which resemble cloisters, and bridges and stepping-stones spanning and surrounding waterlily tanks and pools and fountains. At one end of this landscape-cum-water garden is Heslington Hall, an Elizabethan mansion with an eighteenth-century topiary garden and gazebo. There is no harsh division between them: the large abstract shapes of the yew topiary form an ideal backcloth to the modern sculpture, canal, large lily pool and walks shaded by trees.

UPTON HOUSE

MAP F

near Banbury
1m (2km) south of Edge Hill, 7m (11km) north-west of Banbury, on west side of Stratford-upon-Avon road A422
Owner: The National Trust
Tel: Edge Hill (029 587) 266
Open several days a week from Easter to end September
(peak months June and September)
Plants for sale

The gardens lie behind the seventeenth-century Hornton stone house, all the more enjoyable for being initially hidden and containing a number of period features and surprises. When you round the corner of the house, your first sight is of a wide lawn and dramatic cedar trees, a stage seemingly suspended above the park and the double avenue of chestnuts and oaks on the brow of a hill. Balustraded terraces are between the lawn and the house, which was remodelled in the 1920s when the second Viscount Bearsted bought it. The terraces are planted with catmint, ceanothus and the Scots rose 'Williams' Double Yellow'; there are beds of variegated fuchsias edged with santolina at one end.

Instead of succumbing to the temptation to walk to the end of the lawn and peer over the brink, take the path to the west of the terraces. Curtained by old yews, it zig-zags down to a combe. The stew ponds made in the late seventeenth century by Sir Rushout Cullen (who laid out the 'bones' of the present garden) still stand in the sheltered valley. The ponds were fed by a spring spurting from Monk's Well. The top pond is now a bog garden, lush with moisture-loving plants such as bamboos and primulas, and ornamental trees and groups of shrubs on the surrounding lawn add interest. The middle pond is now a goldfish pool, and the farthest has been drained and planted with cherries, a pretty but restrained contrast to what lies around the corner.

Below the top lawn and high retaining wall, a series of terraced gardens are framed by hedges, their walls draped with climbers and linked by flights of steps. A long lake divides this highly-cultivated south-facing slope from the park which rises beyond. Like the garden in the combe, this comes as a delightful surprise, no hint having been given that the L-shaped valley had been developed in any way. The various compartments contain rose and paved gardens, the original ornamental vegetable garden, and superb mixed and herbaceous borders. Double flower borders flank a grass path running down one side of the slope, and another lies along the terrace below the retaining wall. Blue and yellow flowers, the Bearsteds' racing colours, feature strongly, and there are geum, phlox and asters (the National Collection of *A. ericoides*, *amellus* and *cordifolius* cultivars is here). Another lake, graced by a small classical temple thought to have been built in the late eighteenth century, stands a mile from the house. This can be reached from the public footpath off the main Banbury road.

VICAR'S MEAD

MAP H

Hayes Lane, East Budleigh
2m (3km) north of Budleigh Salterton. From A376, Newton Poppleford to Budleigh Salterton road, turn off west for East Budleigh. Hayes Lane opposite the 'Sir Walter Raleigh'
Owners: Mr and Mrs H. F. J. Read
Tel: Budleigh Salterton (039 54) 2641
Open several days a year for charity between April and September by appointment
Plants for sale

A surprisingly young and vigorous garden spreads and rises away from the fifteenth-century cob and thatched house, its full potential having been realised only recently. It is not difficult to understand why, for it is set on a slope whose steepness would discourage most garden-makers. The only level stretch of ground is the lawn in front of the house; the remainder is on a precipitous north-facing sandstone escarpment.

Unusual tender plants, a good number having come from Chile, grow in a border beneath a thatched cob wall on one side of the lawn; its contents will immediately alert enthusiasts that this garden is created by expert plantsmen. Rare and unusual plants abound at Vicar's Mead, the commonplace being an oddity.

The National Collections of *Dianella*, *Libertia*, *Liriope* and *Ophiopogon* and over eighty different varieties of hosta can be seen in the three and a half acres, as well as an extraordinarily wide collection of specimen trees. These decorate the wooded escarpment and areas of open ground on various plateaus, their size and beauty an encouragement to those chary of planting trees

they feel they will never see mature — all are under ten years old. Many have been grown from seed and have made good progress, despite the low rainfall of the area. The cultivation of the slope necessitated making zig-zag paths, bridges and steps up to the plateaus and over ravines, and bulbs, ferns and wild flowers have been encouraged to naturalise throughout. Wherever possible, roses and clematis have been planted to clamber into trees, and on a small area of level ground behind the house is a sheltered scree garden and a fernery set into the rock face.

VINE HOUSE

MAP E

Henbury, Bristol
4m (6½km) north-west of Bristol centre, off the A4018; near the 'Salutation Inn' in Henbury
Owners: Professor and Mrs T. F. Hewer
Tel: Bristol (0272) 503573
Open a few days a year for charity and by appointment throughout the year

Having been developed by the present owners since 1947, the two-acre garden boasts a fine, and now mature, collection of specimen trees. The majority stand at the far end of the garden, in an informal glade set against a backdrop of woodland. One can assess and appreciate the growing habit and merits of specimens in their prime — an *Aesculus parviflora*, *Picea omorika pendula*, and many different cornus, magnolia and prunus. Beside the informal lawn between the house and glade are beds of unusual shrubs, trees and herbaceous perennials; tree peonies are much in evidence and hellebores make lush growth in a shady area. A path leads through to the 'wild' garden or glade, which has several layers of interest. Beneath the specimen trees grow flowering and other shrubs such as witch-hazels, and the ground is carpeted with spring bulbs, cyclamen and primroses. Plantsmen will take their time inspecting each and every part of the borders and glade; all will appreciate the peaceful atmosphere and 'natural' character of a garden so close to the city centre.

The formal Victorian garden at Waddesdon.

WADDESDON MANOR

MAP F

Waddesdon, near Aylesbury
6m (9½km) north-west of Aylesbury on A41
Owner: The National Trust
Tel: Aylesbury (0296) 651211/651282
Open regularly from late March to October

It was in 1874 that Baron Ferdinand de Rothschild, a collector of fine art and furniture, bought the Waddesdon estate and commissioned the French architect Hipolyte-Alexandre-Gabriel-Walter Destailleur, to build the awe-inspiringly ornate mansion on top of Lodge Hill. Designed in the flamboyant French Renaissance style, the 'chateau' and its priceless contents had to be offset by equally impressive surroundings. Once again Baron Ferdinand turned to France and employed the garden designer Elie Lainé to lay out the bones of the park, the detailed design of the formal gardens being planned by Baron Ferdinand and his gardeners. Transforming the cone-shaped hill into a platform where the grand mansion and formal gardens could stand involved massive earth-moving. To ease and speed up the work of levelling the site and transporting the stone for building, a fourteen-mile stretch of single-track railway was built for a cable engine, and a team of sixteen Percheron mares were imported from Normandy. Special carts were made to carry up thirty-foot semi-mature trees, which were then lowered into place by chains. This was almost unheard of at the time and instantly gave the property the required, well-established look.

Supremely Victorian in concept, the park and gardens were planted with cedars, Wellingtonias, spruces, pines and native trees, whose quantity and size are an impressive features of Waddesdon today. Though now modified, the formal gardens on the terraces are still wonderfully opulent and typical of the Victorian preparedness to display wealth. The parterres were planted twice a year, the urns four or five times, with tender flowers raised in scores of heated greenhouses. Lady Warwick wrote in her memoirs that a thunderstorm ruined the geraniums while she was staying at Waddesdon, but by the following morning the damaged plants had all been removed and 'the gardens had been completely transformed.'

The commanding position of the house and terraces, and the flowing lines and spacious feel of the informal gardens have an unembarrassed grandeur; there is nothing mean or petty about any aspect. Shrubs are planted in bold groups and the proportions of rare and unusual conifers and deciduous trees are perfect. Fountains — the eighteenth-century Italian Triton and Nereids and Pluto and Prosperine on the terraces — ornamental ponds and statuary play an important role. Walks lead to features like the pretty wrought-iron pergola draped with roses, the daffodil valley and the splendid aviary. This is delicately ornate and was built to resemble one in the garden of the baron's childhood home in Frankfurt. It is a charming period feature, with its pavilions and grotto, and still houses free-flying macaws; it also has its own hornbeam-hedged garden planted with 'Iceberg' roses. These period gardens may not be 'easy to relate to', but you can revel in their Victorian grandeur.

WAKEHURST PLACE

MAP J

Ardingly, near Haywards Heath
1m (2km) north of Ardingly on the B2028
Owners: The Royal Botanic Gardens, Kew/The National Trust
Tel: Ardingly (0444) 892701
Open throughout the year
(peak seasons spring, summer and autumn)

The country home of the Royal Botanic Gardens, Kew, Wakehurst's five hundred acres contain an outstanding range of rare and interesting temperate plants and trees. Possibly the greatest garden of the rich Sussex Weald, the vast horseshoe-shaped curve of land offers wonderfully varied terrain for the display of plants of all kinds. There are intimate enclosed areas, spacious level lawns, dramatic ravines and rocky outcrops, woodlands, ponds, streams and a lake; the acid, water-retentive soil, climate

One of the fountains on the terrace at Waddesdon.

thing is well labelled and almost inhumanly well tended. The simplicity of expansive lawns and sheets of water provide a contrast to the excitement to be found in the ravine, water and valley gardens and the Himalayan glade threaded by a stream and ponds. Here the species rhododendrons grow much as they would high in the Himalayas, their impressive proportions and exotic blooms ideally offset by the dramatic surroundings. Various hybrids add to the mounds of colour.

The water gardens are thickly planted with rare indigenous and other exotic species, their proportions, textures and colours being imaginatively blended. There are polygonums from Nepal, Asiatic candelabra primulas, native bull-rushes, reed grasses and sedges, striking maples, unusual willows, magnolias and stuartias. The woodlands are carpeted with bulbs and bluebells in spring and fired with colour in autumn by unusual deciduous and native trees. The majestic conifers in the twelve-acre pinetum, varying in shape from the drooping Brewer's weeping spruce to the stiff skirts of cedars, can be appreciated at any time of the year.

The heath garden, one of the earliest features made by Gerald Loder, offers much more than its name might suggest. Set around, and growing out of, the tightly-clipped mounds of heaths are Australasian and South American plants he collected — tender myrtles like a pink-flowering leptospermum, flowering shrubs from Chile, the delicate white-flowering hoheria from New Zealand, fothergillas which produce brilliant autumn colour, maples, conifers and dwarf rhododendrons. Beside the house are the more intimate, enclosed gardens, the recently re-planted walled garden, dedicated to Sir Henry Price, fragrant with herbs and herbaceous and other flowering plants, and the Pleasaunce with its clipped yew hedges, formal flower beds, ornamental pool and fountain.

Wakehurst Place should be visited time and again at different times of the year; it is better digested in modest mouthfuls, with the excellent guide book to hand rather than in great gulps.

and clean atmosphere provide complementary conditions to those of Kew.

Despite the age of the sixteenth-century house, the garden is a twentieth-century creation. In 1903 the estate was bought by Gerald Loder, later Lord Wakehurst, who immediately embarked on developing its potential. He was President of the Royal Horticultural Society and a keen collector of temperate trees and shrubs, rhododendrons being particular favourites. These and many indigenous plants from New Zealand and Chile thrived in the conditions at Wakehurst. By the time of his death in 1936, the garden was considered one of the finest in the country. The property was then bought by Sir Henry Price, who continued to beautify the gardens with newly-introduced and other plants. He left it to the National Trust in 1963, who leased it to the Royal Botanic Gardens in 1965.

A plantsman's paradise, they offer an unrivalled opportunity to admire wild species collected from all over the world. The way these have been planted and grouped enhances the natural beauty of the terrain and recreates the atmosphere of the plants' natural habitats. The generosity of the planting is another major feature, subjects like ground-coverers and smaller plants having been massed rather than dotted; the overall effect is lush and flourishing. Every-

WALLINGTON HALL

MAP A

Cambo, Morpeth
12m (19km) west of Morpeth on B6343, 6m
(9½km) west of Belsay A696, take B6342 to
Cambo
Owner: The National Trust
Tel: Scots Gap (067 074) 283
Open daily throughout the year
(peak months June to August)

The gardens at Wallington seem perverse: instead of the highly cultivated areas being placed around the house, they lie hidden behind walls in the north-eastern corner of the estate. In the eighteenth century it was not unusual for kitchen gardens to be set some distance from the house; a century later they were transformed into ornamental flower gardens.

Built by Sir Walter Calverley Blackett in 1760, this walled garden replaced an earlier one unwisely placed in a frost pocket, where the garden pond now stands. Plans in the house show how Sir Calverley intended his garden to look, and much of the work carried out is still visible today. It has been suggested that 'Capability' Brown advised on the garden. He was certainly born (and trained as a gardener) at nearby Kirkhale, but there is no real evidence of his having worked here. Informal walks in the then-fashionable landscape manner strike out from the house to east and west wood. They wind through mature beech woodland, open up with vistas to a stone screen and triumphal arch known as the arches and lead to the portico house and various waterlily and other ponds edged with irises and kingcups.

Sir George Trevelyan inherited Wallington in 1879 and he and his wife, Lady Mary, created the charming walled garden which has been so beautifully restored and planted by the National Trust. The sympathetic colouring, presence of water and layout of this hidden garden are delightful surprises. The terrace is exuberant with roses, the walls draped with climbers; borders are filled with flowering plants and shrubs whose colouring has been carefully blended. The rocky banks of an underground stream which surfaces in the garden are almost completely smothered with alpines and dwarf plants.

There are ornamental ponds, eighteenth-century lead figures thought to have been brought to Wallington from the Blackett's home in Newcastle, a hedged enclosure planted with ornamental trees, and an impressive conservatory. Built by Sir George, this is scented by heliotrope, and shelters splendidly large fuchsias and tender and exotic climbers like bougainvillea. At its rear is the owl house, built in 1765, which was originally the gardener's bothy.

WATERHOUSE PLANTATION

MAP J

Bushey Park, Hampton
To the West of the Chestnut Avenue in Bushey
Park, off A308
Owner: Department of the Environment
Tel: London (01) 977 1328
Open daily throughout the year
(peak season April to June)

Water plays an important role here: without it, it is doubtful if the gardens would have come into being. Needed to feed the splendid waterworks at Hampton Court, in 1683 it was channelled from a tributary of the Colne and along the man-made Longford River through the park. In 1949 the Superintendent of the Palace gardens, J. W. Fisher, began developing a woodland garden, and used the river to form streams and a lake. These emphasise the soothing atmosphere and beauty of the now mature garden. In late spring the mature rhododendrons, camellias and azaleas capture the attention in glades and beside the walks, where there are also specimen trees and flowering shrubs. The waterside is decorated with moisture-loving plants like primulas, irises and rogersias, and shafts of sunlight filter through the canopy of mature trees to highlight colourful subjects.

WATERPERRY GARDENS

MAP F

Waterperry, near Wheatley
2½m (4km) from A40 (M), turn off at Wheatley,
and follow Tourist Board signs from Wheatley
Owner: Waterperry Horticultural Centre
Tel: Ickford (084 47) 226
Open continuously throughout the year
Plants for sale

Once the home of the well-known Horticultural School run by Miss Beatrix Havergal, the gardens of Waterperry display a wide range of plants. The school ceased to exist in 1970 but the gardens have retained their educational purpose, being used for day-release and amateur courses. They also include a nursery and a plant centre, so visitors seeking plants can assess the habits and size of mature species in the ornamental gardens, and take note of the conditions in which they thrive.

The walled gardens behind the house shelter the nursery, glasshouses, conservatory containing a mature orange tree, beds of herbs, shrubs and trained fruit trees, as well as propagating units. Beyond lies the flower garden, around lawns shaded by mature cedars and an ancient copper beech. A long herbaceous border is beneath the redbrick kitchen garden wall, draped with climbers; a path at the lower end leads to the rock garden planted with unusual dwarf conifers. Spring bulbs and wild flowers line the informal walks beside the River Thame, and island and other beds of herbaceous plants provide bright splashes of colour and a chance to compare the merits of different varieties. There are beds of shrubs and heathers and an orchard of fruit trees, bushes and canes, including the Royal Sovereign strawberry which won many medals at Chelsea for Waterperry.

During World War II the school's energies were concentrated on food production, though Miss Havergal saw to it that her students were trained in all aspects of horticulture. The knowledge of alpine plants of one of her students, Miss Valerie Finnis, gave birth to the alpine nursery, which now includes the National Collection of *kabschia* saxifrages.

WAYSTRODE MANOR

MAP J

Cowden, near Edenbridge
4½m (7km) south of Edenbridge on B2026 turn
off at Cowden Pound
Owners: Mr and Mrs Peter Wright
Open several days a year for charity and by
appointment for parties
(peak months late April and early June)
Plants for sale

An avenue of chestnuts introduces this well-balanced and beautifully maintained garden. It covers eight acres, two of which are woodland, and belongs to a fourteenth-century house nestling into its sheltered surroundings. Owned and developed by enthusiastic plantsmen, it is full of interesting plants and attractive features — an arbour, a laburnum arch and a wisteria walk. Full advantage has been taken of the string of hammer ponds, and the autumn foliage of the North American oaks has been enhanced by a good collection of more recently planted specimen trees. There are subtle but definite divisions between one area and another; vistas have been formed by groups of trees and yew hedges, and various borders have been planted with colour themes.

There is a small formal garden of grey- and silver-leafed plants, and old-fashioned roses abound: they climb into trees, intertwine with clematis and mingle with herbaceous and other plants in borders. The large number of specimen trees have plenty of space on the lawns to display their individual characteristics and beauty; parts of the lawns are carpeted with bulbs, primroses and cowslips in spring. New and interesting plants are constantly added, though rhododendrons take time to establish themselves on the heavy clay. A water garden is planned.

WESTBURY COURT GARDEN

MAP F

Westbury-on-Severn
9m (14km) south-west of Gloucester on A48
Owner: The National Trust
Tel: Westbury-on-Severn (045 276) 461
Open several days a week from Easter to end October

The formal water gardens at Westbury were built by a country gentleman, Maynard Colchester, between 1696 and 1705, in the Dutch style then fashionable. They are unusual for having survived intact the onslaught of the eighteenth-century landscape movement, and were neglected in the nineteenth and early twentieth centuries. When the National Trust acquired them in 1967, little could be seen of their original design; the Palladian house built to complement them had long been demolished. By 1971, restoration of the gardens was complete (the site of the house has been used for an old people's home.)

The garden is still young, and the yew hedges intended to divide the space into digestible small compartments are still too small to do so. The Tall Pavilion no longer has the house to match its large scale, and it sticks up out of the garden somewhat forlornly. The garden is walled in, which should create a feeling of cosy enclosure; the *clair-voies*, which were intended to provide a view of picturesque (flat) countryside, now look on to a less than idyllic main road. Time, will remedy these defects, as the yew and other foliage grow to a more appropriate scale.

There are notes of real grandeur in the design, however: the long view up one of the two canals to the tall pavilion, framed by alternating yew pyramids and holly balls; the statue of Neptune in the other, T-shaped canal; the grotesquely large urns and pineapples framing the *clair-voies*; and the ordered view of the garden from the immaculately restored tall pavilion.

The garden repays detailed inspection. To the right of the 'T'-shaped canal is a Dutch-style parterre more rectilinear and simpler in design than the French. Surrounding it a grove of quince trees is planted in a quincunx pattern. A small walled room, overlooked by a baroque gazebo, is planted with nearly a hundred species of plants known in England before 1700, and a fine collection of roses. No wall is uncovered: the west wall houses espaliered apples, pears, and plums; and the north an exuberant border.

With a little imagination the baroque aspects of Westbury can be reconstructed and enjoyed. They should be because they are one of the few baroque pieces to have survived. However, do not expect to be intimidated by some Versaillesque vision — Westbury is on an English scale, and is full of the delights of many small-scale gardens.

WEST DEAN GARDENS

MAP I

West Dean, Chichester
5m (8km) south of Midhurst on A286, turn south at West Dean
Owner: The Edward James Foundation (HHA)
Tel: Singleton (024 363) 303
Open daily from April to end September
Plants for sale

Once the home of the late Edward James, the early eighteenth-century house designed by James Wyatt is now a college of arts and crafts. The South Downs are the backcloth to this flint-faced house, which is surrounded by thirty-five acres of gardens, where handsome and venerable trees play a major part. Specimen trees — the *Ginkgo biloba*, paulownia or foxglove tree, contorted hazels and willows, weeping beech and box — and vast conifers, tulip trees, cork and red oaks and horse chestnuts lend stature and dignity to the gardens, and almost constitute an arboretum. Vast cedars form pools of shade on the lawns spreading away from the back of the house; pale feathery maples hang over the sunken garden and its raised beds of roses, and on either side of a long pergola are magnificent specimens of cut-leaf beeches.

An important feature of the gardens, the pergola was designed by Harold Peto, who had a particular talent for such Italianate features. It leads up to a pavilion, whose stone pillars and wooden supports are draped with honeysuckle, clematis and roses, and the edges of the path are embroidered with pinks and other low-growing subjects. A walk across the lawn, behind massive yew hedges, leads past herbaceous borders into the wild garden. This becomes increasingly natural in character. Unusual trees, conifers and yews shade the walks which frequently cross the streams that eventually run into a fast-flowing river. An intriguing feature is one of two large tree-stumps which Edward James had encased in glass fibre and resin by the sculptor Ralph Burton.

The garden at the front of the house blends into the parkland beneath the downs, and a number of mature trees decorate the lawns. The old walled kitchen garden, a short distance from the house, is being transformed into an ornamental flower garden of mixed borders and dwarf box hedges. Espaliered fruit trees grow against the walls and a collection of old-fashioned shrub roses, which thrive on the alkaline soil, has also been planted. A good selection of these is on sale in the nursery section of the walled garden.

WEST GREEN HOUSE

MAP I

Hartley Wintney
1m (2km) west of Hartley Wintney, 10m (16km)
north-east of Basingstoke, 1m (2km) north of A30
Owner: The National Trust
Tel: Bookham (0372) 53401
Open a few days a week from Easter to September
(peak seasons spring and summer)

The garden which surrounds the modest and charming eighteenth-century house is one of pure delight. It marries the best and most-loved qualities of an intimate and profuse cottage garden with the style and elegance of an early-eighteenth-century garden. The choice of plants and the way they have been used derive from the former, the framework, architectural features

and detail from the latter.

The design is a series of walled or hedged enclosures. The most formal of these are the parterre with its box balls and spirals, a vista to a stone column designed by Quinlan Terry, the terraced, rectangular lawn with its yew, hornbeam and Portugal laurel hedges, and the yew *allée* with the orangery at one end and rustic monkey house at the other. Beyond these is the walled garden, half of it devoted to a romantic bower of flowers. Borders are divided into sections by paths and box-edged beds and lawns, and spill over with spring bulbs, then soft and lovely peonies, shrub roses, phlox and clematis. Rambling roses romp into old fruit trees and over two delicate white pavilions against the walls. A *potager*, or ornamental vegetable garden, fills the other half of this delightful garden, 'room'. Either side of a central path lined with lavender and fragrant standard *Viburnum carlesii* stand black-framed hexagonal fruit cages of strawberries, currant bushes and peach trees. Radiating away from them are blocks of vegetables and shapely subjects like rhubarb. Old-fashioned terracotta forcing pots, lead handlights and a stone roller stand at the ready nearby.

The garden which has been developed by the National Trust's tenant, Lord McAlpine, has been given many features with an eighteenth-century flavour, an unusual addition being the Nymphaeum. Designed by Quinlan Terry, its fountain, basin and lead statues set in niches have a classical appearance, the whole resembling a romantic feature in an eighteenth-century landscape garden. Reached through the 'moon gate' in the wall of the flower garden, it lies at the far end of the wilderness garden planted with roses and shrubs, bulbs and martagon lilies. This is a mixture of the wild and the formal, and is decorated with statues and formal ponds.

Beyond the walled garden is the lake, especially made for wildfowl. It is not open to the public, but can be admired from a distance — its island reached by a Chinese-style bridge, the grotto and the Doric gazebo on the far bank. Like the recently-planted avenues of sweet chestnuts and limes, the lake links the garden to the parkland beyond.

The walled garden through the moon gate at West Green House.

WEST LODGE PARK

MAP J

Cockfosters Road, Hadley Wood
On A111 1m (2km) from M25 (exit 24) signposted
Cockfosters
Owner: Beales Ltd
Tel: London (01) 440 8311
Open a few days a year for charity and by
appointment
(peak seasons spring and summer)

Once a favourite hunting ground of Elizabeth, I,
the thirty-six acres of parkland at West Lodge
now belong to a country-house hotel. When
the present owner came here in 1945, the park
was in a sorry state but boasted some fine old
trees — an eighteenth-century arbutus, venerable oaks, towering swamp cypresses and many
conifers planted during the Victorian era. These
add stature to the young Beale Arboretum concentrated in ten acres of the park. Over three
hundred species have been planted here since
1965, from the relatively tender *Paulownia
tomentosa* whose flowers can be caught by late
frosts, to rare conifers and deciduous trees from
all over the world — Caucasian wingnuts, un-

usual robinias, gleditsias, and the National Collection of *Carpinus betulus* cultivars. Flowering trees such as magnolias and cornus and those with fine autumn colour — styrax and maples — have been planted, and sorbus, birch, larch and acacias are all well represented. This arboretum will grow in interest as the trees establish themselves on the heavy London clay; it should provide a source of inspiration for those who have not yet considered planting unusual species in their own gardens.

WESTONBIRT ARBORETUM

MAP F

Tetbury
On A433 3½m (5½km) south-west of Tetbury
Owner: The Forestry Commission
Tel: Westonbirt (066 688) 220
Open daily throughout the year from 10 a.m. to
sunset (or 8 p.m.)
(peak month October)
Plants for sale

Exploration of this exceptional five-hundred-acre arboretum is a humbling experience. The age and impressive size of so many specimens and the way they have been grouped prompt a new appreciation of the beauty and diversity of trees. It warrants frequent visits, preferably at different times of the year.

It was begun in 1829 by Robert Stayner Holford of Westonbirt House, at a particularly exciting time in the plant world. Planthunters like David Douglas were risking their lives in North American Indian country and elsewhere to collect seed for those hungry to grow new specimens in this country. Some of the massive conifers, like the Douglas fir, sequoia and pines, date from this time; successive generations of the Holford family added to the collection as new discoveries were made. They perpetuated Robert Holford's aim to create an arboretum scientifically arranged but aesthetically pleasing.

By 1940 the collection was considered the most comprehensive in Europe; but by 1956, when the Forestry Commission took it over, it

had suffered neglect, some of its fine specimens had been ransacked, and it was in danger of being lost altogether. Thanks to their skill and energy, its majestic avenues were saved and its glades and groves restored. It now displays thirteen thousand catalogued trees and shrubs, and seventeen miles of path weave through the superb collections, planted in specific groups or mixed with those which flower or colour.

The groves of Japanese maples, some of them over a hundred years old, are a magnificent sight in autumn; the brilliant, glowing colour of their feathery skirts or finely textured mounds light up openings in the dark woodland. Sheltered by belts of holm oaks, yews and laurels, the arboretum boasts many champion trees, those which are the tallest or largest of their kind in the country. The soil is sufficiently lime free for ericaceaous plants to be in evidence; magnolias, azaleas, camellias and large mounds of rhododendrons provide splashes of colour beneath the canopy of trees.

Obviously many of the original introductions are now coming to the end of their lives and replacement planting is a constant task, and new collections, such as that of ornamental cherries in the Hillier Glade, are being developed. To ensure that future generations will have the opportunity to study and enjoy this comprehensive collection in the years to come, land on the far side of the valley, known as silk wood, has been planted with a range of trees and shrubs of particular interest to the expert. This oak woodland, with its hazel coppice, is covered with wild flowers in spring. There is an excellent Visitors' Centre near the entrance to the arboretum, offering a wide range of easily-digestible historical and dendrological information.

WESTON PARK

MAP F

Weston-under-Lizard, near Shifnal
6m (9½km) east of Telford off A5
Owner: The Earl of Bradford (HHA)
Tel: Weston-under-Lizard (095 276) 207
Open a variable number of days depending on the
month
(peak months May and June)

For those interested in fine landscapes and architecture, Weston Park is of particular interest. The landscape was laid out by 'Capability' Brown in 1762 for Sir Henry Bridgeman. Typical of so much of his work and reflecting his visionary powers, it is a noble composition of a wide serpentine lake, belts of woodland and vistas through cleverly-placed clumps and single trees. At one time the huge sweeps of lawn would have run to the very walls of the house, but a nineteenth-century Italianate garden of terraces and formal bedding, urns and topiary now overlooks the landscape. A balustraded arc of the terraces contains a magnificent oriental plane tree planted, it is thought, when the house was built in 1671. These trees were first cultivated in this country in the sixteenth century and are known to live to a great age. Its branches spread over nearly a quarter of an acre and form a vast mound of fresh green foliage.

Temple wood, with its mature native trees and rhododendrons, is a backcloth to a focal point in the landscape, — the Temple of Diana. It was designed by James Paine, and its interior is decorated with panels depicting the goddess hunting. The Roman bridge and small domed temple overlooking temple pool are also by Paine, whose successful collaboration with Brown made pictures which are a sympathetic blend of architectural and living features.

WEST WYCOMBE PARK

MAP F

West Wycombe
At west end of West Wycombe, south of Oxford Road
Owner: The National Trust
Tel: High Wycombe (0494) 24411
Open on different days of the week depending on the season

There is a lightheartedness and frivolity about Sir Francis Dashwood's elegant landscape garden, which is lacking in the more thought-provoking and bold eighteenth-century landscapes of William Kent or 'Capability' Brown. Though inspired, like Kent, by all he had seen on his various Grand Tours — the classical ruins and Italian *campagna* — it reflects Dashwood's colourful character and his obvious enjoyment of life, and does not try to make political or moral statements. It is not difficult to imagine the *fêtes champêtres* and other entertainments held here in those times, the mock battles on the lake and masques (which the present Sir Francis Dashwood has revived in recent years).

The first Sir Francis, later Lord le Despencer, was a colourful and contradictory character. As a young man he was an inveterate traveller, notorious for being a founder of the Hell Fire Club and a member of the Prince of Wales's set, but he became a respected politician, a founder member of the Dilettanti Society and a Fellow of the Royal Society and Society of Antiquaries. The landscape is largely his work and is an important example of the semi-formal style of the early landscape movement.

West Wycombe Park lies in a valley of the Chiltern Hills, overlooked on one side by the Palladian house set on high ground and on the other by the church and hexagonal mausoleum crowning West Wycombe Hill. A focal point beyond the landscape, the labyrinthine caves below this hill were once the secret meeting place of the Hell Fire Club. A stream was dammed to form the great lake which stands centre stage; meandering and formal walks and vistas across undulating lawns lead to the various neo-classical architectural features, placed to 'delight the eye'. The most eyecatching of these is the music temple with its Doric colonnade, set against a backdrop of trees, which stands on an island in the lake. It was designed by Nicholas Revett and is the focal point of the landscape viewed from the house. Seen from below the cascade flowing out of the lake, it seems to be a temple floating on water. The reclining nymphs, on piers either side of the cascade, perversely turn their backs on this romantic picture, preferring the sight of the tumbling water. Daphne's temple, also overlooking the lake, and Venus's temple, on a mound in the woodland near the broad walk, are thought to have been designed by John Donowell.

On the high ground south and east of the house is the impressive temple of Apollo — a vast arch of flint and stone bearing the motto of the Hell Fire Club; the round temple by Revett, and the noble east portico of the house. This is a copy of the Villa Rotonda by Palladio, and an ideal spot to admire the landscape. At the far end of the ha-ha which divides the park from the landscape, the temple of the winds rises above shrubs and trees; it was one of the first buildings in this country designed to resemble an antique Grecian temple. Note the outsize doorway which predates the building by about fifty years and adorned the south front of the house before it was remodelled.

The landscape was little altered after Sir Francis's death. On Humphry Repton's advice, the woodland was thinned at the end of the eighteenth century, but restoration work by the National Trust and the replacement planting of trees have ensured that this splendid landscape garden looks much as it did in its heyday.

WHATTON

MAP F

Loughborough
4½m (7km) north of Loughborough on A6,
turn west
Owner: Lord Crawshaw (HHA)
Tel: Loughborough (0509) 842268
Open from Easter to end September on Sundays
and Bank Holiday Mondays and by appointment
for parties
Plants for sale

Predominantly Edwardian in character, the fifteen acres of gardens are a slight distance from the late-nineteenth-century house. There are herbaceous borders, ornamental rose gardens, a large lake, a wild garden and a four-acre arboretum, planted by the owner, which blends with the mature blue cedar and other handsome trees. An unusual feature is the Chinese garden, set in a clearing of the woodland. Created by the first Lord Crawshaw at the end of the nineteenth century, unlike other oriental gardens made then, it is not decorated with a tea-house and pools overhung with maples but with a collection of bronze ornaments. Buddhist memorial lamps, figures and animals shaded by parasols,

and a large central urn entwined with a dragon were acquired by Lord Crawshaw in China and are an intriguing and unexpected addition to the country-house garden.

THE WILLOWS

MAP F

5 Rockley Avenue, Radcliffe-on-Trent
6m (9½km) east of Nottingham, north of A52.
From High Street post office turn into Shelford
Road, over railway bridge, 300yds (280m)
opposite bus shelter turn left into Cliff Way, then
second right
Owners: Mr and Mrs R. A. Grout
Tel: Radcliffe-on-Trent (060 73) 3621
Open several days a year and by appointment for
charity
(peak months April to June)
Plants for sale

Only the most attractive and interesting varieties of plants have been given space in this small plantsman's garden. It is behind a modest semi-detached house and measures only sixty-two by twelve yards, but gives the impression of being several times that size, thanks to its imaginative design and clever use of colour. Various focal points have been created, and island beds and curved borders, divided by grass paths have colour themes. Dark purples and crimsons near the house fade to soft pink, and golds and blues melt into pale lemon and apricot shades, creating a feeling of length. An area devoted to shade-tolerant plants, a small peat bed, a rockery, stone troughs, a pond and a herb garden, have all been incorporated without giving the garden a bitty or fragmented character.

Having been used to tending a much larger plot, the owners must have found it difficult to choose which of their precious plants should be included, but if they contributed to the overall picture room was found for new and rare specimens. Plants with variegated foliage are special favourites; there are fifty different species and cultivars of snowdrop and other species bulbs, and a wide collection of hardy plants. Sturdy shrubs and trees are hosts to climbers and in the front garden space has been found to grow unusual ivies and hollies, dwarf willows, alpines and species bulbs in an area of scree.

WINDLE HALL

MAP B

St Helens
5m (8km) from Junction 23 of M6, off East Lancs Road A580 via bridge from south side of St Helens
Owner: Lady Pilkington
Open for charity a few days a year and by appointment
(peak months July and September)

A brilliant profusion of roses makes a warm welcome in this much-loved private garden which stands like an island divided by fields and roads from intense urban development. The old walled kitchen garden and surrounding five acres have been developed since 1961 by Lady Pilkington and her late husband Sir Harry, and apart from the admirable collection of roses, contain a rockery and tufa rock grotto, imaginatively planted herbaceous borders, specimen and fruit trees, smooth lawns and a bluebell wood. Roses clamber over pergolas, up poles and walls, and beds of hybrid teas, such as 'Sir Harry Pilkington', create a lively and happy picture.

WINKWORTH ARBORETUM

MAP J

Near Hascombe, Godalming
2m (3km) south-east of Godalming on east side of B2130
Owner: The National Trust
Tel: Guildford (0483) 893032
Open daily during daylight hours
(peak seasons spring and autumn)

Covering almost one hundred acres, this twentieth-century arboretum is one of the most favoured walking places for miles around — with good reason. It was originally five acres of forgotten woodland on a steep hillside running down to two lakes, and was developed and extended by Dr Wilfred Fox. Work began before World War II and continued until 1952 when he generously gave the arboretum to the National Trust.

The setting is dramatic, as is the way shrubs and trees have been planted in bold groups; there are also spectacular views of the Hambledon Hills. Dr Fox's first love was autumn colour and it is then, as well as in the spring, that a visit is recommended. The major display of autumn colour is found in the bowl of the wood. The burning foliage of trees like maples, liquidambars, *Nyssa sylvatica* or tupelo trees and cercidiphyllums from Japan (whose dying foliage fills the air with the scent of warm caramel) light up the woodland and form glowing patches of red, yellow and orange.

In spring there are the flowering cherries and magnolias, rhododendrons, camellias and pieris, and a wide collection of unusual sorbus. A long flight of steps, ninety-three in all, becomes a triumphal walk down the hillside, flanked by banks of dazzling magenta, shocking pink, purple and white evergreen azaleas, and vast swathes of bluebells carpeting the oak woodland. There is something to see at all times of the year, a permanent and seductive quality of the arboretum being its lack of pretension. The natural beauty of the site and wood is never overwhelmed by its unusual and often visually exotic contents.

Spring in a woodland garden.

WINLLAN

MAP E

Talsarn, near Lampeter
On B4342 8m (13km) north-north-west of
Lampeter
Owners: Mr and Mrs Callan
Tel: Aeron (0570) 470612
Open by appointment from May to August for
charity
(peak months mid-May to mid-July)

Set in the beautiful Aeron valley, this young six-acre garden is of special interest to naturalists. It was once swampy land covered in gorse and brambles, and has now been cleared and transformed into a wild garden. Enthusiastic botanists and conservationists, the owners have made a pond, cleared and planted the river banks and meadows and created suitable habitats for wild animals and plants. Lawns run down from the house to the pond edged with flag irises and purple loosestrife. An island has been made for nesting waterfowl, and along a well-drained bank of rough grass, violets, heath spotted orchids, primroses, ragged robin and ox-eye daisies have been encouraged to naturalise. A small wood of birches, willows, rowans, red oaks and field maples has been planted to attract birds, and wild grasses and herbs — ideal food for caterpillars — flourish in the far meadow. The rosebay willow herb along the river bank attracts the hawk moth, and numerous nesting-boxes have been placed in the willows and alders which hang over the water.

WISLEY GARDEN

MAP J

Near Woking
Off A3 7m (11km) from Guildford
Owner: The Royal Horticultural Society
Tel: Guildford (0483) 224234
Open throughout the year. Sundays for members
and their guests only
Plants for sale

There is so much to see and to learn in this outstanding all-year-round garden that it merits visiting time and again. As might be expected of the garden owned by The Royal Horticultural Society, the two hundred and fifty acres reflect the highest standards of all aspects of horticulture. Immaculately kept, extraordinarily diverse in content and imaginatively designed, Wisley is not only aesthetically pleasing, but a source of inspiration and practical ideas for the enthusiast.

Having occupied a site in Chiswick for eighty years, the Society moved to Wisley in 1903, thanks to the generosity of Sir Thomas Hanbury. Sir Thomas had bought the property on the death of its previous owner, Mr George F. Wilson, and the six acres Wilson originally cultivated still stand as the core of the garden. He was a talented amateur, one of what was known as the Surrey School of gardeners, whose garden-making style was much influenced by William Robinson, chief advocate of the return to the 'natural' or 'wild' garden. Wilson made full use of the unspoilt woodland set on acid soil and the rich variety of hardy plants being introduced at that time, and created what he described as 'a place where plants from all over the world grow wild'. The area of oak woodland below the rock garden, which he planted with fine shrubs and trees, can still be seen today and is appropriately known as the wild garden. The acid soil of this woodland garden had a rich dressing of leaf mould, unlike most parts of the garden, which are set on fine sand, dry out rapidly and are in constant need of mulching.

The gardens flow away from the nineteenth-century half-timbered house, now converted to offices and laboratories. Somehow, the 'private' nature of both the house and the extensive gardens has been preserved, and the ever-increasing visitors are able to relate to the whole with ease. The style of the gardens near the house is predominantly formal, the planting relaxed and generous. Terraced lawns below the house are draped with tender climbers, the pink and cream-splashed foliage of an *Actinidia kolomikta* and various ceanothus. A long canal with a water spout extends to a loggia, which masks from view the two walled gardens beyond. The first of these contains a parterre, the second a fountain surrounded by borders filled with old-fashioned roses, climbers, herbaceous and silver-leafed plants. Designed by Geoffrey Jellicoe and Lanning Roper, the canal and intimate garden 'rooms' are a relatively recent addition and form a contrast to the 'naturalness' beyond. The alpine meadow is jewelled with wild flowers and spring bulbs and a lush and colourful array of moisture-loving plants grows on the banks of the stream which separates the woodland and the rock gardens.

The rock garden was built by Pulham and Son, in 1911, of Sussex sandstone; its impressive proportions and appearance vaguely resemble the Giant's Causeway. Veined with paths and enlivened with waterfalls and pools, it is covered with alpines, species bulbs, dwarf conifers and many other low-growing subjects which peep out of crevices in the rock and grow on scree or in small beds. One of the most absorbing features at Wisley, it is at its best in April and May. Above is the alpine house where specimens can be admired at close quarters; others are arranged in beds or sinks in the immediate area.

The woodland garden on Battleston Hill is also at its best in spring, when the collection of unusual rhododendrons, specimen and ornamental trees and azaleas come into flower; later in the season interest is provided by the bold plantings of hostas interspersed with lilies. In summer, the one-hundred-and-forty-yard mixed borders come into their own, together with generous displays of modern and old-fashioned roses.

Model vegetable gardens are hidden behind high hedges; island beds of annuals are set in a lawn, an ornamental herb garden and a collection of demonstration gardens is laid out to suit people's various needs and tastes, one being designed especially for the disabled. A short distance away are the glasshouses, the propagating, service and trials houses and the display house built in 1970, which has three separate sections. There is a pool of aquatic plants in the intermediate section and beds of temperate plants, daturas and tender climbers, such as the dazzling bougainvillea. The cool house displays a colourful succession of pot-grown plants, polyanthus and chrysanthemums, the warm section at the far end being lush with exotics.

At the outer edges of the garden are the trial grounds, where the merits of different varieties of flowers and vegetables can be judged (fruit trees and bushes are displayed elsewhere), the young jubilee arboretum and the superb heather garden by the lake and pinetum. These are just a sample of what can be seen at Wisley, and new features are always being added as garden-making tastes and methods change. There is an excellent and informative guide book on sale, which suggests seasonal walks of varying lengths.

WOLLATON HALL

MAP F

Nottingham
2½m (4km) West of Nottingham City Centre, off the A609 approach by car from Wollaton Road.
Owner: Nottingham City Council
Tel: Nottingham (0602) 281133
Open daily throughout the year
(peak months July and August)

Wollaton Hall, one of the most splendid Elizabethan prodigy houses in the country, stands on a hill surrounded by parkland. It was built for Sir Francis Willoughby by Robert Smythson, of Hardwick Hall fame. The elaborate decoration of the house is offset by the impressive stature of many fine trees in the park, the handsome avenue of limes, cedars and beeches, and the horse chestnuts which provide shade for the herd of fallow and red deer. A formal garden of one acre stands on the terraces to the south of the house, where spring and summer bedding and a rose garden provide bright splashes of colour. The camellia house, constructed in 1823 of cast iron — an early example of a building of this kind — overlooks an immaculately-kept pattern of formal flower beds and clipped yew topiary. Camellias, at their best from February to May, still decorate this conservatory, which cost a staggering £10,000 to build and a further £1400 to stock. Woodland and lakeside walks can be enjoyed in the five-hundred-and-fifty-acre parkland; Wollaton Hall is a tranquil and beautiful oasis amid sprawling urban development.

WOODPECKERS

MAP F

Marlcliff, near Bidford-on-Avon
Between Bidford-on-Avon and Cleeve Prior off
B4085
Owners: Dr and Mrs A. J. Cox
Tel: Bidford-on-Avon (0789) 773416
Open by appointment for charity throughout the
year
(peak months April, June and July)
Plants for sale

The majority of gardens open to the public belong to old manor houses, stately homes, and picturesque cottages; surprisingly few, considering how much new building is done each year, are attached to modern houses. Woodpeckers is a welcome exception and full of good ideas for those making a garden from scratch. Built by the present owners in 1967, the house is surrounded by a two-and-a-half-acre plot only two hundred yards from the River Avon. It was designed to blend into the surrounding pastureland and water-meadows, and is mainly an informal plantsman's garden, not bounded by a hedge or a wall. Alpines grow in stone troughs on the terrace, on areas of scree and in well-drained beds constructed of railway sleepers near the house. Large island beds on the lawn have been planted with carefully-chosen plants to give year-round interest, or are devoted to a colour theme.

Old-fashioned shrub roses feature widely, grown singly in rough grass or in a formal yew-hedged rose garden whose painted trellis, brick paths and central sundial have a period flavour. There is a water garden and a potager, or ornamental vegetable garden, patterned with decorative and unusual vegetables. There are standard gooseberries and currants, and old varieties of trained apple trees form arches at each corner. An arbour behind a small white garden is a creamy froth of the 'Rambling Rector' rose, and a white montana clematis, and roses 'Bobbie James' and *longicuspis* romp into apple trees. A circular greenhouse shelters tender subjects: a variegated trachelospermum, a pomegranate

and *Clematis florida* 'Sieboldii', *C. fosterii*, and *C. armandii*, which are saved from summer scorching by the foliage of a vine. There is something to see here at all times of the year, and the garden is a good example of how formal and period features can blend into an essentially twentieth-century creation.

WOODSIDE

MAP H

Higher Raleigh Road, Barnstaple
On outskirts of Barnstaple. A39 to Lynton, turn
right 300yds (280m) above fire station
Owners: Mr and Mrs Mervyn Feesey
Tel: Barnstaple (0271) 430 95
Open several days a year for charity and by
appointment
(peak months May to July)

This two-acre plantsman's garden is high above the town on a steep south-facing slope. Converted from rough ground twenty-three years ago, it is on acid soil, extremely shallow in certain areas, which requires constant mulching. Thanks to the Gulf Stream and shelter provided by a thick belt of trees, the garden enjoys a microclimate which enables a surprising number and fascinating range of tender and rare plants to flourish. Many originated in the southern hemisphere and have been grown from seed sent from botanic and other gardens all over the world. Acid-loving plants, monocots, plants with unusual foliage and rare specimens which defy easy identification give this informal 'green' (rather than floriferous) garden year-round shape and interest. It is primarily a collection of intriguing specimens and not a garden planted for effect. New plants are constantly added to the woodland, and to the raised and scree beds around the lawn. The dry surface of the scree beds provides ideal conditions for many tender, low-growing subjects, whose foliage would be damaged by lying on wet ground in winter.

WREST PARK

MAP G

Silsoe
On A6 9m (14½km) north of Luton.
Owner: English Heritage
Tel: Cambridge (0223) 358911
Open at weekends only from April to end
September

One of the best examples of an early eighteenth-century formal garden to have survived the on-slaught of the landscape movement, Wrest Park is currently being restored. The work of reinforcing the distinctive character of the various layers will probably take twelve to fifteen years: the French-style formality of the garden laid out in 1706, once a spectacular water par-terre; the river made by 'Capability' Brown in the mid-eighteenth century; and the Italianate terraces added in the nineteenth. Although it reflects the garden-making styles of different periods, it does not present a jumbled picture, the later additions being developed to harmonise with the existing formal gardens laid out for the Duke of Kent.

As it was falling into decay, the house was demolished by Earl de Grey in the 1830s and replaced by a French-château-style mansion set three hundred and fifty metres back. Italianate terraces decorated with statuary and matching parterres, designed by the earl, were made to link the house to the formal gardens. A central path lined with Portugal laurels was aligned on the long canal stretching into the far distance. The canal is the backbone and centrepiece of the whole — a long stretch of water forming a superb vista, channelled between lawns and banks of mature trees, to a domed pavilion designed by Thomas Archer. Used for entertaining, this beautiful baroque building conceals rooms in its dome and offers fine views over the gardens. The woodland either side of the canal is cut by straight rides and *allées* in the process of being re-aligned; you will find various features, such as urns, summerhouses, and a Chinese temple and bridge on the east side.

'Capability' Brown was employed between 1758 and 1760 to improve the park and gardens but forbore from making radical changes. It is not known whether that was due to sensitivity to the beauty of the formal gardens or because he was discouraged from doing so by the flat and uninteresting terrain, but he turned his attention to the outlying formal canals. He 'naturalised' these by transforming them into a river, forming a link between the park and the gardens. The water comes from a bath house, which was used for plunging into rather than for swimming.

Other architectural features are the Palladian bowling green house and orangery by Clephane in the upper gardens which, post-dating the 1830s, display period features such as a Victorian arboretum. When these gardens were bought by the government in 1949 they were saved on the brink of extinction, much of the ground having been ploughed up during World War II. Their current restoration is in the hands of Land Use Consultants who are carrying it out gradually, so as not to disturb their ecological balance. Wrest Park has a rich patina of period garden-making styles and these have had to be carefully researched and assessed.

YORK GATE

MAP B

Back Church Lane, Adel, Leeds 16
Behind Adel Church on Otley road out of Leeds,
A660
Owner: Mrs Sybil Spencer
Tel: Leeds (0532) 678 240
Open a few days a year and by appointment for
charity

Those who complain that an acre of ground does not give them enough scope should visit this exceptional garden and be revitalised by all they see here. It is difficult to believe, having explored its many and different 'rooms', that only an acre has been covered.

Designed by a man and planted by a woman, as are some of the best gardens in the country, the bones are predominantly formal and the planting relaxed; it would not be pretentious to find similarities between it and the gardens of

Hidcote and Sissinghurst. Of equal interest to the garden designer and the plantsman, the gallery of small but sensitively painted formal and informal 'pictures' seems neither cramped nor lacking in harmony. Each flows naturally into the other, vistas and surprises being encountered along the way. Taken individually, any of these gardens could be translated to a smaller plot and not found wanting.

The narrow herb garden, its double borders backed by yew hedges, planted with fragrant herbs, balls of golden box and corkscrew yews; the shady dell lush with moisture-loving plants; borders of irises; restrained *allées* that cool the eye; a white and silver garden; a nut walk; a peony bed; a paved garden decorated with sinks

of alpines and bonsai and the water garden — all are separate entities. Taken as a whole the garden has a flowing quality due to the owner's sure eye for what is apt. Though unusual plants abound, they are never allowed to disturb the tightrope balance between design and content.

Carefully chosen and placed to reinforce the mood and style of each area are an enviable collection of period and other man-made features — an old stone font, a slate sundial, a barley-sugar stone column, a summerhouse, attractive garden seats and stone sinks. The same care has gone into the choice and use of materials for paths and terraces, and an original and highly successful ground-covering agent is used in the small pinetum. Large grey pebbles cover

Yew topiary and hedges at York Gate.

Espaliered pyracanthus against the house at York Gate.

the surface of the beds, cutting down on maintenance, creating a subtle oriental effect and forming an ideal background to the diverse shapes and textures of the rare and unusual conifers. A greenhouse has a collection of succulents and cacti and the uniformly high standards of all aspects of the garden, extend to the potting shed, which is decorative as well as being practical, its eaves hung with period garden and agricultural implements and old-fashioned baskets.

The herb garden at York Gate, a garden influenced by Lawrence Johnston's Hidcote.

The Garden Makers

SIR JOSEPH BANKS 1743–1820
Botanist, plant-collector, patron

A gentleman of some means, Sir Joseph Banks's interest in and study of botany (triggered at an early age by finding and devouring his mother's copy of Gerard's *Herball* led to his eventually becoming President of the Royal Society and Honorary President of the Royal Botanical Gardens at Kew. Much to be seen at Kew today is due to his energy and enthusiasm. He circumnavigated the world with Cook on the *Endeavour*, a journey fraught with dangers not the least of which was that of being eaten alive by hostile natives. His experiences on this and other expeditions made him particularly well qualified to instruct and inspire later planthunters.

He was a talented entrepreneur, expert at enlisting the help of key figures to ensure the success of an enterprise, and consequently furthered greatly the interests of horticulture. He engineered the purchase of the valuable Linnaeus library and herbarium, and was one of the seven men who met at Hatchard's bookshop in Piccadilly on 7 March 1804, an historic meeting which saw the birth of what is now known as the Royal Horticultural Society. One of his less-successful ventures was to introduce bread-fruit to the West Indies as a cheap source of food for the negro slaves. If the botanist sent by Banks with Captain Bligh on the *Bounty* had not been instructed to raise breadfruit from seed in Tahiti, the crew might not have mutinied. The five months spent on this seductive island waiting for the seedlings to grow strong enough for the final leg of the journey made the crew reluctant to return to the rigours of life at sea.

SIR CHARLES BARRY 1795–1860
Architect and landscape gardener

Soon after completing his training as a surveyor, Charles Barry, son of a stationer, set off on a tour to study European architecture. The knowledge and inspiration he gained from this extensive trip influenced his future work enormously. On his return he set up his own practice and made a name for himself as a fine architect, particularly in the then fashionable Gothic style. The Houses of Parliament are the best-known example of his work.

He adopted the same elaborate style when designing gardens. The Victorians had become impatient with the purity of the eighteenth-century landscapes which surrounded their mansions, and commissioned Barry to create ornate terraces and flower gardens. These provided a link between the house and the landscape which, in the cases of Bowood and Harewood House, had been created by 'Capability' Brown (*see* entry). Brown would have hated the desecration of his work, but the Victorians found the austerity of his landscapes, which lapped the walls of these houses, distasteful and inhuman. Barry favoured massed bedding-out plants forming intricate and brightly-coloured carpets on the terraces below the house. Fortunately, his clients could afford to raise, in their new and extensive greenhouses, the vast quantities of plants needed to fill these formal beds. He set a trend for fanciful and work-intensive flower beds still seen in public parks today.

SIR REGINALD BLOMFIELD
1856–1942

Architect and garden designer

Reginald Blomfield's books on garden design, particularly *The Formal Garden in England* published in 1892, did much to advance his career and reputation. His style was architectural and formal; decorative plant material was subservient to the overall design, which had strong symmetrical lines, stonework and yew topiary and hedges being major ingredients. His approach to garden-making was diametrically opposed to that of William Robinson (*see* entry), chief advocate of the then increasingly popular wild and natural look. They inevitably crossed swords and criticised each other's views vehemently in print, though it was said, ironically, that there was not a straight line in Blomfield's own garden and not a curved one in Robinson's.

Blomfield's work can be seen at Godinton Park, where the shape of the clipped yew hedges perfectly echoes the gables of the house; Athelhampton is also a good example of the style he promoted, though it was actually designed by Inigo Thomas, his assistant in producing *The Formal Garden in England*.

SIR CHARLES BRIDGEMAN d. 1738

Landscape designer

Bridgeman's early life is a mystery though it is thought that he had worked with London and Wise before 1709 and was involved with the gardens at Blenheim. Not only was he a talented draughtsman and surveyor, but he was adept at

Athelhampton, a formal garden in the style of Reginald Blomfield.

advising on the modification of the formal gardens of the period. The cost of their upkeep was considerable and this doubtless encouraged the birth of the landscape movement, which was overseen by Bridgeman. A friend of some of the important writers and artists of his day, his work was possibly influenced by Alexander Pope, who supported the change in garden-making fashion from the autocratic and formal to the natural and romantic. Though still formal, Bridgeman's designs contained simplified versions of the ha-ha (*see* Glossary) which, in the hands of William Kent (*see* entry) and 'Capability' Brown (*see* entry), became widely used. Severe boundary walls were banished and a degree of harmony achieved with the surrounding landscape. In the intimate or wooded parts of the garden Bridgeman used more naturalistic design and winding as opposed to straight paths.

In 1728 he followed Henry Wise as Royal Gardener, a post he held until his death. Though little of his work now survives, remnants of the garden he laid out for Lord Cobham can be seen at Stowe. The outlines of his formal flower beds can be made out on the lawn during a drought and his hexagonal lake is still a major feature, though its lines were softened by William Kent. A recently restored feature of his is the dramatic amphitheatre which overlooks the lake at Claremont.

LANCELOT 'CAPABILITY' BROWN 1716–83
Landscape gardener and architect

No other gardener or designer has so dramatically and profoundly influenced the landscape of this country; Lancelot 'Capability' Brown's heroic work was extraordinarily extensive and had particularly long-lasting qualities. He was born of humble parents in Kirkhale, Northumberland, and remained at school rather longer than usual in his circumstances, leaving to work as a gardener at nearby Cambo. In 1739 he moved to Buckinghamshire to work for Sir Richard Greville, but left a year later to become head kitchen gardener to Sir Richard's brother, Lord Cobham, at Stowe. He rose rapidly to become head gardener and directed the revolutionary

work being carried out there by William Kent (*see* entry).

His energy and capacity for work were breathtaking — he surveyed, designed and supervised the radical changes to a huge number of properties, as well as being Surveyor and Manager of His Majesty's gardens and waters at Hampton Court from 1764 onwards. He also became a proficient architect and, with his son-in-law Henry Holland, built a number of Palladian-style mansions which ideally suited the style of his landscapes.

His work as a landscape designer followed a strict pattern, its major elements being huge expanses of undulating greensward sweeping right up to the house; lakes formed by damming rivers and streams; clumps and belts of trees and, where appropriate, the inclusion of classical architectural and other manmade features such as cascades. His nickname 'Capability' was due to his unrivalled eye for the 'capabilities' for improvement a property might offer.

This talent, allied to a very persuasive manner, won him a constant flow of commissions. Transforming a work-intensive formal garden into a 'natural' landscape where livestock could graze made economic sense, but the owner who paid vast sums to create valleys and hills, plant thousands of young trees and remove a village was unlikely to see his investment mature. But he bowed to fashion, planted for posterity and was captivated by the charm of 'Capability' Brown's honesty, his practical and hard-working nature, and the innovative practice of subcontracting while assiduously overseeing work meant that no owner was duped or felt cheated. Scores of formal seventeenth-century gardens were wiped out by Brown and his purist style; his uncompromising attitude earned him many critics, but you cannot make a cake without cracking eggs. It is doubtful anyway whether those work-intensive gardens would have stood the test of time as his landscapes have done.

The trees he planted have already disappeared or are about to die. Having been precisely planted to enhance and create vistas, their replacement is not easy; we are possibly the last generation to see his landscapes as he intended. Subsequent additions and changes have been made to some of these, but they still reflect his genius: Bowood, Longleat, Blenheim, Claremont, and Harewood House.

PERCY CANE 1881–1976
Garden designer and writer

Percy Cane's education involved the study of art, architecture, horticulture and agriculture, and prepared him well for his career as a garden designer. His plant knowledge and artistic eye ensured that his work not only looked good but 'worked' practically and suited the period and setting of the house. He was adept at creating formal and natural areas which, though separate entities, were skilfully linked to make a flowing rather than a fragmented picture. His gardens often have a long central vista forming a unifying backbone to sections of varying types — terracing, stonework, yew hedges and shrubs creating judicious divisions between one area and another. The sometimes large and undecorated open spaces between were important elements in the design. He likened a garden to an art gallery, each picture suitably framed and hung, and no two styles clashing. He owned and edited *My Garden Illustrated* and *Garden Design* and was awarded Royal Horticultural Society medals for his exhibition gardens at Chelsea Flower Show. A long-lasting example of his work can be seen at Dartington Hall.

Henry Moore figure in Percy Cane's garden at Dartington Hall.

SIR WILLIAM CHAMBERS 1726—96

Architect and writer

William Chambers was born in Sweden of Scottish parents. In his youth he joined the Swedish East India Company and travelled extensively in the Far East; he then changed tack and studied architecture in Paris and Italy. In 1755 he came to England and set up practice in London, and rose to become Surveyor General and Comptroller of His Majesty's Works in 1782. He was always considered a good classical architect and his work at Kew and the books he wrote — *Dissertation on Oriental Gardening* and *Design of Chinese Buildings*, for example — made his name. There are still several of his buildings in the Royal Botanic Garden at Kew, the 163-foot pagoda, temples of Bellona and Aeolus, the Roman arch and the orangery. He was a great advocate of the Chinese style for garden buildings (there was a vogue for chinoiserie at the time), and his descriptions of such gardens in his *Dissertation* were a veiled criticism of the work of his *bête noir*, 'Capability' (*see* entry) Brown rather than an accurate picture of an authentic oriental garden. He considered Brown ill-educated and lacking in taste and his feelings did not improve when Brown was chosen by Lord Clive to design the gardens at Claremont.

DAVID DOUGLAS 1799—1834

Planthunter

Born at Scone, the son of a stonemason, Douglas was a stubborn and taciturn character whose craze for natural history led him to leave school at ten years old and work in Lord Mansfield's nearby garden. His talent as a botanist led him to join the staff of the Botanic Garden at Glasgow in 1820, where he caught the eye of the Regius Professor, William J. Hooker. Hooker was quick to recommend him to the secretary of the Horticultural Society, Joseph Sabine, who commissioned Douglas to observe and collect plants for the Society.

Douglas made three expeditions to America, large tracts of which were still unexplored and wild. His courageous determination to collect, observe and log as much plant, zoological and geological information as possible led him through appalling hardships and danger, and resulted in his returning home with more new introductions than anyone before him. His life was threatened by unfriendly Indians, grizzly bears, fevers, harsh weather and lack of food. He travelled for weeks through country never before been seen by a white man and, often, much weakened, he lost through misadventure all he had collected. Once, his canoe broke up and he was spun in a whirlpool for over an hour before being tossed on to the bank, alive but empty-handed. Frustrated and tired, on his third expedition he decided to rest and explore the Hawaiian islands, where he was found in a trap gored by a wild bull, his faithful terrier guarding his collecting-box and mourning his master with howls. He introduced so much we now take for granted in our gardens that a list is too long to include, but the Douglas fir, together with many other conifers, is a magnificent memorial to the man, and the tiny *Limnanthes douglasii* is a reminder that nothing was too small for his meticulous attention.

JOHN EVELYN 1620—1706

He was a man of such extraordinarily varied interests and talents that a label would misrepresent him. His books on gardening, and the comments in his diaries regarding plants he had seen and gardens he had visited, are frequently quoted. He was enthusiastic about the introduction of new plants from abroad, published a translation of *The Compleat Gard'ner* written by La Quintinie, Louis XIV's gardener at Versailles, and wrote a practical guide to gardening called *Kalendarium Hortense, or Gardener's Almanac*. Nothing remains of his garden at Sayes Court in Kent, which, much to his chagrin, was ill-used by Peter the Great to whom he lent the property for a period. His cherished holly hedge was apparently ruined when the rowdy Russian was pushed through it in a wheelbarrow!

REGINALD FARRER 1880–1920

Writer, traveller, botanist, planthunter and gardener

Born at Ingleborough in Yorkshire of well-to-do parents, Farrer was a sickly child, with a hare lip and a speech impediment which kept him at home until he went to Balliol College, Oxford, at the age of seventeen. The formative years spent at home were not detrimental to his education; they allowed him to develop an interest in botany. By the age of sixteen he had created a rock garden in an old quarry and contributed a note to *The Journal of Botany* on *Arenaria gothica*, a soapwort, which he had found at Inglethorpe, its only known British habitat.

Soon after leaving Oxford, Farrer set off for Japan and embarked on a life which produced entertaining, informative and original books which described his travels, gardening and plant-hunting experiences, and gave advice on alpine and rock plants and the art of making a success-ful rock garden. He scoured the Alps on plant-hunting trips with E. A. Bowles and, under the guidance of William Purdom who had collected for Veitch and Sons, made an expedition to north-west Kansu in China in 1914, in search of new rock plants. Portly and moustachioed, a scholar who enjoyed his creature comforts rather than a natural adventurer, he nevertheless weathered and wrote with humour about their exploits.

World War I halted the expedition but, unfit for active service, Farrer completed his compre-hensive work, *The English Rock Garden*. In 1919 he set out once again, to upper Burma with Euan Cox. They found little of interest, the rain and generally unhealthy climate making the area as inhospitable to rock plants as it was to people. Cox returned home, but Farrer decided to con-tinue. He fell ill and died on 17 October, his coolie, Dragon, reporting that he died 'without giving any pain or trouble to us'. Farrer's ex-peditions saw the introduction to this country of plants such as *Gentiana farreri*, *Viburnum fragrans* or *farreri*, *Buddleia alternifolia* and *Rosa farreri*, 'The Threepenny-bit Rose', as well as many lilies and primulas.

MARGERY FISH 1892–1969

Gardener and writer

A latecomer to gardening, Margery Fish began her first garden at East Lambrook Manor in 1938. She filled it with what in time became a unique collection of old-fashioned cottage garden plants, unusual herbaceous plants and those with silver or variegated foliage. Designed to give all-year-round interest the predominantly informal cottage garden became a home for wild and florist's flowers which might otherwise have become extinct. The books she wrote describing these and her garden-making experiences still prove a source of inspiration and mark her out as a pioneer in the field of conservation.

GEORGE FORREST 1873–1932

Botanist and planthunter

A tough and dour Scot, Forrest was one of the most successful planthunters in China and Tibet, sending home over thirty thousand specimens during his career. He was recommended by the Edinburgh Botanic Gardens to the wealthy industrialist A. K. Bulley (whose garden at Ness is now the University of Liverpool Botanic Garden). He made seven trips to China and Tibet, all financed by various patrons, and he came to feel more at home in those parts of the world than in Scotland. He frequently faced appalling dangers as Europeans were considered 'white devils' and were hunted down, tortured and killed by Tibetan guerrillas, the majority of whom were Buddhist monks. On one trip all but one of his native plant-collectors were murdered together with a French missionary party, but Forrest escaped. Travelling at night, almost starving and suffering agonising pain from an injury to his foot, he reached base.

He was expert at training and organising his native workers, winning their confidence and friendship and this contributed greatly to the success of his expeditions. He died of heart failure while shooting snipe in Yunnan. *Pieris forrestii* and quantities of other plants, attest to his skills, and he introduced an impressive number of rhododendrons which, though not all hardy in Britain, were the parents of hundreds of modern hybrids which now adorn our gardens.

ROBERT FORTUNE 1812–80
Gardener and planthunter

While in charge of the Horticultural Society's hot-houses at Chiswick House, Robert Fortune was chosen to go to China to collect a specific list of plants. China had opened its doors to foreigners, and the opportunity to study and return with many plants previously only heard of was too good to miss. He embarked on *The Emu*, with a salary of one hundred pounds a year plus five hundred pounds for expenses. Fortune found the Chinese arrogant and proud, and disliked them, but he fulfilled his brief and more, and returned home with a dazzling collection of new plants. He had seen the brilliant colours and amazing quantity of azaleas tumbling down mountainsides, the cultivation of chrysanthemums, and the dwarfing of conifers.

He made a further trip to China for the East India Company, to study the then secret tea industry, which the company hoped to introduce to Northern India. He disguised himself as a native, and was successful in getting the information needed. Fortune was the first planthunter to use the Wardian Box, which ensured that the majority of plants collected survived the long journey home. Among the now common garden plants which Robert Fortune introduced were the Japanese anemone (used to decorate Chinese graves), tree peonies, primulas, weigela, forsythia, azaleas and chrysanthemums.

GERTRUDE JEKYLL 1843–1932
Garden designer, artist and writer

The style of gardening Gertrude Jekyll introduced and the books she wrote are as popular today as they were in her lifetime; she is a living legend. With William Robinson (*see* entry), she transformed the overdressed and garish Victorian garden into a sensitively composed picture that worked with nature, not against it. The new middle class who were building their country houses in the home counties could readily identify with their message. It suited the size of their gardens and their pockets, and the current taste in design influenced by the arts and crafts movement. It also accommodated the wealth of new hardy and perennial plants being introduced

from abroad. The message spread quickly — stiff and pretentious gardens disappeared and an altogether softer look prevailed.

Born of wealthy parents in London, Gertrude Jekyll was brought up and made her home in Surrey. She was encouraged from an early age to take an interest in her surroundings and soon developed an interest in the local traditional crafts, cottage gardens and gardening. Initially, these were hobbies for the well-educated and cultured young lady who was training to become an artist, but they had a profound effect on her work as a garden designer. In her thirties, her eyesight — never good — began to deteriorate. Threatened with blindness, she was advised to give up her ambitions as an artist. Her love of gardening came to the rescue and her enjoyable hobby became a hugely successful career. She was already contributing articles to William Robinson's gardening magazines and had forged friendships with fellow gardeners and with the young architect, Edwin Lutyens, with whom she was to work so closely in the future.

The names Lutyens and Jekyll soon became synonymous with all that was most desirable in house-building and garden-making: the house he built for her at Munstead Wood and the garden she made around it were the fruit of their combined talents. They planned scores of country gardens: he supplied the framework which blended with the design of the house and she the fine embroidery. Her artist's eye and awareness of the effects of light on shape, texture and colour banished the harsh contrasting colours of Victorian bedding-out, and substituted luxuriant borders with carefully-graded, blending colours. Jekyll knew how to marry different textures and the benefits of using grey and other foliage plants — hostas, bergenias, acanthus — to produce effective pictures. Working with nature, she encouraged roses to rampage into trees and the cultivated garden to melt gently into the surrounding woodland or countryside. She advocated the use of unpretentious and previously ignored old-fashioned cottage-garden plants, shrub and rambling roses, and she experimented with and used newly introduced shrubs and perennials, though the overall effect always took precedence.

315

Pergola at Hestercombe designed by Edwin Lutyens.

Her books — *Wood and Garden, Home and Garden, Colour Schemes for the Flower Garden* and many others — are considered bibles on garden-making. Much of their success lay in the fact that she did not theorise but wrote from her own experience. The famous painting of her boots, by Sir William Nicholson, now in the National Portrait Gallery, represents perfectly this down-to-earth woman who would stand no nonsense. She certainly did not believe in 'green fingers', knowing that the beauty of a garden depended on hard and well-directed work. She understood plants and their needs and knew there were no easy answers to achieving the effect of a garden painted rather than slaved at. Because of her earthy qualities, Jekyll was ultimately more successful and influential than the (often eccentric) Robinson in popularising the 'natural' garden. She never ceased to think of herself as an amateur and the increasing army of amateurs found her message inspiring and her garden-making experiences sympathetic. Gardens showing her influence can be seen throughout the country: one planted to her original plans can be seen at Hestercombe.

GEOFFREY ALAN JELLICOE 1900–
Architect, landscape architect, writer

Geoffrey Jellicoe studied architecture at the Architectural Association School. Well known for his designs for public spaces such as Hemel Hempstead New Town and the President Kennedy Memorial at Runnymede, he also laid out and improved a large number of private gardens. He is one of this country's most respected landscape architects, has written a number of books on the subject and is a founder member of the Institute of Landscape Architects. Examples of his work can be seen at Pusey, Hever Castle, Sandringham, Mottisfont Abbey and the Royal Horticultural Society's garden at Wisley.

LAWRENCE JOHNSTON 1871–1958

A highly cultured but shy man, it was through the innovative garden he made at Hidcote Bartrim that Lawrence Johnston influenced so greatly the garden-making style of this century. Other inventive garden-makers before him had been tempted to write books to publicise their ideas, but Johnston was singular in his reticence, generous to his friends with plants and knowledge and without any desire to advertise his talents. He was born in Paris of American parents and his early years were spent in France. The formality of French culture in gardens as in all else, doubtlessly influenced his taste. He went to Cambridge in his early twenties, became a British subject in 1900 and, after fighting in the Boer War, bought the two-hundred-and-eighty acre estate at Hidcote. He made the garden from scratch — a superb arrangement of walks and intimate rooms. Having repaired the neglect suffered by the garden during his absence in the war years, he joined Major Collingwood Ingram, the cherry expert, on a plant-collecting expedition to South Africa, and George Forrest on another to Yunnan. He also created a garden in the South of France called Serre de la Madonne, where he made his home in 1948, having given Hidcote to the National Trust.

WILLIAM KENT 1685–1748
Landscape designer, architect and painter

Though many factors bring about the birth of a new concept, William Kent was the chief innovative force of the eighteenth-century landscape movement. A Yorkshireman of humble birth, he became an apprentice sign-writer to a coach-building firm in Hull, and his artistic talents were spotted by wealthy patrons. Their generosity enabled Kent to spend the next nine years of his life in Italy, during which he studied painting, travelled and absorbed the art and architecture of the country. It was also in Italy that he met his lifelong patron and friend, Richard Boyle, third Earl of Burlington. They travelled together, and were bowled over by the buildings of Andrea Palladio (*see* entry) and inspired by the paintings of Claude (*see* entry) and Poussin. On their return to England, Lord Burlington secured royal and other sought-after commissions for Kent, whose talents as a painter, landscape designer and architect were soon much in demand. Instead of advocating that Palladian architecture be surrounded by Italianate gardens, Kent designed 'natural' idyllic landscapes similar to the Arcadian scenes depicted in Claude's views of the Italian campagna. He was not a gardener like Brown or Repton (*see* entries), with a sound knowledge of trees and plants, but he was the first to use the ha-ha to great effect, create serpentine lakes, banish straight lines and place classical-style buildings and symbolic objects at strategic points to evoke a series of emotions or make political statements. It was important that visitors followed prescribed paths to enjoy the impact and beauty of the numerous features.

Ambitious and likeable, the young Yorkshireman became a sophisticated friend of the scores of wealthy aristocrats he worked for. His landscapes became the status symbol of the time, even if they did not (as at Lord Burlington's villa in Chiswick) surround a Palladian building. Much of his work was added to by later exponents of the art, such as 'Capability' Brown (*see* entry). Clarement and Stowe are examples of this, but his work on the gardens of Rousham is a true and unaltered monument to his genius.

The loggia in William Kent's landscape garden at Rousham.

ROY LANCASTER 1937–
Botanist, plant-collector and writer

Having worked for his native Bolton Parks Department before and after National Service in Malaya, Roy Lancaster furthered his botanical education by working for the University Botanical Garden at Cambridge. This led to his employment by Hillier and Sons, and in 1970 he was made the first Curator of their gardens. He has studied and collected plants from India, Greece and Persia and, through television, books and articles, has done more to inform and excite the layman about plants and plant-collecting, than anyone before him. In 1972 he was awarded the Veitch Gold Memorial Medal for services to horticulture.

ANDRE LE NOTRE 1613–1700
Gardener, designer, painter, engineer and mathematician

Son and grandson of respected gardeners, André Le Nôtre was the best known and most innovative of seventeenth-century gardeners. He never visited Britain, but his influence was widespread and the English aristocracy who visited or were exiled in France scrapped their modest knots on their return and emulated his grand symmetrical style of garden making.

The seventeenth-century English garden designers and nurserymen, London and Wise, were strongly influenced by the sophistication of Le Nôtre's style and were much in demand to create similar, though never quite such ostentatious, examples in England.

LONDON AND WISE
Nurserymen and garden designers

George London (d.1714) had worked for Charles II and the Bishop of London (enthusiastic gardener and plantsman, Henry Compton) before he founded a nursery in Brompton Park, Kensington in 1681. Six years later he was joined by Henry Wise (1653–1738) and the two enjoyed an outstandingly successful partnership. Now the site of the Kensington museums, at its zenith the nursery covered over one hundred acres and supplied the greatest gardens in the land with all they needed to furnish their French-style formal gardens, many of which were also designed by the two men. London had seen Le Nôtre's masterly creations in France and both were fortunate in being recommended to the aristocracy by influential men of the time, which ultimately led to royal patronage. Wise, as gardener to Queen Anne, performed his royal duties and managed the nursery, while London travelled the country on horseback surveying the gardens of the nobility.

Their names became synonymous with formal gardens decorated with elaborate parterres, clipped evergreen trees, pleached *alleés*, fountains and statues. They were renowned for the variety of fruits they stocked; when their gardens at Blenheim and Hampton Court were surveyed, the list included: fourteen varieties of cherries and apricots, fifty-eight of peaches and nectarines, thirty-eight of plums, eight of figs, twenty-three vines and twenty-nine varieties of pear. Most of their work was destroyed in the eighteenth-century landscape movement, Melbourne Hall being one of the few left relatively untouched. Traces of their style can be seen at Blenheim, Chatsworth and at Hampton Court.

CLAUDE LORRAINE 1600–82

The pictures of Claude Lorraine (Claude Gellée), Nicolas Poussin (1594–1665) and Gaspard Poussin (1615–75) together with Salvator Rosa (1615–73), played a key role in the birth of the eighteenth-century landscape movement. Their idyllic interpretations of the Italian countryside depicted ruins, temples and classical figures in legends which represented Arcadia, an idealised version of an innocent and happy country life. Sought out by gentlemen on their Grand Tours, these paintings and the architecture of Andrea Palladio (*see* entry), did much to swing the pendulum of fashionable garden design from the intensely formal to the romantic and pastoral. Both styles were equally contrived but their effects could not have been more different.

JOHN CLAUDIUS LOUDON
1783–1843
Gardener, writer, painter, naturalist and architect

Loudon was a major influence on gardens and gardening during his lifetime. With the rise of a prosperous middle class during the Industrial Revolution, the primary demand was no longer for a rich man's Reptonian landscape but for a fairly modest garden to flatter the proliferating suburban and country villas. Loudon's books, magazines (the first of their sort) and designs guided — even dictated — the transitional steps of this revolution. He was a Scot, well-educated, single-minded and a demon for work. His wife Jane, who was also an author of respected gardening books, was his amanuensis and resident secretary. He had had his right arm amputated in the hope that this would alleviate rheumatic pains.

The style of garden Loudon advocated was the 'gardenesque': an ordered, well-thought-out design incorporating smooth lawns and dry paths which displayed 'the individual beauty of trees, shrubs and plants' and exhibited 'the art of the gardener'. He stressed the importance of providing what he called 'conveniences'. These included well-located seats, beds of scented plants, songbirds and even elements and features which could be enjoyed by invalids. The greenhouse and ferneries were now popular features, and much advice was given on how to choose and use them. He designed arboreta, cemeteries and public parks, recommending that sycamore, plane and almond trees might be used more widely instead of endless, dreary evergreens.

Towards the end of his life he suffered ill-health and financial troubles but still worked constantly, dying on his feet as he was dictating yet another book. His influence is still apparent in public parks and in small and large villa gardens which have retained their stone-edged flower beds and curling paths.

SIR EDWIN LUTYENS 1869–1944
Architect and landscape gardener

The foremost architect of his day, Edwin Lutyens collaborated with Gertrude Jekyll (*see* entry) to create a new and highly popular style of garden design. The bones of these gardens were architectural, their planting subtle and informal. The house and garden blended, particularly when Lutyens had designed the house. Stone and brick were used imaginatively and mixed to form terraces, steps and formal areas, and to link the two elements harmoniously.

The partnership between Jekyll and Lutyens was extraordinarily fruitful; he supplied the design and she the planting plan, and on occasion her practical good sense tempered the charming young man's wilder ideas. He shared her desire to use local materials and traditional craftsmen whenever possible and thanks to her friendship and good connections his career prospered and commissions abounded. Initially he designed country houses, such as Miss Jekyll's own at Munstead Wood in Surrey, but within a short time his commissions became grander and of a more public nature. The Cenotaph in Whitehall was inspired by a feature in the garden at Munstead Wood, and his vice-regal buildings in Delhi are witness to his energy and inventiveness. Examples of his work can be seen at Castle Drogo, Folly Farm and at Hestercombe.

THOMAS MAWSON 1861–1933
Landscape architect

Thomas Mawson had an impoverished childhood and left school at the age of twelve. He spent the next decade working for a succession of diverse, but ultimately beneficial, businesses: his uncle's building firm, a Lancaster cabinet-maker, a nurseryman and a landscape gardener. When he established the Lakeland Nurseries at Windermere with his two brothers, the skills he had learnt were harnessed together and flourished. The nursery became as well known for its stock of plants as for the design service it offered, and news of his talent spread. Apart from private gardens, he designed public parks and was eventually involved in town planning both here and abroad. His books on garden-making and landscape architecture enhanced his reputation.

Mawson's style was more architectural than horticultural, his forté being the use of wood and stone to build features in predominantly formal

The garden designed by Edwin Lutyens and Gertrude Jekyll at Hestercombe House.

gardens. Though on the edge of decay, the long, stylish pergolas at The Hill in Hampstead, the series of enclosed gardens at Dyffryn, and the less formal, but beautifully designed, gardens at Graythwaite Hall attest to his unusual combination of skills.

W. A. NESFIELD 1793–1864
Garden designer

The son of a Durham clergyman, William Andrews Nesfield was a successful and sought-after designer who, like Sir Charles Barry, favoured Italianate terraces embroidered thickly with intricate parterres. His first career was as an engineer in the army, but by the age of twenty-three he had decided to retire and become a painter of seascapes and landscapes. His reputation as a painter, and later as a garden designer, secured him the commission to work at Kew, where he laid out the formal beds and rose garden next to the Palm House, the Syon vista and the Broad Walk. He was also asked to lay out the Royal Horticultural Society's new garden in Kensington, which he dressed with coloured gravels and box planted to represent the rose, thistle, leek and shamrock. His forté was for intricate parterres but these fell out of fashion and little of his work survives except at the

Royal Botanic Garden at Kew (where his formal beds have been modified), at Broughton Hall, Holkham Hall and the maze at Somerleyton Hall.

ANDREA PALLADIO 1518–80
Architect

An Italian whose work was based on his interpretation of the principles of proportion and simplicity laid down by the ancient Roman writer Vetruvius, Palladio's influence on English classical architecture was profound. Inigo Jones was the first to be excited by his now universally admired buildings when he visited the Italian town of Vicenza and devoured his book, *Quatro libri dell' architettura*. By the beginning of the eighteenth century the Grand Tour was an established part of a young gentleman's education and many others were inspired by the classical beauty of Palladio's work. His book was translated into English, (edited by the architect Colen Campbell) and promoted the use of the classic style in this country. Richard Boyle, third Earl of Burlington, William Kent's patron, took up the torch and became the chief exponent of Palladianism, a style which remained popular for more than a century; Burlington's villa at Chiswick is still considered one of the finest examples in England. Inevitably, gardens, as well as houses were adorned with classical buildings, the famous Palladian bridge at Stowe being a prime example.

SIR JOSEPH PAXTON 1801–65

Landscape gardener, architect, engineer and politician

A true Victorian, Paxton was one of the most versatile, ingenious and industrious men of his day. Son of a Bedfordshire farmer, his gardening talents were revealed to the Duke of Devonshire when Paxton was working at the Chiswick gardens of the Horticultural Society, who leased the land from the duke. He employed the young man to work for him at Chatsworth, and a fruitful relationship was forged.

Paxton stated that between half past four and nine o'clock on his first morning at Chatsworth, he had scaled a garden gate, surveyed the whole garden, put men to work and breakfasted with a Mrs Gregory and her niece with whom he instantly fell in love and determined to marry — a propitious start. Once settled, he began creating features which would make Chatsworth renowned: the Emperor fountain, waterworks, immense rock formations, an arboretum, the Great Stove, which did so much to popularise the growing of exotics in this country, and the conservatory housing the giant water lily *Victoria amazonica*. The success of the glasshouse was to inspire his greatest achievement, the construction of the Crystal Palace, the major feature of the Great Exhibition of 1851.

In today's parlance Paxton would be classified as a workaholic and a versatile one at that. In addition his routine duties as head gardener, then agent, at Chatsworth, he designed a number of public parks, was editor of his popular gardening magazines, *Horticultural Register* and *Paxton's Magazine of Botany*, was involved in the building of railways, advised on road transport in the Crimea, redesigned and built three villages on the Chatsworth estate and, in 1854, became a Member of Parliament. It is not surprising that he died of overwork in the year he left Parliament, seven years after he had retired from Chatsworth when his friend and master died.

You can see examples of his work at Chatsworth, Tatton Park and at Somerleyton Hall.

HAROLD AINSWORTH PETO 1854–1933

Architect and garden designer

The son of a railway contractor, Sir Samuel Morton Peto, Harold Peto became an architect and designer who was not only constantly in demand but was respected by fellow workers in the field, no matter how different their styles

Sir Joseph Paxton's rockwork in the garden at Chatsworth.

might be. Gertrude Jekyll and William Robinson, who both favoured 'natural' gardens, admired his formal style which echoed that of the Italian Renaissance gardens. He used water, stonework, terraces and classical artefacts such as Ionic pillars and colonnades to great effect, creating a classical picture which was not out of place in the English countryside. His gardens had a pleasing simplicity which prevented their looking overdone or purposeless. Though man-made features were important elements he believed in keeping a balance between them and the plant material used. He was a knowledgeable and discerning plantsman and his garden at Iford Manor reflects his ideals and taste: it is laid out with terraces decorated with classical statuary and ornaments. His masterly design for the water garden at Buscot Park is stylish but restrained, making it both dramatic and tranquil.

HUMPHRY REPTON 1752–1818
Landscape gardener, architect

Repton had a good grammar school education in Bury St Edmunds and in Norwich, and, at the age of twelve, was sent to Holland to learn a foreign language which would be of use to him later in life. Young Humphry returned with much more than that: he came back a sophisticated sixteen-year-old, his musical and artistic talents well developed. He spent a short period working for a textile merchant, then managed

A formal terrace walk in Harold Peto's own garden at Iford Manor.

his own merchandising firm; its prosperity and an inheritance prompted him to retire to the country with his wife, to enjoy the life of a gentleman. This was not a long-term success: a mixture of bad luck and bad planning forced him to seek another source of income. He decided to combine his artistic talents and his knowledge of the countryside and present himself as a landscape gardener. Thanks to influential friends, he soon became the most sought-after designer of his time.

He began by walking in the footsteps of 'Capability' Brown (*see* entry) and created purist landscapes, but he gradually found a style of his own. Towards the end of his life he was laying out gardens which were taking tentative steps towards the Victorian 'gardenesque' style, later popularised by Repton's admirer, J. C. Loudon (*see* entry). Repton differed from Brown in that he did not apply the same formula to every situation; he believed that a house and its surroundings should be in harmony. Each situation demanded different treatment and, though the pursuit of beauty was the consistent aim, he realised that a garden was not static but changed constantly. The seasons were taken into account, as was the light at different times of day and the needs of everyday life. He was no rigid purist, but a superb interpreter, able to adapt himself to the changing character of the countryside, the lie of the land, various styles of architecture and other immutable considerations. He favoured terraces, flower beds, a more imaginative use and choice of trees and also turned his hand to architecture, in conjunction with William Wilkins, Nash and lastly with his son, John Adey Repton. His business relationship with Nash was ruined when Nash took advantage of Repton's goodwill and also took credit for some of his ideas.

When he was commissioned to improve a property, Repton did a survey and presented his client with a unique and effective sales device, a leather-bound 'Red Book'. In it he had painted views of the garden as they were, with flaps to show the changes he proposed. These were superimposed on the 'before' view and demonstrated how the garden would look 'after' his alterations. Few of these beautiful 'Red Books'

still survive; those which have are now of great value.

Considering his popularity as a landscape gardener, he deserved to accumulate a fortune, but whether it was due to gentlemanly lack of astuteness or just bad luck he did not. Much liked and always facing misfortune with equanimity, he died from the effects of a carriage accident sustained several years before. These are examples of his work at Sheringham Hall, Attingham Park, Ashridge and at Tatton Park.

WILLIAM ROBINSON 1838–1935
Landscape gardener, writer and editor

Always somewhat secretive about his origins, William Robinson, protagonist in a revolution in garden design, was probably born of humble protestant Irish parents. On leaving school he was apprenticed as a garden-boy in County Kerry, and rose to head gardener. Suddenly, for an unknown reason, he intentionally exposed a mass of tender plants in the conservatories to the winter cold, upped and left. He arrived in London in 1861 and took charge of the hardy herbaceous section of the Royal Botanic Gardens in Regent's Park (site of the present Queen Mary's Rose Garden). The collection and care of English wild flowers was another of his duties, and gathering and studying these lit the spark which fired Robinson's zealous advocacy of 'natural' and wild gardens.

A passionate lover of the countryside, he abhorred the contrived and overdone design of Victorian gardens, filled with what he called 'pastry work gardening'. It was not only the way bedding-out plants were used that he loathed, but the plants themselves. He wanted to see only hardy plants, both indigenous and recently introduced, grown in a natural manner, in woodland and pastoral settings. He was an admirer of J. C. Loudon (*see* entry) and agreed with him that the individual plant should be valued, though Robinson's ideas eventually meant the death of Loudon's 'gardenesque' style. He wanted to do away with conservatories, stoves and greenhouses and the use of Latin names for plants, though the alternatives he suggested were often bizarre. Robinson flooded the market with his books and magazines to which others of like

Cottage garden planted with unpretentious native plants as advocated by William Robinson.

mind contributed — Canon Ellacombe, Dean Hole and Gertrude Jekyll, who was editor of his magazine, *The Garden*, for several years. His two most widely-read books were *The Wild Garden* and *The English Flower Garden*. Sales of these and the magazines, plus profits from astute property investments, enabled him to buy Gravetye Manor in Sussex.

He had left the Royal Botanic Garden at the age of twenty-nine to pursue his career as a garden writer, but on his purchase of Gravetye he consulted the head gardener, Robert Marnock, on the design of his new garden. He practised what he had preached but not always with success — daffodils did not naturalise where he intended they should, and herbaceous plants did not thrive when planted in hedges. Gravetye also contained many of the plants of which he disapproved; his greatest critic, the formal landscape architect, Reginald Blomfield (*see* entry) would have found surprising formal elements in Robinson's garden.

It is difficult to gauge the strength of his message; like many zealots, he was often his own worst enemy. He overstated his case and was often eccentric and contradictory, but he changed the face of gardens in this country at the beginning of the century. He lit the torch Gertrude Jekyll was to carry in a more acceptable, practical and ultimately effective way.

LANNING ROPER 1912–83
Garden designer and writer

An American by birth, Lanning Roper came to this country in 1948, having studied fine art at Harvard. He worked at Kew and at the Royal Botanic Gardens, Edinburgh, became assistant editor of the Royal Horticultural Society Journal and from 1951 to 1975 was *The Times* garden correspondent. In 1957 he wrote *The Successful Town Garden* and in 1961 *The Gardens in the Royal Parks at Windsor*. He advised on the improvement of many private properties and, appropriately, the gardens to the new American Museum at Claverton Manor, as well as a number of National Trust properties such as Scotney Castle and Waddesdon Manor. His work can also be seen at the Royal Horticultural Society's garden at Wisley and at Englefield House.

VITA SACKVILLE-WEST 1892–1962
Gardener and writer

The Honourable Victoria Sackville-West was born at Knole in Kent, the only child of the third Lord Sackville. She loved her ancient home passionately and was heartbroken that she would not inherit it. This led her to find a home of her own and to create a garden which has influenced the style of garden-making in this country ever since. When she and her husband, Harold Nicolson, left their first house, Long Barn in Kent, they moved to the derelict Sissinghurst Castle and began to create one of the most beautiful gardens in England. She had been inspired by the extended cottage-garden style of Hidcote, and determined to create another on similar lines. Harold Nicolson designed the bones of the garden, its axial paths and hedges, while she planted the intimate 'rooms' within this framework. Her ideal was to marry maximum formality of design with maximum informality of planting. Her eye for colour and sympathetic plant associations, and success in giving the garden year-round interest, make Sissinghurst exceptional.

Her gardening articles for The *Observer* popularised her taste in plants and garden-making and became so popular with amateur and professional alike that they have sold in book form ever since. Her articles were as informative as they were entertaining and easy to read. She wrote from her own experience and had a talent for summoning up pictures of plants, like her description of the blooms of a *Magnolia grandiflora* resembling 'white doves nestling in large glossy leaves'. Apart from her many non-gardening books, she wrote two long poems, 'The Garden' and 'The Land', both of which were enormously popular.

GRAHAM STUART THOMAS 1909–
Gardener, botanist, garden adviser, writer and painter

Having studied horticulture at the University Botanic Garden in Cambridge, Graham Stuart Thomas's career has covered so many aspects of the gardening world that it is hard to pin-point one in particular. Indisputably he has made an enormous contribution to the development and care of the gardens of the The National Trust. As their Gardens Adviser from 1956 to 1974, he was instrumental in the restoration of many of this country's finest examples. Immense problems were posed in preserving their character and historical integrity while ensuring that the costs of work and maintenance were not excessive.

He has written many books, particularly on his first love, shrub roses, and illustrated others with his paintings and drawings, as well as advising on private gardens. He has been awarded the Royal Horticultural Society's Victoria Medal of Honour, the Veitch Memorial Medal for services to Horticulture, and a Gold Medal for his paintings and drawings. You can see some of his work at Sezincote, Mottisfont Abbey and in numerous other National Trust gardens.

THE JOHN TRADESCANTS: the Elder c1570–1637; the Younger 1608–62
Gardeners, plant-collectors and botanists

John Tradescant and his son introduced more new plants to this country during their lifetime than any plant-collector before them. John the Elder was gardener to the Cecil family at Hatfield and at Cranborne, both of which still show his influence. He was encouraged by the Cecil family to travel widely in Europe seeking new fruits and vegetables, and inevitably he discovered new decorative plants at the same time. The black Mulberry, so important to the silk industry, was brought back from France, as were vines and roses. He visited North Africa and Russia — the first botanist to do so — and comments in his journal on the quantities of *Helleborus alba* to be found there. He became Keeper of His Majesty's gardens at Oatlands in Surrey and was appointed Keeper of the Oxford Botanic Garden in 1637, but died before he could take up the appointment. In his house, known as The Ark, he kept a 'Closett of Rarities' gathered from the many countries he and his son had visited. This was later acquired by the scientist Elias Ashmole, and went to form a fascinating part of the Ashmolean Museum.

John the Younger, a scholar at King's School Canterbury, became his father's talented as-sistant and succeeded him as Keeper of His Majesty's gardens. Also a traveller and plant-collector, he made several voyages to Virginia, returning with a wealth of plants now familiar in our gardens, their provenance long since forgotten — Virginia creeper, cornflowers, lupins, Michaelmas daisies and the spiderwort, *Tradescantia virginiana*. A memorial to the two men now exists in the form of a museum and a replica seventeenth-century garden, planted with the flowers they would have known, at St Mary-at-Lambeth, London.

SIR JOHN VANBRUGH 1664–1726
Architect

Vanbrugh's experience as actor and playwright might well be a clue to his later success as an architect and designer of gardens. His baroque buildings were not as exaggeratedly exuberant and mannered as his Restoration plays, but they reflected a vitality and absence of shyness in making a bold statement. The superb proportions and adornment of Blenheim Palace are a confident and noble celebration of Marlborough's victory; the belvedere at Claremont is wonderfully effective in its size and placement, and the rotondo at Stowe is perfect in its proportions. Another superb example of his work is Castle Howard, and he is said to have influenced the design of the house and garden at Duncombe Park.

VEITCH

Had it not been for the several generations of the Veitch family and their famous nursery, many now-familiar plants would not have been introduced so easily to this country. The prosperity of their nursery enabled them to train and send plant-collectors, such as William and Thomas Lobb, E. H. Wilson and William Purdom, to seek out new and beautiful plants to satisfy the insatiable appetites of their many clients.

John Veitch (1752–1839) was a Scot who originally set up the nursery in Devon, where he worked for Sir Thomas Acland at Killerton. Succeeding generations of the family expanded the business, eventually forming two different companies, Robert Veitch and Son in Exeter

Reproduction Elizabethan knot garden at Hatfield House, where John Tradescant the Elder was gardener to the Cecils.

and James Veitch and Sons in Chelsea; the latter also ran several specialised nurseries in Surrey. The business embraced the design and laying out of gardens, the breeding of plants, the introduction of new species and varieties, and it ultimately became famous for its collections of orchids and other tender plants. By 1914 the London firm's fortunes had seriously declined and the business was closed down, but the Exeter branch continued until 1969 before being sold.

The name of this enterprising family is remembered annually when the Royal Horticultural Society selects 'those who have helped in the advancement and improvement of the science and practice of horticulture', and award the Veitch Memorial Medal.

FRANCIS KINGDON WARD
1885–1958
Botanist and planthunter

Son of the Professor of Botany at Cambridge University he, unlike the majority of plant-collectors, had the advantage of absorbing naturally and being encouraged to pursue botanical knowledge from an early age. He and George Forrest (*see* entry) came to be considered the great twentieth-century collectors, both introducing many new plants of high quality. A confident and friendly man, Ward was thorough in the field, always observing the habits of any plants he found. He was also a talented geologist and photographer and the author of ten books describing his adventures and work.

His first two expeditions were made for the seed firm Bees Ltd; the following twenty — to Burma, Tibet, India and north and west China — were on behalf of wealthy private patrons. Rhododendrons, primulas, lilies, gentians and poppies (the blue poppy *Meconopsis betonicifolia* being particularly noteworthy) made up the main part of his introductions. During World War II his botanical knowledge and experience of living rough were put to good use teaching soldiers at a jungle-survival school what they could and could not eat.

ELLEN ANN WILLMOTT 1858–1934
Gardener, horticulturist and writer

Now remembered chiefly as the author of the twenty-five-part illustrated work, *The Genus Rosa*, the wealthy Miss Willmott's garden at Warley Place was famed in its time for its wide collection of rare plants. She was born at Spring Grove, Sir Joseph Banks's old home in Middlesex, and brought up at Warley, a property in Essex which had once belonged to John Evelyn. Both she and her sister shared their mother's enthusiasm for gardening. Ellen Willmott was ambitious and imperious, and her critics claimed that she bought rather than earned her reputation as a horticulturist, but her success in acquiring and raising an exceptional collection of plants was never disputed. World War I changed her fortunes; she could no longer afford to keep eighty-five gardeners at Warley or to finance planthunting expeditions, and she had to sell her properties in Italy and France.

Miss Willmott was rewarded for her contribution to horticulture by admission as the first woman member of the Linnaean Society and by being awarded the Victoria Medal of Honour by the Royal Horticultural Society. When the Society was offered Sir Thomas Hanbury's garden at Wisley, Miss Willmott was one of its first trustees. The garden at Warley no longer exists, though her influence can be seen in her sister's garden at Spetchley Park; part of her original collection of roses found a home at Nymans. An example of her garden design work can be seen in the rock garden at Newby Hall.

Vanbrugh's bridge over 'Capability' Brown's lake at Blenheim.

Bodnant, a garden filled with trees and shrubs introduced by turn-of-the-century planthunters Wilson, Forrest, Kingdon Ward and Rock.

E. H. WILSON 1876–1930

Plant-collector

Ernest Henry, or 'Chinese' Wilson as he came to be known, was an exceptionally successful plant-collector. Without the wealth of trees and plants he introduced, our gardens today would be much impoverished. He was born in Gloucestershire and rapidly progressed from working in a Warwickshire nursery to being recommended by the Director of Kew to collect plants for the famous nursery of James Veitch and Son (*see* entry). He was only twenty-two at the time, and Veitch and Son were at the height of their success, so his talents as a botanist and potential as a

planthunter must have been highly regarded. Part of his commission was to seek out specifically and return with the seed of the dove or handkerchief tree, *Davidia involucrata*. He failed to track this down on his first expedition, returning with Davidias of a different variety, but he did eventually secure seed of this admired tree.

Wilson's meticulous approach to his work and his ability to get on with the Chinese, at a time when the Boxer troubles strained relations, contributed hugely to the success of the expeditions he made for Veitch. In his efforts to bring back the regale lily he almost lost his life: his leg, fractured by a falling boulder, turned gangrenous before expert medical attention could be reached, but he cheered on the bearers who were carrying him and insisted that a mule train on the same narrow path, but moving in the opposite direction, should step over his stretcher rather than try to pass and possibly prompt a landslide. His leg was saved but he suffered for the rest of his life from what he called his 'lily limp'.

The Director of the Arnold Arboretum in Boston, Professor Charles Sargent, advised him and became a close friend of his, and from 1907 he collected for the arboretum, eventually becoming its Keeper on Sargent's death in 1927. He held this post until his death in a car crash in 1930, an ironic end for a man who had risked his life so often in the field. His books and his outstanding number of plant introductions are now familiar to the gardener — *Prunus serrula, Clematis montana rubens, Cornus kousa, Cotoneaster horizontalis* and *Magnolia wilsonii* are but a handful.

The potting shed at York Gate.

A Glossary of Garden Terms

ALLÉE

A typical feature of the seventeenth-century formal garden which originated in France, the *allée* (or alley) is a straight walk or avenue. Sometimes edged by clipped hedges or avenues of trees such as limes, it leads to a focal point or feature such as an urn or a statue from which other walks radiate. Undecorated and sublimely simple in design, *allées* were originally a restful contrast to the intensely cultivated and intricate parts of a strict formal garden. The *allée* might pretend to be a natural, even on occasion a pastoral feature, but its symmetry gives it away as being manufactured by man. Melbourne Hall still retains its original French-style design, with numerous *allées* leading to the garden's outer reaches.

BEE-BOLES

Alcoves set into old walls where the straw beeskeps were placed to protect them from the weather. They were built from Tudor times to the mid-nineteenth century and were usually near ground level, facing south. Their curved shape echoes that of the skep itself, which was set at a slight tilt to allow access for the bees. Thirty of these alcoves can be seen set in the wall which divides the topiary garden from the Carolean garden at Packwood and there are old-fashioned straw bee-skeps housing working bees in the white, wooden bee-house at Attingham Park.

BELVEDERE

A tower-like building which offers fine views of the garden, landscape and surrounding countryside. Some stand on their own, like that built by Vanbrugh on a hill above the landscape garden at Claremont; others rise like a turret from the house itself. The word belvedere literally means 'beautiful' view.

BOSKETS

Blocks or wedges of woodland between axial avenues and rides. A feature of the outer reaches of seventeenth-century French-style gardens, the woodland gave a 'natural' look to what was, in reality, a highly artificial layout. Boskets, thickets or shrubberies were also used to decorate areas between the symmetrical or winding paths of wilderness gardens. Examples can be seen at Melbourne Hall, Blickling Hall and Wrest Park.

CLAIR-VOIE

A grille or opening set in a wall or hedge, giving a 'clear view' to the countryside beyond, or a run of iron railings set between piers in a wall, fulfilling the same purpose. Usually at the end of a walk or *allée* they were used to lengthen a vista. There is an example of an early Dutch-style *clair-voie* at Westbury Court.

COLD BATHS, BATH-HOUSES, PLUNGE-POOLS

Though not as commonly seen as the swimming pools of today, these small stone baths were fashionable features of seventeenth- and eighteenth-century gardens. Designed to accommodate at most two crouching rather than outstretched bodies their obvious use was to cool down on a hot summer day. A plunge into the cold waters of such a pool was also considered good for the health, a physician of the day recommending that it was 'good against headaches, strengthens and enlivens the body, is good against vapours and impotence'. The eighteenth-century vogue for landscapes decorated with classical buildings might also have

The Belvedere at Claremont.

inspired the gentlemen of that time to ape the ancient Greeks or Romans, who attended the baths not only to cleanse themselves but to exchange high-minded ideas and gossip. It is possible to imagine the cold bath at Rousham being used in such a way, but the *raison d'être* of that at Packwood is less clear. The pool was usually placed near a source of running water, which flowed through or fed it and prevented its becoming stagnant and unhealthy.

CRINKLE-CRANKLE WALL

A serpentine wall, usually of brick, the bays of which provide shelter for tender shrubs or fruit trees. Originating in the eighteenth century, it was built to run from east to west, its curved design giving extra strength.

EYECATCHER

A building set at a considerable distance from the garden and house, a distant focal point which adds interest to the surrounding landscape. These structures are often eccentric in design; what may seen to be a ruined building set against the skyline on high ground, can be a purpose-built folly. The arched facade at Rousham and the folly at Mount Edgecumbe are examples; others are Alfred's tower at Stourhead, the Corinthian arch at Stowe, the domestic and simple dovecote at Hodnet Hall and the column at Blenheim.

FOLLY

Follies come in all shapes and sizes: ruins, pyramids, temples, grottoes, even hermit's cells. They were built to provoke as varied a collection of reactions. Many reveal the idiosyncrasies of their owners, having been built to their design, rather than that of an architect. The intriguing features in the landscape at West Wycombe Park reveal as much about the life and character of Sir Francis Dashwood as they do about fashionable eighteenth-century garden-making. They seldom fulfilled a useful purpose, being constructed to impress or amuse, but were important features of the landscape garden.

GROTTO

A cavern-like structure, as difficult to build as it is prone to decay. It was a popular feature of eighteenth-century landscapes, designed to promote feelings of gloom or excitement, and was often made of or housed a collection of scientific interest — minerals, shells, corals or fossils. Few have survived intact but a very large example is being renovated at Painshill. The grotto is beside the lake, and a long passage leads to a great hall once highly decorated with minerals, which sparkled in the light reflected off the water. At nearby Claremont, a smaller grotto is also being restored and a fine example marks the source of the river Stour at Stourhead. Another, at Goldney House, is sunk beneath the ground and contains a seated figure of Neptune.

HA-HA

An admirable device, first used in France, which prevents livestock from invading the garden while preserving an unbroken view over open countryside. The boundary to the garden is formed by a deep ditch. The garden side of it is sheer and lined with a retaining wall while the bank of the outer side is sloping. The garden designer Charles Bridgeman introduced a simplified version of the ha-ha to this country and from then on it became an almost indispensable feature of the landscape garden. It gained its name from its surprise element. In discovering the design and the seemingly invisible boundary, visitors would exclaim 'Ha-Ha'.

ICE HOUSE

A dry, underground, man-made cavern where ice was stored. At a convenient distance from the house, it lay beneath a mound of earth shaded by trees. The first was built in this country in 1660 in St Jame's Park by Charles II who had doubtless been impressed by such practical constructions during his exile in France. Some ice houses were topped by elegant buildings, others were simple half-barrel-shaped storage spaces with sunken entrances, ease of access being vital. The refrigerator is a relatively recent invention, so it is easy to understand why these constructions were popular with the wealthy; those less fortunate had to rely on travelling ice carts. An interesting example, covered by a tent-like roof of thatched heather, is at Scotney Castle, and others are at Killerton, Ham House, and Tapeley Park. The interior of the ice house at Sutton Park has been lit to enable the visitor to examine its construction.

KNOT

An intricate pattern of beds filled with herbs, flowers, coloured stones, gravel or sand, and edged with low-growing plants like santolina, box, lavender and rosemary. Dating from the fifteenth century, they were placed near the house, so that the beauty of their design could be admired from upstairs windows. The knot would often display the owners' initials, crest or emblem, or the decorative design of plaster or woodwork ceilings in the house would be copied. There are 'closed knots', composed of intricately-entwined hedges and more loosely-designed 'open knots' of beds filled with flowers, herbs or gravel. A large and authentically-planted example is at Hatfield House, another at Little Moreton Hall. One composed solely of dwarf box can be seen at Barnsley House, and a recent example at Sledmere incorporates the initial S into the design.

The seventeenth-century dovecote that acts as an eyecatcher at Hodnet Hall.

The grotto at Stourhead.

MAZE

The historically correct name for a puzzle of twisting, hedged corridors is a labyrinth; the name maze was originally used for a similar puzzle which was a design of paths divided by clipped turf. Thought from ancient times to have a religious or mystical significance, these popular and intriguing features can be seen at Chenies Manor, Grey's Court, and Doddington Hall. There are labyrinths at Hampton Court, Somerleyton Hall and at Hatfield House.

MOUNT

An artificially created hill or mound, the mount was a common feature of Tudor gardens and was constructed either as a 'look-out' to the land which lay beyond the secure confines of the garden, or as a point from which a fine view of the garden could be enjoyed. The mount at Packwood House affords a splendid view over the topiary garden, as does that in the Queen's garden at Kew.

ORANGERY

A forerunner of the greenhouse and conservatory, the orangery was built to house not only orange trees but other exotics or evergreens which might be damaged or killed off by severe weather. It was almost always elegant in design and had a certain prestige value: few could afford to buy such plants, and those who could wanted to display them with style. It is thought that oranges first appeared during the latter half of the sixteenth century; chroniclers John Aubrey and John Evelyn both wrote of seeing them in the gardens of the nobility. Being evergreen, they were as decorative in winter as in summer, when, set in ornamental tubs, they were wheeled out into the garden to add elegance to the seventeenth-century, French-style gardens. Orangeries which still house orange trees can be seen at Saltram, Tatton Park, and Peckover where the small and unpretentious orangery houses venerable and fruitful specimens.

PARTERRE

Of French origin, the parterre took over from the smaller, usually enclosed, knot garden in the seventeenth century. On level ground, formal geometric beds edged with dwarf box or cotton lavender are filled with low-growing flowers, coloured stones or gravel. They were laid out where they could easily be admired from the house and possibly add to its grandeur. Many were designed by London and Wise, but the landscape movement saw their demise, when vast formal gardens were swept away and replaced by landscapes which lapped the walls of the mansion. Only a handful of parterres survived this period, but the Victorian era saw their revival when fashion once again demanded that the house be surrounded with formal and often extravagant features. Lavish numbers of brightly coloured plants, raised in greenhouses, filled the intricate embroidery of flower beds, creating impressive and flamboyant effects which often resembled, highly coloured patterned carpets. This style of planting is still popular in many public parks and is much harder to execute than might be imagined. There are good examples at

The fleur-de-lys knot garden at Broughton Castle.

Holkham Hall, Oxburgh, Tatton Park, Castle Ashby and Waddesdon.

PATTE-D'OIE

Translated, *patte-d'oie* means goose's foot, which perfectly describes the way paths, avenues or *allées* fan out from a central point. They were a popular feature of seventeenth-century French-style gardens and can be seen at Hampton Court, Ham House and Melbourne Hall.

PLEACHING

The interwining and training of the branches of a line of trees to form a hedge or screen on stilts. These sometimes form tunnels, their neat and symmetrical character giving them a masonry-like appearance. Usually composed of hornbeam, lime or yew, such hedges are often a feature of formal period gardens and are known to have adorned Tudor gardens.

POTAGER

A French-style ornamental vegetable garden as attractive as it is productive. Vegetables mixed with flowers are still used to great effect in the splendid formal gardens at Villandry in France, edging beds and contributing to an intricate pattern. The modern *potager* is on a much smaller scale and its produce is grown to be eaten, not purely for decoration. The idea of planting flowers and vegetables together has not been customary for a considerable time, but intricate, formal gardens are making a come-back and the *potager* could again become a popular feature. The difficulties of designing and maintaining it are considerable because the plant content is constantly being cropped and the painstakingly-created design being decimated. The skilful choice and placing of subjects is essential. A good example can be seen at Barnsley House, where Rosemary Verey has followed an eighteenth-century design incorporating espaliered and trained fruit trees, standard gooseberry bushes, herbs and unusual and colourful varieties

The maze or 'labyrinth' at Chatsworth.

of vegetables. The beds, divided by a pattern of brick paths, are varied in shape and are small enough to be tended with ease. There is another at West Green House, which boasts decorative hexagonal fruit cages and ornamental beds of fruit and vegetables.

ROOT HOUSE

A nineteenth-century rustic summerhouse made from the gnarled base and trunks of trees. Usually thatched, sometimes with heather, according to the Victorian garden writer John Claudius Loudon they should look man-made and not as though they had 'grown'. The materials used made them cheap to construct and suited the current vogue for the 'rustic' look. An example can be seen at Spetchley Park, a garden which particularly reflects late Victorian and Edwardian taste.

STEW OR FISH POND

Medieval in origin, these ponds were an easily accessible source of fresh fish which could be eaten during the harsh winter and early spring when other sources of food had been exhausted. A feature of ancient abbey gardens, many of them still survive — but few in their original form. They have been converted into formal ponds or water gardens, and can be seen at Forde Abbey, Upton House and at Barrington Court.

STOVE HOUSE, GREENHOUSE, CONSERVATORY

As exotic fruits and plants were introduced during the seventeenth century, partially-glazed houses were built where tender plants, particularly evergreens (hence the name greenhouse), could be overwintered. They were originally heated with open fires, pans of coals or Dutch stoves, but the noxious fumes damaged the plants. Gradually more sophisticated and indirect forms of heating by means of outside stoves, were introduced. By the end of the Victorian era — the heyday of the grand conservatory — complex and ingenious methods of regulating their temperature had been devised. It was also realised

Joseph Paxton's wallcases at Chatsworth.

with ferns, tropical plants, song birds and water features, and rapidly became as typical a period feature as the aspidistra. Novels and plays of the time frequently featured dramatic or romantic scenes enacted in conservatories, their jungle-like nature making them ideal spots for sharing secrets, smoking in peace or plighting one's troth. The majority of these domestic conservatories have now disappeared and have made a comeback only in the last decade. While not containing the impressive collections of plants they used to hold, they make useful and attractive extra rooms and have become, once again, status symbols.

The modern greenhouse, retaining its practical rather than aesthetic character, is used mainly for the propagation of plants and is heated to a lesser degree and with greater ease. Like the gardens of today, greenhouses have shrunk. They are no longer hidden behind the walls of the vegetable garden and some designs are attractive rather than purely functional. Excitingly designed, equipped and filled glasshouses can be seen in the Royal Botanic Gardens at Kew, at the Royal Horticultural Society's garden at Wisley and, appropriately, at Chatsworth. Early nineteenth-century examples are at Bicton and Syon Park.

that the plants needed maximum light and suitable ventilation to thrive, as well as heat, and the abolition of the glass tax in 1845 saw the arrival of glazed roofs.

This was an exciting time for plantsmen as an ever-increasing number of exotic plants were being introduced from abroad, and those who could afford to erect large glasshouses scrambled to raise the first specimens in this country. Thousands of half-hardy bedding-out plants also had to be raised each year, to fill the then fashionable formal beds around the house. Wealth was not felt to be embarrassing, but was something to display, so extravagantly-filled and expensive-to-run glasshouses became important status symbols. The most impressive of these was built by Sir Joseph Paxton at Chatsworth. It covered an acre of ground and a coach and pair could be driven through it with ease. Paxton also built a special glasshouse to house the prized Victoria Regina waterlily, *Victoria Amazonica*, the first to flower in this country, and this construction was to inspire his finest creation, the Crystal Palace.

Sadly, none of these glasshouses exists today, but Decimus Burton's Palm and Temperate Houses at Kew give an idea of what they were like. Dramatically scaled-down editions were soon seen as important adjuncts to the well-appointed Victorian mansion. They were filled

*An area of ornamental vegetable gardening at
Heale House.*

The garden of eccentric topiary at Levens Hall.

'TAPESTRY' HEDGE

A hedge composed of several different kinds of hedging material, both evergreen and deciduous, which has varied texture and colour. One surrounds the fuchsia garden at Hidcote; it is composed of variegated and green holly, copper beech, yew and box. Another can be seen at Chilcombe House.

TOPIARY

Evergreen shrubs and trees clipped into shapes such as pyramids, balls, birds or even more ambitious forms. The Romans clipped box into various shapes and topiary was a common feature of medieval gardens — a contrast to the wild forests beyond. Popular in Elizabethan and Jacobean gardens, box, rosemary, whitethorn and privet were used to decorate knot gardens; yew was not considered a suitable material until the beginning of the eighteenth century. The reign of William and Mary saw the zenith of fanciful topiary, when all manner of real and imaginary architectural and animal shapes were created, but they disappeared with the birth of the landscape movement. The vogue was for the 'natural' rather than the contrived look and topiary became non-U, only to surface again with the arts and crafts movement at the turn of this century.

Much of the topiary to be seen today is not as old as might be imagined: yew does live to a great age, but it is not as slow-growing as is generally thought. There are huge and uneven yew hedges and tunnels dating from Elizabethan times, some of which were originally topiary, but much that is passed off as ancient was planted in the eighteenth and nineteenth centuries. The extraordinary topiary at Levens Hall was never intended to reach such large proportions, having originally decorated a knot garden, and this is true too of the unique picture at Packwood House. In both cases shapes have been added; the dating of the composition at Packwood is something of a mystery and may well be another case of an overgrown dwarf topiary garden. The strong, geometric yew shapes at Athelhampton and the shaped hedge at Godinton are turn-of-the-century examples and though topiary is not much seen in modern gardens, it appears as imaginative single or paired features and is becoming increasingly popular.

TREILLAGE

Structures created out of trellis, square or diamond-shaped wood or metal lattice work. An early form of garden decoration, *treillage* can be ornate and, apart from acting simply as a screen, can be formed into such features as arbours, pillars, obelisks and arches. It is effective in creating false perspectives and a greater feeling of space in a building or a small garden or courtyard. The rose gardens at Shugborough and Cliveden are both decorated with delicate *treillage*.

TROMPE L'OEIL

An 'eye-deceiver' which can create an illusion of space, length or volume. The ha-ha is a superb example, as it so effectively gives the impression of a garden melting into the landscape, the livestock grazing on its far side being prevented from entering the garden seemingly by magic. The placing and grouping of trees in a landscape, narrowing or widening of avenues, grading and shape of steps, placing of lakes on low ground, and use of trellis in small enclosed spaces, can create the illusion of limitless space and form false perspectives which add beauty and grandeur to a garden or landscape. An eighteenth-century picturesque landscape was designed to resemble a romantic, classical dream which in itself might be a *trompe l'oeil*. Nymphs and satyrs did not inhabit the wood, grottoes were not actually filled with horrors nor did gods frequent the temples, but one was led to think they might.

VISTA

A view channelled down an avenue of trees, between hedges or the folds of a valley. At the end of this contrived channel, other 'vistas' down further avenues often come into view, or a feature such as a folly or eyecatcher creates a focal point. A standard feature of seventeenth-century formal gardens, they have been used ever since

The terrace gardens flowing away from Newby Hall.

as a means to tempt us onwards through a garden, and often to take advantage of the 'borrowed' wild or rural landscape beyond its confines.

WILDERNESS

A misleading name for a highly-contrived part of the garden set beyond the formal area around the house. In the seventeenth century the ground was laid out with a pattern of straight paths which radiated from a central point and were lined with hedges, while pleached or ornamental trees and flowering trees and shrubs were planted in the spaces between the walks. There is an early example of a wilderness at Ham House. In the nineteenth century their design became more relaxed, the paths becoming serpentine rather than straight, with the spaces in between filled with then-popular evergreen shrubs, such as laurels and rhododendrons.

Maps

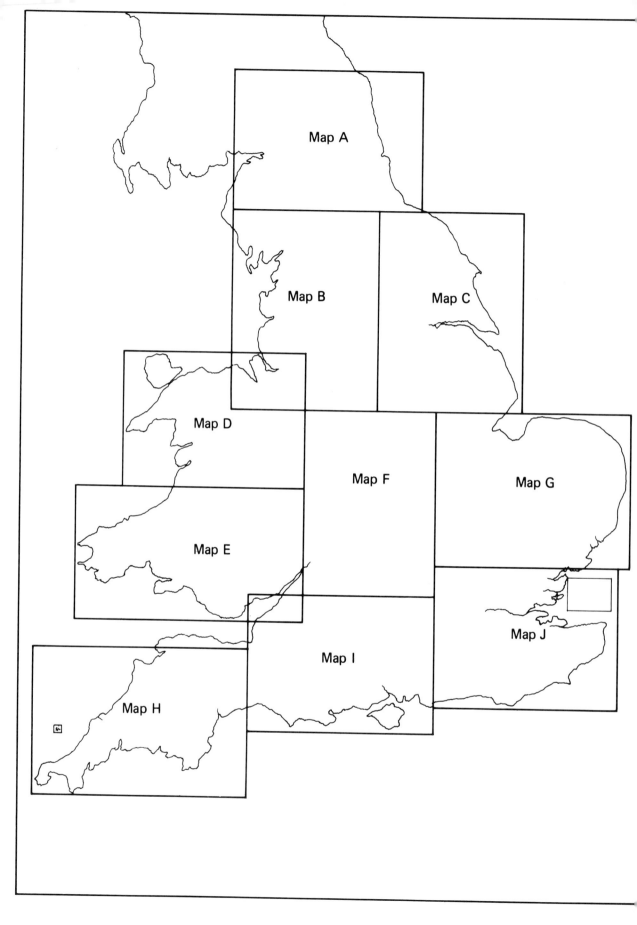

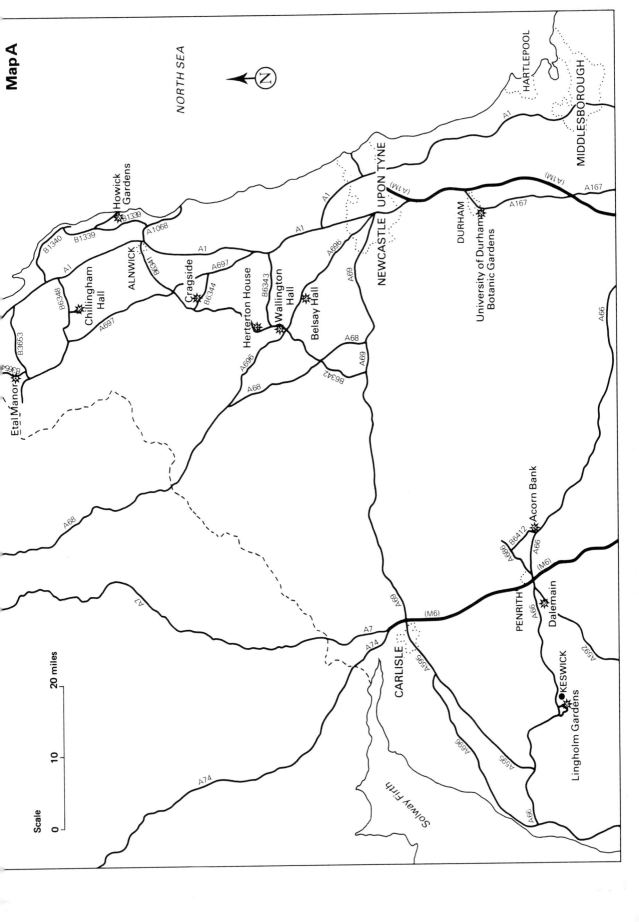

Map A

NORTH SEA

N

MIDDLESBOROUGH

HARTLEPOOL

A1

A19

A167

A167

(A1M)

(A1M)

A1

DURHAM

University of Durham
Botanic Gardens

NEWCASTLE UPON TYNE

A69

A696

A1

A696

Howick Gardens

B1339

B1340

B1339

A1068

ALNWICK

B6341

A1

Cragside

A697

B6344

Herterton House

B6343

Wallington Hall

Belsay Hall

A68

A69

A696

A68

B6342

A69

B6348

A697

Chillingham Hall

A1

B3653

Etal Manor

B3663

A68

A68

A7

A66

A66

B6412

Acorn Bank

A686

A66

(M6)

Dalemain

PENRITH

A66

A592

A66

A595

KESWICK

Lingholm Gardens

A591

A595

A596

CARLISLE

A69

(M6)

A7

A74

A74

Solway Firth

Scale

0   10   20 miles

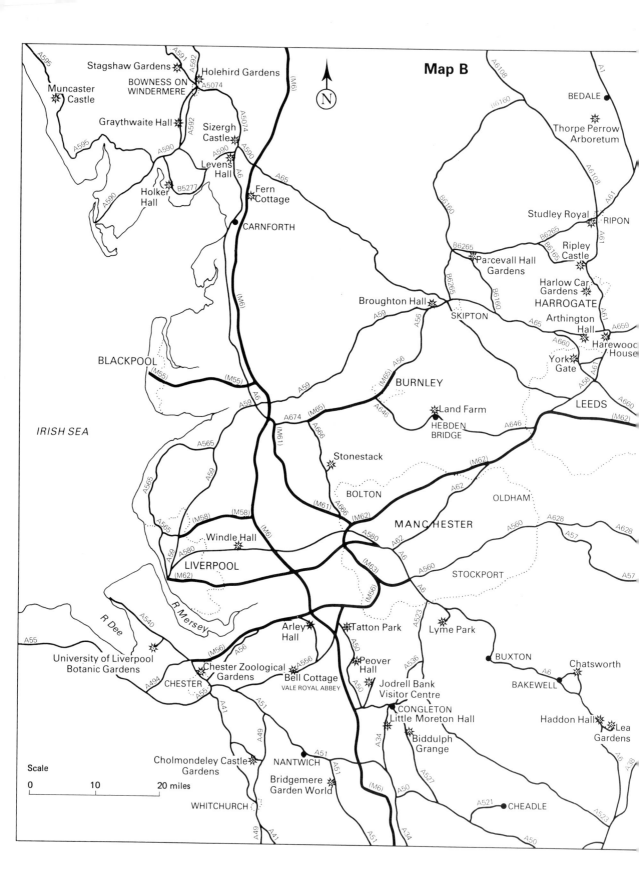

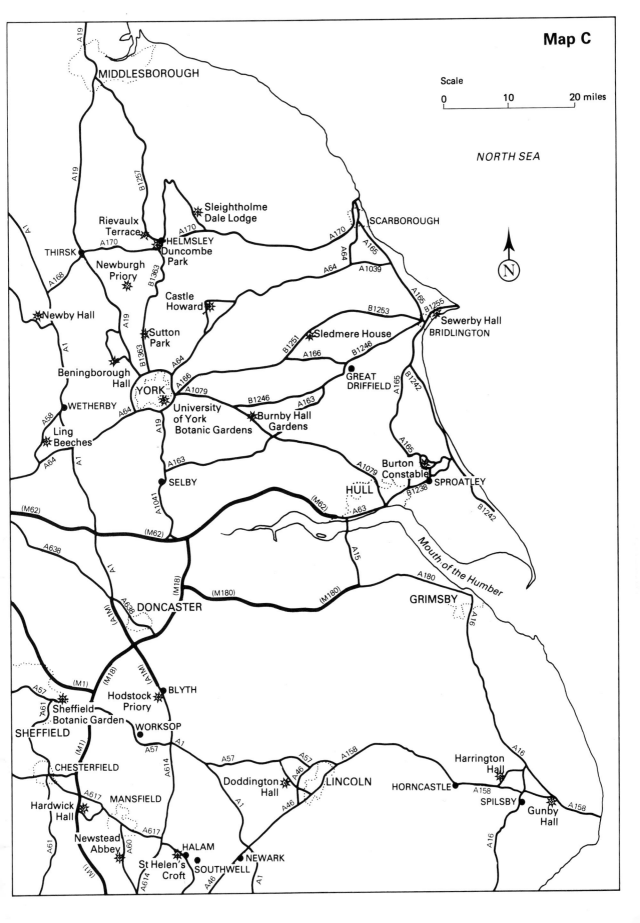

Map C

Scale

0   10   20 miles

NORTH SEA

N

MIDDLESBOROUGH

A19

B1257

SCARBOROUGH

Sleightholme
Dale Lodge

A170

A170

A165

Rievaulx
Terrace

THIRSK

A170

HELMSLEY
Duncombe
Park

A64

A1039

Newburgh
Priory

B1363

A168

Castle
Howard

B1253

A165

B1255

Sewerby Hall
BRIDLINGTON

Newby Hall

A19

Sledmere House

B1251

A166

B1246

Sutton
Park

A64

A166

GREAT
DRIFFIELD

A165

B1242

Beningborough
Hall

A1

A1079

YORK

University
of York
Botanic Gardens

B1246

A163

Burnby Hall
Gardens

A165

WETHERBY

A58

A64

A19

Ling
Beeches

A163

A1079

Burton
Constable

SPROATLEY

B1238

B1242

A64

A1

SELBY

A1041

HULL

A63

(M62)

(M62)

(M62)

Mouth of the Humber

A638

A15

A180

(M18)

(M180)

(M180)

GRIMSBY

A16

DONCASTER

A638

(A1M)

A1

(M1)

A57

Hodstock
Priory

BLYTH

A16

A61

Sheffield
Botanic Garden

(M18)

(A1M)

WORKSOP

A1

Harrington
Hall

A16

SHEFFIELD

(M1)

A57

A614

A57

A57

A158

A57

CHESTERFIELD

Doddington
Hall

A46

LINCOLN

HORNCASTLE

A158

SPILSBY

A158

A617

MANSFIELD

A1

A46

Gunby
Hall

Hardwick
Hall

A61

A617

HALAM

A60

A16

Newstead
Abbey

A614

St Helen's
Croft

SOUTHWELL

NEWARK

A46

A1

(1M)

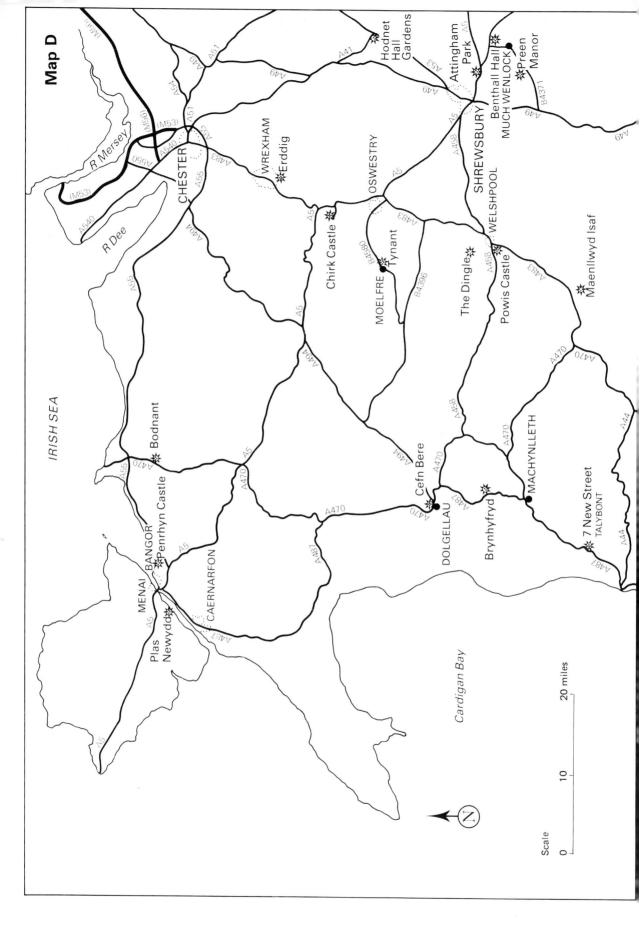

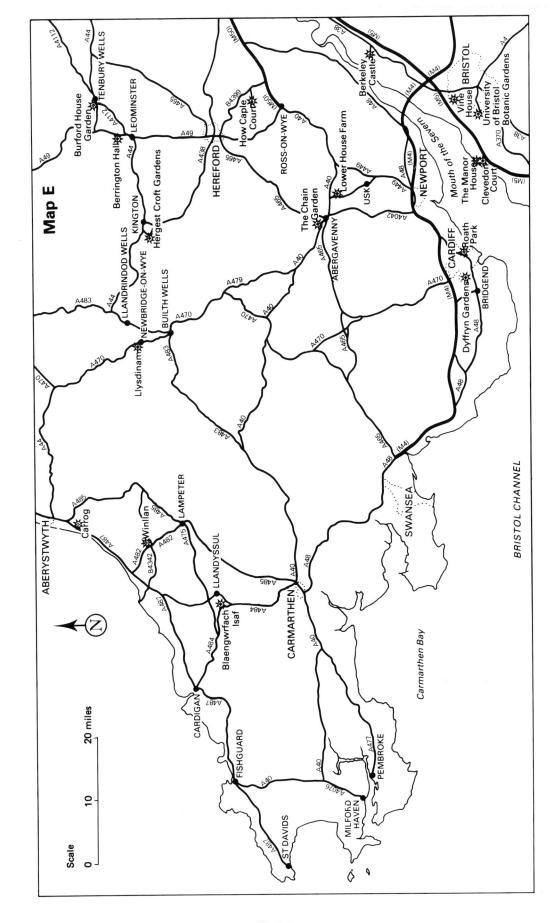

Map E

Scale
0   10   20 miles

N

ABERYSTWYTH

Caffog

A485

A487
A482
Winllan
B4342
A482

A475
LAMPETER

A484
LLANDYSSUL

Blaengwrfach Isaf

A487
CARDIGAN

A487
FISHGUARD

A40
ST DAVIDS

A487

A40

A40
CARMARTHEN

A484
A485
A48
A40

A476
A4076
MILFORD HAVEN

A477
PEMBROKE

Carmarthen Bay

A48 (M4)
A48
SWANSEA

A44
A470

A483
A44
LLANDRINDOD WELLS

Llysdinam
NEWBRIDGE-ON-WYE
A483
BUILTH WELLS
A470

A479
A470
A40

A483
A40

A470
A465
A40

A465
The Chain Garden
ABERGAVENNY
A40

A49
A44
Burford House Garden
A4112
TENBURY WELLS
A44
Berrington Hall
LEOMINSTER
A49
A44
KINGTON
Hergest Croft Gardens

A438
HEREFORD
A465

B4399
How Caple Court
A449 (M50)
A465
ROSS-ON-WYE
A40

Lower House Farm
A449
USK
A40
A4042

A470
A465
A48
Dyfryn Gardens
CARDIFF
Roath Park
A48
BRIDGEND
A470

A48 (M4)
A465

A38 (M5)
Berkeley Castle
A48
A38 (M4)

(M4)
(M5)
Vine House
University of Bristol
BRISTOL
Botanic Gardens
A4
A370
A38

Mouth of the Severn
NEWPORT
The Manor House
Clevedon Court
(M5)

BRISTOL CHANNEL

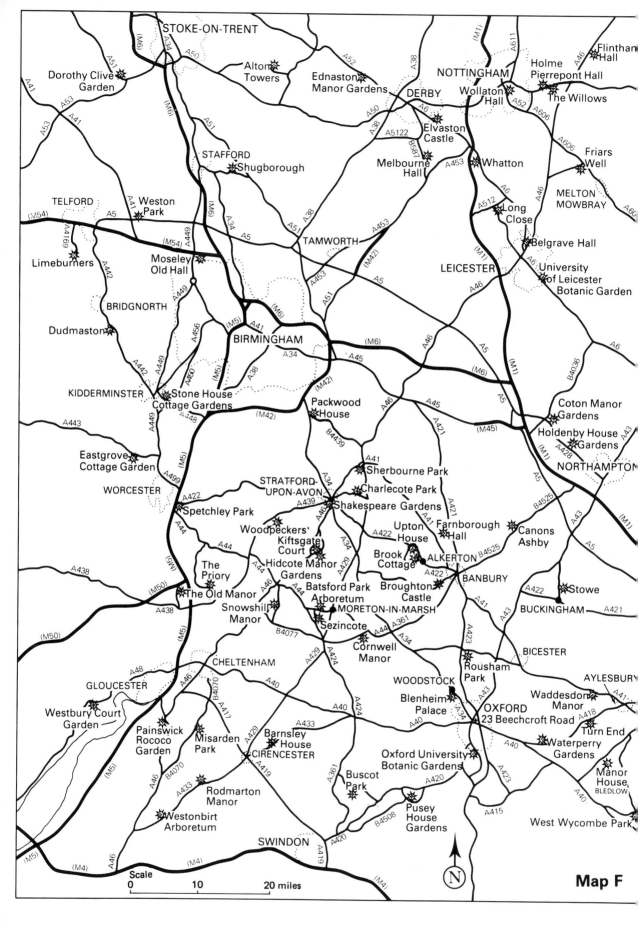

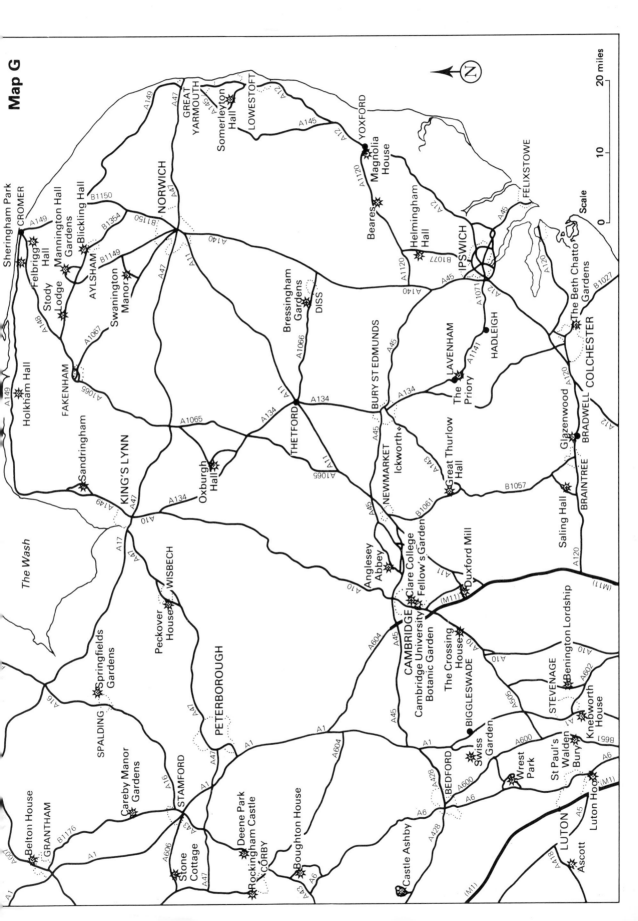

Map G

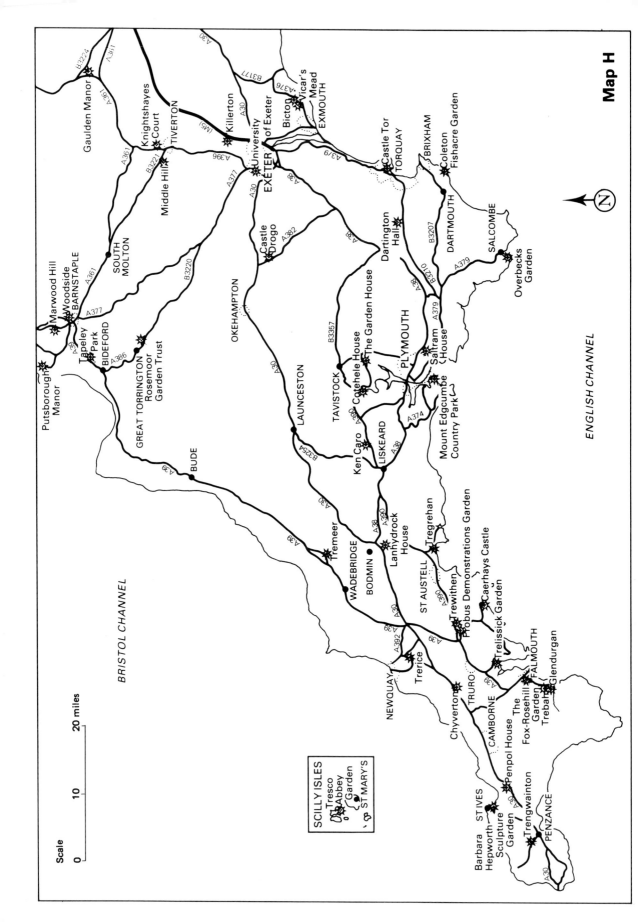

Map H

N

ENGLISH CHANNEL

BRISTOL CHANNEL

Scale

0   10   20 miles

SCILLY ISLES
Tresco
Abbey
Garden
ST MARY'S

Gaulden Manor
Knightshayes
Court
TIVERTON
Killerton
University of Exeter
Bicton
Vicar's
Mead
EXMOUTH
Castle Tor
TORQUAY
BRIXHAM
Coleton
Fishacre Garden
Middle Hill
SOUTH
MOLTON
EXETER
Castle
Drogo
Dartington
Hall
DARTMOUTH
SALCOMBE
Marwood Hill
Woodside
BARNSTAPLE
Tapeley
Park
BIDEFORD
GREAT TORRINGTON
Rosemoor
Garden Trust
OKEHAMPTON
The Garden House
PLYMOUTH
Saltram
House
Overbecks
Garden
Putsborough
Manor
BUDE
LAUNCESTON
TAVISTOCK
Cotehele House
Mount Edgcumbe
Country Park
Tremeer
WADEBRIDGE
BODMIN
Lanhydrock
House
Tregrehan
Ken Caro
LISKEARD
Probus Demonstrations Garden
Caerhays Castle
Trewithen
ST AUSTELL
Trelissick Garden
Trerice
NEWQUAY
Chyverton
TRURO
CAMBORNE
Penpol House
The
Fox-Rosehill
Garden
FALMOUTH
Trebah
Glendurgan
Barbara
Hepworth
Sculpture
Garden
ST IVES
Trengwainton
PENZANCE

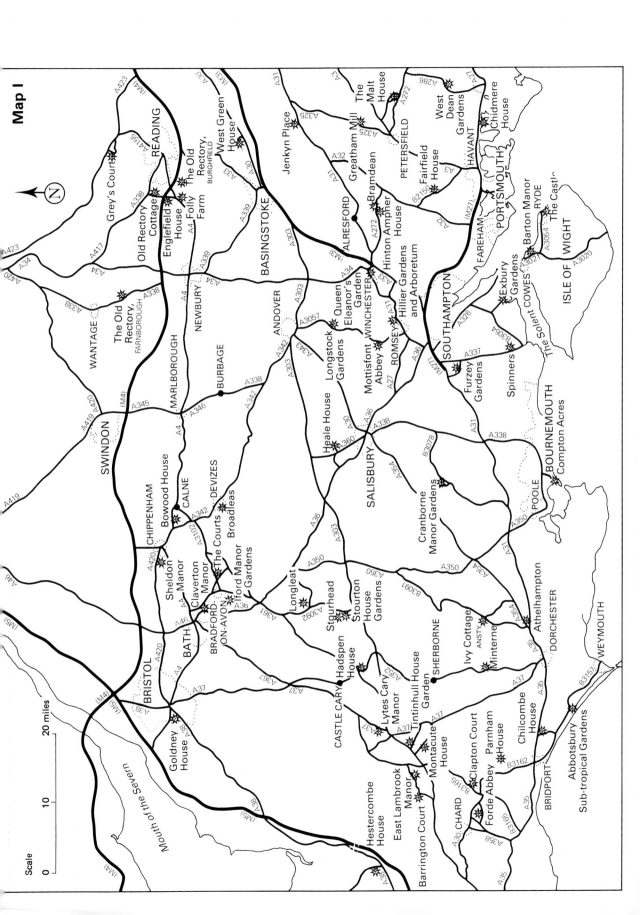

Map I

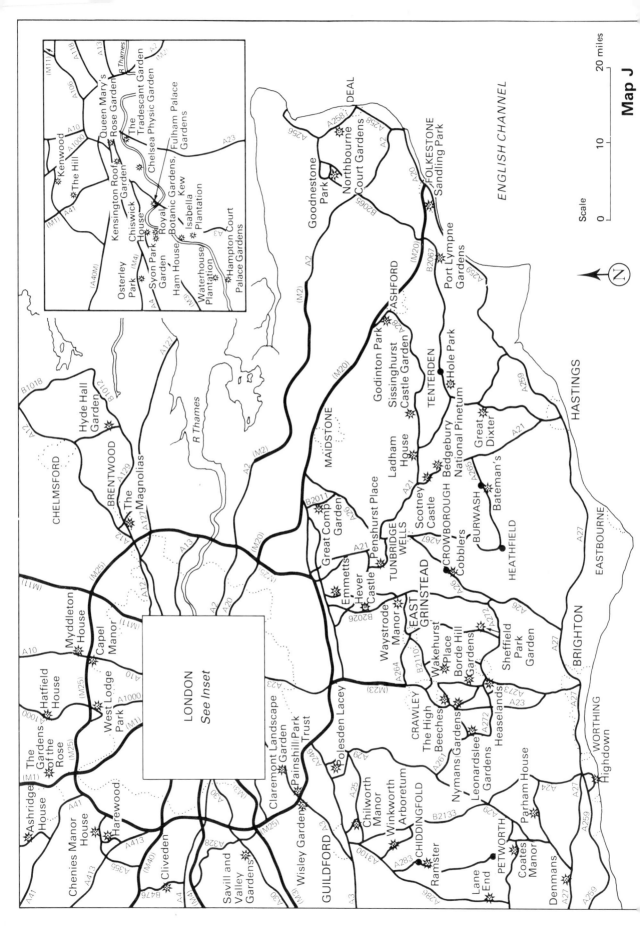

Map J

ENGLISH CHANNEL

Scale

0   10   20 miles

N

LONDON
See Inset

Inset labels:
Kenwood
The Hill
Queen Mary's Rose Garden
The Tradescant Garden
Chelsea Physic Garden
Fulham Palace Gardens
Kensington Roof Garden
Chiswick House
Syon Park
Royal Botanic Gardens, Kew
Isabella Plantation
Osterley Park
Ham House
Waterhouse Plantation
Hampton Court Palace Gardens

Map labels:
DEAL
Goodnestone Park
Northbourne Court Gardens
FOLKESTONE
Sandling Park
Port Lympne Gardens
ASHFORD
Godinton Park
Sissinghurst Castle Garden
TENTERDEN
Hole Park
Bedgebury National Pinetum
Great Dixter
Ladham House
Penshurst Place
Scotney Castle
CROWBOROUGH
Cobblers
BURWASH
Bateman's
HEATHFIELD
HASTINGS
EASTBOURNE
MAIDSTONE
Great Comp Garden
TUNBRIDGE WELLS
Emmetts
Hever Castle
Waystrode Manor
EAST GRINSTEAD
Wakehurst Place
Borde Hill Gardens
Sheffield Park Garden
CRAWLEY
The High Beeches
Nymans Gardens
Leonardslee Gardens
Heaselands
BRIGHTON
WORTHING
Highdown
Chilworth Manor
Winkworth Arboretum
CHIDDINGFOLD
Ramster
Lane End
PETWORTH
Parham House
Coates Manor
Denmans
GUILDFORD
Wisley Garden
Painshill Park Trust
Polesden Lacey
Claremont Landscape Garden
CHELMSFORD
Hyde Hall Garden
BRENTWOOD
The Magnolias
R Thames
Ashridge House
Chenies Manor House
Cliveden
Harewood
The Gardens of the Rose
Hatfield House
West Lodge Park
Myddleton House
Capel Manor
Savill and Valley Gardens

Road numbers: A12, A13, A127, A10, A41, A413, A355, A476, A4, A355, M1, M25, M11, A1000, A414, B1018, B1012, A129, M2, A2, A20, M20, M23, A23, A21, A22, A26, A27, A24, A29, A25, A3, A31, A272, A264, A267, A265, A259, A28, A258, A256, B2065, B2067, A20M, A2070, B2026, B2011, A251, B2110, A261, B2133, A283, A286

Index

Index of gardens (by county)

Note: page numbers in italic type refer to illustrations;
map references are in bold type

ENGLAND

AVON

Claverton Manor (Claverton, nr Bath) 100–1, **I**
Clevedon Court (Clevedon, nr Bristol) 101, **E**
Goldney House (Lower Clifton Hill, Bristol) 135, **I**
Manor House, The (Walton-in-Gordano, nr Clevedon) 196, **E**
University of Bristol Botanic Garden (Bracken Hill House, North Road, Leigh Woods, Bristol) 284, **E**
Vine House (Henbury, Bristol) 289, **E**

BEDFORDSHIRE

Luton Hoo (Luton) 191, **G**
Swiss Garden (Old Warden) 270–1, **G**
Wrest Park (Silsoe) 305, **G**

BERKSHIRE

Englefield House (Theale, nr Reading) 122, **I**
Folly Farm (Sulhamstead, nr Reading) 127–9, **I**
Old Rectory, The (Burghfield, nr Reading) 211, **I**
Old Rectory, The (Farnborough, nr Wantage) 211–12, **I**
Old Rectory Cottage (Tidmarsh, nr Reading) 212, **I**
Savill and Valley Gardens (The Great Park, Windsor) 246–7, *247*, **J**

BUCKINGHAMSHIRE

Ascott (Wing, nr Leighton Buzzard) 45, **G**
Chenies Manor House (Chenies, nr Amersham) 91, **J**
Cliveden (Taplow, nr Maidenhead) 101–2, **J**
Harewood (Harewood Road, Chalfont St Giles) 145, **J**
Manor House, The (Bledlow, nr Princes Risborough) 195, **F**
Stowe (Buckingham) 268, **F**
Turn End (Townside, Haddenham, nr Aylesbury) 283, **F**
Waddesdon Manor (Waddesdon, nr Aylesbury) *290*, 291, *292*, **F**
West Wycombe Park (West Wycombe) 299–300, **F**

CAMBRIDGESHIRE

Anglesey Abbey (Lode, nr Cambridge) 42–3, **G**
Cambridge University Botanic Garden (Cambridge) 78, **G**
Clare College Fellows Garden (Cambridge) 98–9, *100*, **G**
Crossing House, The (Meldreth Road, Shrepresh, nr Cambridge) 109, **G**
Duxford Mill (nr Duxford) 116–18, **G**
Peckover House (North Brink, Wisbech) 220–1, **G**

CHESHIRE

Arley Hall and Gardens (nr Northwich) 43–4, **B**
Bell Cottage (Vale Royal, Whitegate, Northwich) 55, **B**
Bridgemere Garden World (Bridgemere, nr Woore and Nantwich) 72, **B**
Chester Zoological Gardens (Upton, Chester) 91, **B**
Cholmondeley Castle Gardens (Malpas, nr Whitchurch) 95–6, **B**
Jodrell Bank Visitor Centre Gardens (nr Holmes Chapel) 176, **B**
Little Moreton Hall (nr Congleton) 187–8, **B**
Lyme Park (Disley, nr Stockport) 191–2, **B**
Peover Hall (Over Peover, nr Knutsford) 224, **B**
Tatton Park (Knutsford) 272–3, *274*, **B**
University of Liverpool Botanic Gardens (Ness, Neston, South Wirral) 286–7, **B**

CORNWALL

Barbara Hepworth Sculpture Garden (Barnoon Hill, St Ives) 47–8, *48*, **H**
Caerhays Castle (Gorran, nr St Austell) 77–8, **H**
Chyverton (Zela, nr Truro) 96, **H**
Cotehele House (St Dominick, nr Saltash) 105–6, **H**
Fox-Rosehill Garden, The (Melvill Road, Falmouth) 129–30, **H**
Glendurgan (Helford, Mawnan Smith, nr Falmouth) 134–5, *134*, **H**
Ken Caro (Bicton, nr Liskeard) 176, **H**
Lanhydrock House (Bodmin) 183, **H**
Mount Edgcumbe Country Park (Cremyll) 202, **H**
Penpol House (Penpol Avenue, Hayle) 221, **H**
Probus Demonstrations Garden (Probus, nr Truro) 231, **H**
Trebah (Mawnan Smith, nr Falmouth) 276, **H**
Tregrehan (Par) 276–7, **H**
Trelissick Garden (Feock, nr Truro) 277, **H**
Tremeer (St Tudy, nr Bodmin) 277–8, **H**
Trengwainton (nr Penzance) 278, **H**
Trerice (St Newlyn East, nr Newquay) 280
Trewithen (Grampound Road, nr Truro) 281–2, *282*, **H**

CUMBRIA

Acorn Bank (Temple Sowerby, nr Penrith) 41–2, **A**
Dalemain (Ullswater, nr Penrith) 110, **A**
Fern Cottage (Holme, nr Carnforth) 127, **B**
Graythwaite Hall (Graythwaite, nr Ulverston) 136–8, **B**
Holehird Gardens (Patterdale, Windermere) 165–6, *166*, **B**
Holker Hall (Cark-in-Cartmel, Grange-over-Sands) 167, **B**

358

Index of people

Note: this index includes references both to garden
designers and makers and to historical figures;
page numbers in italic type refer to illustration captions.